TO KNOW GOD AND THE SOUL

TO KNOW GOD AND THE SOUL

Essays on the Thought of Saint Augustine

ROLAND J. TESKE, S.J.

The Catholic University of America Press
Washington, D.C.

Copyright © 2008
The Catholic University of America Press
All rights reserved
The paper used in this publication meets the minimum requirements of
American National Standards for Information Science—Permanence of Paper
for Printed Library Materials, ANSI Z39.48-1984.
∞

LIBRARY OF CONGRESS CATALOGING-IN-PUBLICATION DATA
Teske, Roland J., 1934
   To know God and the soul : essays on the thought of Saint Augustine /
Roland J. Teske.
      p. cm.
   Includes bibliographical references and indexes.
   ISBN-13: 978-0-8132-1487-0 (cloth : alk. paper)
   ISBN-13: 978-0-8132-2877-8 (pbk : alk. paper)
   1. Augustine, Saint, Bishop of Hippo.   I. Title.
BR65.A9T44 2007
230'.14092—dc22   2006022031

For my colleagues in the Department of Philosophy at Marquette University, past and present

CONTENTS

Acknowledgments	ix
Introduction	xi
Abbreviations	xvii

PART I: AUGUSTINE & NEOPLATIONISM

1. Augustine as Philosopher: The Birth of Christian Metaphysics	3
2. The Aim of Augustine's Proof That God Truly Is	26
3. Spirituals and Spiritual Interpretation in Augustine	49
4. Love of Neighbor in Augustine	70

PART II: GOD & SPEAKING ABOUT GOD

5. Properties of God and the Predicaments in *De Trinitate* 5	93
6. Augustine's Use of *Substantia* in Speaking about God	112
7. Divine Immutability in Augustine	131

PART III: CREATION & BEGINNINGS

8. The Motive for Creation according to Augustine	155
9. Problems with "The Beginning" in Augustine's Sixth Commentary on Genesis	165
10. Augustine's View of the Human Condition in *De Genesi contra Manichaeos*	180

PART IV: THE SOUL & TIME

11. Augustine on the Incorporeality of the Soul in Letter 166	197
12. The World-Soul and Time in Augustine	216
13. *Vocans temporales, faciens aeternos:* Augustine on Liberation from Time	238

14. The Heaven of Heaven and the Unity of
    Augustine's *Confessiones*   259

Bibliography   275
Index of Names   287

ACKNOWLEDGMENTS

The previously published articles included in this volume are here listed together with their original publication information. I thank the editors of the various journals for granting permission to reprint the articles and acknowledge the respective journals as copyright holders.

"Saint Augustine as Philosopher: The Birth of Christian Metaphysics," *Augustinian Studies* 23 (1992): 7–32.

"The Aim of Augustine's Proof That God Truly Is," *International Philosophical Quarterly* 26 (1986): 253–268.

"Spirituals and Spiritual Interpretation in St. Augustine," *Augustinian Studies* 15 (1984): 65–81.

"Love of Neighbor in St. Augustine," *Studia Ephemeridis "Augustinianum"* 26. Congresso Internazionale su S. Agostino nel XVI Centenario della Conversione. Roma, 15–20 settembre 1986. Atti III, pp. 81–102.

"Properties of God and the Predicaments in *De Trinitate* V," *The Modern Schoolman* 59 (1981): 1–19.

"Augustine's Use of 'Substantia' in Speaking about God," *The Modern Schoolman* 62 (1985): 147–163.

"Divine Immutability in St. Augustine," *The Modern Schoolman* 63 (1986): 233–249.

"The Motive of Creation according to St. Augustine," *The Modern Schoolman* 65 (1988): 245–253.

"Problems with 'The Beginning' in Augustine's Sixth Commentary on Genesis," *University of Dayton Review* 22.3 (1994): 55–68.

"St. Augustine's View of the Human Condition in *De Genesi contra Manichaeos*," *Augustinian Studies* 22 (1991): 141–155.

"Saint Augustine on the Incorporeality of the Soul in Letter 166," *The Modern Schoolman* 60 (1983): 220–235.

"The World-Soul and Time in St. Augustine," *Augustinian Studies* 14 (1983): 75–92.

"*'Vocans Temporales, Faciens Aeternos'*: St. Augustine on Liberation from Time," *Traditio* 41 (1985): 36–58.

"The Heaven of Heaven and the Unity of St. Augustine's *Confessions*," *American Catholic Philosophical Quarterly* 74 (2000): 29–45.

INTRODUCTION

This volume contains fourteen previously published articles on Augustine of Hippo written over the past twenty-five years. The articles are grouped around four themes that have been my chief topics of interest: Augustine and Neoplatonism, God and Speaking about God, Creation and Beginnings, and the Soul and Time. My early interest in Augustine was strongly influenced by the writings of Robert O'Connell, S.J., who awakened me to an awareness of the influence of Plotinus upon Augustine's thinking, especially in Augustine's early works. At times the Plotinian influence did not fit well with the Christian faith so that Augustine had to revise his views on a number of points over the years from the period at Cassiciacum in 386 just before his baptism to his latest works against Julian of Eclanum just before his death in 430. Some scholars would say, and have said, that Robert O'Connell was wrong and has led me and others into similar errors in reading Augustine, especially with regard to the fall of the soul. Ronnie Rombs's book, *Saint Augustine and the Fall of the Soul: Beyond O'Connell and his Critics*,[1] has, I believe, thrown considerable light on the debate and may well get Augustine scholars beyond the current state of the dispute. In any case I wrote the articles in this volume convinced that Augustine held a real fall of the soul in his early writings up to and including his *Confessiones* (hereafter *conf.*). I could have profited from Rombs's distinction between a cosmogonic, a metaphysical, and a moral sense of the soul's fall, since I now see that Augustine himself in his earliest writings held a fall in all three senses, but soon abandoned the cosmogonic sense of the fall and eventually retained only a moral sense of the fall.

1. Washington, DC: The Catholic University of America Press, 2006.

Scholars approach Augustine from many perspectives—as philologists, as historians, as patrologists, as theologians, and as philosophers—to mention some of the most significant. And the results are correspondingly diverse. Although I had the usual theological training for the priesthood, my further academic training was in philosophy, and my specialization was modern philosophy, specifically British Hegelianism and its opponents. I like to think that my exposure to modern philosophy, and especially early analytic philosophy, sharpened my abilities to be able to read thinkers like Augustine with a clarity that others with other backgrounds may not have. Others, of course, are likely to think that Francis Herbert Bradley (on whom I wrote my dissertation) and his ilk have twisted my mind. Exposure to some analytic philosophy also made me somewhat intolerant of philosophers who either banished from philosophy whole branches of philosophical thought or declared doctrines of Augustine and Aquinas simply unintelligible nonsense. For better or worse this volume offers the readers some of what I regard as my best efforts at understanding Augustine, a man and a thinker I have admired and grown in admiration for over the last quarter-century.

Toward the end of his life Augustine wrote an extraordinary work, the *Revisions (Retractationes),* in which he reexamined and commented on all of his books. Unfortunately he was not able to complete the sequel, in which he planned also to review his sermons and letters. In the introduction to each article I too endeavor to revise or review what I have written in it, indicating in some cases that I may have overstated or understated my position or failed to be sufficiently aware of or open to other views. Augustine's *Revisions* was not a recanting or retracting of what he had said—at least in most cases, although his words about his early work, *De immortalite animae,* which was written shortly after his baptism, are disarmingly frank: "It is first of all so obscure because of its complexity and the brevity of its arguments that it wearies even my mind when I read it, and I scarcely understand it myself."[2] At other times Augustine seems to try to put a better spin on what he wrote than the text itself seems to justify, such as when the Pelagians appealed to some things that Augustine himself had said on freedom of the will. I hope that my attempt to offer a *retractatio* of some of my articles will put them in a better perspective and that I can exhibit the same sort

2. *Retractationes* 1.5.1.

of intellectual candor as the bishop of Hippo did. On the other hand, Augustine commented on all of his books, while I have the advantage of choosing the articles that in retrospect I regard as some of my best work.

My study of Augustine was in some sense thrust upon me when the Department of Philosophy at Marquette University needed someone to teach the graduate course on Augustine in the late 1970s. Since I was at that time quite innocent of much knowledge of Augustine, I began my study of him by focusing upon his earliest works and only gradually worked my way through most of his middle and later works. Hence, I knew relatively little of his mature works on grace in the controversy with the Pelagians until I read and translated those works in the late 1980s and early '90s. Had I known the anti-Pelagian works better, some of my earlier articles would have had a different slant, for example, on the meaning of "spiritual person," though what I wrote remains true for the early works, even if it does not present the whole truth for the later Augustine.

Etienne Gilson once said that Augustine never changed any of his basic views. "We have never discovered the slightest philosophical change in any of his essential theses. Saint Augustine fixed his main ideas from the time of his conversion—even we believe regarding grace."[3] Most contemporary scholars, on the contrary, maintain that Augustine changed on many of his basic views, especially on freedom and grace, and that he should be read from a genetic or historical point of view. I now believe that Augustinian scholars are still at times insufficiently attentive to the development of Augustine's thought. The definition of time, for example, which plays such an important role in book 11 of the *conf.*, is not found elsewhere in the bishop's works. I now suspect that attempts to reconcile the definition of time from book 11 with what he says about time in his later works may simply overlook the fact that Augustine had moved on. For, as I saw it and still see it, that definition implies a cosmogonic sense of the fall of the soul, which Augustine had, I now think, already begun to move away from in the *conf.* So too, the theory of "causal reasons," which is found only in *De Genesi ad litteram,* may have simply represented a stage in Augustine's thought that he soon left behind. Hence,

---

3. E. Gilson, *The Christian Philosophy of Saint Augustine,* trans. L. E. M. Lynch (London: Victor Gollancz, 1960), 364n49.

scholars will, I believe, need to give greater attention to the development of Augustine's thought than had been previously suspected.

Despite their deficiencies in some respects, the articles collected in this volume do represent the core of what I learned in studying Augustine over the past quarter-century. All told, I have some forty articles, book chapters, and encyclopedia entries and one book on Augustine as well as the introductions to my translations of the anti-Pelagian works, the anti-Manichaean works, the *Letters,* and a volume of works against various heresies.[4] Due to limitations on this volume's size, I obviously had to omit a good number of articles, including some of my more recent articles on more theological topics, to which I turned when working with the works on grace. Hence, if one identifies Augustinian thought with the bishop of Hippo's doctrine of grace, original sin, and the damage to human nature stemming from Adam's sin, one will find very little in these articles that is Augustinian in that sense. On the other hand, because I came to know the later works against the Pelagians and especially the four works against the so-called Semi-Pelagians only somewhat late in my study of Augustine, I was able to remain in untroubled love with his thought—something that has surprised a few of my friends who more or less identified Augustine with his doctrine of predestination. More recently, in working with Prosper of Aquitaine, I have come to see how even so ardent an Augustinian as Prosper was in the late 420s soon came to a far less rigorous Augustinianism than the elderly bishop of Hippo had himself held in his last years.[5] In fact, Prosper's *De vocatione omnium gentium,* written around 450, is characterized by such a marked departure from the stricter views of the elderly bishop that many have wrongly, I have argued, attributed the work to someone other than Prosper.[6] The facts of the matter seem rather that, once settled in Rome as a friend and secretary to Leo the Great, Prosper found that he did not

---

4. The translations are available in the *Works of Saint Augustine: A Translation for the Twenty-First Century* (Hyde Park, NY: New City Press). The translations are also available online in the Past Masters Series. For the complete list of my writings on Augustine, see the Philosophy Department website at www.marquette.edu.

5. See Letters 225 and 226, which Prosper and Prosper's friend Hilary wrote to Augustine, in which they complain in a rather fawning fashion about the monks of Province who found the hard-line Augustinian doctrine on grace and predestination a bit too much and were, therefore, disloyal to Augustine and his teaching.

6. See my "The Augustinianism of Prosper of Aquitaine Revisted," *Studia Patristica* 43, ed. F. Young, M. Edwards, and P. Parvis (Leuven: Peeters, 2006), 491–503.

have to be more Augustinian than the pope. Hence, it was perhaps not altogether bad that I began my work with Augustine's earlier works and focused upon his more philosophical thought and the Plotinian framework in which his thought developed. The earlier Augustine, as I read him, was an exciting intellectual adventurer who faced immense philosophical challenges from the anti-intellectual church of Africa and from Stoic and Manichaean corporealism, who found solutions to many of his problems in Plotinian spiritualism, who often enough soon found elements of Platonism in conflict with the Christian faith, but who eventually got things straight, always landing on his feet and squarely within the faith of the Catholic Church, of which he stands as the greatest of the Western Fathers.

ABBREVIATIONS OF THE TITLES OF AUGUSTINE'S WORKS CITED

c. Acad.	Contra Academicos
c. adv. leg.	Contra adversarium legis et prophetarum
an. et or.	De anima et ejus origine
quan.	De animae quantitate
b. vita	De beata vita
civ. Dei	De civitate Dei
conf.	Confessiones
con. Max	Conlatio cum Maximino Arianorum episcopo
cons. Ev.	De consensu Evangelistarum
cont.	De continentia
div. quaes.	De diversis quaestionibus octoginta tribus
doc. Chr.	De doctrina Christiana
duab. an.	De duabus animabus
en. Ps.	Ennarationes in Psalmos
ench.	Enchiridion ad Laurentium de fide, spe et caritate
ep. (epp.)	Epistulae
ep. Jo.	In epistulam Joannis
c. ep. Man.	Contra epistulam Manichaei quam vocant fundamenti
c. Fel.	Contra Felicem Manichaeum
f. et symb.	De fide et symbolo
c. Fort.	Acta contra Fortunatum Manichaeum
Gn. litt.	De Genesi ad litteram
Gn. litt. imp.	De Genesi ad litteram imperfectus liber
Gn. adv. Man.	De Genesis adversus Manichaeos
haer.	De haeresibus

imm. an.	De immortalite animae
Jo. ev. tr.	In Johannis evangelium tractatus
lib. arb.	De libero arbitrio
mag.	De magistro
c. Max.	Contra Maximinum Arianum
mend.	De mendacio
c. mend.	Contra mendacium
mor.	De moribus ecclesiae Catholicae et de moribus Manichaeorum
mus.	De musica
nat. b.	De natura boni
ord.	De ordine
pecc. merit.	De peccatorum meritis et remissione et de baptismo parvulorum
praed. sanc.	De praedestinatione sanctorum
c. Prisc.	Contra Priscilianistas
qu. Ev.	Quaestiones Evangeliorum
retr.	Retractationes
c. Sec.	Contra Secundinum Manichaeum
s.	Sermones
s. Dom. mon.	De sermone Domini in monte
Simpl.	Ad Simplicianum
sol.	Soliloquia
spec.	Speculum
spir. et litt.	De spiritu et littera
Trin.	De Trinitate
util. cred.	De utilitate credendi
util. jejun.	De utilitate jejunii
vera rel.	De vera religione

OTHER ABBREVIATIONS

AS	Augustinian Studies
BA	Bibliothèque augustinienne
PL	Patrologia Latina

I

Augustine & Neoplatonism

1

AUGUSTINE AS PHILOSOPHER

The Birth of Christian Metaphysics

When Allan Fitzgerald, O.S.A., invited me to give the 1992 Saint Augustine Lecture at Villanova University, I chose to speak in defense of an Augustinian philosophy, because I was convinced that Augustine not only had a philosophy, but also made a very significant contribution to metaphysics in Western thought by introducing the concepts of incorporeal being and of timeless eternity, concepts that the West has so successfully absorbed that their source is often forgotten. I perhaps did not give sufficient credit to Saint Ambrose, whose preaching was certainly imbued with such Neoplatonic ideas, but I still believe that the books of the Platonists provided Augustine with the ability to articulate such philosophical concepts, which Augustine certainly heard about in the preaching of the bishop of Milan. But who ever learned metaphysics from the homilies of a bishop? I never intended to imply that Augustine's philosophy was limited to the two issues that I singled out, but I still believe that they do represent his two most significant contributions to metaphysics in the sense of the science that transcends bodily and temporal reality.

A distinguished Augustine scholar, Goulven Madec, has said, "The history of patristic philosophy has only a precarious status. It lacks a principal object; for there is no 'patristic philosophy.'"

He immediately adds, "and the Fathers of the Church are not 'philosophers' in the commonly accepted sense."¹ Certainly, he is correct in maintaining that the Fathers of the Church are not philosophers in the sense commonly accepted today. However, it is not nearly so clear that the Fathers of the Church were in no sense philosophers or that there is no philosophy to be found in the Fathers of the Church. Regardless of the claim about the Fathers of the Church in general, I shall argue that Augustine of Hippo was a philosopher in some sense and that there is an Augustinian philosophy, even in the sense of philosophy commonly accepted today. I shall first examine what Augustine understood by philosophy; then I shall ask whether there is in Augustine a philosophy in the contemporary sense. Finally, I shall suggest what I consider the principal features of Augustine's legacy to Western philosophy.

WHAT AUGUSTINE MEANT BY PHILOSOPHY

Augustine provides a nominal definition of philosophy as "the love of wisdom" or "the pursuit of wisdom."² While a philosopher of the late twentieth century certainly recognizes and can probably accept such a definition, if one listens further to what Augustine says about philosophy, one finds the *philosophia* of which he speaks to be both something familiar and also something quite unfamiliar, something much the same and something quite different from what is today meant by philosophy. I will suggest one reason why at least some today find themselves at home with what Augustine meant by philosophy; then I want to point out two ways in which what Augustine meant by philosophy differs from what most of us take philosophy to be.

I suggest that we find the *philosophia* of which Augustine speaks something familiar, because he saw philosophy as a continuation of classical Greek philosophy, as something rooted in and carrying on the very best of Greek philosophy. Augustine began to burn with the love of wisdom from the time of his reading Cicero's *Hortensius,* which con-

---

1. Goulven Madec, "La christianisation de l'hellenisme. Thème de l'histoire de la philosophie patristique," in *Humanisme et foi chrétienne. Mélanges scientifiques du centenaire de l'institut catholique de Paris* (Paris: Beauchesne, 1976), 399–406, here 399 (my translation).

2. See *c. Acad.* 2, 3, 7; *ord.* 1, 11, 32; *ep.* 139, 30.

tained an exhortation to this love of wisdom.³ He tells us that he began to desire "the immortality of wisdom with an incredible ardor of heart" and "began to rise up to return to" his God.⁴

This conversion to philosophy, begun with the reading of the *Hortensius*, reached a high point in the momentous encounter with the *libri Platonicorum* in 386, when the fire kindled by the *Hortensius* flamed out incredibly.⁵ But what was this *philosophia* that so aroused Augustine's love? In the closing sections of *Contra Academicos* (hereafter *c. Acad.*) he presents a brief history of philosophy, beginning with Socrates and Plato, through the later Academy and Plotinus, and continuing down to his own time. Plato, he tells us, added to the moral teaching of Socrates a knowledge of natural and divine reality, derived from Pythagoras and other wise men, and crowned it with dialectic, which is either itself wisdom or its indispensable condition. Hence, Augustine adds that "Plato is said to have put together the complete discipline of philosophy."⁶ Augustine singles out the features of the Platonic system that are for his purposes most significant: "that there are two worlds: one the intel-

---

3. *Conf.* 3, 4, 7. The *Hortensius* survives only in fragments, many of which are contained in the writings of Augustine. The fragments have been edited by Michel Ruch, *L'Hortensius de Cicéron: Histoire et reconstitution* (Paris: Belles Lettres, 1958). See Goulven Madec, "L'*Hortensius* de Cicéron dans les livres XIII–XIV du *De Trinitate*," *Revue des études augustiniennes* 15 (1969): 167–171, where Madec argues that Augustine may have derived his definition of wisdom as "rerum humanarum divinarumque scientia" (*Trin.* 14, 1, 3) from the *Hortensius,* though it is clearly found in other works by Cicero.

4. *Conf.* 3, 4, 7: "immortalitatem sapientiae concupiscebam aestu cordis incredibili et surgere coeperam, ut ad te redirem." See also Robert J. O'Connell, "On Augustine's 'First Conversion' Factus Erectior (*De beata vita* 4)," *AS* 17 (1986): 15–29.

5. *C. Acad.* 2, 2, 5. In "Verus Philosophus Est Amator Dei: S. Ambroise, s. Augustin et la philosophie," *Revue des sciences philosophiques et théologiques* 61 (1977): 549–566, here 560, Goulven Madec has said, "L'*Hortensius* a lancé Augustin dans la quête de la sagesse; il a ouvert à son esprit un espace de liberté."

6. *C. Acad.* 3, 17, 37: "Igitur Plato adiciens lepori subtilitatique Socraticae, quam in moralibus habuit, natualium divinarumque rerum peritiam, quam ab eis quos memoravi diligenter acceperat, subiungensque quasi formatricem illarum partium iudicemque dialecticam, quae aut ipsa esset aut sine qua omnino sapientia esse non posset, perfectam dicitur composuisse philosophiae disciplinam." See also *civ. Dei* 8, 4, where he again sketches in outline the history of philosophy and gives the same central position to Plato. He claims that, while Pythagoras excelled in the contemplative part of philosophy, Socrates excelled in the active part. "Proinde Plato utrumque iungendo philosophiam perfecisse laudatur, quam in tres partes distribuit: unam moralem, quae maxime in actione versatur, alteram naturalem, quae contemplationi deputata est; tertiam rationalem, qua verum discernatur a falso."

ligible world in which Truth dwells, and this sensible world, which, it is clear, we perceive by sight and touch. The former is the true world; this one is similar to it and made in its image. From the intelligible world the Truth, so to speak, shines forth and becomes, as it were, clear in the soul that knows itself. But of this world, not knowledge, but only opinion can be generated in the minds of the foolish."[7] Later in his history of philosophy, Augustine points out that "the doctrine of Plato, which is purest and brightest, has banished the clouds of error and has shone forth, especially in Plotinus." Plotinus was so kindred a soul to Plato that he seemed to be Plato come back to life.[8] By his own time Augustine claims that "there has all been filtered out one teaching that is the true philosophy. It is not the philosophy of this world, which our sacred mysteries rightly detest, but of the other intelligible world."[9]

Furthermore, in *De ordine* (hereafter *ord.*) Augustine makes it quite clear that Christ himself taught what was for Augustine the core of Platonic philosophy, namely, that there was another intelligible world besides this world known to the senses. He says, "Christ himself does not say, 'My kingdom is not of the world,' but 'My kingdom is not of this world,'" thus indicating that "there is another world far removed from these eyes."[10] Through his brief history of philosophy Augustine clear-

---

7. *C. Acad.* 3, 17, 37: "Sat est enim ad id, quod volo, Platonem sensisse duos esse mundos, unum intelligibilem, in quo ipsa veritas habitaret, istum autem sensibilem, quem manifestum est nos visu tactuque sentire; itaque illum verum, hunc veri similem et ad illius imaginem factum, et ideo de illo in ea quae se cognosceret anima velut expoliri et quasi serenari veritatem, de hoc autem in stultorum animis non scientiam sed opinionem posse generari."

8. *C. Acad.* 3, 18, 41: "Adeo post illa tempora non longo interuallo, omni pervicacia pertinaciaque demortua os illud Platonis, quod in philosophia purgatissimum est et lucidissimum, dimotis nubibus erroris emicuit maxime in Plotino, qui Platonicus philosophus ita eius similis iudicatus est, ut simul eos vixisse, tantum autem interest temporis, ut in hoc ille revixisse putandus sit."

9. *C. Acad.* 3, 19, 42: "sed tamen eliquata est, ut opinor, una verissimae philosophiae disciplina. Non enim est ista huius mundi philosophia, quam sacra nostra meritissime detestantur, sed alterius intellegibilis."

10. *Ord.* 1, 11, 32: "Esse autem alium mundum ab istis oculis remotissimum, quem paucorum sanorum intellectus intuetur, satis ipse Christus significat, qui non dicit: 'regnum meum non est de mundo' sed: 'regnum meum non est de hoc mundo.'" Later in his *retr.* 1, 3, 2, Augustine expresses his displeasure at this interpretation of Christ's words and sees that it would have been better to understand him as referring to the new heaven and new earth. However, he adds: "Nec Plato quidem in hoc errauit, quia esse mundum intellegibilem dixit, si non vocabulum, quod ecclesiasticae consuetudini in re illa inusitatum est, sed ipsam rem velimus attendere. Mundum quippe ille intellegibilem nuncupavit ipsam rationem sempiternam atque incommutabilem, qua fecit Deus mundum."

ly indicated that what he calls the true philosophy, the philosophy of the intelligible world, is in continuity with the best in Greek thought, namely, that of Plato and Plotinus. Later in *De civitate Dei* (hereafter *civ. Dei*) Augustine's appraisal of the achievements of the Platonic philosophers is no less laudatory. They recognized, he tells us, that "the true God is the author of reality, the source of the light of truth and the bestower of beatitude."[11] The Platonists "saw that God was not a body, and, therefore, transcended all bodies in their search for God." They "saw that nothing subject to change is the highest God and, therefore, transcended every soul and all spirits subject to change in their search for the highest God."[12]

Plato taught that the wise man imitates, knows, and loves this God and becomes blessed by participating in him.[13] There is no need to look at the position of any other philosophers; "none of them have come closer to us than the Platonists."[14] Most of us, I suspect, can agree with Augustine that Plato and Aristotle and Plotinus were philosophers and that we too mean by philosophy the sort of thing that Plato, Aristotle, and Plotinus did.[15] But what we mean by philosophy also differs from what Augustine meant in at least two very important ways. First, philosophy for Augustine meant a whole way of life. When Augustine said that "a human being has no other reason for philosophizing except to be happy,"[16] he meant by *philosophari* not the pursuit of a particular academic discipline, but a whole way of life dedicated to the pursuit of wisdom. With an exaggeration perhaps needed to prevent us

---

11. *Civ. Dei* 8, 5: "verum Deum et rerum auctorem et veritatis inlustratorem et beatitudinis largitorem esse dixerunt."

12. Ibid. 8, 6: "Viderunt ergo isti philosophi, quos ceteris non inmerito fama atque gloria praelatos videmus, nullum corpus esse Deum, et ideo cuncta corpora transcenderunt quaerentes Deum. Viderunt, quidquid mutabile est, non esse summum Deum, et ideo animam omnem mutabilesque omnes spiritus transcenderunt quaerentes summum Deum."

13. Ibid. 8, 5: "Si ergo Plato Dei huius imitatorem cognitorem amatorem dixit esse sapientem, cuius participatione sit beatus, quid opus est excutere ceteros?"

14. Ibid.: "Nulli nobis quam isti propius accesserunt."

15. Augustine knew that some had claimed that Plato and Aristotle held that same doctrine; see *c. Acad.* 3, 19, 42: "non defuerunt acutissimi et solertissimi viri, qui docuerunt disputationibus suis Aristotelem ac Platonem ita sibi concinere, ut imperitis minusque attentis dissentire videantur." He is perhaps alluding to the lost work of Porphyry that bore such a title. See "Porphyrios," by R. Beutler, in *Real-Encyclopädie den classischen Altertumswissenschaft*, vol. 22, pt. 1 (Stuttgart: Metzler, 1953), cc. 284–285.

16. *Civ. Dei* 19, 1, 2: "nulla est homini causa philosophandi, nisi ut sit beatus."

from assuming that we know what the ancients meant by *philosohia,* one scholar has said that "philosophy means something entirely different in Graeco-Roman antiquity from what it does today."[17] Following what Pierre Hadot has written, A. H. Armstrong has put it this way with greater balance: "[F]or most ancient philosophers, philosophy was a comprehensive and extremely demanding way of life, requiring, certainly, the intense study of the whole of reality, but designed to lead, not simply to what we should call an 'intellectual' or 'scientific' understanding of the nature of things, but to the attainment of that human goodness, including or consisting in wisdom, but a transforming wisdom, which can alone bring about human well-being."[18]

With such a view of philosophy in mind, Augustine reminds Romanianus of his frequent insistence that he "regarded no fortune as favorable save that which bestowed the leisure to philosophize *(otium philosophandi),* no life as happy save that which is lived in philosophy."[19] A life lived in philosophy required *otium,* which we correctly, but very inadequately, translate as "leisure." André Mandouze says that, besides leisure and the material resources needed to ensure it, *otium* requires "above all the interior availability *(disponibilité)* without which there is neither tranquility of soul nor peace of mind, two things indispensable for withdrawal into oneself and the recollection of God."[20] It was for the sake of such *otium* that Alypius kept steering Augustine away from marriage, warning that "we could by no means live together a life of secure leisure in the love of wisdom, as we had long desired," if Augustine took a wife.[21]

Years later, in looking back on the time at Cassiciacum, Augustine

---

17. Ilsetraut Hadot, "The Spiritual Guide," in *Classical Mediterranean Spirituality,* vol. 15 of *World Spirituality: An Encyclopedic History of the Religious Quest* (New York: Crossroad, 1986), 436–59, here 444.

18. A. H. Armstrong, *Expectations of Immortality in Late Antiquity,* The Aquinas Lecture, 1987 (Milwaukee: Marquette University Press, 1987), 21. Armstrong refers to Pierre Hadot's *Exercises spirituels et philosophie antique* (Paris: Études augustiniennes, 1981).

19. *C. Acad.* 2, 2, 4: "nullam mihi videri prosperam fortunam, nisi quae otium philosophandi daret, nullam beatam vitam, nisi qua in philosophia viveretur."

20. André Mandouze, *Saint Augustin. L'aventure de la raison et de la grâce* (Paris: Études augustiniennes, 1968), 194 (my translation).

21. *Conf.* 6, 12, 21: "Prohibebat me sane Alypius uxore ducenda cantans nullo modo nos posse securo otio simul in amore sapientiae viuere, sicut iam diu desideraremus, si id fecissem."

described it as *Christianae vitae otium:* the leisure of Christian life.²² And soon after his return to Africa, in writing to Nebridius, Augustine used the marvelous phrase *deificari in otio* (to become God-like in leisure)²³ to describe his aim in withdrawing from the troubled journeys of this world in order to "think of that one last journey which is called death."²⁴ Georges Folliet claims that "Augustine speaks as a Christian convert, but the description of the asceticism he envisages and the expressions he uses make one suspect that his present ideal for life is much closer to that of the wise man presented by the Neoplatonic philosophers than to that of the Gospel."²⁵ Folliet has perhaps overemphasized the Neoplatonic influence upon Augustine's ideal for the life he and his companions were beginning to lead at Thagaste, a life that others see as the cradle of Western monasticism.²⁶ Later in his life Augustine said that "the true philosopher is a lover of God,"²⁷ for the true philosopher loves that Wisdom which, or rather who, is God. We must remember that for Augustine what one loves necessarily transforms the lover into itself.²⁸ Thus in loving God, one is transformed into or becomes God.²⁹ Hence, Augustine's goal at Thagaste of "becoming God-like" is simply the goal of the life of philosophy. The life of philosophy is, after all, a life in love with wisdom, "but of a transforming wisdom"—to use Armstrong's words—of that Wisdom that transforms one into God, into a child of the Most High.

Certainly, the *otium* of Thagaste is Christian and monastic, but it

---

22. *Retr.* 1, 1.
23. *Ep.* 10, 2.
24. Ibid.: "de illa una ultima, quae mors uocatur, cogitantis."
25. Georges Folliet, "'Deificari in otio.' Augustin, *Epistula* 10, 2," *Recherches augustiniennes* 2 (1962): 225–236, here 226 (my translation).
26. See Mandouze, *Saint Augustin,* 207–209, where the author emphasizes the advance represented by *deificari in otio* over the ideal of Cassiciacum and insists that the *otium* of Thagaste includes the framework of religious life and communal sharing of goods. See also George Lawless, *Augustine of Hippo and His Monastic Rule* (Oxford: Clarendon Press, 1987), 51, where Lawless says of the *otium* described in *vera rel.* 35, 65 that it "is a far cry from the leisure of the philosophers."
27. *Civ. Dei* 8, 1: "verus philosophus est amator Dei."
28. *Div. quaes.* 35, 2: "Et quoniam id quod amatur afficiat ex se amantem necesse est, fit ut sic amatum quod aeternum est aeternitate animum afficiat. Quocirca ea demum vita beata est quae aeterna est. Quid vero aeternum est quod aeternitate animum afficiat nisi Deus?"
29. *Ep. Jo.* 2, 14: "quia talis est quisque qualis eius dilectio est. Terram diligis? terra eris. Deum diligis? quid dicam? Deus eris? Non audeo dicere ex me, Scripturas audiamus: 'Ego dixi, Dii estis, et filii Altissimi.'" See also *s.* 120, 1.

is also, I believe, clearly in continuity with the dedication to the life of philosophy envisioned at Cassiciacum. In any case, to dedicate oneself to philosophy, in order to become God-like in leisure, was far more like entering monastic life than selecting a major in college or even a program of graduate studies. This is the first respect in which the *philosophia* of Augustine is quite different from the contemporary meaning of philosophy.

The second way in which what Augustine called philosophy differs from what most moderns understand by philosophy has to do with the task and the content of philosophy. In one passage Augustine tells us that philosophy has a twofold question: "one about the soul, the other about God. The first makes us know ourselves; the other that we know our origin. The former is sweeter to us; the latter more precious. The former makes us worthy of happiness; the latter makes us happy."[30] That is, as aiming at the happy life, philosophy has no concern with this world of bodily things, but only with God as our goal and ourselves as returning to him.[31] Philosophy is not the path for everyone, but for the very few. Philosophy promises reason to these few, setting them free and teaching them "not only not to hold those [i.e., the Christian] mysteries in contempt, but to understand them, and them alone, as they should be understood."[32] Thus the content that philosophy brings the very few to understand is identical with the mysteries of the Christian faith. The true and genuine philosophy has, Augustine claims, "no other task than to teach what is the principle without principle of all things and how great an intellect remains in it and what has flowed forth from there for our salvation without any lessening of its being."[33] Augustine explicitly

---

30. *Ord.* 2, 18, 47: "Cuius duplex quaestio est, una de anima, altera de deo. Prima efficit, ut nosmet ipsos noverimus, altera, ut originem nostram. Illa nobis dulcior, ista carior, illa nos dignos beata vita, beatos haec facit."

31. See *c. Acad.* 1, 1, 3: "Ipsa docet et vere docet nihil omnino colendum esse totumque contemni oportere, quidquid mortalibus oculis cernitur, quidquid ullus sensus attingit. Ipsa verissimum et secretissimum Deum perspicue se demonstraturum promittit et iam iamque quasi per lucidas nubes ostentare dignatur."

32. *Ord.* 2, 5, 16: "Philosophia rationem promittit et vix paucissimos liberat, quos tamen non modo non contemnere illa mysteria sed sola intellegere, ut intellegenda sunt, cogit." Goulven Madec, "A propos d'une traduction de *De ordine* II, v, 16," *Revue des études augustiniennes* 16 (1970): 179–185, where Madec argues convincingly that *sola* modifies *mysteria* rather than *philosophia*.

33. Ibid. 2, 5, 16: "nullumque aliud habet negotium, quae vera et, ut ita dicam, germana philosophia est, quam ut doceat, quod sit omnium rerum principium sine

identifies these three with the Father, Son and Holy Spirit, which "the venerable mysteries . . . proclaim, neither confusing them, as some do, nor treating them unjustly, as many do."[34] Thus, the whole task of philosophy is to understand the Christian Trinity as the source of being, of truth, and of salvation. It does not take too much stretching to see in this early text the "rerum auctorem, veritatis inlustratorem et beatitudinis largitorem" of the *civ. Dei*. Thus the whole content of philosophy for Augustine is the triune God of Christianity.

Philosophy is the love of wisdom, and as early as the *c. Acad.* Augustine appeals to Cicero's definition of wisdom as "the knowledge of things human and divine."[35] In the *De Trinitate* (hereafter *Trin.*), following Saint Paul in 1 Corinthians 12:8, Augustine distinguishes wisdom and knowledge so that wisdom *(sapientia)* is knowledge of things eternal and knowledge *(scientia)* is knowledge of things temporal. *Scientia* is not knowledge of just anything temporal, but only of that "by which the saving faith, which leads to true happiness, is born, nourished, defended and strengthened."[36]

Madec has noted that this distinction between *sapientia* and *scientia* "is not without analogy with the double function that Cicero assigns to philosophy in the *Hortensius:* the practice of the virtues and contemplative wisdom."[37] Thus, in *c. Acad.* 1, 7, 20, the knowledge of things

---

principio quantusque in eo maneat intellectus quidve inde in nostram salutem sine ulla degeneratione manaverit."

34. Ibid.: "quem unum Deum omnipotentem, cum quo tripotentem patrem et filium et spiritum sanctum, veneranda mysteria, quae fide sincera et inconcussa populos liberant, nec confuse, ut quidam, nec contumeliose, ut multi, praedicant." Here I find Madec's argument for following the edition of P. Knöll persuasive. I also agree with Madec's claim that *confuse* and *contumeliose* refer to the doctrine of the Sabellians and of the Arians respectively; see Madec, "A propos d'une traduction," 182–184. Frederick Van Fleteren, however, suggests that it is Porphyry whom Augustine has in mind; see his "Authority and Reason, Faith and Understanding in the Thought of St. Augustine," *AS* 4 (1973): 33–71, here 48–49.

35. See *c. Acad.* 1, 6, 16: "Non enim nunc primum auditis, 'Sapientiam esse rerum humanarum divinarumque scientiam.'" Augustine repeats that definition four or even five times in the first book. See Madec, "L'*Hortensius* de Cicéron," here 169.

36. *Trin.* 14, 1, 3: "Verum secundum hanc distinctionem qua dixit Apostolus: 'Alii datur sermo sapientiae, alii sermo scientiae' (1 Cor 12:8), ista definitio dividenda est ut rerum divinarum scientia proprie sapientia nuncupetur, humanarun autem proprie scientiae nomen obtineat . . . huic scientiae tribuens, sed illud tantummodo quo fides saluberrima quae ad veram beatitudinem ducit, gignitur, nutritur, defenditur, roboratur."

37. Madec, "L'*Hortensius* de Cicéon," 170 (my translation). Madec adds, "Mais la *scientia* augustinienne assume précisément la fonction pratique de la philosophie."

human is "that by which one knows the light of prudence, the beauty of temperance, the strength of courage, and the holiness of justice."[38] It is, I suggest, Augustinian wisdom in the proper sense, which is the content of philosophy, that is, knowledge of the eternal God: Father, Son and Holy Spirit, while knowledge in the proper sense embraces the means of the soul's return to God, the temporal dispensation by which God has offered us salvation.[39] Or, as Augustine has often expressed it, the great Neoplatonists have seen from afar the Fatherland to which we must return.[40] They have come to know the eternal reality of God, but in their pride they have failed to know the way to attain the Fatherland.[41] That way is the humanity of Christ, who as God is also the goal. As human, he is our knowledge; as divine, he is our wisdom. What philosophy can attain, and what the great Platonists have attained, is the knowledge of God's eternal reality; what philosophy cannot attain is the knowledge of the temporal dispensation and the humanity the Word has assumed, which is also the way, indeed the only way, of re-

---

38. *C. Acad.* 1, 7, 20: "Illa est humanarum rerum scientia, qua novit lumen prudentiae, temperantiae decus, fortitudinis robur, justitiae sanctitatem."

39. Madec claims that the true philosophy included the Incarnation of the Word. In "Connaissance de Dieu et action de grâce. Essai sur les citations de l'*Ep. aux Romains* 1, 18–25 dans l'oeuvre de saint Augustin," *Recherches augustiniennes* 2 (1962): 273–309, here 283, he says, "Augustin a reconnu dans la doctrine du Verbe incarné la 'seule doctrine philosophique parfaitement vraie' et 'la philosophie véritable et authentique' qui a pour tâche l'intelligence des mystères." He refers to *c. Acad.* 3, 19, 42, where Augustine says, referring to the intelligible world: "cui animas multiformibus erroris tenebris caecatas et altissimis a corpore sordibus oblitas numquam ista ratio subtilissima revocaret, nisi summus Deus populari quadam clementia divini intellectus auctoritatem usque ad ipsum corpus humanum declinaret atque submitteret, cuius non solum praeceptis sed etiam factis excitatae animae redire in semet ipsas et resipiscere patriam etiam sine concertatione potuissent." I am in complete agreement with Madec that without humble faith in the Incarnate Word, souls could never attain the Fatherland, even if they saw it from afar. The Platonists certainly did not know or were too proud to take the way, but faith in the Incarnation belongs to *scientia* as opposed to *sapientia*, to the way as opposed to the goal. *Philosophia* concerns the *aeternalia Dei*, not the temporal dispensation. See my "The Link between Faith and Time in St. Augustine," in *Augustine: Presbyter Factus Sum*, ed. J. Lienhard, E. Muller, and R. Teske (New York: Peter Lang, 1993), 195–206.

40. *Jo. Ev. tr.* 2, 4: "Viderunt quo veniendum esset. . . . Illud potuerunt videre quod est, sed viderunt de longe." *Trin.* 4, 15, 20: "nonnulli eorum potuerunt aciem mentis ultra omnem creaturam transmittere et lucem incommutabilis veritatis quantulacumque ex parte contingere . . . de longinquo prospicere patriam transmarinam."

41. *Trin.* 4, 15, 20: "Sed quid prodest superbienti et ob hoc erubescenti lignum conscendere de longinquo prospicere patriam transmarinam? Aut quid obest humili de tanto intervallo non eam videre in illo ligno ad eam venienti quod dedignatur ille portari?"

turn.[42] Thus from his earliest writings Augustine saw the need for the Incarnation of the Word if souls—"blinded by the abundant darkness of error and stained with the deepest filth of the body," were to be "able to return to themselves and see again their fatherland."[43]

We have seen that *philosophia* for Augustine was a wisdom in continuity with the best in classical Greek thought, but that it differed from what it means for us in the twentieth-first century insofar as it involved a whole way of life aimed at true happiness and embraced as its content only the Christian mysteries. On the other hand, Augustine is quite clear that, if philosophy can know the eternal God as the source of our being, knowledge, and beatitude, philosophy cannot provide the way of attaining God. For that we need faith in Christ, our knowledge, who is also our wisdom.

CAN THERE BE AN AUGUSTINIAN PHILOSOPHY?

The most serious objections to the claim that there is such philosophy in Augustine stem from Augustine's clear claim that one must first believe in order to understand.[44] Etienne Gilson has made the strong claim that "we know of no single instance where Augustine allowed reason to dispense with faith as its starting point.... This is the reason why belief in God precedes even proof of His existence."[45] Augustine's insistence that one must first believe in order to understand would seem

---

42. See *conf.* 7, 9, 13–14, where Augustine contrasts what he found in the *libri Platonicorum* and what he did not find there. What he found there were the *aeternalia Dei;* what he did not find there was the temporal dispensation by which we are saved. See also *cons. Eu.* 1, 35, 53: "Ipse est nobis fides in rebus ortis qui est ueritas in aeternis." *Trin.* 13, 19, 24: "Scientia ergo nostra Christus est, sapientia quoque nostra idem Christus est. Ipse nobis fidem de rebus temporalibus inserit; ipse de sempiternis exhibet ueritatem. Per ipsum pergimus ad ipsum, tendimus per scientiam ad sapientiam; ab uno tamen eodemque Christo non recedimus, 'in quo sunt omnes thesauri sapientiae et scientiae absconditi'" (Col 2:3).

43. *C. Acad.* 3, 19, 42; see above note 39.

44. Augustine read in Is 7:9: "Nisi credideritis, non intellegetis." He cites the text for the first time in *lib. arb.* 1, 2, 4 and then again in *lib. arb.* 2, 2, 6 and *mag.* 11, 37.

45. Gilson, *The Christian Philosophy of St. Augustine*, 34. Gilson points to *mor.* 1, 2, 3, 1311–1312, where he claims Augustine uses the faulty method of beginning with reason—a method that Gilson oddly views as Manichaean. Gilson comments, "He only resigns himself to stoop to the madness of the Manichaeans by provisorily adopting their method, even as Jesus Christ submitted to death to save us" (ibid., 265n31).

to prejudice the case against anything like an autonomous philosophy within his thought. "Faith seeking understanding" is, after all, the classical description of the movement of theology rather than of philosophy. Moreover, the case for an independent philosophy is aggravated by an important change in Augustine's thought. Scholars frequently speak of Augustine's conversions in the plural.[46]

Besides the momentous events of 386–387 that led to his being baptized and becoming a servant of God, there is Augustine's conversion to Manichaeism in 373. But there is another turning point in Augustine's life that has been described as his final conversion.[47] In 396, while writing to Simplicianus, Augustine came to realize that faith is a gift of God. Much later, in writing to the monks of Provence, Augustine admits that he had "other thoughts on this question" and that God "revealed to me the means of solving the problem, when . . . I was writing to bishop Simplician."[48] Prior to the time of *Ad Simplicianum* (hereafter *Simpl.*),

---

46. See Jean-Marie Le Blond, *Les conversions de saint Augustin* (Paris: Aubier, 1950); François Masai, "Les conversions de saint Augustin et les débuts du spiritualisme en Occident," *Le Moyen Âge* 67 (1961): 1–40; Leo C. Ferrari, *The Conversions of Saint Augustine* (Villanova: Villanova University Press, 1984).

47. See Ferrari, *The Conversions*, 70ff. A. Pegis refers to this conversion as Augustine's second. See Anton C. Pegis, "The Second Conversion of St Augustine," in *Gesellschaft, Kultur, Literatur: Rezeption und Originalität im Wachsen einer europäisschen Literatur und Geistigkeit* (Stuttgart: Anton Hiersemann, 1975), 79–93.

48. *Praed. sanc.* 4, 8. Ferrari takes Augustine's use of *revelare* in this passage in a strong sense. He speaks of the revelation as "a tremendous transformation in the very foundations of Augustine's thought. Furthermore, it was no conclusion reached on the basis of mere human reasoning. Indeed, as Augustine tells us, it was a veritable revelation to him from God Himself, as he struggled to answer the question of Simplicianus" (Ferrari, *The Conversions,* 77). However, Augustine uses *revelare* in the preceding paragraphs of *praed. sanc.,* and he does so in dependence upon Paul's words, "And if on some point you think otherwise, God will reveal this to you as well; only, let us walk in the truth that we have already attained" (Phil 3:15–16). Augustine applies this text to the monks of Provence, saying that, if they cling to the truths they already hold that separate them from the Pelagians, "if they think otherwise with regard to predestination, God will reveal this to them as well" (*praed. sanc.* 1, 2). Surely Augustine is not promising these monks an exceptional revelation from God, but simply the intellectual clarification that comes from prayerful pursuit of the truth, which is always for Augustine a divine gift. See as well Augustine's use of this text in *ep.* 120, 1, 4, where Augustine can hardly be promising Consentius an exceptional revelation of the doctrine of the Trinity. On the other hand, Peter Brown's statement, "when Augustine speaks of an idea having been 'revealed' to him, he means only that he has reached the inevitable conclusion of a series of certainties . . . —an experience not unknown to speculative thinkers today" (*Augustine of Hippo: A Biography* [Berkeley and Los Angeles: University of California Press, 1969], 282n2) seems to offer a too naturalistic interpretation that overlooks the fact that for Augustine it is God "who gives understanding" (see *praed. sanc.* 1, 2).

he thought "that the faith by which we believe in God is not a gift of God, but something that we have from ourselves."⁴⁹

At that time he thought that we needed grace in the sense that we needed to have the Gospel preached to us, but "I thought that it was entirely up to us that we should consent to the Gospel preached to us, and that we had it from ourselves."⁵⁰ Hence, from 396 on Augustine regarded the assent of faith to the Gospel as a gift of God, while prior to that time he thought of the assent as merely a reasonable act of human practical reason. Prior to 396 Augustine had distinguished human authority and divine authority as grounds for belief, and he had distinguished divine and human objects of belief.⁵¹ But he had not distinguished the assent of belief that is a gift of God from the assent that is merely a reasonable human act.

What then is the relevance of this final conversion to my topic? Prior to 396 believing was, in Augustine's eyes, a matter of reasonable human assent, whether one relied upon divine or human authority, whether what one believed was what God spoke or what another human spoke. Hence, believing in order to understand was a method open to every reasonable human being and, for that reason, a philosophical method. Masai describes Augustine's pre-396 position as a philosophical fideism in the sense that one must begin with faith, albeit a philosophical faith.⁵² Masai sees in the revelation of 396 the birth of theology and refers to Augustine's position after 396 as a theological fideism, because one begins with faith, but a faith that is a gift of God and not, therefore, something that is entirely up to us or that we have from ourselves as human beings. Masai concludes, "Beginning in 396, Augustine acknowledged in the act of faith as well as in its object a divine origin and nature. But *ipso facto* the philosophical character of Augustinian thought is found to be compromised. As it rests entirely upon the foundation of a light freely given by God, it cannot keep the pretense of

---

49. *Praed. sanc.* 3, 7: "errarem, putans fidem qua in Deum credimus, non esse donum Dei, sed a nobis esse in nobis."

50. Ibid. 3, 7: "ut autem praedicato nobis evangelio consentiremus, nostrum esse proprium, et nobis ex nobis esse arbitrabar."

51. See *ord.* 2, 9, 27: "Auctoritas autem partim divina est, partim humana, sed vera firma summa est, quae divina nominatur."

52. The term "fideism" is, I believe, unfortunate; like the term "ontologism," it carries misleading historical overtones and recalls the fideism of Huet (1630–1721) or the traditionalism of Bonald (1754–1840) and of Lamennais (1781–1854), in accord with which all knowledge had to begin with an act of faith.

addressing human reason as such; it becomes necessarily a knowledge reserved for the faithful alone. In brief, the philosophy of Augustine has from that time been transformed into theology."[53] Obviously the question of whether there can be an Augustinian philosophy becomes more difficult once the act of believing is seen to be a free gift of God and not something entirely up to us so that we can believe if we want to do so. It is not merely that prior to 396 Augustine did not consider the question of our beginning to believe as a grace; rather, he tells us that he had regarded beginning to believe as something within our power. In a footnote Masai wonders whether it is conceivable to restore within the strictly Augustinian perspective a Christian philosophy alongside theology.[54] He dodges an answer, while noting that an answer to this question depends upon the solution of other problems raised by divine illumination and, more generally, the relation between nature and grace.

On the other hand, the existence of philosophy in Augustine has also had its defenders. In the second BA edition of *De magistro* (hereafter *mag.*) and *De libero arbitrio* (hereafter *lib. arb.*), F. J. Thonnard, while admitting that Augustine did not formally create a philosophical system, holds that it is possible to make explicit Augustine's philosophy. He points to three conditions of an Augustinian philosophy that were articulated by Fulbert Cayré:

if the philosophical questions that Saint Augustine has dealt with were studied by him in a rational manner and not merely from the perspective of faith; 2) if these questions include all the major problems posed by every philosophy worthy of the name; 3) if the solutions that he brings to them are tied together by common principles capable of giving to the whole a solid coherence. If these are fulfilled, there is in Saint Augustine a true philosophy that can be separated from his theology, even if he himself has not separated them.[55]

I agree with Cayré that the three conditions for the existence of philosophy are sufficient and sufficiently met in the works of Augustine for one to speak of an Augustinian philosophy. But I think one can go further and say that there has to be within Augustine's strictly theological

---

53. Masai, "Les conversions de saint Augustin," 36–37.
54. Ibid., 37.
55. See the note: "La philosophie augustinienne," in the second edition of BA 6, 514–517, here 517. In the third edition by G. Madec, this note is omitted, perhaps because of Madec's conviction that there is no patristic philosophy.

thought an autonomous philosophy that is an indispensable condition of the possibility of his theology. Masai is surely correct that a proper solution to the question of whether there can be an Augustinian philosophy depends upon the wider questions of nature and grace, or of reason and faith.

There was a time in the not so distant past when in Catholic circles philosophy and theology were sharply distinguished, so much so that philosophical ethics, for example, was said to be the sort of moral guidance that would have been applicable if we were living in a state of pure nature, that hypothetical state which has never existed, but would have existed if human beings were not destined for a supernatural end. Theologians such as Karl Rahner and Henri de Lubac have done much to correct the view that revelation and grace are purely extrinsic additions to nature.[56]

Rahner has argued that the possibility of revelation requires that man, as the hearer of the word of God, have a natural self-understanding independent of special revelation in order to be able to hear and understand God's word. He claims that theology "necessarily implies philosophy, i.e., a previous . . . self-comprehension of the man who hears the historical revelation of God."[57]

Furthermore, he maintains that "that self-clarification of man's existence which we call philosophy can certainly be 'pure' philosophy in the sense that it does not take any of its material contents and norms from . . . revelation."[58] But even apart from such a transcendental deduction of the necessity of a philosophy for understanding the revealed word of God, one can, I believe, argue that in Augustine there are philosophical truths that human reason can know independently of accepting in faith God's revelation of those truths. These truths would be analogous to what Thomas Aquinas called the *praeambula fidei*. Let me briefly sketch my reasons for this claim. First, even after 396, when God revealed to Augustine that the act of believing is a gift of God and not something within simply human power, it does not seem to be the case that every act of believing is a gift of God. Indeed Augustine implies that faith

---

56. See my "Rahner on the Relation of Nature and Grace," *Philosophy and Theology*, disk supplement 4, 4 (1989): 109–122.

57. Karl Rahner, "Philosophy and Theology," in *Theological Investigations*, vol. 6 (Baltimore: Helicon, 1969), p. 73.

58. Ibid., p. 78.

need precede reason only "in certain things pertaining to the doctrine of salvation which we cannot yet perceive by reason."[59]

Second, Augustine groups the objects of belief *(credibilia)* into three classes. He speaks of things that must always be believed and can never be understood, of things that are understood as soon as they are believed, and of things that are first believed and later understood. The first class of objects of belief includes all historical events of which we were not ourselves witnesses. The second class includes "all human reasonings either in mathematics or in any of the disciplines." The third class of objects of belief includes truths about "the divine realities that can only be understood by the pure of heart."[60] Augustine thought that one might, for example, understand a theorem in geometry as soon as one accepted it as true. Certainly, the second class of *credibilia* are supernatural in terms neither of the object believed nor of the authority one believes nor of the act of believing as a special gift of God.[61]

Third, Augustine credited the great Greek philosophers with having come to a knowledge of God and of human destiny. Though at one point he entertained the idea that Plato had come into contact with God's revelation to the Jewish people, he clearly stated that they came to a knowledge of the eternal reality of God from the things God had made.[62] Hence, I believe that one can maintain that there is in Augustine—and indeed there must be in Augustine—a philosophy, and a philosophy that can be recognized as philosophy even in the sense in which we speak of philosophy today. One could, of course, so define philosophy that Augustine's thought is automatically excluded. But any such definition could, I fear, banish from the realm of philosophy the works of Hegel and Aquinas, Kierkegaard, and even Descartes as well.

---

59. *Ep.* 120, 1, 3: "Ut ergo in quibusdam rebus ad doctrinam salutarem pertinentibus, quas ratione nondum percipere valemus, sed aliquando valebimus, fides praecedat rationem."

60. *Div. quaes.* 48: "alia quae mox ut creduntur intelleguntur, sicut sunt omnes rationes humanae vel de numeris vel de quibuslibet disciplinis; tertium quae primo creduntur et postea intelliguntur qualia sunt ea quae de divinis rebus non possum intelligi nisi ab his qui mundo sunt corde."

61. Thus in *ep.* 120, 1, 5, Augustine seems to say that there are some truths that we know to be true and cannot believe once an account has been given. "Sunt autem quaedam, quae cum audierimus, non eis accommodamus fidem et ratione nobis reddita vera esse cognoscimus, quae credere non valemus."

62. *Civ. Dei* 8, 12: "Sed undecumque ista ille [Plato] didicerit, sive praecedentibus eum veterum libris siue potius, quo modo dicit Apostolus, quia 'quod notum est Dei manifestum est in illis.'"

AUGUSTINE'S LEGACY TO WESTERN PHILOSOPHY

Any attempt to sum up the core of Augustine's legacy to Western philosophy is bound to be incomplete and perspectival. I intend to touch upon three topics, one an attitude, the other two matters of doctrine. The attitude that I want to single out is a deep appreciation for human intelligence. Prior to Augustine, at least in the African Church, the spirit of Tertullian was still regnant—Tertullian who asked what Athens has to do with Jerusalem, what the Academy has to do with the Church, Tertullian who claimed that we have no need for a curiosity going beyond Christ Jesus or for inquiry going beyond the Gospel.[63] When Augustine warns of bishops and priests who "avoid unveiling the mysteries or, content with simple faith, have no care to know more profound truths," he indicates the anti-intellectual atmosphere within the *Catholica* that helped push him into the Manichaean fold.[64] From his own conversion to Manichaeism Augustine learned how dangerous it could be to meet the human desire to know with ridicule instead of respect.[65] In his *Gn. litt.* he again and again indicates his respect for the inquiring mind by refusing rashly to claim knowledge or to give up on its pursuit.[66]

Let me offer two examples of Augustine's respect for the human intellect's desire to know. First, years after Augustine's ordination to the episcopacy, Consentius wrote to Augustine that he thought "that the truth about God's reality ought to be grasped by faith rather than by reason."[67]

---

63. Tertullian, *De praescriptione haereticorum* 7: "Quid ergo Athenis et Hierosolymis? Quid academiae et ecclesiae? . . . Nobis curiositate opus non est post Christum Iesum nec inquisitione post evangelium."

64. *Mor.* I, I, I: "Nec, si ea discere cupiens, in aliquos forte inciderit vel episcopos vel presbyteros, vel cujusmodi Ecclesiae catholicae antistites et ministros, qui aut passim caveant nudare mysteria, aut contenti simplici fide, altiora cognoscere non curarint, desperet ibi scientiam esse veritatis, ubi neque omnes a quibus quaeritur docere possunt, neque omnes qui quaerunt discere digni sunt." See *util. cred.* 1, 2, 4, for Augustine's claim that it was the demand for belief prior to understanding that lured him into Manichaeism.

65. We perhaps have a reflection of such ridicule in Augustine's refusal to give the answer that someone gave to the question about what God was doing before he created the world, namely, that he was preparing hell for people who ask profound questions; see *conf.* II, 12, 14: "'Alta,' inquit, 'scrutantibus gehennas parabat.' Aliud est videre, aliud ridere. Haec non respondeo."

66. See the note: "Le charactère aporétique du De Genesi ad litteram," in BA 48, 575–580.

67. *Ep.* 119, 1: "ego igitur cum apud memet ipsum prorsus definerim veritatem rei divinae ex fide magis quam ex ratione percipi oportere."

Otherwise, Consentius suggests, only the likes of philosophers would attain beatitude, and he argues that "we should not so much require a rational account of God as follow the authority of the saints."[68] In response Augustine warns with regard to the Trinity against following the authority of the saints alone without making any effort to understand. "Correct your position," he says, "not so that you reject faith, but so that what you already hold by solid faith, you may also see by the light of reason."[69] Augustine adds, "Heaven forbid that God should hate in us that by which he made us more excellent than the animals. Heaven forbid, I say, that we believe so that we do not accept or seek a rational account, since we could not believe unless we had rational souls."[70] He cites Saint Peter's warning that we should be ready to give an account of our faith and urges Consentius to "a love of intelligence" *(ad amorem intelligentiae)*. His words, *Intellectum uero valde ama:* "Have a great love for the intellect," echo down the centuries as a charter for Christian dedication to intellectual pursuits, first of all, in theology, but also in what we today identify as philosophy and the sciences.[71]

Second, no one would claim that Augustine was a philosopher of science, but his care to interpret Scripture in such a way as to avoid a contradiction with what has been scientifically proven has been admired by a scientist as great as Galileo. In *Gn. litt.,* while dealing with the shape of the heavens, Augustine manages to ask a question that cannot on the surface fail to strike us, who live in the age of space exploration, as naive. "What does it matter to me," he asks, "whether the heaven encloses the earth like a sphere . . . or only covers it from above like a lid?"[72] Yet he worries that someone might find in the Scripture

---

68. Ibid.; "si enim fides sanctae ecclesiae ex disputationis ratione, non ex credulitatis pietate adprehenderetur, nemo praeter philosophos atque oratores beatitudinem possideret."

69. *Ep.* 120, 1, 2: "corrige definitionem tuam, non ut fidem respuas, sed ut ea, quae fidei firmitate iam tenes, etiam rationis luce conspicias."

70. Ibid. 1, 3: "Absit namque, ut hoc in nobis Deus oderit, in quo nos reliquis animantibus excellentiores creavit absit, inquam, ut ideo credamus, ne rationem accipiamus sive quaeramus, cum etiam credere non possemus, nisi rationales animas haberemus."

71. Ibid. 1, 6 and 3, 13. It is important to bear in mind that Consentius's principal difficulty was purely philosophical, namely, to conceive of God as an incorporeal being, as we shall see shortly.

72. *Gn. litt.* 2, 9, 20: "Quid enim ad me pertinet, utrum caelum sicut sphaera undique concludat terram in media mundi mole libratam, an eam ex una parte desuper velut discus operiat?"

what seems opposed to clearly seen rational arguments and, as a result, give up all belief in the Scriptures. He warns that "the Holy Spirit who spoke through the [authors of Scripture] did not intend to teach human beings matters of no use for their salvation."[73] He faces the Psalm text that God "has stretched out the heaven like a skin" (Ps 103:2), which seems contrary to the view that the heaven is spherical. Augustine even envisages the case in which some are able to prove with indubitable arguments that the heaven is spherical and says, "Then we must prove that what our books say about the skin is not contrary to those rational truths; otherwise, there will be another contradiction between this text and the other passage of Scripture in which it says that the heaven was hung as a vault (see Is 40:22)."[74] In writing to Christine of Lorraine, Galileo cites the text from Augustine and adds, "From this text we see that we need no less care to show how a passage of Scripture is in agreement with a proposition demonstrated by natural reason than to show how one passage of Scripture agrees with another contrary to it. . . . One must admire the circumspection of this saint who manifests such great reserve in dealing with obscure conclusions or those of which one can have a demonstration by human means."[75]

Let me, then, turn to two points of philosophical doctrine. In writing to Caelestinus in 390 or 391, Augustine offers a brief, but important summary of his worldview: "Accept this priceless, but tiny gem *(quiddam grande, sed breve)*. There is a nature changeable in places and times, such as the body, and there is a nature not changeable in place at all, but changeable only in time, such as the soul, and there is a nature which cannot change either in place or in time. This is God."[76]

Robert O'Connell has pointed to this three-tiered view of reality

---

73. Ibid.: "sed spiritum Dei, qui per eos loquebatur; noluisse ista docere homines nulli saluti profutura."

74. Ibid. 2, 9, 21: "demonstrandum est hoc, quod apud nos de pelle dictum est, veris illis rationibus non esse contrarium; alioquin contrarium erit etiam ipsis in alio loco scripturis nostris, ubi caelum dicitur velut camera esse suspensum."

75. Galileo Galilei, "Lettre à Christine de Lorraine, Grand-Duchesse de Toscane (1615), traduction et présentation par François Russo," *Revue d'histoire des sciences et de leurs applications* 17 (1964): 332–366; cited from BA 48, 177n20 (my translation). Galileo also cites *Gn. litt.* 1, 17, 37; 1, 19, 38–39, 41; 2, 10, 23; 2, 18, 38; 2, 28, 43.

76. *Ep.* 18, 2: "Sane quoniam te novi, accipe hoc quiddam grande et breve: est natura per locos et tempora mutabilis, ut corpus, et est natura per locos nullo modo, sed tantum per tempora etiam ipsa mutabilis, ut anima, et est natura, quae nec per locos nec per tempora mutari potest, hoc Deus est."

with the utterly immutable God at the top and souls mutable only in time in the middle and bodies mutable in both time and place at the bottom as the controlling idea in Vernon Bourke's presentation of Augustine's view of reality.[77] Contained in that *quiddam grande et breve* that Augustine offered to Caelestinus are two doctrines that lie, I suggest, at the heart of Augustine's philosophical legacy to the Western world: his concept of nonbodily realities, such as the soul and God, and his concept of nontemporal reality, such as the utterly unchanging reality of God. As a nature that is immutable in place must be free from any spatial extension, so a nature that is immutable in time must be free from any temporal distension. Prior to Augustine, at least in Western Christianity, there was no philosophical concept of incorporeal being, of being that is whole wherever it is *(totus ubique)*. Once again the philosophical views of Tertullian and the corporealism of the Stoics were the common philosophical patrimony of the West.[78] In the West prior to Augustine, the term "spirit" was, of course, used in the Bible, in medicine, and in philosophy. But when the meaning of spirit was spelled out, it seems to have meant a subtle kind of body, not something nonbodily. So too, we use "spirits" to refer to a beverage, and pneumatic tires are certainly bodily.[79] In holding that God and the soul were bodily, the Manichees

---

77. Robert J. O'Connell, S.J., *Imagination and Metaphysics in St. Augustine* (Milwaukee: Marquette University Press, 1986). O'Connell is referring to Bourke's *Augustine's View of Reality* (Villanova: Villanova University Press, 1964).

78. See Gérard Verbeke, *L'évolution de la doctrine du pneuma, du stoïcisme à s. Augustin* (Paris: Desclée de Brouwer; and Louvain: Institut supérieur de philosophie, 1945). Verbeke attributes the concept of spirit as incorporeal to the influence of Scripture. F. Masai more correctly, I believe, recognizes the term as biblical, but attributes the concept to Neoplatonism. See Masai, "Les conversions de saint Augustin," 17. For the Stoic view that whatever is, is a body, see E. Weil, "Remarques sur le 'matérialisme' des Stoiciens," in *Mélanges Alexandre Koyré*, vol. 2, *L'aventure de l'esprit* (Paris: Hermann, 1964), 556–572. Weil argues that corporealism more accurately describes the Stoic position than materialism. With Augustine too, the term "materialism" should be used with care, since matter is present in everything changeable, such as souls, though souls are not bodily. See *conf.* 12, 6, 6.

79. See Masai, "Les conversions de saint Augustin," 15–23, for his account of the spiritualization of spirit. Just as most of us who are believers do not require a philosophical concept of nonbodily reality when we pray to God, so the Christians of the first centuries had no need for such a concept of God or of the soul in their lives. So too, prior to the Arian controversy, there was no need for a concept such as the consubstantiality of the Father and the Son, but once the question arose whether or not the Son was a creature, the technical term and concept were needed. In Augustine's case, it was the problem of evil that necessitated a concept of God as nonbodily. After all, if all that is, is bodily, then either God is an infinite body and evil is in God, or God is finite and evil is

were not being singular, but rather were in full accord with the common philosophical view of the age.[80]

Even the Arians whom Augustine encountered seem to have thought of God as corporeal.[81] From Consentius's letter to Augustine already mentioned, we can see that even this budding theologian could not quite see how God was bodiless.[82] We also know that Augustine encountered in the young layman Vincentius Victor, a convert from Donatism, a thinker who explicitly held that the soul was corporeal.[83] Even after Augustine's time the doctrine of the incorporeal nature of the soul was not universally accepted. Thomas Smith points to Faustus of Riez and Cassian as examples in fifth-century Gaul of thinkers who held the corporealist position on the nature of the soul.[84] Augustine's spiritualist understanding of God and the soul, however, became the dominant view in the West for centuries to come. Indeed, the Augustinian revolution was so effective that many anachronistically suppose that the concept of spiritual reality is biblical and explicitly contained in the Christian revelation.[85]

---

another body. The former view means that God is not all good; the latter approximates the Manichaean position.

80. Masai says, "La vérité est qu'avant Augustin, il est vain de chercher dans l'Afrique chrétienne un spiritualisme au sens moderne du terme: le Stoïcisme de Zenon y règna sans contest . . ." ("Les conversions de saint Augustin," p. 19). For the Manichaean position, see *c. ep. Man.* 20, 22, where Augustine calls the Manichees "carnal minds," "qui naturam incorpoream et spiritualem cogitando persequi vel non audent vel nondum valent." So too, he admits in *conf.* 4, 16, 31, that he himself had thought of God as a "bright and immense body" and that he himself was "a part of that body."

81. See, for example, *c. Max.* 2, 9, 2, where Augustine accuses Maximinus of a carnal interpretation of "in sinu Patris" (Jn 1:18): "Sinum quippe tibi fingis, ut video, aliquam capacitatem majoris Patris, qua Filium minorem capiat atque contineat: sicut hominem corporaliter capit domus, aut sicut sinus nutricis capit infantem." See my paper, "Heresy and Imagination in St. Augustine," *Studia Patristica* 27, ed. Elizabeth A. Livingstone, 400–404 (Leuven: Peeters, 1993).

82. See *ep.* 119, 5, where Consentius writes to Augustine, "ais non tamquam aliquod corpus debere cogitare Deum . . . sed sicut iustitiam vel pietatem corpoream cogitare non possumus . . . ita et Deum sine aliqua phantasiae simulatione, in quantum possumus, cogitandum." See also Robert J. O'Connell, *The Origin of the Soul in St. Augustine's Later Works* (New York: Fordham University Press, 1987), p. 94.

83. See *an. et or.* 4, 12, 17—14, 20. See also the notes to the text, which show the linkage to Tertullian's position, as well as the note: "Une théorie stoïcienne de l'âme," BA 22, 837–843.

84. See Thomas A. Smith, "Augustine in Two Gallic Controversies: Use or Abuse?" in *Augustine: Presbyter Factus Sum* (New York: Peter Lang, 1993), 43–55. See also Ernest Fortin, *Christianisme et culture philosophique au cinquième siècle: La querelle de l'âme humaine en Occident* (Paris: Études augustiniennes, 1959).

85. Masai, for example, points to M. Testard who, in speaking of the young Augustine, mentions that he totally lacked certain beliefs fundamental to the Christian faith, such as

The second philosophical doctrine that Augustine bequeathed to the West is the concept of eternity as timelessness, as a mode of existence that is whole all at once *(tota simul)*, without past and without future.[86] Once again, as in the case of spirit, there is in the Bible the language of eternity in the sense of a duration that is everlasting, a duration without beginning or, at least, without end. So too, there was in earlier Greek philosophy the concept of a world without beginning or end.[87] Only with Plotinus do we find a philosophically articulated concept of eternity as timeless duration.[88] But prior to Augustine, at least in the West, there does not seem to have been in any Christian author a philosophically articulated concept of eternity as a timeless present.[89] Even if Gregory of Nyssa did anticipate Augustine in adopting the Plotinian concept of eternity into Christian thought, Augustine certainly remains the source of the concept for the Christian West.

Just as Augustine needed the philosophical concept of incorporeal reality if he was going to be able to deal with the Manichaean questions about the ontological status of evil, so he needed the concept of timeless eternity to handle their questions about what God was doing before he created the world.[90] Unless one has a concept of God as a reality

---

the spiritual nature of God and the soul (Maurice Testard, *Saint Augustin et Cicéron* [Paris: Études augustiniennes, 1958], 1:101; Masai, "Les conversions de saint Augustin," 13).

86. For the texts on eternity in Augustine, see my "*'Vocans temporales, faciens aeternos'*: St. Augustine on Liberation from Time," *Traditio* 41 (1985): 29–47.

87. See Aristotle, *De caelo* 2, 1, 283b26–32.

88. For the Plotinian source of the concept of timeless eternity, see W. Beierwaltes, *Plotin über Ewigkeit und Zeit* (Frankfurt am Main: V. Klostermann, 1967), 198–200, and also my "'Vocans temporales,'" 29–47.

89. The only Christian thinker prior to Augustine to have used the Plotinian concept of eternity in his speculative thought seems to have been Gregory of Nyssa. See David L. Balás, "Eternity and Time in Gregory of Nyssa's *Contra Eunomium*," in *Gregor von Nyssa und die Philosophie,* ed. Heinrich Dörrie, Margarete Altenburger, and Uta Schramm (Leiden: E. J. Brill, 1976), 128–155. Balás concludes, "Most historians of philosophy would consider St. Augustine as the first Christian thinker who adopted [the strict notion of eternity]. Priority surely belongs to Gregory of Nyssa. In fact the famous definition of Boethius: 'interminabilis vitae tota simul et perfecta possessio' could easily be put together from Gregory's texts" (147). The *Contra Eunomium* is dated between 380 and 383, but a direct influence of Gregory upon Augustine seems less likely than the dependence of Augustine upon Plotinus and the Neoplatonic Christians of Milan. B. Altaner concludes that Augustine knew no work of Gregory of Nyssa; see his "Augustinus und Gregor von Nazianz, Gregor von Nyssa," in *Kleine Patristische Schriften,* ed. G. Glockmann (Berlin: Akademie Verlag, 1967), p. 285.

90. E. Peters, "What Was God Doing before He Created the Heavens and the Earth?" *Augustiniana* 34 (1984): 53–74.

not extended in length, breadth, and depth, one cannot maintain that God is infinite and that evil is not in God, unless, of course, one takes the radical option of denying the reality of evil. So too, unless one can think of God's eternity as a duration not extended beyond the present into past and future, one is faced with the prospect of an idle or sleeping God who wakes up and in a burst of energy creates the world. Peter Brown speaks of Augustine's discovery of spiritual reality in reading the *libri Platonicorum* as "the evolution of a metaphysician."[91]

Brown adds, "[A]nd his final 'conversion' to the idea of a purely spiritual reality, as held by the sophisticated Christians in Milan, is a decisive and fateful step in the evolution of our ideas on spirit and matter."[92] It was certainly that, but I suggest that it was also the birth of Christian metaphysics in the West, if one may use such an Aristotelian term for so Platonic an offspring. It was the philosophical doctrine of Augustine on the spirituality of God and the soul and on the eternity of God that pervaded Western Christian thought for centuries to come. Both of these doctrines were found in Neoplatonism prior to being taught by any Christian thinker, and the Christian faith was proclaimed and taught for the better part of four centuries before there emerged a clear concept of God and the soul as nonbodily and of God as timeless. Hence, these doctrines cannot have been derived from the Christian revelation; they must rather be philosophical doctrines independent of revelation, however useful they may have come to appear as means for articulating the word of God. Just as the desire to know, or the love for intelligence, is part of the nature of human beings, so the doctrine of the incorporeal nature of the human soul and of God and the doctrine of the eternity of God are matters of philosophical, not revealed, knowledge.

CONCLUSION

I have tried to show what Augustine meant by philosophy and have argued that there is in Augustine philosophy even in the contemporary sense. Finally, I have tried to show that Augustine's philosophical legacy to the West has been very rich, though there is, of course, much, much more in Augustine than philosophy and he is much more than a philosopher.

91. Brown, *Augustine of Hippo*, p. 86.
92. Ibid.

2

THE AIM OF AUGUSTINE'S PROOF THAT GOD TRULY IS

Augustine's proof of the existence of God in lib. arb. *has met with a variety of interpretations, but no matter how one looks at it, it is a far cry from the sort of demonstration found in Saint Thomas's* Summa of Theology, *where the influence of Aristotle and Aristotelian science is clearly seen. In this article I argue that Augustine's purpose was not so much to prove that there is a God, as to lead his readers to understand what sort of God there is, namely, one who is nonbodily and nontemporal. I wrote another article, which was published in the* Proceedings of the Jesuit Philosophical Association, *in which I argued less successfully that Augustine could not have intended to prove the existence of God in* lib. arb. *at all. In recent years I have turned some of my attention to Henry of Ghent, a Neoaugustinian of the thirteenth century, and I have found in Henry a defense of Augustine's arguments for the existence of God that is, I think, quite compatible with my interpretation in the present article of what Augustine was doing in* lib. arb. *Although Henry, unlike Augustine, knew a great deal about Aristotelian science and accepted Aristotle's arguments for the existence of God, his own metaphysical proof is rather a guiding of the student to an intellectual insight into the existence and nature of God than an Aristotelian demonstration of God's existence.*

The heart of book 2 of *lib. arb.* aims to show "how it is manifest that God is."[1] All the commentaries that I have been able to consult speak of this section as a proof for the existence of God or even as *the* Augustinian proof for the existence of God, though they differ considerably in their assessment of the success of the proof.[2] Yet "how it is manifest that God exists" seems a strange way to refer to a conclusion arrived at by mediate reasoning many pages long. And the conclusion that "God is and truly is" suggests that the "is" in question may be a far richer notion than that expressed in the proposition that God is.[3] What I shall argue

---

1. The Latin, "quomodo manifestum est Deum esse," is translated in a variety of ways, some emphasizing the idea of proof, others the evidence of the existence of God. In BA 6 F. J. Thonnard translates the words as "comment prouver avec évidence l'existence de Dieu?" *On the Free Choice of the Will,* trans. by Anna S. Benjamin and L. H. Hackstaff (Indianapolis: Library of the Liberal Arts, 1964), translates it as "how it is proved *(manifestum)* that God exists." In *St. Augustine: The Problem of Free Choice* (Westminster, Md.: Newman Press, 1955), Mark Pontifex says, "how it is clear that God exists." And in *Die frühen Werke des heiligen Augustinus* (Paderborn, 1954), Carl Perl translates it as "wie wird das Dasein Gottes offenbar." Though I have consulted, of course, various translations, especially those in the BA edition of Augustine's works, the translations throughout are my own, except in the case of the *conf.,* where I have used John K. Ryan's translation (Garden City, N.Y., 1960), though with occasional emendations.

2. For example, BA 6 introduces subtitles, such as "Demonstratur Dei existentia" and "Démonstration de l'existence de Dieu" (220–221). Yet in the notes Thonnard observes that there is a lack of rigor in the proof such as one finds in the five ways of Saint Thomas (521). And he also points out that there is a lengthy digression in the midst of the argument. Mark Pontifex speaks of "St. Augustine's argument for the existence of God" and notes that Augustine's "argument is not systematic in the sense that the Thomist proofs are systematic, and a number of questions are left unanswered" (261). Etienne Gilson, in *Christian Philosophy,* also speaks of "Augustine's proof," which he calls a demonstration (18). However, he notes that Augustine's "method unquestionably gives the impression of being slow and tortuous, but the numerous intermediate steps it places between its starting point and conclusion are not indispensable to the mind that has once mastered it" (18). Charles Boyer, S.J., deals with the *lib. arb.* argument in *L'idée de vérité dans la philosophie de saint Augustin* (Paris: Beauchesne, 1940), where he calls it "une démonstration en règle de l'existence de Dieu" (64). See also his "La preuve de Dieu Augustinienne," *Archives de philosophie* 7 (1930): 103–141, where he argues against an ontologist interpretation of *lib. arb.* In *Dieu présent dans la vie de l'esprit* (Paris: De Brouwer, 1951), F. Cayré devotes the fifth chapter to explaining the Augustinian proof and limits himself to *lib. arb.* 2 and the parallel texts in *vera rel.*

3. Though in many ways Augustine seems here to offer a proof for the existence of God very much along the lines of the Thomistic proofs, there are serious reasons, I believe, to read the Augustinian argument in a quite different sense. Gilson, for example, warns that Augustine's "proofs of God's existence proceed entirely on the level of essence rather than on the level of existence properly so-called" (*Christian Philosophy,* 21). He adds, "Faithful to the tradition of Plato, St. Augustine thinks less about existence than

here is that to hold that the central section of *lib. arb.* 2 is concerned merely with proving that there is a God is to miss a great deal. For I believe that an equally important, if not the most important, goal of this section is to lead the reader to conceive of God as a spiritual substance, immutable and eternal.[4] There are a number of reasons that, I believe, can be urged in favor of this thesis. Though perhaps no one of them is of itself sufficient, the cumulative effect is, I believe, highly persuasive.

AUGUSTINE'S MAIN INTELLECTUAL CONCERN AT THIS POINT

In this section I want to argue that the main intellectual problem that Augustine faced during the years prior to and immediately after 386 was not the existence of God, but the nature of God as a spiritual being. I shall first trace what he called "almost the sole cause of my error" (*conf.* 5, 10, 19) and then show that, though conceiving of God as a spiritual substance was a serious problem for Augustine, knowing that there is a God certainly was not.

Lib. arb. was begun while Augustine was still in Rome before his return to Africa. Though the second and third books may well be somewhat later, the work was completed by the time of his ordination as a bishop.[5] At the time at which he wrote *lib. arb.,* he was still very

---

about being . . . [he] wanted above all else to stress the obligation which the mind has of explaining the spurious *esse* known in experience by a supreme *Vere Esse*, i.e., by a being which fully deserves the title 'being'" (21).

4. In "Les conversions de saint Augustin," F. Masai speaks of the whole of *lib. arb.* 2 as an ascent from the sensible to the intelligible (26), and he singles out 2, 8, 20–24 as a proof of immateriality (24n41). However, I have not found any author who maintains the thesis that I am arguing for, namely, that the central thrust of *lib. arb.* 2 is to bring the reader to conceive of God as a spiritual substance. Indeed, Boyer, in *L'idée de vérité*, 65, argues that to deal with Augustine's proof for God's existence, one should separate it from such other questions as "les théories de la vision de Dieu, de l'illumination, de la participation, de l'essence divine," though he admits that they are often found together. This move, of course, presupposes as *un point de départ* a thesis that is almost the direct opposite of the conclusion for which I am arguing.

5. Augustine tells us in the *retr.* 1, 9, 8, that he began the *lib. arb.* while he was still in Rome. Since book 2 is a revision of the first, it was surely somewhat later. However, the style of the second seems closer to that of the first than to that of the third. That Augustine says that "the second and third books were completed when I could, after I had been ordained a priest at Hippo" (ibid.) by no means rules out the possibility that much of the second book was finished quite early. See P. Séjourné, "Les conversions de saint

much concerned with Manichaeism and its theological objections to the Catholic faith, and so it is understandable that Augustine would in these early writings respond to the Manichees and try to win over his Manichaean friends to his newly found faith, especially since he had lured many of these same friends into Manichaeism. Hence, one would expect that these early writings reflect Augustine's own theological problems prior to 385–386 and the solutions to them that he discovered. However, Augustine did not differ with the Manichees over whether or not there was a God, but over whether or not God was bodily. Furthermore, if, as we shall see, the inability to conceive a spiritual substance is the main ground for Augustine's becoming and staying a Manichee, then there is even stronger reason to suppose that he is here concerned with conceiving of God as a spiritual substance.

In reading *conf.* 3 through 7, one can hardly miss the recurrence of one theme, namely, Augustine's complaint about his inability to conceive a spiritual substance. Indeed texts that mention this inability abound from *conf.* 3, 4, 7, where after reading the *Hortensius* he begins to burn with a fierce love of wisdom and begins to rise up to return to his God, until *conf.* 7, 9, 13, where he first encounters the *libri Platonicorum*. If one thinks anachronistically, it is easy to suppose that this inability to conceive a spiritual substance is a personal intellectual blindness largely due to a life of sin and pleasure.[6]

However, such was not the case. Verbeke's study of the notion of *pneuma* has shown that until the time of Augustine there simply was not present in the Western Church a concept of the spiritual in the sense of a noncorporeal substance.[7] Masai's article amends Verbeke's conclusion

---

Augustine d'après le De Libero Arbitrio I," *Revue des sciences religieuses* 89–90 (1951): 359–60, and R. O'Connell, *St. Augustine's Early Theory of Man, A.D. 386–391* (Cambridge, Mass.: Belknap Press, 1968), 53.

6. Masai quotes Testard's expression of surprise that the early Augustine seemed to lack an awareness of some basic Catholic beliefs, such as the spiritual nature of God and the soul (Masai, "Les conversions de saint Augustin," 13; Testard, *Saint Augustin et Ciceron,* 110). Recently Alvin Plantinga supposed that no one in the history of philosophy except perhaps David of Dinant and Thomas Hobbes thought that God was material; A. Plantinga, *Does God Have a Nature?* (Milwaukee: Marquette University Press, 1980), 38–39. Such unawareness of the development of spiritualism in the West is reflected in the recent *Proceedings of the American Catholic Philosophical Association* (1978) on the topic of "Immateriality," in which Augustine seems not to have even been mentioned.

7. Verbeke, *L'évolution de la doctrine.*

insofar as he attributes the source of the concept of spirit in the technical sense to the influence of Neoplatonism.[8] Whereas Verbeke sees the origin of the concept of spirituality in the biblical revelation, Masai more plausibly attributes it to Augustine's contact with the writings of Plotinus.

Anthropomorphism in the Catholica

That there was no clear doctrine of the spiritual nature of God in the African Church would seem to follow from the fact that Augustine believed for nine years that the Catholic Church held that God was in the form and shape of a human being. That is, if an intelligent man in search of the truth—and surely Augustine was such a one—could be so long "mistaken" about what the Catholic Church held, it would seem reasonable to suppose that this was due to the fact that there was no doctrine of divine spirituality taught in the African Church.[9]

When Augustine began his search for wisdom, he was clearly put off by the demands for faith and intellectual humility (*conf.* 3, 5, 9). He found a literal reading of Scripture posed problems that were only exacerbated by the baiting questions of the Manichees, who promised a Christian wisdom without having to believe. The Manichees asked the young reader of the Scriptures whether God was confined by a bodily shape and had hair and nails (*conf.* 3, 7, 12). At that time he did not know that God was a spirit and that our being made in God's image did not mean that God has our shape. According to *conf.* 6, 3, 4, it was only nine years later in the Milan of Ambrose that he found that the *Catholica* did not hold, as he had thought, that God was "limited by the shape of the human body." Under the influence of Ambrose's preaching

---

8. Masai, "Les conversions de saint Augustin," 16–23. "Il faut inverser les rôles que cet historien de la philosophie attribue au platonisme et au christianisme, dans le processus de spiritualisation de l'esprit. C'est le platonisme qui a élaboré la conception—d'origine manifestement philosophique—d'intelligence, de pensée, d'esprit. Mais ces notions grecques n'avaient pas encore pénétré dans les milieux qui traduisirent la Bible ou conçurent le Nouveau Testament. C'est seulement par la suite, surtout à partir du IIIe siècle, que la philosophie spiritualiste trouva, en Plotin notamment, des interprètes capables de l'imposer à l'attention générale" (17).

9. There was, of course, the biblical sense of "spirit" prior to the time of Augustine, though that sense by no means implied an immateriality such as Augustine derived from his contact with the Platonists. One must remember that Tertullian insisted that God is a body, even if he is a spirit. "Quis negabit Deum corpus esse, etsi Deus spiritus est?" (*Adversus Praxean* 7; cited by Masai, "Les conversions de saint Augustin," 18).

he came to regard as "infantile nonsense" what he had thought was the doctrine of the Church, namely, that God was confined "in a space, however, high and wide, yet bounded on every side by the shape of human members" (*conf.* 6, 4, 5). Again in *conf.* 6, 11, 18, he says, "One great hope dawned: the Catholic faith does not teach what we once thought and what we vainly accused it of. Her learned men hold it blasphemy to believe that God is limited by the shape of the human body." If Augustine believed for nine years that the Catholic Church held an anthropomorphic view of God, such a view of God must have been fairly common among the faithful of the African Church in which he grew up.[10] After all, we do know that there existed at the time of Augustine a monastery of anthropomorphite monks in Egypt who were regarded as little more than eccentric.[11]

However, one need not go beyond Augustine to find evidence of such anthropomorphism in the Church. For, in *mor.* 1, 10, 17, Augustine admits that there are within the Church children *(pueri)* not in time, but in virtue and prudence, who "think of God in a human form and suppose that he is such." These little ones are still nurtured at the breasts of mother Church. Augustine also admits that within the ranks of the Manichees "no one is found who limited the substance of God by the shape of the human body"—an opinion than which there is none more abject. Such a text seems to imply that there are within the *Catholica* many little ones whose idea of God is that of a very large man. Within the Church they are safe, while the Manichees, though not having such a crass view of God, have separated themselves from the Church. So too in *Contra epistulam Manichaei quam vocant fundamenti* (hereafter

---

10. In *St. Augustine's Confessions: The Odyssey of Soul* (Cambridge, Mass.: Belknap Press, 1969), 18–20, Robert O'Connell describes the "conservative" African Catholics who resisted Augustine's Plotinian understanding of the faith. "African Christianity especially seems to have been conservative in tendency, suspicious on principle of any such flight toward philosophical *intellectus* of the faith" (19).

11. "Il convient d'ailleurs de le souligner, à l'époque même d'Augustin il subsistait encore—et aux portes d'Alexandrie!—des orthodoxes convaincus du caractère corporel de la divinité. Sur l'importance de ces 'anthoropomorphites' ... on peut consulter la monographie recente de A. Favale: Theofilo d'Alessandria, ... mais en ayant évidemment soin de considérer ces moines égyptiens, non comme de grossiers novateurs, mais comme les représentants *attardés* d'une mentalité antérieure à la diffusion du spiritualisme plotinicien et à son incorporation dans le patrimonie intellectel de la chrétienté" (Masai, "Les conversions de saint Augustin," 21n36).

c. ep. Man.), he asks his readers to compare with the Manichees—not the spiritual Catholics who can "see that the divine substance and nature is not stretched out in space"—but "our carnal and little ones, who are commonly wont, when they hear certain members of our body in allegory, as when God's eyes or ears are mentioned, to picture God, as a result of freedom of the imagination, under the shape of a human body" (*c. ep. Man.* 23, 25).

Here Augustine clearly gives preference to those "who think of [God] in a human form cloaked in its kind with the highest dignity," as opposed to the Manichees, who think of God as a mass diffused everywhere infinitely except where it gapes open before the land of darkness. For the carnal ones will, if they remain in the Church, be fed with milk until they grow strong enough to abandon the material images of God and to think of spiritual things. The Manichee, however, must cease to be a Manichee in giving up his imaginings.[12]

Even in a text as late as the *In Johannis evangelium tractatus* (hereafter *Jo. ev. tr.*), Augustine clearly implies that the "carnal" or "animal" men in the Church think of God as bodily and even imagine "the Father in one place, the Son standing in another before him and pleading for us . . . and the Word producing words on our behalf, with a space between the mouth of the speaker and the ears of the hearer."[13] Even "spiritual" men by reason of the habit of bodies have to drive away such corporeal images like "pesky flies from the interior eyes" of the mind. Augustine in this text interprets the Pauline "spiritual" as opposed to

---

12. This is a significant argument for the convert to Neoplatonism. For the *Catholica* can embrace both the carnal and the spiritual, though the former are little children compared to adults. Manichaeism, however, cannot include the spirituals, for once one conceives of God as an incorporeal substance he has ceased to be a Manichee. It strikes me that this passage also throws light upon Augustine's state of mind described in *c. Acad.* 2, 2, 5, where he says that after the discovery of Neoplatonism, he turned to Saint Paul convinced that such men as the apostles could not have lived as they did if their teaching and writing were opposed to "this so great a good," namely, Neoplatonic spiritualism. See John J. O'Meara, *St. Augustine: Against the Academics* (Westminster, Md.: Newman Press, 1950), 177–178n24. Augustine's excitement is surely due to his previous conviction that the Church was tied to a bodily view of God, which would, therefore, have been opposed to "huic tanto bono." Finally, it is interesting to note Augustine's ambivalence with regard to anthropomorphism, for though he brands it as the most abject of opinions and as one the learned in the Church regard as blasphemy, he still finds it tolerable in the little ones in the Church and even ascribes to it a certain dignity in comparison to the Manichaean position.

13. *Jo. Ev. tr.* 102, 4.

"carnal" or "animal" in terms of the ability or inability to think of God as an incorporeal and immutable substance.[14]

Thus it seems that Augustine's belief that the *Catholica* held an anthropomorphic view of God was correct, at least with regard to the vast majority of the faithful, especially if the "spirituals" were only those who, under the influence of Neoplatonism, were able to think of God as an incorporeal substance. After all, in Milan Augustine discovered that it was the learned men of the Church who rejected an anthropomorphic view of God. Moreover, O'Connell has argued convincingly that Augustine's Platonizing version of Christianity met with considerable resistance among the "conservative" Christians of the African Church.[15]

Manichaean and Stoic Materialism

Though Augustine never could accept an anthropomorphic view of God, he did hold a corporeal view of God for at least nine years while he was an auditor in the Manichaean sect. He admits that he thought that God was "an immense shining body" and that he was "particle of that body" (*conf.* 4, 16, 31). He tells us that at Rome "I wished to meditate on my God, but I did not know how to think of him except as a vast corporeal mass, for I thought that anything not a body was nothing whatsoever. This was the greatest and almost the sole cause of my error. As a result, I believed that evil is some substance" (*conf.* 5, 10, 19–20). And in another similar text he says, "If I were only able to conceive a spiritual substance, then forthwith all those stratagems would be foiled

---

14. Ibid.; see also *Jo. Ev. tr.* 103, 1. Also see Solignac's note, "Spirituels et charnels," in the BA 14, 629–634. Also see O'Connell, *St. Augustine's Confessions*, 162–172, esp. 172n5, for a criticism of Solignac's view. The text from *Jo. Ev. tr.* is cited by neither author; yet it clearly ties "being a spiritual" to Neoplatonism through the ability to think of God as an incorporeal substance. There is a moral or ascetic dimension to the animal/spiritual distinction. However, it is the intellectual dimension that seems to have been neglected, perhaps largely because the novelty of the *spiritalis intellectus* that Augustine was proposing has been forgotten. It is startling to hear the saint tell his congregation: "cogitantes in hac presenti turba Caritatis Vestrae necesse est ut multi sint animales," even though these "animales" are simply those who "nondum se possunt ad spiritalem intellectum erigere" (*Jo. Ev. tr.* 1, 1).

15. O'Connell, *St. Augustine's Confessions*, 19–20, 156. In *S. Aurelii Augustini Confessionum Libri XIII* (Turin: Marietti, 1948), Joseph Capello notes, "Afri eo mentem amicam corporibus habebant ut Tertullianus ipse scripserit in *de carne Christi* II: 'Nihil est incorporale nisi quod non est'" (p. 151).

and cast out of my mind. But this I was unable to do" (*conf.* 5, 14, 25).

He thought of God and evil as "two masses opposed to one another, each of them infinite, but the evil one on a narrower scale, the good on a larger" (*conf.* 5, 10, 20). God, he believed, was infinite on all sides except where he was limited by the realm of darkness. Thus the Manichaean God was a bodily mass infinite in every direction except on the side where it was bordered by the evil mass. In *c. ep. Man.* 21, 23, Augustine tells us that the Manichees offered the example of a cross-shaped bread to aid the imagination of their followers. Three parts were white and infinitely extended in every direction except on the side where the black part rests.[16] Such a view of God was what Augustine held more or less firmly for a period of nine years. As we have seen, he attributes the cause of his errors to his inability to conceive a spiritual substance.

Augustine's passage from Manichaeism to Catholicism was not by any means direct. Rather, he was briefly caught in the skepticism of the Academy, and also he seems to have come to hold a corporealism not unlike that of Stoicism and his African predecessor, Tertullian. For at the beginning of *conf.* 7, where Augustine is already well along in terms of his return to the Catholic faith, he presents a conception of God as infinitely extended in all directions. He again complains that he "could conceive of no substantial being except such as those that I was wont to see with my own eyes" (*conf.* 7, 1, 1).

By this time Augustine believed that God was incorruptible, inviolable, and immutable, since he clearly saw that to be such was better than to be corruptible, violable, and mutable, even though he as yet did not know how he knew this.[17] He thought of God "as something corporeal, existent in space and place, either infused into the world or even diffused outside the world through infinite space.... For whatever I conceived as devoid of such spatial character seemed to me to be nothing, absolutely nothing, not even so much as an empty space" (*conf.* 7, 1, 1). Clearly Augustine has distanced himself from the Manichaean view of God insofar as he now no longer holds two oppos-

---

16. See BA 13, p. 674, where A. Solignac describes the Manichaean doctrine of *cuneus*, or wedge, by which the realm of darkness cuts into the realm of light.

17. It is interesting to note that Augustine seems to have come to this insight prior to his contact with Neoplatonism, though the latter has often been blamed for his "static" conception of God.

ing substances, but one substance and that unbounded. Thus he seems to have adopted a Stoic corporealism and to have thought of God as "a great corporeal substance, existent everywhere throughout infinite space, which penetrates the whole world-mass, and spreads beyond it on every side throughout immense, limitless space" (*conf.* 7, 1, 2). Thus the earth and the heavens and every thing in them would "have" God, who would fill all bodies, just as the sun penetrates and fills the air. Such a view of divine omnipresence, however, he later realized, entailed that larger things held a larger part of God and smaller things a smaller part (*conf.* 7, 1, 2).

Several paragraphs later Augustine tells us that he imagined the whole of creation as a huge but finite mass and thought that God "encircled it on every side and penetrated it, but remained everywhere infinite" (*conf.* 7, 5, 7). He pictured God as an infinite sea and creation as a huge but finite sponge "filled in every part by that boundless sea." Such would seem to be the view that he labels in *conf.* 7, 14, 20 as idolatry. For he tells us that when he turned from Manichaean dualism, his "soul fashioned for itself a god that filled all the places in infinite space. It thought that this god was you . . . and became the temple of its own idol." Thus the early part of *conf.* 7 bears the mark of Augustine's dalliance with Stoicism. God is first seen as "diffused" throughout the world, and then the imagery is turned about so that the world is seen as in God. But in both views God and the world are spatial.[18]

In this section I have tried to present what Augustine speaks of as the sole cause of his error, namely, his inability to conceive of a spiritual substance. He explicitly claims that, because he could not conceive a spiritual substance, he came to regard evil as a substance opposed to God.[19] We have seen that he always rejected an anthropomorphic view

---

18. In *Early Theory*, 98, O'Connell mentions with regard to this text the familiar earmarks of Stoicism: the allusions to air and sunlight. Their penetration of the bodies situated in them furnished frequent Stoic analogies for the divine presence to all limited beings. Bathed in this presence, they are, in addition, all "governed both inwardly and outwardly by Your secret inspiration"—the *pneuma* central to classic Stoic thought. See also on this point: Gérard Verbeke, "Augustin et le stoïcisme," *Recherches augustiniennes* 1 (1958): 67–89, especially 79–80.

19. Fortunatus's question "Is there something outside of God, or is everything in God?" (*c. Fort.* 5), it seems to me, throws light on how Augustine viewed the connection between the inability to conceive a spiritual substance and the positing of evil as a substance. For the question implies that God is extended such that anything is either inside

of God and shunned the Catholic Church for many years because he believed that Catholics were anthropomorphites. On the other hand, he held for nine years a dualistic materialism, and even when he gave up Manichaeism, he still was left with a materialism, even though of a Stoic sort. It was only through contact with the *Platonici* that he was able to come to a concept of God as a spiritual being, and there is every reason to believe that Augustine's problem in conceiving a spiritual substance was not personal, but due to the lack of such philosophical concepts in almost the whole Western Church.[20]

Now the fact that this was Augustine's main intellectual problem does not, of course, force us to interpret the core of *lib. arb.* 2 as a *manuductio* toward a spiritual conception of God, for an author need not always discuss his more urgent problems. However, when one adds to this the fact that whether or not there is a God was never an urgent question either for Augustine or, he thought, for his contemporaries, it becomes more likely that his aim in *lib. arb.* 2 is at least also to bring us to conceive of God as a spiritual substance.

God Known to All

Though the endeavor to prove the existence of God has at least since the Middle Ages been one of the main concerns of philosophy, it was not such for Augustine. He did not personally experience the question of God's existence as a genuine problem for himself. He tells us that he always believed that God exists and has providential care for us. "Sometimes I believed this more strongly and at other times in a more feeble way. But always I believed both that you are and that you have care for us" (*conf.* 6, 5, 7–8; see also *conf.* 7, 7, 11). But Augustine also held that God "is everywhere hidden, everywhere available to all *(publicus)*, whom no one can know as he is, whom no one is permitted

---

or outside of God. Since Augustine admittedly could conceive of nothing real except extended body (*conf.* 7, 1, 2) and since he could not bring himself to deny the reality of evil—for otherwise our fear of evil would be a greater evil (*conf.* 7, 5, 7), we see that he was faced with the choice of either placing evil in God or making it another substance outside of God. Since he could not locate evil in God, he was forced to hold a finite God who is limited by an evil substance.

20. There was, of course, already a Neoplatonic Christianity in Milan that included Ambrose. However, apart from this nucleus there simply was no spiritual concept of God or of the soul in the Western Church.

not to know" (*en. Ps.* 74, 9). If no one is allowed to be ignorant of God, then there would seem to be something quite otiose about a proof for the existence of God, especially one that runs on for so many, many paragraphs.[21]

And this is not an isolated text. In his *Jo. ev. tr.*, Augustine says that the God of all creation "could not be entirely unknown even to all the nations before they believed in Christ. For such is the power of the true divinity that it cannot be entirely and completely hidden from a rational creature already using its reason. Apart from a few in whom nature has been very depraved, the whole human race admits God as author of this world. Insofar, then, as he has made this world splendid in earth and sky, even before they were imbued with the faith of Christ, God was known to all nations (*Io. ev. tr.* 106, 4)." In commenting on Psalms 13:1, Augustine says that not even those philosophers who think perversely and falsely of God have dared to say that there is no God. And for that reason, Augustine explains, the fool said in his heart that there was no God, for he did not dare to say it aloud, even if it thought it in his heart.[22] In dealing with Psalms 52:1, he says that there are in fact very few who say in their hearts that there is no God.[23]

---

21. There is in Saint Augustine's writings on the existence of God, if not a "contradiction" at least a tension, if I may use the gentler expression. For, while Augustine supposedly offers many arguments that claim to show that God exists, he also holds the doctrine that there is no one who does not know that God exists. I am reminded of the opening lines of the final section of his first *Inquiry*, where David Hume muses over the great number of philosophical arguments "which prove the existence of a Deity and refute the fallacies of atheists," along with the claim by the religious philosopher that there can be no one "so blinded as to be a speculative atheist." The religious philosopher thus is found to be in the odd position of struggling (1) to prove that there is a God so as to rid the world of atheists, and (2) to maintain that there cannot be anything like a speculative atheist for whom a proof of God's existence might be of help. "Knights-errant, who wandered about to clear the world of dragon and giants," Hume quips, "never entertained the least doubt with regard to the existence of these monsters" (Section 12, Part 1). Perhaps one way in which this tension in Augustine's thought might be alleviated is by recognizing that the so-called proofs of God's existence are better viewed as equally emphasizing our coming to a correct idea of the nature of God as a spiritual being.

22. "The fool said in his heart: 'There is no God.' For not even certain sacrilegious and detestable philosophers who thought perverse and false things of God dared to say: There is no God. Therefore, the fool said it in his heart, because no one would dare to say it aloud, even if he dared to think it" (*en. Ps.* 13, 2).

23. "[T]hey are few, and it is difficult to come across a man who says in his heart: There is no God. Nonetheless they are so few that for fear of saying this in a crowd they say it in their heart, because they do not dare say it with their mouth" (*en. Ps.* 52, 2).

Furthermore, Augustine says that all creation proclaims, "God has made us." In preaching on Romans 1:20, he says, "Ask the world, the beauty of heaven, the brightness and order of the stars, the sun . . . the moon; ask the earth fruitful with plants and trees, filled with animals, and beautified with men, and see if they do not respond to you by their meaning, God made us" (*s.* 141, 2, 2). The fact that things change proclaims that they were made, and the beauty of things in this world discloses the beauty of their maker. In other words, the movement from the visible things of this world to God was an easy and spontaneous one for Augustine, though, unlike Plotinus, he did use some sort of argument.[24] But if the existence of God is so readily known and known by almost everyone so that even the fool does not utter aloud that there is no God, is it really likely that Augustine's principal aim in *lib. arb.* was to prove that there is a God?

ARGUMENTS FROM THE TEXT ITSELF

That Augustine aims in *lib. arb.* 2 to show that God is a spiritual being, immutable and eternal, can be argued to from the text itself in a number of ways. First of all, any proof of the existence of God has to start off with some basic idea of what is meant by the term "God," in order to go about showing that there is something to which the term applies. In *lib. arb.* 2, Augustine and Evodius agree that, if there is something superior to our reason—at least if it is eternal and immutable—then that is God. Though Evodius initially protests that God is not "that to which my reason is inferior, but rather that to which no one is superior," he seems willing to accept this, if he finds that "there is nothing above our reason except that which is eternal and immutable" (*lib. arb.* 2, 6, 14).

"Few are found of such great impiety that there is fulfilled in them that which was written, 'The fool says in his heart, "There is no God."' Such insanity pertains to only a few" (*s.* 69, 2, 3).

24. In the BA edition, Thonnard says (519), "Plus exigeant que Plotin, il ne considère pas l'existence de Dieu comme immédiatement évidente, puisqu'il entreprend d'en donner une démonstration rationnelle, en remontant par les divers degrés jusqu'au vrai Dieu, l'UN suprême." So too, in ACW 22, Pontifex says that Augustine "rejected the view of Plotinus that God's existence was immediately evident and needed no rational proof" (254).

What is important to my argument is that Augustine has just pointed out that all bodies are mutable, that the life which animates our bodies is mutable, and that reason itself is mutable. Furthermore, in stating the major premise of the argument, Augustine stresses the noncorporeal vision by which reason discerns its God. Thus whatever is immutable will be both incorporeal and superior to what is highest in us, namely, reason. "If reason—without the use of any corporeal instrument—not through touch, not through taste, not through smell, not through the ears, not through the eyes, and not though any sense inferior to itself, but through itself discerns something eternal and immutable, it ought to admit that it is its God and that it itself is inferior (*lib. arb.* 2, 6, 14)."

If all bodies are mutable and if the proof attains something that is immutable, it follows that that something is not a body. Furthermore, if that immutable and, therefore, eternal something superior to our reason is seen only by noncorporeal eyes and in a noncorporeal discernment, it too must be noncorporeal. Hence, the initial notion of God with which the argument begins is that of a spiritual substance, immutable and eternal, and the goal of the proof, therefore, must be to attain such a being.[25]

Another indication that Augustine was not, in *lib. arb.* 2, merely showing that there is a God, but showing how God is to be thought of can be drawn from the formulation of the conclusion, namely, that "God is and is truly and sovereignly."[26] For, whatever Augustine might mean by "is" when he uses the verb without conscious reflection on its meaning, when he does explicitly reflect on its meaning, he ties *esse* with immutability, self-sameness, eternity.[27] For example, he says, "For anything, of whatever excellence, if it is changeable, is not truly; for true being is not present where there is also nonbeing. For whatever

---

25. This initial notion is not a conceptual grasp of what it is to be an incorporeal being. If it were, there would, of course, be no need for the extended exercise that follows. It is rather a verbal definition or a mere notion whose referent becomes gradually understood *(intellectus)* in the course of the long *manuductio*.

26. "Est enim Deus, et uere summeque est" (*lib. arb.* 2, 14, 39).

27. There are uses of the verb "to be" *(esse)* that seem simply to assert that there is something or someone. Thus, for example, the proof in *lib. arb.* 2, which begins by establishing that Evodius or the individual inquirer exists by means of what has been called the Augustinian *cogito*. However, though creatures are, their being is not true being, for their being is a failing or ceasing to be (*lib. arb.* 3, 7, 21).

can be changed, once it has been changed, is not what it was; if it is not what it was, a certain death has taken place there; something has been slain there that was and is not now (*Io. ev. tr.* 38, 10)." Texts from Augustine that show that true being is closely tied to, if not identical with, immutability and eternity could be produced in great number. For the purpose of this article the following should suffice as both clear and representative.[28]

Therefore, the angel, and in the angel the Lord, had said to Moses who sought his name, "I am who I am. You shall say to the children of Israel: 'Who is' has sent me to you." To be is the name of immutability. For, everything which is changed ceases to be what it was and begins to be what it was not. Only what is not changed has true being, pure being, genuine being. (*s.* 7, 7)

I am called "Is," he said. What is: I am called "Is"? That I remain eternally, that I cannot be changed. . . . Therefore, the immutability of God deigned to express itself by that phrase, "I am who I am." (*s.* 6, 3, 4)

What is unchangeable is eternal; it is always the same way. But what is changeable is subject to time. (*div. qu.* 19)

Hence, Augustine's conclusion, namely, that God is and is truly and sovereignly—at least if the words are taken to mean what Augustine says they mean when he speaks formally—states that God is immutable and eternal and, hence, incorporeal.

The best argument from the text, however, is based upon what Augustine does do in the many paragraphs of *lib. arb.* from 2, 7, 15 to 2, 12, 38. For what he does in these paragraphs is guide his readers to a conceptual grasp of God as a spiritual substance that is present everywhere and whole wherever he is present. That is, he gradually guides his readers to a grasp of the *verum esse* of God, of his immutability and eternity, of his omnipresence and spirituality. And he does this in dependence upon Plotinus's dual treatise on omnipresence, namely, *Ennead* 6, 4 and 5.[29]

---

28. For further evidence, see E. Gilson, "Notes sur l'être et le temps chez saint Augustine," *Recherches augustiniennes* 2 (1962): 205–223.

29. In *Early Theory,* 53–55, O'Connell juxtaposes texts from *lib. arb.* and *Ennead* 6, 5, 10 in order to show that Augustine was well aware of Plotinus's treatises on omnipresence. "The likelihood is that Augustine either had the *Enneads* to hand when writing the *De Libero Arbitrio,* or, at very least, had its turns of phrase quite fresh in memory" (57).

In order to see that Augustine does lead his reader to a conception of God as a spiritual substance, let us turn to the section that immediately follows that in which Augustine and Evodius agree upon the structure of the proof, namely, *lib. arb.* 2, 7, 15. At this point one would expect the argument to get under way. Augustine could simply have argued that there are truths of mathematics and of wisdom that are immutable and according to which we judge and about which we do not judge. Therefore, he could have concluded, there is something immutable and eternal above our reason, which, in accord with the previous agreement with Evodius, should be acknowledged to be God. But instead of immediately appealing to such truths, Augustine introduces a discussion of *commune* and *proprium* with reference to the objects of the bodily senses, a discussion that the BA edition labels as a digression. It can be regarded as a digression, of course, if one insists upon believing that Augustine was chiefly concerned with demonstrating that there is a God. However, one then, it would seem, has also to believe that Augustine cannot compose very well, for if that were the case he rambles off his topic for many a page.[30] In the light, moreover, of O'Connell's study of Augustine's use of Plotinus, it is hard to continue to treat *lib. arb.* 2, 15–33 as "an anomaly to be ignored or as a mere digression."[31]

Rather the discussion in *lib. arb.* 2, 7, 15–19 begins the long *manuductio* by which Augustine guides his reader to the concept of a spiritual substance that is immutable and eternal. First, he points out that each person has his own bodily senses, interior sense, and reason or mind. Yet the objects of our senses of sight and hearing are such that several of us can see the same visible object and hear the same sound. The other senses are not quite the same. For in smelling and tasting something we change the object we smell or taste so that another person cannot taste or smell precisely what I have tasted or smelled. And though two persons can touch exactly the same surface, even the same part of the same

---

30. H.-I. Marrou's comment with regard to the *conf.,* "Augustin compose mal," was one that he himself had soon to retract. See O'Connell, *St. Augustine's Confessions,* 9. But those who see in *lib. arb.* 2 "a digression" (Thonnard), "slow and tortuous" reasonings (Gilson), or a lack of systematic argument (Pontifex) surely imply that Augustine has not put things together very well. Another argument in favor of my thesis is precisely that the alleged digression is to the point and that the allegedly tortuous reasoning is a requisite *manuductio* toward a very difficult concept.

31. O'Connell, *Early Theory,* 53.

surface, they cannot do so at the same time. Augustine points out that two persons cannot both sense what one person in sensing changes and appropriates into himself. What we do not change and make our own in sensing we both can sense either successively by touch or simultaneously by sight or hearing.[32] He sums this up in a rule: "Thus it is clear that those things which we do not change and yet sense by the senses of the body do not pertain to the nature of our senses and, hence, are rather common to us, because they are not turned and changed into what is proper and, so to speak, private to us (*lib. arb.* 2, 7, 19)." He further specifies "proper and private" as "that which belongs to each of us alone and that which each of us alone perceives in himself, because it properly pertains to his nature." And by "common and, so to speak, public" is meant "what is perceived by all perceivers with no corruption or change of itself" (*lib. arb.* 2, 7, 19).

After initiating this discussion on "common" and "proper," Augustine begins to look for something that we can see not by the eyes of the body, but by the eyes of our mind, by our reason, *communiter*, for something that offers itself to all and that is not changed by those to whom it is present, but remains whole and uncorrupted. Thus he turns to consider the law and truth of number and the truths of wisdom. He shows how they are common to all who reason, are immutable, not changed or corrupted or appropriated by any viewer.[33] No one is

---

32. In *Ennead* 6, 4, 12, Plotinus uses the examples of sound and sight to illustrate how participation does not divide the intelligible reality in which the many share. For example, he says,

> A sound is everywhere in the air, a one not divided, but a one everywhere whole, and with regard to vision, if the air passively receives the form [of the visible object], it retains it undivided. But not every opinion agrees with this; let it be said only to show that the participation [of the many] is in one and the same reality. The example of sound makes it clearer how in all the air the form is present whole. For everyone would not hear the same thing, if the uttered word were not whole in every place and if each hearer did not receive it in the same way.

(Unless otherwise indicated, translations from Plotinus are my own, though I have closely followed Bréhier's.)

33. One of the "problems" with the proof has to do with how Augustine moves from the eternal truths of mathematics and of wisdom to the eternal Truth and Wisdom that is God. Thonnard speaks of two modes of being for the eternal truths: "l'un participé dans notre esprit, où elles vivent sous la forme multiple des règles des nombres et de la sagesse; l'autre absolu, dans la source du Verbe, où elles vivent sous la forme parfaite de l'infinie simplicité de la Vérité divine" (BA 6, 521). He argues that to move from the participated mode of multiple truths to the absolute mode of simplicity, one needs the

crowded out, but all can share in truth and wisdom. And as we can each hear the whole of the same sound and each see the whole of what the other sees, so too by our reason each of us can grasp the whole of a truth of mathematics or of wisdom.

In paragraphs 20 through 38, the *commune* and *proprium* theme is sounded again and again. The phrases "communis" and "communiter omnibus" appear well over twenty times in discussing the truths of mathematics and of wisdom. Similarly the phrase "manens in se" occurs frequently, and wisdom and truth gradually emerges in personal guise, indeed in the guise of a beautiful lover.

In *lib. arb.* 2, 12, 33, Augustine explicitly refers back to the discussion of *commune* and *proprium* in 2, 7, 15–19. As what we see in common with our eyes or hear in common with our ears cannot be a part of my nature or your nature, so what each of us sees with the eyes of his mind cannot belong to the nature of either of our minds, but is some third thing upon which each of us gazes. This truth we see in common is superior to our minds, because it is immutable and, "manens in se," it neither increases when we see it nor decreases when we do not (*lib. arb.* 2, 12, 34).[34] Moreover, we do not judge it, but in accord with it.

---

principle of causality, which is, in its Augustinian form, the principle of participation, though he admits that this step is absent from Augustine's argument and that for "l'esprit intuitif d'Augustin" (BA 6, 523), there is hardly need for making this step explicit.

It is interesting to note that for Plotinus the topic of omnipresence is treated in *Ennead* 6, 4 and 5, in the context of the question raised in Plato's *Parmenides* regarding how a Form can be shared by many things and yet not be divided. E. Bréhier says in his introduction to the *Enneads* on omnipresence, "Chez Platon, Parmenides voulait montrer que, faute d'admettre cette vue paradoxale qu'une seule et même chose peut être présente à la fois partout, la participation aux formes était inconcevable: Socrate était donc invité démontrer que cette thèse paradoxale était véritable. C'est précisément ce que tente de montrer Plotin, *en se plaçant précisément au point de vue de Socrate*"; Plotin, *Enneades* VI, Ire Partie (Paris: Belles lettres, 1963), 162.

34. One of Augustine's favorite phrases that he uses in speaking about God is "manens in se." E.g., in *conf.* 7, 9, 14, we find "manentis in se sapientiae"; in *conf.* 6, 11, 17, "in se manens innouat omnia"; and in *conf.* 10, 10, 24, "uerbo tuo in se permanenti." The second phrase is recognized as a quote from Ws 7:27. However, forms of the phrase "manens in se" also appear often in Plotinus, especially in *Ennead* 6, 4 and 5, the double treatise on omnipresence. In *Trin.* 5, 3, 14, Augustine explains that "manens in se" means that in producing the world God remains unchanged. He says there of the Holy Spirit, "And it is written of him that he acts and he acts while remaining in himself; for he is not changed or turned into any of his works." Thus, the expression seems to sum up what O'Connell says of the function of the Eros image in *Ennead* 6, 5. "But, to begin with, a word of explanation on its function in the argument. . . . The relation that Plo-

By *lib. arb.* 2, 13, 35, *Veritas* appears as one we should embrace, enjoy, delight in.[35] In the Truth, in which the highest good is known and held, we are happy or blessed. We cannot lose against our will such truth and wisdom. "For no one can be separated from it by places" (*lib. arb.* 2, 14, 37). "We have what we all enjoy equally and in common. There is no crowding and no failing in it. She welcomes all her lovers without rendering them jealous. She is common to all, yet chaste to each. No one says to another, 'Withdraw so that I can approach; remove your hand so that I can embrace her also. All cling to her; all hold the Self-same'" (*lib. arb.* 2, 14, 37).[36] This wisdom is our food and drink; yet we do not change it into ourselves. Whereas food for the body is changed into something proper and private to the eater, when one partakes of wisdom, he does not change it into himself. "What you take of it, remains whole for me."[37] So too what each of us breathes in of wisdom does not become a part of each of us, but remains "whole and at the same time common to all" *(simul omnibus tota est communis)*. Truth is less like what we touch, taste, or smell, and more like what we see or hear. For each of us hears the whole sound and each sees the whole of what we see.

---

tinus means to exclude is one whereby the superior reality . . . will compose with the beings of the inferior world, becoming a 'form' ap-*prop*-riated by one being to the exclusion of others. Such a relation would prevent its remaining integrally present to each and common to all" (*Early Theory*, 52; see also 56).

35. O'Connell sums up the point well: "Along with both authors' presiding intention of contrasting 'common' possession with individual 'appropriation' of any desired good, the first thing that strikes one on examination of this parallel is the initial identity of basic image: it is a question in both cases of Beauty—in characteristic feminine form—being sought by her many lovers" (*Early Theory*, 56).

36. Both Plotinus and Augustine uses the image of "no crowding" of the lovers around the Truth; so too both authors emphasize that there is no failing or running out on the part of the object loved. Augustine too follows Plotinus's language of "seeing and touching" with his "cernimus et tenemus." The expression "idipsum omnes tangunt" is startling, for *idipsum* is one of Augustine's favorite expressions for God, the Self-same. See James Swetnam's study on Augustine's use of the expression: "A Note on *In Idipsum* in St. Augustine," *The Modern Schoolman* 30 (1952–53): 328–331. There is, of course, a variant reading, "ipsam," which would here mean the Truth; though I believe the first reading is preferable, in either case there is the startling idea of "touching God." Yet such language is Plotinian and even traceable to the *Ennead* on omnipresence. For example, "Yet we must think of how we touch the good with our souls" (*Ennead* 6, 5, 10), and "we see the good and lay hold of it" (*Ennead* 6, 5, 10; the latter quoted from *Early Theory*, 55).

37. Augustine's words seem almost copied from Plotinus's expression: "I do not attain one good and you another, but [we both attain] the same" (*Ennead* 6, 5, 10).

Yet there is a great difference between bodily seeing and hearing and seeing with the mind. "For the whole word is not sounded at once, but stretched out and produced through times . . . and every visible image swells out through places and is nowhere whole. And these things are taken away against our will, and we are prevented from enjoying them by crowding" (*lib. arb.* 2, 14, 38).[38] In the case of Truth and Wisdom we are not elbowed aside by fans pushing to get closer to see and hear better. "She is close to all and everlasting to all who love her and turn to her in the whole world. She is in no place, and yet is nowhere absent. Outside she admonishes; within she teaches. She changes for the better all who behold her; she is changed for the worse by no one" (*lib. arb.* 2, 14, 38).[39]

What Augustine has led us to is a conception of subsistent, personified Truth and Wisdom that is stretched out neither in space nor in time, that is whole in every place and at every time, that remains in herself while making everything new. Thus, Augustine has in this long section of *lib. arb.* 2 led his reader to conceive of a being that is truly, that is noncorporeal, unchanging, and eternal. Had he wished to establish merely that there is a God—something that was never a problem for him—he could have done so without so many paragraphs that have struck many as off the mark, because they had missed the point.

CONCLUDING REFLECTIONS

I have argued that the proof in *lib. arb.* 2 that God is and truly is, is best understood not merely as a demonstration that there is a God, but rather as a *manuductio* toward a conception of God as a spiritual substance that is immutable and eternal. The first part of the article deals with Augustine's main intellectual problem in the years prior to 386–387, namely, his inability to conceive a spiritual substance—an inability, we must not forget, that he shared with the whole Western Church. He

---

38. Augustine's use of "intumescence" with reference to the extension and distension of the world in space and time not merely recalls the association with the fall of the soul into body and time through the "tumor superbiae," but evokes Plotinus's use of *onkos* for "mass" or "body."

39. Augustine's language in speaking about *veritas* and *sapientia* and their *pulchritudo* makes the use of the feminine pronoun seem natural, though the "wisdom and truth" referred to is, of course, the Word, the eternal Christ.

refused to accept the anthropomorphism that he believed was the doctrine of the Catholic Church and accepted Manichaean dualistic materialism, which he held for a period of nine years. In abandoning the Manichaean position, he moved to a Stoic materialism until, in hearing Ambrose preach, he began to realize that the learned men of the *Catholica* did not think of God as bound by the shape of a human body or even as being bodily at all. Only through contact with the writings of the *Platonici* did Augustine find a way to think of God as incorporeal, as present everywhere and whole wherever present.

Secondly, I showed that whether or not there is a God was not a problem for Augustine or, he thought, for hardly anyone else. Even the fool did not venture to say aloud that there is no God. Hence, I concluded that it would seem reasonable to interpret *lib. arb.* 2 as addressing Augustine's main intellectual problem, not the question of whether there is a God, especially if there is supporting evidence in the text itself.

The second part of the paper presents reasons to show that *lib. arb.* 2 does indeed lead Evodius and the reader to a conception of God as incorporeal and immutable, as a substance present everywhere and whole everywhere. The initial notion of God with which the argument begins, the formulation of the conclusion, and the content of the argument itself render it highly likely that Augustine was concerned with the conception of God as a spiritual substance every bit as much as—if not more than—with establishing that there is a God. Especially the clear dependence of *lib. arb.* 2 upon Plotinus's dual treatise on omnipresence, *Ennead* VI, 4 and 5, indicates that Augustine was at least as concerned with the nature of God as with his existence.

In conclusion, I want to suggest that the conclusion that Augustine is at least equally, if not more, concerned with coming to a conception of the nature of God as a spiritual substance, should not, after all, be very surprising. For there is good reason to believe that a philosopher's theory of knowledge is determinative of his theory of being.[40] Lonergan has argued that there is an isomorphism between the structure of knowing and the structure of being, and though I neither presuppose all that he said on the matter to be true nor can undertake a justification of the

---

40. See Bernard J. F. Lonergan, *Insight: A Study of Human Understanding* (London: Longmans, 1958), 399ff.

thesis, there is, nonetheless, something, I believe, intuitively right about the general idea behind the thesis.

Augustine held that human knowing was to be understood in terms of the model of vision. As we have eyes of the body, so there is the mind, the eyes of the soul. What seeing is to the eyes of the body, that understanding is to the eyes of the mind. What visible things are to the seeing of bodily eyes, that intelligible things are to the understanding of the mind.[41]

Whereas for Aquinas there were two basically different acts of the intellect, for Augustine there is basically one sort of intellectual act, and that is conceived on the model of bodily vision. Aquinas distinguished the acts of understanding from the acts of judging, the former leading to answers to questions for understanding, the latter leading to answers to questions for reflection. Thus Thomas could hold that existence is what is grasped as the proper content of the answer to a question for reflection, while form is what is grasped in answering a question for intelligence. And because there is the distinction between types of questions and types of intellectual acts, there is also a distinction on the side of the known between contents of acts of understanding and contents of acts of judging.

However, if one does not distinguish acts of understanding from acts of judging, if, as Augustine did, one sees all intellection as basically a kind of seeing, then there will not be a distinction between the contents of judgment and the contents of acts of understanding. That is, one will regard existence as something to be grasped in an intellectual looking with the eyes of the mind that is not distinguished from what one grasps insofar as one understands what the thing is. For, without the distinction between acts of the intellect, one will be an essentialist in the sense that one will not distinguish existence and essence, *esse* and *essentia*.[42] If one, consequently, holds that to be is to be something, it

---

41. Augustine's elaborately worked out parallel between seeing with the eyes of the body and seeing with the eyes of the mind is well known. See above note 13 for his comparison of bodily images of God with pesky flies that one has to sweep away from the mind's eyes. "Menti hoc est intelligere quod sensui videre" (*ord.* 2, 3, 10). "Ego autem ratio ita sum in mentibus ut in oculis est aspectus. Non enim hoc est habere oculos quod aspicere" (*sol.* 1, 6, 12).

42. In *Trin.* 6, 2, 3, Augustine says that God is undoubtedly "substantia" or "essentia"—what the Greeks call "ousia"—and explains that *essentia* is related to *esse,* as *scientia*

is easy to see why he would interpret a question, such as how is it manifest that God is, as not merely asking whether there is a God, but as asking how God is, that is, as something that is *vere summeque,* that is *Idipsum.* "For he is sovereignly and primarily *(summe ac primitus)* who is utterly immutable and who could say in the fullest sense, 'I am who I am'" (*doc. Chr.* 1, 32, 35).

---

and *sapientia* are related to *scire* and *sapere.* Furthermore, God is "summa essentia" (*vera rel.* 11, 22), and to be "summe ac primitus" is "to be utterly immutable" (*doc. Chr.* 1, 32, 35).

3

SPIRITUALS AND SPIRITUAL INTERPRETATION IN AUGUSTINE

I wrote this article before becoming aware that Augustine came to another understanding of the opposition between the spirit and the letter, which he expressed in his De spiritu et littera *(hereafter* spir. et litt.*) 4, 6. In the course of the Pelagian controversy he came to see that the law or letter killed, while the spirit gave life because it enabled one to fulfill the commands of the law. Had I been aware of this development in Augustine's thought, I could have written a better paper and have been more patient with some of the secondary sources that focused more on his later views or did not distinguish between his earlier and later views. Even in the later works, however, Augustine retained his earlier interpretation of the opposition between a literal and a spiritual interpretation of Scripture, though he gave it a subordinate position. Hence, what I wrote remains true, but certainly not the complete picture. An important factor in overcoming his problems with Stoic and Manichaean corporealism was Augustine's learning to interpret Scripture spiritually rather than literally, and what I wrote still remains valid for Augustine's conversion to Catholicism in the Milanese Church under the influence of the preaching of Ambrose, which was heavily laced with Neoplatonic spiritualism.*

In this article I want to propose a hypothesis about what Augustine meant when he spoke of the "spirituals" as opposed to "the animal or carnal men" in the Church and in speaking of the "spiritual" interpretation of Scripture. I shall offer some evidence that the hypothesis is correct, though within the limits of a short article I obviously cannot prove its correctness. Nonetheless, I believe that sufficient evidence can be mustered to render the hypothesis a highly plausible one.

Perhaps the best way for me to approach the statement of the hypothesis will be to sketch what has led me to formulate it and to regard it as true. While I was working out an article on Augustine's proof in *lib. arb.* 2 that God is and is truly and sovereignly, I concluded that his goal is not so much to establish that there is a God, but to show that God is an incorporeal and immutable substance. Part of my argument rested upon the fact that in the years prior to 386–387 Augustine's main intellectual problem was his coming to conceive of God as an incorporeal substance.[1] His inability to conceive of a spiritual substance was, he admits, "almost the sole cause" of his errors.[2] Furthermore, he insisted that whether or not there is a God was never a personal question for him and that there is no one—or practically no one—who dared to deny that there is a God.[3] Augustine's inability to conceive of a spiritual substance was not a matter of personal ignorance, but the common heritage of the Western Church prior to him.[4] Stoic materialism formed the common philosophical background of the Western world, and it was only as a result of Augustine's contact with Neoplatonism in the Church of Milan that he, and through him the whole Western Church, came to conceive of God and the soul as spiritual substances.[5] Thus,

---

1. From the reading of the *Hortensius* and Augustine's first attempt to study the Scriptures up to his contact with the *libri Platonicorum* in the *conf.*, Augustine mentions again and again his inability to conceive of a spiritual substance. For example, in *conf.* 5, 14, 15, he says, "quod si possem spiritalem substantiam cogitare, statim machinamenta illa omnia solverentur et abicerentur ex animo meo, sed non poteram." Generally I have followed John K. Ryan's translation, though I have modified it in some places, as I have noted.

2. *Conf.* 5, 10, 19.

3. In commenting on the Psalm verse, "The fool says in his heart that there is no God," Augustine points out that even the fool was not so foolish as to say this aloud (*en. Ps.* 13, 2). Even more strongly he says that God allows no one to be ignorant of him (*en. Ps.* 74, 9).

4. Verbeke, *L'évolution de la doctrine*.

5. François Masai, in "Les conversions de saint Augustin," argues that, though Verbeke is correct in regarding Augustine as the first in the Western Church to come to a

his famous "Noverim me, noverim te" (*sol.* 2, 1, 1) was not a prayer to know God's and his soul's existence, but rather to know their nature as spiritual substances.

Now it was in the context of that study that I came across the beginning of the *Jo. Ev. tr.*, where in approaching the lofty doctrine of the Prologue to the Gospel of John, Augustine worries about his flock's ability to grasp what John said. In words whose literal translation never ceases to amuse, Augustine says that there are undoubtedly many *animales* out there among *vestra caritas.* These *animales,* or "natural men" are the *psychicoi* of 1 Corinthians 2:14–3:3 where Saint Paul speaks of the "fleshly" *(sarkicoi),* "natural" *(psychicoi),* and "spiritual" *(pneumaticoi)* persons in the Church. But Augustine goes on to note that the animal or carnal men in the Church are precisely such because they cannot as yet rise to a spiritual understanding *(intellectum spiritualem).*

Now if one grants that Augustine was the source of the concept of a spiritual God in the whole Western Church and if one also admits

---

concept of the spiritual as incorporeal, he is incorrect in attributing to Christianity the "spiritualization" of the concept "spirit":

> il faut inverser les rôles que cet historien de la philosophie attribue au platonisme et au christianisme, dans le processus de spiritualisation de l'esprit. C'est le platonisme qui a élaboré la conception—d'origine manifestement philosophique—d'intelligence, de pensée, d'esprit. Mais ces notions grecques n'avaient pas encore pénétré dans les milieux qui traduisierent la Bible ou conçurent le Nouveau Testament. C'est seulement par la suite, surtout à partir du IIIe siècle, que la philosophie spiritualiste trouva, en Plotin notamment, des interprètes capables de l'imposer à l'attention générale. (17)

Despite the work of Verbeke, scholars seem unable to believe that Christianity was not possessed of a concept of God and of the soul as incorporeal from the very beginning. William A. Schumacher, in *Spiritus and Spirituales: A Study in the Sermons of Saint Augustine* (Mundelein, Ill.: St. Mary of the Lake Seminary, 1957), makes the amazing statement:

> On the doctrine of the spirituality of the human soul rest both the meaning of our present life and our hopes for the life to come; indeed, Christianity may be said to stand or fall with this doctrine, since, once this is established, the truth of the Hereafter follows as a direct consequence. The principal and most important element in divine revelation concerning the human soul is the essential difference between body and soul, and the simple, immaterial, and indivisible character of the latter. (50)

True, once the doctrine of the spirituality of the soul is established, the survival of the soul follows. However, it is not true that the fact of survival—much less, belief in the fact of survival—depends upon that doctrine. If Verbeke and Masai are correct—and it seems that they are—then Christianity survived in the West until the time of Augustine without any doctrine of the soul's spirituality.

that, since such a concept is both a difficult one to grasp and one that stemmed from a school of philosophy at times strongly and explicitly opposed to Christianity, it could easily meet not merely with incomprehension, but also with resistance on the part of the more traditional Catholics, one might come to suspect—as I did—that when Augustine speaks of "carnal or animal men" as opposed to the "spirituals" in the Church he means that the "animal or carnal men" are those who are as yet unable to conceive of a spiritual substance, whereas the spirituals are those who can conceive of a spiritual substance, that is, who can bring to the understanding of faith a central insight of Neoplatonic philosophy.[6] So I also want to propose that by a spiritual understanding of the Scriptures he means an understanding of what is dealt with as nonbodily and nonimaginable.[7] It may be that not every text is open to such an interpretation, but it seems to me that a great many texts are able to be read in that fashion—enough so that I believe that one could say that this is the basic or central meaning.

PREVIOUS INTERPRETATIONS OF *SPIRITUALES*

Before beginning to look at various texts that support this claim, let us look at various other attempts to determine what is meant by the *spirituales* in the Church. Obviously Augustine draws upon the Pauline texts from 1 Corinthians 2 and 3, and many commentators rest content with referring the reader to the scriptural passages on the assumption that Augustine meant what Paul meant. However, others note that Au-

---

6. There are at least two problems with so bald a statement. First, Augustine clearly means something more by "spiritual" than this intellectual aspect of the concept, and I intend to prescind from that "more" in this paper. Second, Augustine himself is anachronistic insofar as he implies that the concept of "the spiritual" stems from the teaching of Christ, as we shall see. Indeed, he attributes this spiritual understanding even to the Old Testament prophets and patriarchs, e.g., *en. Ps.* 72, 6 and *en. Ps.* 103, s. 3, 5.

7. There have been many studies of Augustine's interpretation of Scripture and its multiple senses. I realize that there may well be present in Augustine the four "senses" of the later Middle Ages and that he speaks in *Gn. litt.* 1, I, 1, of what might be taken as those four senses. "In omnibus libris sanctis oportet intueri quae ibi aeterna intimentur, quae ibi facta narrentur, quae futura praenuntientur, quae gerenda praecipiuntur aut moneantur." It may be that there are in Augustine the traditional three spiritual senses, namely, allegorical, anagogical, and moral. I neither affirm nor deny that. What I suggest is that, when Augustine speaks of a spiritual explanation of Scripture, such an explanation involves the conception of God or of the soul as incorporeal realities.

gustine is not merely aware of what Paul meant, but he is aware that he means something quite different from what Paul meant.⁸

Perhaps the most explicit identification ventured is that offered by Courcelle, who argues that it is Paulinus of Nola whom Augustine has especially in mind when he speaks of the "spirituals" to whom he addressed the *conf*.⁹ However, that view both seems too narrow in its specification of the audience for whom the *conf*. were intended and fails to explain why Paulinus and his group should be tagged as "spirituals" in the Church.¹⁰

There are several notes in the BA edition of Augustine's works. For example, in BA 14, 629–634, A. Solignac has a note entitled, "Spirituels et charnels." He points out that the distinction between "spirituales et carnales ecclesiae suae" is related to the question of the spiritual interpretation of Scripture, to which he has devoted the previous note on pages 622–629, since the spiritual interpretation of Scripture is reserved to the spirituals. He goes on to deal with (1) the identity of the spiritual and carnal men, (2) the extent and limits of the judgment by the spiri-

---

8. If one admits that Saint Paul did not have a Neoplatonic concept of spirit as an incorporeal substance—as one should—then it goes without saying that Augustine did not mean what Paul meant. But Augustine seems quite aware that Paul distinguishes between "carnal" and "animal," although he himself does not do so. "The Saint does not pursue Paul's distinction between *homo animalis,* meaning human nature as such, and *homo carnalis,* having the added implication of nature in revolt against God. Augustine knew this *distinction,* but saw little practical value in it; in his eyes, *homo animalis* cannot help becoming *carnalis* (unless aided by God), and thus the difference is negligible"; Schumacher, *Spiritus and Spiritales,* 184. On the other hand, this distinction between "human nature as such" and "nature as in revolt against God" seems quite foreign to Augustine's way of thinking.

9. Pierre Courcelle, in *Recherches sur Les Confessions de saint Augustin* (Paris: E. de Boccard, 1950), maintains, "Tout l'ouvrage est, du reste, à l'usage de lecteurs catholiques, notamment à l'usage des 'spirituels'" (18). He claims that we can go on to identify those Augustine refers to as the "spirituals," to whom the biographical part is addressed (29). And he finally lets the cat out of the bag. "Lorsqu'Augustin mentionne les 'spirituels' qui pourront sourire amicalement en apprenant les bizarres erreurs où il est tombé dans sa jeunesse, il songe sûrement à Paulin surtout" (31–32). I should think that it would make better sense to suppose that these "spirituals" were Neoplatonic Christians, i.e., Christians whose understanding of God and the soul benefited from Neoplatonic spiritualism.

10. In *St. Augustine's Confessions,* 12–22, Robert O'Connell mentions four different audiences for the *conf.:* the Manichees, the Neoplatonists, the "conservative" Catholics, and Augustine's flock at Hippo. In comparison, Courcelle has excessively narrowed the intended audience of the *conf.* and has offered no explanation of why Paulinus and his followers should be tagged as "spirituales."

tuals, and (3) their role in the Church. It is the first topic that is most pertinent. After tying the expression to the Pauline texts, he concludes, "Les spirituals sont donc les parfaits, adultes dans le Christ, capables d'assimiler la nourriture solide des Écritures et de la distribuer à ceux qui leurs sont inférieurs; les charnels sont au contraire les imparfaits, incapables de saisir la profondeur des livres sacrés, mais qui en reçoivent l'enseignement par l'intermédiaire des parfaits" (630). He notes that the distinction between the spirituals and the carnals is not the same as that between the teaching Church and the Church that is taught or as that between the hierarchy and the faithful. Rather the spirituals and the carnals are found to be on both sides of such divisions.[11] He concludes, "La qualité de *spirituel* ne tient donc pas à la *fonction* dans l'Église, mais à la *manière de vivre,* plus profondément au rapport qui s'établit au coeur de chaque membre de l'Église entre lui-même et Dieu" (631).

In BA 72, 837, M.-F. Berrouard has a note on *animalis homo,* where she says that she translated the expression as "l'homme naturel" because she relies on the Pauline sense to which Augustine obviously appeals. Thus she says, "Les chrétiens animaux, ou charnels, sont ceux qui continuent à vivre selon le vieil homme; ils jugent et se comportent comme s'ils n'avaient pas été régénérés par le baptême." This view—correct to some extent, of course—overlooks the intellectual aspect of the animal/spiritual distinction as it is found in Augustine.

T. J. Van Bavel says that the little ones live from faith exclusively and cannot understand. They are reborn in Christ, but are not strengthened by the profound and spiritual knowledge of the Scriptures: "Les spirituels, par contre, sont ceux qui non seulement acceptent la doctrine chrétienne et y croient, mais encore, par révélation de Dieu, la comprennent et la connaissent. Comme exemple de l'intelligence inférieure des petits, Augustin invoque souvent l'incapacité de se figurer Dieu comme un être purement spirituel ou l'incompréhension de la doctrine trinitaire."[12] This statement indeed comes close to the position that I want to maintain. However, Van Bavel does not stress the novelty

---

11. In *St. Augustine's Confessions,* 169–72, O'Connell is critical of Solignac's views regarding the extent of the judgment of the spiritual man and regarding the nature of the Church as hierarchical rather than spiritual. It seems to me that, if my argument is correct, it would support O'Connell's interpretation of the very difficult Book 13 of the *conf.*

12. T. J. Van Bavel, "L'humanité du Christ comme lac parvulorum et comme via dans la spiritualité de saint Augustine," *Augustiniana* 7 (1957): 245–281, here 257.

of the conception of God as a spiritual being. Nor does he tie such a conception to Neoplatonism. Rather he adds to the above statement: "Ainsi, arrive-t-il souvent que le concept *parvulus* signifie que quelqu'un est dans l'erreur au sens spéculatif."[13] Yet, if Augustine was truly the first thinker in the West to conceive of God and the soul as spiritual substances, it is strange to categorize those who have not come to such a conception as having erred speculatively.

Schumacher's study examines every occurrence of *spiritus, spiritualis,* and *spiritualiter* in Augustine's sermons. He finds that *spiritualis* (1) describes nonbodily beings and activities, but claims that in the vast majority of cases it (2) has a specifically Christian sense insofar as it refers to the economy of salvation and various gifts and benefits proper to it. He devotes a whole chapter (182–208) to a consideration of three special uses: the spiritual man, the spiritual body, and the spiritual interpretation of Scripture.

He sees that the spiritual man is distinguished for his understanding of the faith (185) and finds that "intellectores regni coelestis" is the most frequent synonym for "spirituales" in Augustine (188). However, he never ties Augustine's spiritual man with an understanding of God and the soul as incorporeal beings—the sort of understanding that Augustine learned from Neoplatonism. Similarly, he sees that a spiritual interpretation of Scripture comes from the Holy Spirit and is meant for the spiritual life of man, but he does not find that an interpretation is spiritual because it concerns an incorporeal reality, even though he notes that for Augustine the opposites of spiritual understanding are: historical, carnal, and bodily (201).

SPIRITUALS AND CARNALS WITHIN THE CHURCH

Let us begin with Augustine's contact with the preaching of Ambrose. He tells us in *conf.* 5, 13, 13 that he came to Milan and to Ambrose, in whose eloquence he delighted. Gradually, however, the truth of what he was saying seeped into his mind along with the eloquent expression.

---

13. Van Bavel cites *vera rel.* 16, 32 in support of this claim: "Et haec est disciplina naturalis christianis minus intelligentibus plene fide digna, intelligentibus autem omni errore privata." Surely that text cannot imply that what fully deserves the belief of Christians—even of the less intelligent ones—contains error. A little one may fail to understand, but failure to understand does not entail being in error.

He began to think that the Catholic faith could be defended against the Manichaean objections by a spiritual exposition of the Scriptures. "This was especially the case after having heard [Ambrose] resolve one or the other difficulty *(aenigmate)* from the old scriptures, whose sense when I took it literally *(ad litteram)* was killing me. Thus after several passages of those books had been spiritually explained *(spiritualiter expositis)*, I blamed my own despair, in which I had believed that the law and the prophets could in no way be upheld against those who hated them and scoffed at them."[14] In *conf.* 6, 3, 4, Augustine tells us that he heard Ambrose preach every Sunday and gradually became convinced that the objections of the Manichees against the Scriptures could be met. In *De beata vita* (hereafter *b. vita*) 1.4, he tells us that he began to realize from Ambrose's sermons "that one should not think of any body whatever when one thinks of God or when one thinks of the soul, for that is the one thing in reality closest to God." He tells us of his joy in realizing that the law and the prophets did not have to be understood as the absurdities he had thought. "I was glad when I often heard Ambrose speaking in his sermons to the people as though he most earnestly commended it as a rule that 'the letter kills, but the spirit quickens' (2 Cor 3:6). For he would draw aside the veil of mystery and spiritually lay open *(remoto mystico velamento, spiritualiter aperiret)* things that interpreted literally seemed to teach unsound doctrine" (*conf.* 6, 4, 6).

In particular, he gives as an example of the understanding of the spirituals the solution of the Manichaean objection to the statement from Genesis that man was made in God's image. He tells us that he "found that 'man was made by you to your image,' was understood by your spiritual sons, whom you had regenerated by your grace in our Catholic Mother, not as though they believed and thought of you as limited by the shape of the human body—although what a spiritual substance would be like I did not surmise even in a weak and obscure manner"

---

14. Many translations speak of allegorical or figurative interpretation in dealing with this passage. For example, Ryan says, "various passages ... explained ... by way of allegory." Frank Sheed says, "I had heard explained figuratively several passages." However, though *aenigma* can mean "allegory," *aenigmate soluto* is better translated as I have done following the BA edition, "après avoir entendu bien des fois resoudre l'une où l'autre des difficultés que présent les anciennes Écritures." In this passage the *aenigma* is the problem solved, not the solution of the problem, and the problem is solved by spiritual explanation.

(*conf.* 6, 3, 4). Hence, he came to admit that he "barked for so many years . . . against the fantasies of a carnal imagination" (ibid.). Thus Ambrose's spiritual interpretation of Scripture concretely meant in the case of the verse from Genesis that Augustine could think of God as an incorporeal substance and thus could realize that our being made in his image did not entail God's having a human shape or being imaginable. It is very much to the point of my argument that Augustine follows immediately with a description of God as having the Neoplatonic characteristics of a spiritual being that is whole everywhere. "But you, most high and most near at hand, most secret and most present, in whom there are no members, some greater, others smaller, who are everywhere whole and entire, who are never confined in place, and who surely are not in our corporeal shape, you have yet made man to your own image. And behold, from head to foot he is contained in space!" (ibid.)

At first reading one is likely to think that "your spiritual sons" are simply all who were "regenerated by your grace in our Catholic Mother," that is, all the baptized.[15] However, in *conf.* 6, 11, 18, he tells us that it is the learned *(docti)* in the Church who "hold it blasphemy to believe that God is limited by the shape of the human body." Thus, when he says that "the Catholic faith does not teach what we once thought," namely, an anthropomorphism, the Church that teaches this is the learned in the Church, and the learned or "spirituals," I suggest, are those who have come to a conception of God and of the soul as incorporeal realities, that is, those who have attained some grasp of Plotinus's doctrine on incorporeal reality. That is, Augustine is not saying anything about the faith of the average cleric or lay person, who were certainly—insofar as they reflected on the question—materialists, as Tertullian had been. After all, the *animales* in the congregation at Hippo were surely catechumens or already baptized in the Church.

That there were many in the Church who could not or at least did not rise to a spiritual understanding of God is confirmed by *De moribus ecclesiae Catholicae et de moribus Manichaeorum* (hereafter *mor.*) 1, 10, 17, where we find that Augustine admits that "there are found among us

---

15. That such is not the case is clear from a text such as: "Sunt enim in Ecclesiis etiam hi qui non iam lacte potantur, sed vescuntur cibo, quos idem Apostolus significat dicens: 'Sapientiam loquimur inter perfectos' (1 Cor 2:6); sed non ex his solis perficiuntur Ecclesiae, quia si soli essent, non consuleretur generi humano" (*en. Ps.* 8, 5).

some children *(pueri)* who think of God in a human form and suppose that he is so—an opinion than which there is none more abject, but there are found many elders who see with their mind that his majesty remains inviolable and immutable not merely above the human body, but also above the mind itself." These "ages" are not a matter of time, but of virtue and prudence. He admits that no Manichaean is an anthropomorphite, but the Catholic Church "supports [her little ones] as infants at the breast . . . and they are nourished and brought to full manhood and then arrive at the maturity and white hairs of wisdom" (ibid.). Augustine uses the Pauline texts on children as contrasted with adult believers to describe the difference within the Church between those who were not and those who were able to understand God not merely as incorporeal, but as immutable.

In *c. ep. Man.* 23, 25, Augustine asks his Manichaean reader to compare with the Manichees: "not the *'spirituales'* of the Catholic faith, in whom the mind—as far as possible in this life—sees that the divine substance and nature is not stretched out in places and with any limits of lines, but . . . ones who are commonly wont, when they hear certain members of our body in an allegory, as when God's eyes or ears are mentioned, to picture God, as a result of freedom of the imagination, under the shape of a human body." A bit further on he concedes that he laughs at *(derideo)* carnal men who cannot yet think of spiritual things *(cogitare spiritualia)* and think of God under human shape. Yet the little ones in the Church who "think of God under human form cloaked, after its kind, with the highest dignity" think in a more tolerable and worthy fashion *(tolerabilius et honestius)* of God than the Manichee who thinks of him as a mass infinitely extended in every direction except where it is limited by evil.[16]

Furthermore, the little ones in the Catholic Church will grow up nourished by her milk, and eventually they begin to "understand spiritually *(spiritualiter)* the allegories and parables of Scripture and gradually realize that God's powers are fittingly mentioned in one place by the word 'ears,' in another by the word 'eyes,' and in yet another by the

---

16. Two reasons for this might be suggested: one, that the limited God of the Manichees is mutable, violable, and corruptible—something that Augustine came to abhor—and two, that Word did, after all, become flesh and, as such, is the *lac parvulorum*, as we shall see in the final section.

words 'hands' and 'feet'" (ibid.). The further they progress in such understanding, the more they are confirmed in their Catholicity. However, the Manichee who surrenders his imaginings about God has thereby ceased to be a Manichee. This point was one of tremendous importance for Augustine since a Manichee who transcends his imagination and thinks of God as incorporeal can no longer be a Manichee. The *Catholica,* however, has her "little ones," but also has her "spirituals." Indeed, mother Church nourishes the little ones so that they may come to the maturity of wisdom.[17]

Thus there seems to be reasonably clear evidence that he links being a "spiritual" in the Church with being able to conceive of God as incorporeal, as a substance not stretched out in places or times, just as there is reasonably clear evidence that links being "animal" or "carnal" or "a little one" in the Church with having an anthropomorphic or at least corporeal concept of God.[18] For the "carnal" and "little ones" are precisely the sort that Augustine himself had been prior to his contact with the Platonists, namely, easy targets for Manichaean objections such as Fortunatus later posed to Augustine: "Is there something outside of God, or is everything in God?" (*c. Fort.* 5). For as long as one is convinced that to be real is to be a body, one is caught on the dilemma of either locating evil in God or locating it outside of God. Caught by

---

17. This is perhaps a major part of the reason for Augustine's joy in finding that the teaching of the Catholic Church was not opposed to *huic tanto bono,* namely, the doctrine of the Neoplatonists. See O'Meara, *St. Augustine,* 177–178n24.

18. There are many other texts that might be cited. Let me mention but two that are both relatively short and clear. "Parvuli enim erant, et nondum spiritaliter diiudicabant, quae de rebus non ad corpus, sed ad spiritum pertinentibus audiebant" (*Jo. Eu. tr.* 103, 1). "Omnia quippe dicta sunt hic, quae si intellegantur secundum humanum sensum carnaliter, nihil aliud nobis facit anima plena phantamatis, nisi quasdam imagines velut duorum hominum Patris et Filii, unius ostendentis, alterius videntis; unius loquentis, alterius audientis, quae omnia idola cordis sunt; quae si iam deiecta sunt de templis suis, quanto magis deicienda sunt de pectoribus christianis?" (*Jo. Eu. tr.* 19, 1).

Augustine goes so far as to say that some philosophers of this world—surely, the Neoplatonists—"saw what St. John says, namely that by the Word of God all things were made . . . and that God has an only-begotten Son through whom everything exists. They were able to see that which is, but they saw from afar" (*Jo. Eu. tr.* 2, 4).

Yet he never calls such men "spirituals." It would seem that the influence of Neoplatonic spiritualism might be—in the mind of Augustine—a necessary condition for being a spiritual, but it is not a sufficient condition. In fact, Augustine reproaches them for their pride in refusing to accept the cross of Christ, the necessary *lignum* for crossing the sea of this world to the fatherland they glimpsed from afar.

the first horn, one has to surrender the thesis that God is all good; but caught by the second, one has to surrender the thesis that God is infinite. Hence, one is faced either with a God who is evil at least in part or with a God who is limited by evil outside of himself.

Let us turn to another text that, I believe, clearly supports my thesis, namely, *Jo. Ev. tr.* 102, 4. Augustine there has been commenting on John 16:25, where Jesus said, "I have spoken these things to you in proverbs; the hour is coming when I will no longer speak in proverbs, but will openly speak of my Father."[19] He argues that the text does not refer to the afterlife and concludes that it remains that Jesus is to be understood to have promised to make his disciples spiritual from carnal or animal men, although we will not yet be such as when we will have a spiritual body.

This transformation of the apostles from "carnals" to "spirituals" is attributed to the reception of the Holy Spirit. However, not everyone who has received the Holy Spirit is a spiritual. It seems that, besides having received the Holy Spirit in baptism, one must have also attained an understanding of the incorporeal nature of God. Augustine then cites a series of quotations from 1 Corinthians. *"Homo animalis,"* he goes on to tell us, "does not perceive what pertains to the Spirit of God" (1 Cor 2:14). "He hears what he hears of the nature of God so that he is not able to think of anything other than a body, however huge and immense, however bright and beautiful, still a body. Therefore, to him whatever things are said of the incorporeal and immutable substance of wisdom are proverbs—not that he considers them as proverbs, but because he thinks just as do those who are accustomed to hear and not to understand proverbs" (*Jo. Ev. tr.* 102, 4). On the other hand, a *spiritualis*—even if he sees in life only through a glass and partially "sees nonetheless—not by any sense of the body, not by any imagining thought which receives or forms likenesses of any bodies, but by the most certain understanding of the mind—that God is not a body, but spirit, so that when the Son speaks openly of the Father, he who speaks is seen to be of the same substance [as him of whom he speaks]" (ibid.). Then those

---

19. *Proverbia*, though usually translated as "parables," might be better translated as "dark saying" or "riddle," since he seems to offer the following as an example. "Quis vadit ad eum qui cum illo est? Sed hoc intelligenti est verbum, non intelligenti proverbium" (*Jo. Ev. tr.* 103, 2).

who ask in his name do not "imagine by a lightness or weakness of mind that the Father is in one place, the Son in another standing before him and asking on our behalf" (ibid.). Thus the spirituals enjoy a kind of intellectual vision of God; they grasp that God is not a body, but spirit. They do not imagine the Father and the Son as standing apart in space or suppose that "the Word . . . makes words on our behalf" when he intercedes for us with the Father.

Augustine realizes that even the spiritual man is prey to such imaginings, and he uses a marvelous image to insist: "Whatever of the sort occurs to spiritual men when they think of God as a result of their being used to bodies, they drive away from the interior eyes—by denial and rejection—like pesky flies. Thus they come to rest in the purity of that light, with which as witness and judge they reject as false those very images that rush before their inner gaze" (ibid.).

One danger of such an imaginative approach to God can be seen by the fact that Augustine implies in this text that the sameness of substance between the Father and the Son is seen and understood only if they are grasped as nonbodily.[20] Thus, such imagining, the work of a carnal understanding, can be seen as a source of heresy.

This section of the paper has attempted to show that there is some reasonably good evidence to tie the spirituals in the Church to those in

20. There are passages in which Augustine links carnal understanding with heresy. In at least some of these passages there is the suggestion that a lack of spiritual understanding is at the root or heart of the heretical view. Thus, for example, in commenting on Ps 130:2, Augustine says that "infirmi" who try to grasp what they are still incapable of grasping, at times think that they have grasped what they have not and think themselves wise. "Hoc autem contigit omnibus haereticis; qui cum essent animales et carnales, defendendo sententias suas pravas, quas falsas esse non potuerunt videre, exclusi sunt de Catholica" (*en. Ps.* 130, 9). Instead of clinging to the humanity of Christ, they try to rise up to grasp the Word. Augustine takes the Arians as an example. "Illi autem haeretici volentes disputare de eo quod non poterant capere, dixerunt quia Filius minor est quam Pater, et dixerunt quia Spiritus Sanctus minor est quam Filius; et fecerunt gradus, et immiserunt in Ecclesiam tres deos" (*en. Ps.* 130, 11). In dealing with the Arian interpretation of Jn 5:19 (*Jo. Ev. tr.* 18, 5), Augustine says to the heretics that he will come down "ad carnalem sensum tuum, ita interim cogito ut tu." He then imagines the Son watching the hands of the Father "ut quomodo viderit eum fabricare, sic et ipse tale aliquid fabricet in operibus suis." Thus he accuses the Arian: "Carnali sapore et puerili motu facis tibi in animo Deum facientem, et Verbum adtendentem, ut cum fecerit Deus, faciat et Verbum." Thus the subordination of the Son to the Father results from imagining the Son watching the hands of his craftsman Father to learn how he too might make things. Although pride and earthly desires impede the heretic's understanding, it is intellectual failure, it seems, that is at the heart of the Arian error.

the Church who have some grasp of a spiritual substance, that is, those whose way of thinking about God has been reformed by Neoplatonism. The animal or carnal men, on the other hand, though in the Church, are those who are as yet unable to rise to a spiritual understanding of God and of the soul.

SPIRITUAL INTERPRETATION OF SCRIPTURE

Since it is the spirituals who can interpret Scripture spiritually and the carnals who cannot, this section is closely linked to the preceding one.[21] I shall limit this section to dealing with several examples of what Augustine himself calls a spiritual exposition or understanding of Scripture, for the wider use of "spiritual sense" to refer to allegorical, analogical, and moral senses—however appropriate for the whole tradition of the Middle Ages—need not and, if I am correct, does not square with Augustine's use of the expression.[22] This point has been, I believe, partially established by what we have seen Augustine say about Ambrose's preaching.

There can be no doubt that spiritual understanding of Scripture is linked with the reception of the Holy Spirit.[23] It is, moreover, for the spiritual life of the faithful in some sense.[24] What I am arguing is that, besides the spiritual source and the spiritual purpose, an understanding of Scripture is spiritual because of the sort of interpretation it is, that is, because it involves grasping some incorporeal reality or understanding what is said in an incorporeal sense. Indeed, among the texts that Schumacher cites, there is the following: "For it pleased the Lord our God to exhort you through us to the point that in all these things which are said as of a bodily and visible creature, we seek something spiritually hidden so that we may rejoice when we have found it" (*s.* 3, 2).

I hope to show that at least a number passages in which Augustine

---

21. Cf. Solignac, "Spirituels et charnels," 629–630.
22. Schumacher recognizes that Augustine's terminology does not coincide with that of a later age. "Augustine and his contemporaries borrowed this division of 'proper' and 'spiritual' senses from the rhetoric of their age, and used it as a much wider and more flexible classification than is possible with our rigid modern stratification of 'senses' of Scripture"; Schumacher, *Spiritus and Spirituales*, 199.
23. See *Jo. Ev. tr.* 97, 1 and 102, 4.
24. Schumacher, *Spiritus and Spirituales*, 202.

speaks of spiritual understanding are spiritual in an intrinsic sense insofar as they involve an understanding of God or the soul as incorporeal or interpret the corporeal things mentioned as referring to incorporeal things —something that Augustine learned to do from Neoplatonism.

Let us turn to a few passages of Scripture in which Augustine presents us with a spiritual interpretation. One of the Old Testament passages that the Manichees used as a standard objection to the Catholic acceptance of these Scriptures was Genesis 24:2–3, where Abraham has his servant place his hand under his thigh and swear by the God of heaven. For the Manichees such a text proved that the Patriarchs were "dirty old men," as Peter Brown put it.[25] And from Secundinus's Letter to Augustine, we know that this passage was one of those raised as an objection to the "spiritual" young Augustine. Secundinus could say, "I knew that you always hated such stuff. I knew you were one who loved lofty things."[26]

Augustine responds to this objection in *Contra Secundinum Manichaeum* (hereafter *c. Sec.*) 23, in saying that Abraham, in bidding his servant so to swear, prophesied that "the God of heaven would come in the flesh that was propagated from that 'thigh.'" He attacks the Manichees for their concern about the Son of God being harmed by the womb of the Virgin, though their doctrine has God contained in the womb of every female, whether human or beast. He mocks their horror at the "thigh" of the Patriarch, as though that *membrum* could not be chastely touched.

The carnal interpretation of the passage is fairly clear; the servant swore by placing his hand on the Patriarch's genitals. However, Augustine understands the passage to refer to Abraham's prophesying Christ's coming in the flesh from the seed of Abraham. Yet this interpretation does not seem to be particularly spiritual in the sense of incorporeal. Nonetheless, if we turn to *Jo. Ev. tr.* 43, where Augustine is dealing with Christ's words that Abraham rejoiced to see my day, we find that Augustine appeals to Genesis 24 as indicating when Abraham saw not merely Christ's temporal day in which he came in the flesh, but his eternal day. Hence, Abraham knew Christ not merely as one to come

---

25. Brown, *Augustine of Hippo*, 50. Brown has "put forth thy hand over my loins" as the translation of Gn 24:2.
26. The translation is from Brown, *Augustine of Hippo*, p. 50.

in the flesh, but as the eternal Word: "ineffable Light, Word that lasts, splendor shining upon devout minds, unfailing wisdom, God remaining with the Father and at some time to come in the flesh without leaving the Father's bosom. All this Abraham saw" (*Jo. Ev. tr.* 43, 16). Thus, Augustine maintained that Abraham was one of the spirituals.[27]

Another example of "spiritual understanding" is the Christian interpretation of the commandment to observe the Sabbath. Augustine says that those who objected to Christ's healing on the Sabbath "understood the observance of the Sabbath carnally and thought that God after the labor of making the world has been subsequently as if asleep and that he therefore made holy that day upon which he began his rest" (*Jo. Ev. tr.* 20, 2). Augustine says that we Christians spiritually observe the mystery *(sacramentum)* of the Sabbath that was commanded the Fathers by abstaining from servile work, that is, from sin, and by having spiritual tranquility in our heart. Thus, to correct the idea that God has slept after the effort of creation, Jesus told them that his Father works up to now. In that way a spiritual understanding of the Sabbath avoids the imagery of God resting from his labors of creation and involves a nonbodily observance, that is, peace of soul and avoidance of sin.

A third example of spiritual understanding concerns Jesus' words about the necessity of eating his flesh and drinking his blood. Augustine tells us that the disciples who found this a hard saying were scandalized because in their folly *(stulte)* they understood this carnally *(carnaliter illud cogitauerunt)*, that is, "they thought that the Lord was about to cut off and give them pieces of his body to eat" (*en. Ps.* 98, 9).[28] Augustine tells us that the Lord instructed those who remained with him. "Understand spiritually what I said. You are not going to eat this body that you see and drink that blood which they will shed who will crucify me. I have given you a mystery *(sacramentum)*; spiritually understood, it will give you life. Though it must be visibly celebrated, it should be invisibly understood."[29] Augustine here explicitly appeals to a spiritual

---

27. See above note 6. In *Jo. Ev. tr.* 43, 16, Abraham is said to see with "the eyes of the heart" not merely Christ's temporal day, but "diem Domini qui nescit ortum, nescit occasum."

28. Augustine makes the same point even more crudely in *Jo. Ev. tr.* 11, where he speaks of cutting up, cooking, and eating his flesh like that of a lamb.

29. Such a statement might seem to play havoc with a eucharistic realism. However, Augustine's problem with a bodily presence of Christ in the Eucharist, it strikes me, is not unlike that of Descartes—and perhaps for the same reason, namely, that for both to

understanding of Christ's words as necessary. And that spiritual understanding involves a noncarnal or even a nonbodily presence of Christ in the Eucharist. He is there spiritually.

A final example of spiritual understanding has to do with the prophecy of Jonah that in three days Nineveh will be overthrown. Augustine says that the text must be understood spiritually if the truth of Scripture is to be saved. Thus, though the city was not physically overthrown, it was spiritually overthrown insofar as the people repented of their sins.[30] Here it is the interior act within the incorporeal soul that saves the truth of the prophecy.

This section has shown that a number of passages from Scripture that Augustine explains spiritually involve the grasp of God or the soul as incorporeal substances. Thus there is some evidence to link what Augustine meant by a spiritual understanding of Scripture with the influence of Neoplatonism.

CHRIST FOR THE SPIRITUALS AND FOR THE CARNALS

When Schumacher begins to specify the objects of the spirituals' knowledge, he mentions that besides the general expressions, such as *regnum coeleste, divina,* and *mandata Dei,* that the "Person of Jesus Christ, and Him Crucified, is a special object of this understanding."[31] Now it is certainly true that Christ is a special object of knowledge for the "intellectores regni coelestis, aeterni," but Augustine says something much more interesting that just that. He says that for the little ones in the Church, that is, for the *carnales* and *animales,* the humanity of Christ is the milk by which they must be nourished because they are not capable of taking solid food. On the other hand, the little ones in the Church are expected to grow up, to become adults or *spirituales,* so that they can be nourished by the Word himself, who is the food of angels.[32] Thus the *lac parvulorum* is the humanity that Christ assumed and

---

be a body is to be extended in three dimensions. Perhaps because for Augustine to be a body meant to have three dimensions, he had to understand Christ's presence in the Eucharist as a spiritual presence.

30. "Si carnaliter intelligas, falsum videtur dixisse: si spiritualiter intelligas, factum est quod dixit Propheta. Eversa est enim Nineve" (*s.* 361, 20).

31. Schumacher, *Spiritus and Spirituales,* 189.

32. This theme of the humanity of Christ as the *lac parvulorum* is found in numerous texts. Van Bavel's article is an excellent study of the topic. Among the main texts in

by which he feeds the little ones. But we are not meant to remain little ones all our lives; we are meant to grow up and be nourished by solid food, by the Word, by the *panis angelorum*. Hence, Augustine implies that the flesh that Christ has assumed, his humanity, all his historical actions including his crucifixion and death, are merely the nourishment of the little ones who are as yet incapable of the solid food. He implies that we should be gradually weaned from the *lac parvulorum* and that it is a bit disgraceful for one to be still at the breast when one ought to have grown up. He implies that when one is a spiritual, he eats the food of angels and has no more need for the humanity of Christ.[33]

In the concluding section of this paper, however, I do not intend to focus upon the role of the humanity of Christ. My thesis in this paper is that for Augustine a *spiritualis* in the Church is one who brings to the faith an understanding that, under the influence of Neoplatonism, can think of God and the soul as spiritual or incorporeal substances. On the other hand, an *animalis* or *carnalis* is one without a spiritual understanding of God or the soul.

In *Jo. Ev. tr.* 98 Augustine asks whether the spirituals have a doctrine that they conceal from the carnal men in the Church. While 1 Corinthians might seem to imply that there is such a doctrine, Augustine fears the consequences of admitting an esoteric doctrine that might readily cloak over and excuse moral wickedness.[34] He begins his response by pointing

---

which Augustine treats this theme are: *en. Ps.* 8, 5; *en. Ps.* 33, 6; *en. Ps.* 130, 9–12; *en. Ps.* 119, 2; *en. Ps.* 117, 22; and *Jo. Ev. tr.* 98, 1–8.

33. This is the clear implication of all the texts I have read on this point, except for *In Ioan. Ev.* 98, 6, where, as we shall see, Augustine suddenly realizes what the metaphor of mother's milk entails for the lasting significance of the humanity of the Word. Van Bavel notes, "Cette doctrine, dans toute sa simplicité, n'offre aucune difficulté. Les problèmes surgissent seulement lorsque saint Augustin prétend que l'homme doit dépasser ce stade et tendre à la nourriture des adultes. Au moyen de lait, le petit doit croître pour manger du pain. Ce pain n'est autre que le Verbe de Dieu"; Van Bavel, "L'humanité du Christ," 255. Augustine puts into the mouth of Christ as he is about to ascend to the Father the following words: "Expedit vobis ut haec forma servi auferatur a vobis; caro quidem factum Verbum habito in vobis, sed nolo me carnaliter adhuc diligatis, et isto lacte contenti semper infantes esse cupiatis" (*Jo. Ev. tr.* 94, 4). He is even more emphatic when he insists that for those who want to understand the Word, "non eis sufficiat caro, quod propter eos Verbum factum est, ut lacte nutrirentur" (*En. Ps.* 177, 22).

34. "Si autem dixerimus: Habent, timendum et cavendum est, ne sub hac occasione in occultis nefaria doceantur, et spiritalium nomine, velut ea quae carnales capere non possunt, non solum excusatione dealbanda, verum etiam praedicatione laudanda videantur" (*Jo. Ev. tr.* 98, 1).

out that the very flesh and blood of the Crucified is not thought of in the same way by the carnals as by the spirituals, "for the former it is milk, for the latter it is food. If the latter hear no more, they do understand more. For what is equally received in faith by both is not equally grasped by their minds" (*Jo. Ev. tr.* 98, 2). Augustine appeals to Paul's statement that Christ crucified is a scandal to the Jews, folly to the Gentiles, but to those who have been called it is the power and wisdom of God, "but the carnal little ones hold this only on faith, while the more capable spirituals also see this by understanding" (ibid.). Hence, Augustine insists that both spirituals and carnals hear the same teaching, though each receives it according to his capacity. The carnals lack the "spiritual understanding" that the spirituals possess (*Jo. Ev. tr.* 98, 3). Thus when Paul judged that he could speak at Corinth only of Christ crucified and that he could not speak to them as spirituals but as carnals, the spirituals among them heard the same teaching, but understood it differently. "Animalis homo," that is, one who is humanly wise, Augustine tells us, does not grasp "what belongs to the Spirit, that is, what grace the cross of Christ confers upon believers. He thinks that that cross only succeeded in offering an example to be imitated by us struggling even unto death for the truth" (ibid.).

Such men do not know, Augustine tells us while quoting Paul, how Christ crucified was "made for us by God wisdom, justice, sanctification, and redemption" (1 Cor 1:30). But it is in Hebrews 5:12–14 that Augustine finds the further clue as to the nature of the solid food of the perfect, that is, the wisdom that Paul spoke to the perfect at Corinth. The perfect are "those who have their faculties trained by habit to separate good from evil" (Heb 5:14). "Those with a weak or untrained mind can only do this if they are sustained by a certain milk of faith so that they may believe the invisible things that they do not see and the intelligible things they do not understand" (*Jo. Ev. tr.* 98, 4). Hence, such little ones are easily carried off by promises of knowledge to the empty and sacrilegious tales of the Manichees "so that they think of good and evil only by bodily images and think that God is but a body and can only think of evil as a substance" (ibid.). Thus we see that the little ones—the carnal or animal men in the Church—are those who cannot rise to an understanding of God as incorporeal and who thus are liable to fall prey to the same Manichaean challenges as Augustine had before he learned to think as a Neoplatonist. The spiritual man, on the other hand, understands that "evil is a falling away of mutable substances from God—the immutable and sovereign substance who made them from nothing" (ibid.).

The little one in the Church is first given milk, that is, the Symbol and the Lord's Prayer.[35] The Catholic faith is to be preached to both carnal and spiritual, but matters of deeper understanding should not be mentioned since they are too burdensome for the little ones. But the food of the spirituals is not contrary to the milk of the little ones. Augustine points out that it is solid food that becomes milk for the infant through the mother's flesh.[36] "Thus acted mother Wisdom herself, which, though it is the solid food of the angels on high, deigned somehow to become milk for the little ones, when the Word became flesh and dwelt among us. But Christ the man, who by his true flesh, true cross, true death and true resurrection is called the pure milk of the little ones, when he is grasped well by the spirituals, is found to be the Lord of the angels. Hence, the little ones ought not so to be nursed that they never understand Christ as God, nor ought they to be weaned so that they abandon Christ as man."[37] Suddenly Augustine seems to have realized that the metaphor of milk and solid food would have the spirituals in a position to do without the humanity of Christ. He tells us that the metaphor of a mother's milk is not quite right and that we would do better with the image of a foundation. "For Christ crucified is both milk to the infants and food for those advancing."[38] Much earlier Augustine had come close to holding the Porphyrian doctrine that every body is to be fled from. See *Soliloquia* (hereafter *sol.*) 1, 24. Of this passage Augustine admits in the *Retractationes* (hereafter *retr.*) 1, 4, 3,

---

35. *Jo. Ev. tr.* 98, 5. This is the only reference I have found that makes concrete what the doctrine given to the little ones was.

36. This image is found in *conf.* 7, 8, 24, where Augustine speaks of wisdom becoming milk through the flesh. It is not insignificant that that image occurs immediately after his contact with the books of the Platonists.

37. The expression "mater ipsa sapientia" referring to the Word who became flesh and thus milk for us little ones is somewhat startling (*Jo. Ev. tr.* 98, 6).

38. This is the only text in which Augustine explicitly corrects the implications of his metaphor. Elsewhere he seems quite content with regarding Christ's humanity and his historical actions as something to be transcended. In the other texts the humanity of Christ is the *via* by which we ascend to the Word and, it seems—if one may borrow a metaphor from a later mystic—a ladder to be thrown aside once it has been climbed.

"Et in eo quod ibi dictum est, *penitus esse ista sensibilia fugienda,* cavendum fuit ne putaremur illam Porphyrii falsi philosophi tenere sententiam, qua dixit, *omne corpus esse fugiendum.*" That certainly is a doctrine inimical to the Incarnation. But he says in *De doctrina Christiana* (hereafter *doc. Chr.*) that we should not cling to the humanity of Christ. "No reality *in via* ought to hold us, when not even the Lord himself, insofar as he deigned to be our way, wanted to hold us, but to pass on, lest in our weakness we should cling to temporal realities, even if they have been assumed and carried by him for our salvation" (*doc. Chr.* 1, 34, 38). And in *Trin.* 13, 19, 24, we find that wisdom has to do with eternal things, while science concerns what is temporal. Thus, "all those things which the Word made flesh did and suffered for us in time and place . . . pertain to knowledge, not to wisdom." Obviously one builds upon a foundation; whereas, one gives up mother's milk.

Hence, the spiritual knows Christ not merely as man, but as creator. He knows how to think of God as an incorporeal substance. The little ones do not have a different Gospel preached to them; there is no esoteric Christianity for the spirituals. However, there is a vast difference in understanding, and one of the main factors in that difference in understanding on the part of the spiritual man is the influence of Neoplatonism.

4

LOVE OF NEIGHBOR IN AUGUSTINE

In Augustine's De vera religione *(hereafter* vera rel.*) I found an amazing account of love of neighbor that is highly spiritual in the sense that the neighbor we should love is a soul. In this work Augustine says that we should love our neighbor as ourselves and insists that we are not our bodies. Hence, one should not love another on the basis of any bodily relationship. He seemed in this work to take quite literally Christ's words about hating father, mother, and so on. In* doc. Chr., *however, which is not much later than* vera rel., *a quite different interpretation of the love of neighbor emerges, in which bodily relationships are taken as God-given directions for our love of others. I suggest that one of the factors that explains Augustine's move away from a highly Platonic view of what it is to be a human being was his realization of what Saint Paul had said in Ephesians 5 about no one hating his own flesh. Hence, the article illustrates one way in which Augustine rapidly moved away from an aspect of Neoplatonism that he came to realize was incompatible with Christianity.*

In his *retr.* Augustine tells us, "Whoever reads my works in the order in which they were written will perhaps discover how I made progress in writing" (Prologue, 3). Such a statement obviously implies that there is progress and development in what he has written. This article will explore but one way in which Augustine made progress, namely, in his understanding of the command to love one's neighbor as oneself. To be even more specific, it will deal with the object of love of neighbor, when one loves his neighbor as one ought.[1] In doing so, it will cast light upon Augustine's philosophy of man from the perspective of his understanding of love of neighbor.

The investigation of this topic will principally focus upon two works, *vera rel.* and *doc. Chr.* For in these two works Augustine deals with the nature of love of the neighbor and does so both extensively and in a way that opens up, I believe, a fascinating perspective on his changing view of man.[2] Though these two works were written within less than a decade of each other, the thoughts that they present on the second of the two great commandments seem quite different.[3] It will be one of

---

1. We know that Augustine changed on this point from *retr.* 1, 26, where he modifies his claim, "Charitatem voco, qua amantur ea quae non sunt prae ipso amante contemenda: id est, quod aeternum est, et quod amare ipsum aeternum potest. Deus igitur et animus quo amatur, charitas proprie dicitur purgatissima et consummata, si nihil aliud amatur" (*div. quaes.* 36, 1). We will return to this text later. See below notes 6 and 37.

2. The discussion of love of neighbor in *vera rel.* runs from 45, 83 to 48, 93. The relevant texts in *doc. Chr.* run from 1, 22, 20 to 1, 35, 39. There are, of course, numerous other texts in which Augustine deals with love of neighbor. I have chosen to focus on these because they reveal, I believe, better than any others how Augustine made progress on this point. Though the topic of love in Saint Augustine has received extensive treatment, many of these studies have focused upon the question of whether Christian love of God can be eudaimonistic or teleological or must be unselfish or deontological. For example, Anders Nygren's *Agape and Eros* (Philadelphia: Westminster, 1953); John Burnaby's *Amor Dei: A Study of the Religion of St. Augustine* (London: Hodder and Stoughton, 1938); Ragnar Holte's *Béatitude et Sagesse: Saint Augustin et le problème de la fin de l'homme dans la philosophie ancienne* (Paris: Études augustiniennes, 1962); Gunnar Hultgren's *Le commandement d'amour chez Augustin: Interprétation philosophique et théologique d'après les écrits de la période 386–400* (Paris: J. Vrin, 1939).

Oliver O'Donovan, *The Problem of Self-Love in St. Augustine* (New Haven: Yale University, Press, 1980), has a chapter entitled "Your Neighbor as Yourself" (112–136). However, his central concern is not the nature of love of neighbor or the development of Augustine's thought on the topic. Indeed, when he does refer to *vera rel.,* he interprets it as a demand that we love in our neighbor "bare humanity" (113). "We are required to *estimate* our neighbor *as equal humanity*" (114). This obscures the fact that Augustine is saying that we love in the neighbor only his soul.

3. The *vera rel.* was written after Augustine's return to Africa from Rome. In *c. Acad.* 2, 3, 8, Augustine promised Romanianus a treatise on the true religion. "Ce traité ne verra le jour qu'après plusieurs années. Entre temps, il y aura la mort de Monique, le séjour à Rome, la conversion complète d'Augustin. Rentré à Thagaste, en 388, il a fondé une communauté religieuse et entamé la lutte contre les manichéens.... Le *De vera religione* vient naturellement couronner, vers 390, tout ce travail de pensée. Peu après, Augustin sera ordonné prêtre, à trente-six ans." *Oeuvres de Saint Augustin,* 8: lre Série: Opuscules, texte, traduction et notes par J. Pegon, S.J. (Paris: Desclée de Brouwer, 1951), 12.

The dating of the *doc. Chr.* is somewhat more complicated, for though Augustine

my aims here to determine just how radically the two works differ on love of neighbor; yet even a cursory glance at a few texts seems to reveal that Augustine's view on love of neighbor underwent profound changes between 389 and 397. While in *vera rel.* 46, 89, to love one's neighbor as oneself is to love him as a soul, since "bodies are not what we are," in *doc. Chr.* 1, 26, 27, love of neighbor is a love for the whole that includes body and soul. Similarly, in *vera rel.* 46, 88, love of neighbor should not be based upon temporal relationships; whereas, in *doc. Chr.* Augustine says that God has given us such temporal relationships to help us direct our love to its correct object. In *vera rel.* 46, 86 and 89, we are told that we ought not to love our bodies, though in *doc. Chr.* 1, 28, 29, we find that we love our bodies by a natural law God has given us.

What I intend to do in this article is, first, to examine the account of love of neighbor in *vera rel.* Then I shall turn to the account of love of neighbor in *doc. Chr.*, which I shall emphasize less, because it is better known and less startling.[4] Finally, I shall venture an explanation for the apparently radical change in the way in which Augustine dealt with love of neighbor, which is surely tied in some way to a gradual moderation of his early enthusiasm for Neoplatonism.

LOVE OF NEIGHBOR IN *DE VERA RELIGIONE*

The discussion of love of neighbor in *vera rel.* arises out of Augustine's argument that even the three basic vices, lust, pride, and curiosity,

---

tells us in *retr.* 2, 4, 7, that he found the *doc. Chr.* still incomplete when he was writing the review of his works and that he then set off to complete it, some have asked whether he did not at that point completely revise the part that he had written some thirty years earlier. See Dom de Bruyne, "Itala de saint Augustin," *Revue Bénédictine* 30 (1913): 301–303, and P. Courcelle, *Les lettres grecques en Occident de Macrobe à Cassiodore* (Paris: de Boccard, 1948), 149–150. Bardy dates the completion of *doc. Chr.* at 426–427. The first two books and up to 3, 25, 35 of the third were completed by the end of 396 or the beginning of 397. In BA 12, 577, Bardy rejects the hypothesis of de Bruyne and Courcelle that "Saint Augustin a corrigé complètement vers 426 ce qu'il avait déjà écrit. Il s'est borné à ajouter ce qui manquait." Bardy also refers to H.-I. Marrou's rejection of Courcelle's and de Bruyne's view in *Saint Augustin et la fin de la culture antique*, 4th ed. (Paris: E. de Boccard, 1958), 708, though Marrou simply says that he does not find it necessary to suppose that "le texte de la première partie ait été entièrement remanié lors de la reprise de l'ouvrage."

4. Etienne Gilson, in *Christian Philosophy*, presents a good treatment of love of others based on *doc. Chr.* He gives, however, no indication that there is quite another view presented in the earlier *vera rel.* See 165–168. Moreover, neither Hultgren nor O'Donovan seems to recognize any significant difference between the two works.

can lead us back to God. Pride, for example, manifests a desire for unity and power in passing, temporal things. From this idea Augustine takes up the Stoic theme that the wise man is not conquered by any adversity. He tells us that we all want to be unconquered—and rightly so, for our soul has been made by God and to God's image.[5]

Augustine maintains that, had we kept God's commands, no one would conquer us. However, he adds—in words that seem to imply that we personally sinned in Adam, "We shamefully consented to the words" of the woman who now gives birth in pain, while we toil upon the earth and are overcome by everything that upsets us. We do not want to be conquered by another man: our equal; but we are easily conquered by a vice: something far inferior. "A man who has conquered his vices cannot be conquered by a man. For he is not conquered unless what he loves is snatched away from him by an adversary. Therefore, he who loves only what cannot be snatched away from its lover is surely unconquered and is not tortured by envy" (*vera rel.* 46, 86). Hence, a condition of one's being unconquered is that one not love what can be taken from him against his will. This would seem to imply that if we wish to be unconquered, we should love only God and no temporal and perishing things. For if we love what is temporal and perishing, we love what can be taken away from us.[6] Certainly, if one loves only the immutable and eternal, the object of his love cannot be taken away from him against his will. Indeed, if one loves only the immutable and

---

5. Augustine's "Invicti volumus esse, et recte" (*vera rel.* 45, 84) recalls Cicero's discussion of the Stoic wise man in the *Tusculanae Disputationes* 5, 18: "at nos virtutem semper liberam volumus, semper invictam; quae nisi sunt, sublata virtus est," and in *De finibus*, where he says of the wise man, "Recte eius omnia dicentur, qui scit uti solus omnibus; recte etiam pulcher appellabitur . . . recte solus liber, . . . recte invictus." In *mor.* 1, 24, 43, Augustine refers to Job, that most Stoic of all Old Testament figures, as *invictus*. And in *quan.* 36, 80, he speaks of God as *Dominus invictissimus,* presumably because of his omnipotence and inviolability. See *Gn. adv. Man.* 1, 17, 28, where man's being made to the image of God lies in the power by which he overcomes the beasts, namely, intellect. Man preserves that image by keeping his body in subjection and by being subject to God; thus he retains the middle rank in which he was created. For other Stoic influences on Augustine, see Verbeke, "Augustin et le stoicisme."

6. In *vera rel.* 35, 65, he says, "Loca offerunt quod amemus, tempora surripiunt quod amamus." Though what places offer us is bodies, it would seem that times carry off everything temporal, i.e., bodies and souls. Hence, one sees the point of the text in *div. quaes.* 31, 1 (see above note 1), where the soul and God are the sole objects of charity. The soul's inclusion among what should be loved may rest upon Augustine's view that souls become what they love; thus by loving the eternal, souls become eternal (*ep. Jo.* 2, 14); see below note 28 for further texts on this aspect of love.

eternal, he loves something that is more abundantly offered, the more numerous are its lovers.⁷

But what about love of one's neighbor? Surely our human neighbors are temporal and even perishing beings.⁸ And in loving another human being the manyness of the lovers would surely seem to reduce the possession and enjoyment of each of the lovers. This would seem to hold true even if we are not bodies, but souls, and the love involved is, therefore, spiritual. Nonetheless, Augustine goes on to add, "And he loves his neighbor as himself. Hence, he does not begrudge his neighbor's being what he himself is and even helps him as much as possible" (*vera rel.* 46, 86). This love of neighbor entails two things: that we do not begrudge or envy his being what we are—for example, persons leading a good life or enjoying the truth—and that we help him to attain or share in what we are or have.⁹

What Augustine has said up to this point is certainly problematic; however, he goes on to add: "He cannot lose his neighbor whom he loves as himself, because not even in himself does he love what lies before the eyes or any other senses of the body. Therefore, he has present

---

7. In *lib. arb.* 2, Augustine spent many paragraphs developing a concept of God as a spiritual being through the use of an analogy between the objects of sight and hearing and the truth. For just as many can see and hear the whole of the same thing at once, so the truth offers itself to its many lovers wholly and chastely (*lib. arb.* 2, 14, 37). Like the objects of sight and hearing, truth is common to all and is never the private and proper possession of anyone. See Robert J. O'Connell, *St. Augustine's Early Theory of Man, A.D. 386–391* (Cambridge, Mass.: Belknap Press, 1968), 52–58. Augustine's development of the theme of "common" and "proper" in *lib. arb.* 2 is not the digression that it has been taken to be, if one views Augustine's aim here as the development of the concept of a spiritual reality. See my "The Aim of Augustine's Proof that God Truly Is," *International Philosophical Quarterly* 26 (1986): 253–268.

8. Augustine, of course, thinks of the neighbor as a soul. Unlike God souls are mutable in time; unlike bodies souls are not mutable in place (*ep.* 18, 2). Hence, another soul cannot come to us or go away from us in space. For more on this point, see below notes 12, 14, and 16.

9. Later, in *vera rel.* 47, 90, Augustine offers an example of how one remains unconquered in loving a human being, that is, "cum in eo nihil praeter hominem diligat, id est creaturam Dei ad ejus imaginem factam." For "si quisquam diligit bene cantantem, non hunc aut illum sed tantum bene cantantem quemlibet, cum sit cantator ipse perfectus; ita vult omnes esse tales, ut tamen ei non desit quod diligit, quia ipse bene cantat." If one is envious of a good singer, he loves something else, such as praise, that can be taken from him if another sings well. Augustine goes on to apply this to living well. His point is that if one loves some spiritual good, then he can will all to share it since it is not diminished or changed by any of its lovers. See the long discussion of "common" and "proper" in *lib. arb.* 2.

to himself *(apud se)* the one he loves as himself" (ibid.). Thus the man who is not conquered by any vices loves neither in himself nor in his neighbor what can be seen or sensed by the bodily senses. As we shall see, Augustine interprets loving one's neighbor as oneself not as meaning that one loves one's neighbor as much as oneself, but as meaning that one loves one's neighbor as the sort of reality that one is, namely, a soul.[10] Yet how can it be that, if one loves his neighbor as a soul, he cannot lose that neighbor? Though it is clear that, if one loved his neighbor as a bodily being, the neighbor he loves could be taken from him against his will, since times carry off the bodily things we love,[11] still it is not clear that, if we love in our neighbor only the soul, he cannot be taken from us, but is present to us simply by reason of this love.

This argument that the neighbor that one loves is present to one, because one does not love the neighbor's body, seems to imply not merely that the "real" neighbor is the soul of the other, but that souls can be really present to each other, even though the body of one is not present to the other. That is, spatio-temporal distances and even death need not separate one from another soul that is loved. For souls are spiritual beings and cannot be spatially separated one from another.[12]

---

10. Augustine's statement "corpora vero non sunt quod nos sumus" is coupled with the "tanquam seipsum" of the command to love one's neighbor (*vera rel.* 46, 89). So too when he insists that we should not love someone because that person is a son or spouse, he argues that no one is son or spouse to oneself. Such relationships are carnal and should not be loved, but hated. "Quapropter quisquis in proximo aliud diligit quam sibi ipse est, non eum diligit tanquam seipsum" (ibid.). See also Augustine's very literal interpretation of Lk 14:26 in *s. Dom. mon.* 1, 15, 40–41; see also below note 25.

11. *Vera rel.* 35, 65 (see above, note 6).

12. One might object that souls are in bodies and can, hence, be separated by reason of bodily separation. However, that would be to forget that Augustine clearly maintained that souls cannot move about in space. See *ep.* 18, 2 and *div. quaes.* 3, where Augustine insists that though the soul moves the body in place, it does not itself move in place. In *Imagination and Metaphysics*, 1–2, Robert O'Connell calls attention to the oddness of what Augustine said in *ep.* 18: We "are accustomed to think of our souls as 'in' our bodies so that they move about as our bodies move from one place to another, but Augustine did not think of our souls that way; they were, for him, both everywhere and nowhere, quite literally 'neither here nor there.'" Recall too that in *quan.* 30, 61, Evodius suddenly realizes that the argument has proved that our souls are not in our bodies and that he, therefore, does not know where he is. Augustine points out that "doctissimi homines" have held this view; he is probably referring to the view of Plotinus and other Neoplatonists that the body is in the soul (*Ennead* 5, 5, 9 and 4, 3, 9). So too Marius Victorinus notes that "multi in anima corpus esse dicunt" (*Adv. arianos* 1, 32). Indeed Saint Thomas Aquinas makes the same point in *Summa theologiae* I, q. 8, a. 1 ad 2um.

Though Augustine's claim that the neighbor one loves cannot be taken from him might bear a benign interpretation and merely express the pious thought that "one who loves God with his whole mind *(animo)* knows that what is not lost to God is not lost to him either" (*vera rel.* 47, 91), as Augustine puts it a little later, there are reasons to think that Augustine may have had something else in mind. After all, in that "quiddam grande et breve" that he included in *Epistulae* (hereafter *ep.*) 18 to Celestine in 390 and that has been taken as the keystone of his view of reality, he has insisted that souls can move in time, but not in place.[13] And if our souls are not in our bodies, as Augustine suggested in *De quantitate animae* (hereafter *quan.*) 30, 61, then we might wonder with Evodius whether we know where we are. Furthermore, in that same work he offers the puzzling view of the soul as both one and many.[14] And this view may well underlie the view of friendship that he presents in *conf.* 4, 6, 11. There he says with reference to his dead friend, "I thought that his soul and my soul had been one soul in two bodies," and he seems to have understood literally the poet's "dimidium animae meae"—something that he later found to be embarrassingly silly.[15] Hence, one might find in Augustine's claim that, despite physical separation and death, the neighbor one loves is present to one and cannot be taken away, a reflection of his spiritualist metaphysics, in accord with which the "swellings"

---

13. See *ep.* 18, 2 and Bourke, *Augustine's View of Reality*, 3–5. Bourke does not, however, seem to appreciate the oddness of Augustine's claim about the soul's immutability in space.

14. Thus in *quan.* 30, 61, Evodius suddenly realizes what the argument has established and asks, "Nonne istis rationibus confici potest, animas nostras non esse in corporibus? quod si ita est, nonne ubi sum nescio? Quis enim mihi eripit, quod ego ipse anima sum?" And in *quan.* 32, 69, Augustine tells Evodius that if he should say that the soul is one, Evodius will point out that one person can be happy while another is sad and that one and the same reality cannot be both. If Augustine says that the soul is one and many, Evodius will laugh at him. But if he says that the soul is simply many, Augustine would have to laugh at himself—something still less desirable. That is, the first suggestion is contradictory, but the second is preferable to the third. See Vernon J. Bourke, "St. Augustine and the Cosmic Soul," *Giornale de Metafisica* 9 (1954): 431–440; reprinted in Vernon J. Bourke, *Wisdom from St. Augustine* (Houston: Center for Thomistic Studies, 1984), 78–90; see also my "The World-Soul and Time in St. Augustine," AS 14 (1983): 77–94.

15. See *conf.* 4, 6, 11: "Bene quidem dixit de amico suo 'dimidium animae' suae. Nam ego sensi animam meam et animam illius unam fuisse animam in duobus corporibus, et ideo mihi horrori erat vita, quia nolebam dimidius vivere et ideo forte mori metuebam, ne totus ille moreretur, quem multum amaveram." By the time of the *retr.* 2, 6, 2, he viewed this more as a "declamatio levis quam gravis confessio."

or "tumors" that are our bodies cannot hold separate minds or souls that know and love each other.[16] For if "bodies are not what we are," then we are united or separated not by distances of place, but by knowledge and love. Given his highly spiritual view of man, would it not seem that he could say with regard to the neighbor whom he loved what he said of the God he loved? "There is no place, both backward do we go and forward, and there is no place" (*conf.* 10, 26, 37).[17]

Augustine stresses that "no one is unconquered in virtue of his own efforts, but only in virtue of that immutable law which frees those who observe it. For thus what they love cannot be taken away, and this alone makes them unconquered and perfect. For, if one loves a man—not as oneself, but as an animal or a thing, in order to derive some temporal pleasure or advantage from him, one is enslaved not to a man, but to a vice, because he does not love a man as a man should be loved" (*vera rel.* 46, 87).[18]

But how is a man to be loved as a man? One should not, we are

---

16. Augustine views bodies as swollen in space just as souls are distended in time. In *quan.* 14, 24, Augustine says, "tumor enim non absurde appellatur corporis magnitudo." So too the mind alone can see those natures "quae, ut ita dicam, sine tumoribus esse intelliguntur" (ibid.). He is well aware of the negative connotations of the term, for he later speaks of three sorts of bodily growth, of which the third is "noxium, quod cum accidit, tumor vocatur" (*quan.* 19, 33). Bodies are said to be "tumida loco" (*vera rel.* 30, 56) and leave us with "phantasmata tumoris" (*vera rel.* 35, 65). Moreover, alluding to Sir 9:10, he says that the soul of man in paradise "nondum per superbiam proiecerat intima sua," though he is later said to be "in exteriora per superbiam tumescens" (*Gn. adv. Man.* 2, 5, 6). Furthermore, in *conf.* 7, 7, 11–7, 8, 12, he says of himself, "tumore meo separabar abs te et nimis inflata facies mea claudebat oculos meos." But after being touched by the truth, God's hand, his swelling subsides. "Et sic residebat tumor meus ex occulta manu medicinae tuae." Here the swelling—his body into which he fell through pride—has closed his spiritual eyes to the sight of God. So too it would seem that our bodies close our "eyes" to what our neighbor really is so that in our fallen bodily condition we have to communicate with signs and language. See *Gn. adv. Man.* 2, 5–6 and 2, 32, as well as O'Connell, *Early Theory,* 161–165.

17. There is a passage in *div. quaes.* 35, 1, in which Augustine says that we should not love what can be taken from us while our love for it and enjoyment of it lasts. That which cannot be lacking as long as it is loved is that which one possesses when one knows it. "Id autem est, quod nihil est aliud habere quam nosse." Though he is here speaking of God, it would seem that, if we are souls and love our neighbor as a soul, then we would have our neighbor simply by knowing him.

18. That is, if one loves a man as something less than a soul, that is, as one might love an animal or some possession, for the sake of temporal pleasure or advantage, he loves what can be taken from him and does not love the other person as himself. One "uses" another correctly when he loves the other for the sake of God.

told, love another as a brother according to the flesh, or as a son, or as a spouse, or as any relative or neighbor or fellow citizen. "For that love is temporal. For we would not have such relationships which arise by being born or dying, if our nature had remained steadfast in God's commandments and image and were not relegated to corruption" (*vera rel.* 46, 88). Since it would seem that all human loving at least in this life is done in time and is in that sense a temporal love, Augustine must mean that the problem with loving another as a brother according to the flesh is that such love is a love of what is temporal. Moreover, he seems to imply that our having such relationships is due to the fall.[19] Moreover, he makes it clear that our being in time is due to sin, as is our being in the body.[20] Hence, we need deliverance from time, and Christ has come to free us from time and make us sharers in eternity.[21]

Had we—once again the "we" of all humankind—not disobeyed in paradise, we would not have such carnal relationships. However, now Truth, we are told, is calling us back to our pristine and perfect nature and commands us to resist carnal custom *(carnali consuetudini)*. Indeed, Christ teaches that no one is fit for the kingdom of God who does not hate these carnal relationships *(carnales necessitudines)* (*vera rel.*

---

19. See also *s. Dom. mon.* 1, 15, 40–41, where Augustine also maintains this position, which he later rejected. See *retr.* 1, 13, 8, where in commenting on *vera rel.* 48, 88, he says, "Hunc sensum prorsus improbo, quam jam et superius improbavi in libro primo de Genesi contra Manichaeos (see *retr.* 1, 10, 2). Ad hoc enim ducit, ut credatur illi conjuges primi non generaturi posteros homines nisi peccassent; tanquam necesse fuerit ut morituri gignerentur, si de concubitu maris et feminae gignerentur. Nondum enim videram fieri potuisse ut non morituri de non morituris nascerentur, si peccato illo magno non mutaretur in deterius humana natura; ac per hoc, si et in parentibus et in filiis fecunditas felicitasque manisset, usque ad certum sanctorum numerum, quem 'praedestinavit Deus', nascerentur homines non parentibus successuri morientibus, sed cum viventibus regnaturi. Essent ergo istae cognationes atque affinitates, si nullus delinqueret, nullusque moreretur."

20. In *vera rel.* 20, 38, Augustine says, "Ita homo de paradiso in hoc saeculum expulsus est, id est ab aeternis ad temporalia." But the doctrine of the fall into time is still clearer in 22, 42, where he is arguing that the world should not be considered evil because it is passing. He uses the analogy of a song and points out that in order for one to hear the whole song, the individual notes must pass away. However, most men easily hear a whole verse or even a whole song, but no one can perceive the whole order of the ages. But here is the rub: "Huc accedit quod carminis non sumus partes, saeculorum vero partes damnatione facti sumus." That is, we have become parts of the ages or have entered time as a punishment for having sinned.

21. See my "Vocans temporales, faciens aeternos: St. Augustine on Liberation from Time," *Traditio* 41 (1985): 29–47, for this view of the purpose of the Incarnation and its implications for human existence and time.

46, 88). This carnal custom seems to be not simply a matter of undue sensuality, but the habit or custom that the soul has acquired of being enfleshed. Thus these carnal relationships are those relationships that arise from our being embodied.[22] The implication is, of course, that human souls preexisted their embodiment and fell into body and time by some primordial sin. Augustine realizes that this interpretation of the commandment to love the neighbor might very well strike his readers as a bit harsh. He counters that it should seem more inhuman not to love in a man what is man and to love in him what is son. For in loving a son one loves what belongs to oneself, not what belongs to God. That is, one loves something private and not common. Here again Augustine takes up the Plotinian theme that he used in *lib. arb.* 2, where sin is defined in terms of the love of what is private and one's own instead of what is common and available to all.[23]

Should one think that he can love both his son and the man, Augustine answers that God bids us to love only the man. For no one can, he argues, serve two masters or love perfectly whither we are called unless he hates whence we are called. "Therefore, let us hate temporal relationships, if we burn with a love for eternity. Let a man love his neighbor as himself. For no one surely is to himself father or son or relative or anything of this sort, but only a man. Therefore, he who loves someone as himself ought to love in him that which he is to himself. But bodies are not what we are. Hence, in a man we should not seek or desire

---

22. In *mor.* 1, 22, 40, Augustine says, "Sed inter omnia quae in hac vita possidentur, corpus homini gravissimum vinculum est, justissimis Dei legibus, propter antiquum peccatum, quo nihil est ad praedicandum notius, nihil ad intelligendum secretius." He goes on to say that man loves his body "vi consuetudinis," that is, out of the habit it has acquired of living in it. There is, in this work, another extensive treatment of love of neighbor—a treatment that seems much less austere than that in *vera rel.* For instance, there is considerable emphasis upon corporal works of mercy. I am not at all sure of how to account for such a diversity, though it is tempting to explain the difference in terms of the different views of man. In *mor.* 1, 37, 52, Augustine speaks of man "ut homini apparet." As such he is a soul suited to rule a body, and love for a man involves his body and his soul. But in *vera rel.* "bodies are not what we are." Does *vera rel.* then deal with man as he *is*, as opposed to *mor.*, which considers man as he *appears* to man?

23. In *lib. arb.* 2, 19, 53, Augustine comes to his revised definition of sin; he says, "Voluntas ergo adhaerens communi atque incommutabili bono, impetrat prima et magna hominis bona, cum ipsa sit medium quoddam bonum. Voluntas autem aversa ab incommutabili et communi bono, et conversa ad proprium bonum, aut ad exterius, aut ad inferius peccat." In *vera rel.* 46, 88, he asks, "Quid ergo mirum si ad regnum non pervenit, qui non communem, sed privatam rem diligit?"

the body" (*vera rel.* 46, 89). In support of this claim that we should not desire the body of another, Augustine appeals to Exodus 20:17, where we are commanded not to covet the neighbor's goods or property *(rem proximi tui)*. Thus he implies both that love is a seeking or desiring or coveting and also that the body is a possession of the person rather than a part of the person.

Whoever loves in his neighbor something other than what he is to himself, namely, a soul, does not love him as oneself. That is, the command to love the neighbor as oneself does not mean that one is to love the neighbor with the same amount or same kind of love with which one loves oneself, but that one is to love the neighbor as the sort of reality that one is, namely, as a soul. Not only should human nature, we are told, be loved "without the fleshly condition," but this is so whether that human nature is still to be made perfect or already perfect. That is, what should be loved is the soul of the other, for that is the man or human nature. Even after the Resurrection it is not the body that should be loved.[24] For, as Augustine sees it at this point, relations that we have as the result of the flesh are the result of sin, the fall into body and time. We have another set of relations that are not carnal, but due to our renewal and reformation. "And thus we are all related under one God the Father. And we are fathers to one another, when we care for one another, sons when we obey, but especially brothers insofar as we are called to one inheritance" (*vera rel.* 46, 89). That is, we have acquired a new set of relationships, and these new relationships of sonship under the Father, of paternal care for others, or of filial obedience to others, if loved properly, require that we flee from those based on the flesh.[25]

24. Earlier in *vera rel.* 16, 32, Augustine says of Christ, "Resurrectio vero ejus a mortuis, nihil hominis perire naturae, cum omnia salva sunt Deo, satis indicavit." That would seem to say that the body belongs to human nature, though one might still maintain that the body is a possession, not a constituent, of human nature, which lies in the soul alone. On the other hand, the doctrine of the resurrection would seem to have been one of the grounds for Augustine's abandonment of his early Neoplatonic contempt for the body.

25. Augustine is offering an interpretation of the words of Christ, "Si quis venit ad me, et non odit patrem suum, et matrem, et uxorem, et filios, et fratres, et sorores" (Lk 14:26). He understands Christ to demand that his disciples hate the carnal relationships that we acquired by birth, while we love the soul, human nature free from the carnal condition. See *s. Dom. mon.* 1, 15, 40–41, where he admits that the "little ones" have difficulty with these words, but insists that in the kingdom to which we are called there will be no such relationships. In fact in Christ we acquire a whole new set of relationships. See also *conf.* 9, 13, 37, where the natural relations of Augustine and Monica are seen in their true light.

Augustine explains why a man is unconquered, though he loves a man. One must love in him nothing besides the man, that is, the creature of God made in the image of God. Such a one cannot lack the perfect nature that he loves, since he himself is perfect man. It seems that Augustine is saying that, if one loves in his neighbor only the man, that is, the soul, and that as it was made by God, then one is what one loves. And since a soul cannot be taken away from itself, what one loves cannot be taken away. But this view comes close to losing the significance of the neighbor's being another! He goes on then to show how the unconquered man "uses" friends and enemies. He is benevolent to all and beneficent to those to whom he can be. "He cares for fellow men according to the occasions times offer, if he cannot care for all equally. He does not love an intimate *(familiarem)* more, though he might more readily speak to him, since there is more trust and greater occasion for doing so. He treats those immersed in time better to the degree that he is not himself bound to time. Since one cannot do good to all, though he loves them all equally, he has to do good under pain of injustice to those closer to him" (*vera rel.* 47, 91). However, the closeness or union of soul is greater than that of times and places and, hence, places a greater demand upon our beneficence. "However, the union of soul is greater than that of the times or places in which we are born in this body, but that union is greatest which prevails over all things" (*vera rel.* 47, 91). He seems to envision three degrees of union. The lowest is based on places and times; the *conjunctio animi* is greater; but the greatest of all is the union that prevails over all things.[26] Hence, such an interpretation would seem to neutralize any special claim family or neighbors might have upon our doing good for them, though temporal and spatial relationships might explain and even demand our doing good to those closer to us.[27]

Hence, in *vera rel.* love seems to be understood in the sense of desir-

---

26. Since the soul is superior to the body and since, for Augustine, only God is superior to the soul, it would seem that the union that prevails over all would have to be our union in God.

27. Hultgren notes, "La notion d'amour devient ici extrémêment atténué. La négation de la valeur éternelle des liens naturels a pour effet non seulement d'ôter à l'amour du prochain tout élément sensuel mais de lui enlever encore tout caractère individuel. Il y a lieu de se demander si l'on peut encore parler dans ce cas d'un amour personnel avec une personne comme sujet et une autre comme objet et s'il reste encore en lui quelque chose de la communauté naturelle" (175).

ing or coveting someone or something. Since we become what we love, we should not love anything less than what we are, such as bodies.[28] Benevolence and beneficence toward the neighbor seem to be consequences of loving the neighbor as oneself. It seems that love of neighbor as oneself means love of another as a soul, since one is one's soul. We are not our bodies, and we should love neither our own body nor the body of our neighbor. We have bodies and those temporal relationships consequent upon being born only because of sin, because of which we shall also die. To love others not as other souls, but because they have certain temporal and corporeal relationships to us, that is, as our father or mother or brother or sister or spouse, is not to love them as oneself, for no one is to himself a mother or a father, a brother or a sister, but only a soul. If one loves the relations he has acquired in Christ, he must hate the temporal relations from which he is called. Indeed we have such temporal relations only because of the punishment of sin.

LOVE OF NEIGHBOR IN *DE DOCTRINA CHRISTIANA*

The discussion of love of neighbor in *doc. Chr.* occurs within the context of one of Augustine's clearest presentations of the celebrated *uti-frui* distinction. Augustine maintains that we should enjoy only immutable and eternal things and that we should use all else only so that we may come to enjoy the former.[29] He admits that it is a deep question whether men should "enjoy one another, use one another, or do both" (*doc. Chr.* 1, 22, 20). Though we are commanded to love one another, we are left with the question of whether another man is to be enjoyed, that is, loved for his own sake, or used, that is, loved for the sake of

---

28. Augustine's view that one becomes what one loves would seem to make it at least awkward, if not impossible, for him to speak of "properly" loving something less than what one is. On this view of love, see *div. quaes.* 35, 2, where he says, "Et quoniam id quod amatur, afficiat ex se amantem necesse est; fit ut sic amatum quod aeternum est, aeternitate animum afficiat. Quocirca ea demum vita beata est, quae aeterna est. Quid vero aeternum est, quod aeternitate animum afficiat, nisi Deus?" See too *mor.,* 1, 21, 39 where he says "ei rei quemque conformari quam diligit." In *s.* 121, 1, he says "Amando Deum, efficimur dii: ergo amando mundum, dicimur mundus." So too in *ep. Jo.* 2, 14, he says, "Terram diligis? terra eris. Deum diligis? quid dicam? Deus eris? Non audeo dicere ex me, Scripturas audiamus."

29. See Vernon Bourke's *Joy in Augustine's Ethics* (Villanova: Villanova University Press, 1979), 29–49, for a good discussion of the *uti-frui* distinction.

something else. Augustine holds that we should love another man not for his own sake, but for the sake of God. Hence, we should "use" and not "enjoy" our fellow man.

He goes on to claim that, just as we should love even ourselves for the sake of God, so too we should love our neighbor as we love ourselves, namely, for the sake of God. We should not, however, love everything that is to be used. We should love things that are related to God with us in a certain society, such as, angels and men, or are related to us and require the beneficence of God through us, such as, the body (*doc. Chr.* 1, 23, 22). Here the body is one of the objects we should love; indeed, it is through us, it seems, that God takes care of or exercises his providence over the body.

There are, Augustine states, four things to be loved: first, what is above us, namely, God; second, what we ourselves are, namely, souls; third, what is on a level with us, namely, our neighbor; fourth, what is below us, our bodies. Augustine points out that we do not need commandments to love ourselves or our bodies, for we do so by our very nature (*doc. Chr.* 1, 23, 22). Though in *vera rel.* we were to hate carnal relationships based on our being in the body and in time, here by a natural law we do love and should love our bodies to which we are present in order to mediate God's beneficence.[30]

Augustine finds that Paul's statement in Ephesians 5:29 that no one hates his own flesh supports his claim. He mentions that there are some—perhaps the Neoplatonists or the Manichees—who have expressed the desire to be completely without a body.[31] But he insists that they were deceived. What they really wanted was a body with the incorruptibility and with the quickness that they thought could belong

---

30. One might ask whether love has not changed its meaning. As long as love entails that the lover becomes what he loves, it would seem to be impossible to speak of a correct love of bodies. Here, however, love includes the beneficent care of the lower by higher reality.

31. It is difficult to determine whether Augustine is speaking of the Manichees or the Neoplatonists. However, the Manichaean view went, it would seem, considerably beyond the position described here, since they regarded the body as the substance of evil. See, for example, *civ. Dei* 14, 6. The Platonists, however, laughed at the Christian view of the soul's separation from the body as a punishment (*civ. Dei* 13, 16); in words quite similar to the language of *doc. Chr.,* Augustine argues here that it is not the body, but the corruptible body that is a burden to the soul. See also *civ. Dei* 22, 11, for the Platonist difficulties with the resurrection of the body.

only to the soul. True, there are some men who seem to persecute their bodies by discipline and labor. But they do this—if they do so correctly—not so that they have no body, but so that they have a body under control and ready for the tasks to be done (*doc. Chr.* 1, 24, 24).

Others are misled by a text, such as Galatians 5:20, and wage war against their body as a natural enemy. Paul meant, Augustine tells us, that we should do battle against uncontrolled carnal habit (*indomitam carnalem consuetudinem*), not that we should kill the body. Until the resurrection the flesh lusts against the spirit, and the spirit against the flesh. The spirit resists the flesh, "not through hatred, but through its rule, because it wants what it loves more subject to the better" (*doc. Chr.* 1, 24, 25). Nor does the flesh resist the spirit through hatred, but through the bond of habit inherited from the first parents' sin. But even those who hate their body are not prepared to lose an eye, albeit without pain and without diminishing of vision, unless some other great value were at stake. Augustine says that this proof shows the certitude of Paul's claim that not merely does no one hate his own flesh, but that he "nourishes and cares for it, as Christ does the Church" (Eph 5:29).

Though each of us loves his own body, we still have to learn how to love it and care for it wisely and ordinately. Though we want a healthy and whole body, we can love something more than integrity and health. Many, for example, willingly suffer the loss of organs or limbs for the attainment of other preferred goods. This greater love for something else does not mean one does not love bodily health and integrity (*doc. Chr.* 1, 25, 26). We do not need commandments to love ourselves or our bodies. "We love that which we are and that which is below us, and nonetheless pertains to us, by an immovable law of nature (*inconcussa naturae lege*), which has been promulgated in the beasts as well (for even the animals love themselves and their bodies)" (*doc. Chr.* 1, 26, 27).

But we do need a commandment to love God and to love our neighbor as ourselves. With regard to the latter, Augustine says, "If you understand the whole of yourself, that is, your soul and body, and the whole of your neighbor, that is, soul and body (for man consists of soul and body), no kind of reality is passed over in these two commandments" (*doc. Chr.* 1, 26, 27). Here the body is not merely something that is a possession, that pertains to us, but is something that with soul constitutes a man. Here we love ourselves and our body by an immovable law of nature, though the love of ourselves and of our body is not thereby wise and ordinate. To live in a holy and just way involves having an integral evaluation of reality (to be *rerum integer aestimator*), which implies an ordered love. The hierarchy of being, namely, God, souls, bodies, provides the key. Ordered love means loving God more than souls and souls more than bodies, including our own (*doc. Chr.* 1, 27, 28). It means loving equals equally, that is, other men as ourselves, but more than our body or theirs. A sinner is not to be loved as such, but as a man he is to be loved—like everyone and everything else—because of God.

Though we are to love all men equally, we cannot help all equally. Hence, Augustine says that you "ought especially to be concerned about those who are more closely joined to you according to the opportunities of places and times or any other things as if by lot. For, if you have an abundance of something that you should give to one who has not and you cannot give it to two, then, if you should meet two, neither of whom surpasses the other in need or some other relationship to you, then you could do nothing more just than to choose by lot to which of the two you should give what cannot be given to both. Thus in the case of men, all of whom you cannot help, you should regard how each is able to cling more closely to you in time as a drawing of lots" (*doc. Chr.* 1, 28, 29). Here relationships based on places and times are not to be hated and shunned, but are providential guideposts, like a natural lottery, directing the course of our beneficence.[32] Temporal relationships are no longer called the result of sin and are no longer something from which we should flee or something we all should hate. They are God-given and natural. The closer someone is to us in terms of such relations, the more that person has a claim upon our beneficence.

Hence, by the time of *doc. Chr.* 1 Augustine's view of love of neighbor and of the neighbor we should love has changed. By a law of nature we love our own bodies, though we still have need for an ordered love of ourselves and our bodies. Since we are body and soul, we now love

---

32. Of this passage, Gilson says that there is an order in our love of neighbor, "If we had wealth to give away and saw no reason for giving to one man rather than to another, we should draw lots to find out who was to receive it. Now this drawing of lots has been made for us by nature as God established it: our relatives and especially our close relatives are clearly indicated as the first recipients of our charity"; *Christian Philosophy*, 166.

our neighbor as body and soul, and relations of place and time are positive, not objects of hatred, but directives of love.

A SUGGESTED EXPLANATION

We have seen that Augustine's view of the love of neighbor evolved rather dramatically during the few years between *vera rel.* and *doc. Chr.* In the final section of this article I offer a hypothesis as to the cause of this abrupt shift in view, which involves his coming to speak of the neighbor one should love as a whole composed of body and soul, his explicitly stating that we do and should love our body and, hence, the body of our neighbor, and his regarding temporal relations as positive and God-given signposts directing our beneficence.

It would, first of all, seem reasonable to suppose that this shift represents a move away from a highly spiritual, Neoplatonic view of man to a more Christian view of man in which the body plays a much more significant role.[33] Second, Augustine tells us in his earliest writing that he had resolved never to depart from the authority of Christ.[34] And it seems reasonable to suppose that he never did depart from it, even though he may not have immediately come to realize what the authority of Christ demanded.[35] Third, the importance to him of the Neoplatonic spiritualism was immense, for it was the key to the resolution of all his intellectual difficulties. Without the ability to conceive of a spiritual substance, he had no answer to the Manichees.[36]

---

33. Very early Augustine had seem to favor the Porphyrian view, "Omne corpus esse fugiendum." In *sol.* 1, 14, 24 he said, "Penitus esse ista sensibilia fugienda." See also *quan.* 3, 4: "Ideoque bene praecipitur etiam in mysteriis, ut omnia corporea contemnat, universo huic mundo renuntiet, . . . quisquis se talem reddi desiderat, qualis a Deo factus est, id est, similem Deo." In *doc. Chr.* we find him claiming that we love the body by an unshakable law of nature.

34. "Mihi autem certum est nusquam prorsus a Christi auctoritate discedere: non enim reperio valentiorem" (*c. Acad.* 3, 20, 43).

35. He complains, for example, in *lib. arb.* 3, 31, 59 that he does not know whether the Catholic interpreters of Scripture have taken a position—or what that position is, if they have taken one—with regard to the origin of the soul. So too it is only gradually that he came to realize the implications of Rom 9:11 for the question of prenatal sin. See Robert J. O'Connell, S.J., "Augustine's Rejection of the Fall of the Soul," *AS* 4 (1973): 1–32, esp. 25–26.

36. See the many texts from *conf.* 3 to 7 where Augustine complains of his inability to conceive of a spiritual substance as the sole cause of his errors, especially 5, 10, 19 and

My suggestion is that Augustine came to realize that the authority of Christ demanded a much more positive view of the body and, consequently, a radically different view of love of neighbor. Specifically, I want to suggest that it may have been his reading of Ephesians 5:29 that triggered the change of mind and heart. The suggestion rests in part upon the prominence of that text in the *doc. Chr.* account and its absence from the *vera rel.* account as well as from any other work of Augustine's until almost the time of *doc. Chr.*—at least in a literal interpretation. Moreover, when Augustine reviewed his early statement that one should love only God and the soul, he explicitly appeals to Ephesians 5:29 as a proof-text to justify loving one's own flesh.[37]

I returned to the early writings to search out the first occurrence of that text and found that it is not until almost the time of the *doc. Chr.* that Augustine realizes the literal significance of Paul's saying, "No one hates his own flesh." The earliest reference to Ephesians 5:29—and it is at best a veiled reference to this text—occurs in *De Genesis adversus Manichaeos* (hereafter *Gn. adv. Man.*).[38] Augustine is discussing the sleep God induced in Adam in order to remove the rib with which he made Eve. He stresses that the sleep signifies the interior and hidden contemplation—most removed from every sense of the body—of perfect wisdom.[39] This wisdom consists not merely in the knowledge that

---

5, 14, 25. Here it is crucial to recall that this inability represented not merely a personal problem of Augustine's, but the common philosophical heritage of the whole Western Church until this time. See Masai, "Les conversions de Saint Augustin," pp. 11–15.

37. See *retr* 1, 26, 2, where Augustine is discussing *div. quaes.* 36, 1 (see above note 1). To this he says in retrospect, "Quod si verum est, quomodo ergo apostolus ait: 'Nemo unquam carnem suam odio habuit.'" That is, Augustine was well aware that his view with regard to the object of love of neighbor had changed, and he ties that change to the text from Ephesians, even though he defends his previous statement in terms of the "proprie" he had employed, "quoniam caro diligitur quidem, nec tamen proprie, sed propter animam cui subiacet ad usum. Nam etsi propter seipsam videtur diligi, cum eam nolumus esse deformem, ad aliud referendum est decus eius, ad illud scilicet a quo decora sunt omnia." Nonetheless, the aptness of Paul's statement for refuting the Manichees makes it all the stranger that Augustine does not use this text against them until *cont.* in 395.

38. I had missed this reference on my first reading of the work and returned to find it only because of Robert O'Connell, who assured me it was there. If it is a reference to Eph 5:29, Augustine's spiritual interpretation of the text supports my claim; if it is not a reference to Eph 5:29, then one has to date his first use of that text considerably later.

39. In *Gn. adv. Man.* 2, 11, 16, Augustine tells us that it is easy to understand man's superiority to the beasts, but quite difficult to understand "in seipso aliud esse rationale

there is a distinction in us between that which rules by reason and that which obeys reason, but also in the order by which one rules his flesh and presides over the marriage in himself so that the flesh does not lust against the spirit, but obeys it and thus ceases to be carnal. Augustine then says,

> He correctly filled the place of the rib with flesh in order to indicate by this term the state of love by which each one loves his own soul and is not insensitive so as to contemn it, because everyone loves that over which he presides. For flesh is not mentioned in this passage to signify the lust of the flesh, but rather in that manner in which the prophet says that a heart of stone is taken from the people and a heart of flesh is given (Ez 11:19). The Apostle also speaks in this way, "Not on tablets of stone, but on the tablets of flesh in your hearts" (2 Cor 3:3). For a proper expression is one thing; quite another is a figurative expression, such as we are dealing with here. (*Gn. adv. Man.* 2, 12, 17)

He goes on to insist that whether these things were said figuratively or done figuratively they were not so said or done without reason, but are mysteries and sacraments to be interpreted and understood. If Augustine did have Ephesians 5:29 in the back of his mind when he wrote this, as seems to be the case, he certainly was at great pains not to offer a literal interpretation in accord with which one should love his wife as he loves his own flesh. "Wife" is taken figuratively as that part of the soul that is to obey reason; "flesh" is the carnal appetite within man's soul. And all of this is better grasped by withdrawing from visible things into the *interiora intelligentiae* (*Gn. adv. Man.* 2, 12, 16). Rather than say that everyone loves his flesh—even with the help of the Scripture texts that indicate a positive sense of "flesh"—Augustine says that everyone loves his own soul *(anima)*. Everyone loves that over which he presides *(praeest)*, but he seems unwilling to state what the text quite literally says, namely, that everyone loves his own flesh.

The earliest explicit reference to Ephesians 5:29 that I have been able to find in Augustine is *De sermone Domini in monte* (hereafter *s. Dom. mon.*), written in 393–394. Here Augustine is dealing with Jesus' bidding his disciples to anoint their heads when they fast (Mt 6:17–18);

---

quod regit, aliud animale quod regitur." To see this "non opus est ut oculis istis corporeis, sed quanto quisquis ab istis uisibilibus rebus in interiora intelligentiae secesserit . . . tanto melius et sincerius illud uidet" (*Gn. adv. Man.* 2, 12, 16). That is, the meaning of woman's being made from man is to be understood in a highly spiritual sense.

he says that no one "has correctly *(recte praeceperit)* commanded . . . that we have our heads anointed when we fast. But if all admit that this is most shameful *(turpissimum),* this command to anoint the head and to wash the face must be understood to concern the interior man" (*s. Dom. mon.* 2, 12, 42). He explains that "he anoints the head who rejoices interiorly in mind and reason." One does this who does not seek joy externally so as to rejoice carnally over the praise of men. "For the flesh which ought to be subject is in no sense the head of the whole human nature. 'No one hates his own flesh,' as the Apostle says, when he commands concerning loving one's wife. But the husband is head of the woman, as Christ is the head of the man. Therefore, let him rejoice interiorly in his fast for the very reason that in fasting he who desires to have his head anointed according to this command turns from the pleasure of the world to be subject to Christ" (ibid.). There are several things to note about this text. One, it occurs within a spiritual interpretation of the command to anoint one's head. Two, though Augustine sees that Ephesians 5:29 literally refers to loving one's wife, he applies it to the subjection of the lower appetites in a human being. Three, when he speaks of having one's head anointed, he is playing with the literal meaning of *christos,* that is, anointed, so that such a one has as his head Christ.

The next use of the text is in *cont.,* written in 395. In *cont.* 8, 19 Augustine quotes Paul's "I know that good does not dwell in me, that is, in my flesh" (Rom 7:18). He adds, "Thus he says that he is his flesh. Hence, it is not our enemy, and when its vices are resisted, it is loved, because it is cared for. 'No one ever hates his own flesh,' as the Apostle says." Here for the first time, Augustine seems to understand Ephesians 5:29 as meaning quite literally that a man does not hate his own flesh, and he even identifies the flesh with the person.

Moreover, in *cont.* 9, 22 he uses the text against the Manichees, who in their madness "attribute our flesh to that nation of darkness . . . although the true teacher urges husbands to love their wives by the example of their flesh, just as he urges them to this also by the example of Christ and the Church." Here, the love of one's flesh provides the example of how one should love one's wife, just as Christ's love for the Church provides an example of this.

Let me mention one other text, *De utilitate jejunii* (hereafter *util. je-*

jun.), from 399, where Augustine once again uses Ephesians 5:29 against the Manichees. He quotes Galatians 5:17 and Ephesians 5:29 and then adds, "In that first sentence which I quoted, there seems to be a kind of struggle between two enemies, the flesh and the spirit, because 'the flesh lusts against the spirit and the spirit against the flesh.' But in the latter there is a sort of conjugal union: 'For no one ever hates his own flesh, but nourishes and cares for it, as Christ also does for the Church'" (*util. jejun.* 4, 4). He goes on to challenge the Manichees with regard to Ephesians 5:29: "You suppose the flesh a shackle. Who loves a shackle? You think the flesh a prison. Who loves a prison? 'For no one ever hates his own flesh.' Who would not hate his chain? Who would not hate his punishment? And yet 'No one ever hates his own flesh, but nourishes and cares for it, as Christ also does for the Church.' . . . Everyone loves *(diligit)* his own flesh. The Apostle says so, and everyone experiences this in himself."[40] By this time Augustine has turned a full 180 degrees with regard to the valuation of the flesh.

In conclusion, it seems that Augustine's realization of the import of Ephesians 5:29 was gradual. It was apparently not until the time of *cont.* and *doc. Chr.* that he realized that the implications of the Pauline statement were that man does and should love his own flesh as well as the significance of this for the neighbor one is to love as himself. If this hypothesis is correct, Augustine struggled for a long time before he could read Ephesians 5:29 in a literal sense and "see" its import for oneself and the neighbor whom one is to love as oneself. However, his determination never to depart from the authority of Christ eventually triumphed over his wild enthusiasm for the spiritualism he found in the *libri Platonicorum.*

---

40. Particularly striking is his rejection of the idea that the flesh is a chain, for he had earlier been quite explicit that the body is a chain—indeed, "inter omnia quae in hac vita possidentur, corpus homini gravissimum vinculum est" (*mor.* 1, 22, 40). I have not carefully explored his use of the text beyond 400, though in *ep.* 130, 3, 7, writing to Proba, he uses Eph 5:29 as justification for Paul telling Timothy to take a little wine for his stomach. And in *ep.* 140, 6, 16 he cites Eph 5:29 to explain the fact that even saints want to prolong their lives.

2

God & Speaking about God

5

PROPERTIES OF GOD AND THE PREDICAMENTS IN *DE TRINITATE* 5

In Trin. *5 Augustine provides a set of rules for speaking about God that I found to be not merely intelligible, but brilliant. Hence, I was puzzled over why some contemporary thinkers found his language about God—which is that of classical theism—so unintelligible or at least problematic. I found Augustine's distinction between speaking about God, thinking about God, and the being of God very important. I suggest that one must distinguish between what Augustine understood by accidents and what contemporaries understand by properties, and I argue that Augustine provides a sound account of relative and nonrelative predication about God.*

In *conf.* 4, 16, 28–19, Augustine reports that he read and understood on his own Aristotle's *Categories* when he was only twenty. He says that he then thought that everything that existed "had to be included under these ten predicaments," but that his attempt to understand God by them was a hindrance rather than a help. For at that time he thought that God was subject to his greatness and beauty in such wise that they were in God as in a subject, just as they are in bodies. However, by the time of *Trin.*, Augustine makes extensive use of the Aristotelian categories in speaking about God. Indeed Augustine's use of the categories in speaking about God in *Trin.* has been said by E. Hendrikx in his introduction to *Trin.* to mark the beginning of scholasticism.[1] Hendrikx suggests that Augustine's initial attempt to apply the categories to God was rationalistic in the sense that God was made to conform to a philosophical doctrine, while in *Trin.* Augustine uses the categories as a means for arriving at the truth.[2] Instead of being a philosophical doctrine to which the object must conform, the categories have become a means for coming to know the object, namely, God.[3]

Augustine's use of the Aristotelian categories in speaking about God has been the object of considerable criticism by contemporary philosophers. M. Durrant, for example, has argued that God cannot be sensibly said to be substance and that the Trinitarian formulae "in one substance" or "of the same substance" cannot "have any place in talk about the persons of the Trinity."[4] Richard La Croix has argued that Augustine's account of divine simplicity and immutability is incoherent because he does not provide any criterion for distinguishing relative and nonrelative properties of God.[5] Moreover, there seem to be some inconsistencies in what Augustine says. For example, he claims that there are no accidents in God because nothing happens to him *(nihil ei accidit)* and then later argues that it happens to him *(accidit ei)* in time that he is lord of Israel.[6]

---

1. "C'est ainsi que dans le *De Trinitate* la scholastique a connu son heure de naissance; et c'est à juste titre que M. Marrou en proclame Augustin le précurseur" (BA 15, 16–17).

2. Ibid., 16: "Dialecticien par tempérament, il s'était assimilé, jeune étudiant, la doctrine aristotélicienne des catégories avec une facilité étonnante; tout de suite, mais à tort, il avait voulu l'appliquer à Dieu dans un sens rationaliste."

3. Ibid.: "Mais si dans le *Dialogues* la dialectique, en son point de vue formel, règne encore en souveraine, dans les oeuvres postérieures elle est mise de plus en plus au service de l'objet dont il s'agit. Elle garde sa valeur, non pas tant pour elle-même, que pour l'aide qu'elle peut et doit fournir à la conquête de la vérité."

4. See Durrant, *Theology and Intelligibility*, 122 and 145. Durrant investigates what Aristotle's Metaphysics 8, 1017 b 10–25, has to say on *ousia*. "I shall investigate the above-mentioned passage from the *Metaphysics* with a view to answering the question of whether there is a sense in which God can be said to be substance in the senses of 'substance' provided by the framework. If upon investigation it turns out that God cannot be so said to be, then the question arises as to how the Greek Fathers . . . can maintain the contrary" (46). He argues that they could speak of God as substance only as a result of "a fundamental misinterpretation of the framework within which they were writing" (ibid.). Durrant's procedure in dealing with the use of "substance" by the Greek Fathers and Augustine seems to share the same rationalism that Hendrikx notes in Augustine's early thought.

5. See La Croix, "Augustine on the Simplicity of God."

6. "[N]ihil in eo secundum accidens dicitur, quia nihil ei accidit" (*Trin.* 5, 5, 6). "Certe vel ut Dominus hominis esset ex tempore accidit Deo: et ut omnis auferri videa-

The purpose of this paper will be to attempt to come to some understanding of the use that Augustine makes of the categories or predicaments in speaking about God, especially in *Trin.* 5. Though his chief concern is with the doctrine of the three persons in God, I shall prescind from the doctrine of the Trinity and focus on the non-Trinitarian use of the predicaments. Moreover, I shall prescind from Augustine's claim that God is substance or essence and focus upon his claim that there are no accidents in God. I shall argue that this claim does not mean that God has no contingent properties and that Augustine does suggest a rule for distinguishing what is said of God relatively from what is said of God nonrelatively. Finally, I shall indicate why La Croix's argument that Augustine cannot distinguish relative from nonrelative properties of God fails.

DICERE, COGITARE, ESSE

In order to understand what Augustine is saying in book 5, it is necessary to bear in mind his distinction between speech about God, thought about God, and the being of God. At the beginning of book 5, Augustine says that he is beginning to speak of things that cannot be said by anyone or at least by himself as they are thought. Moreover, our thought itself, when we think of the Trinity, feels itself unequal to that of which we think and does not grasp him as he is. We ought always to think of God, of whom we cannot think worthily. We ought always to speak well of God, though no speaking is able to express him (*Trin.* 5, 1, 1).[7]

Amid what might seem merely a manifestation of Augustine's love for rhetoric, there is implicit a distinction between speaking about God, thinking about God, and the being of God. After telling us that we "should understand God in so far as we are able as great without quantity, as good without quality, as creator without need, as presiding without posture, as containing everything without possession, as whole everywhere without place, as everlasting without time, as making changeable things without any change of himself, and as undergoing no

---

tur controversia, certe ut tuus Dominus esset, aut meus, qui modo esse coepimus, ex tempore accidit Deo" (*Trin.* 5, 16, 17).

7. Augustine plays on the terms *benedictio* and *dictio*, "blessing" and "speaking": "cui laudando reddenda est omni tempore benedictio, et cui enuntiando nulla competit dictio" (*Trin.* 5, 1, 1).

change," he adds that "whoever thinks of God in this way, even though he does not discover what God is, nevertheless avoids as far as possible thinking of him what he is not" (*Trin.* 5, 1, 2). In turning to an Arian objection, he "begins to respond regarding those things which are not said as they are thought, and are not thought as they are" (*Trin.* 5, 3,4). So too in *Trin.* 7, 4, 7, he says that "God is more truly thought than he is spoken of and is more truly than he is thought."

Though it might seem that the point of this distinction between *dictio, cogitatio,* and *esse* is primarily applicable to the mystery of the Trinity, Augustine's example in *Trin.* 5, 1, 2 seems to indicate that the distinction is equally pertinent to speaking about God apart from consideration of the Trinity. From *Trin.* 5, 1, 2 it seems that Augustine recognizes that one can speak of God in terms of each of nine accidental predicaments. That is, one can say that God is great, is good, is creator, presides over creation, contains everything, is everywhere, is everlasting, produces changeable things, and undergoes no change.[8] However, we must not think of God as we speak of God, for even our thought of God is not equal to the being of God. Though we can say that God is great and is good, we must not think of the greatness or goodness of God as a quantity or a quality that inheres in God as in a subject and that is distinct from God. However, even when our thought about God thus corrects our speech about God, our thought about God remains unequal to the being that God is.

The relevance of this distinction can be further illustrated by Augustine's discussion of how God is simple *and* multiple. In *Trin.* 6, 6, 8 Augustine says that God is spoken of with a multitude of names or terms: great, good, wise, happy, true, and whatever else he seems to be said to be not unworthily. Our speech ascribes to God a multiplicity of predicates; however, Augustine maintains that God's greatness is the same thing as his wisdom, and his goodness the same thing as his wisdom and greatness, and his truth the same as all these (*Trin.* 6, 6, 8). In this passage our speech about God *(dictio)* ascribes to God a multiplicity of

---

8. With regard to *passio* one might object that we cannot say that God undergoes anything and that, hence, nothing is said of God according to passion. However, Augustine claims that an affirmation and its corresponding negation are according to the same predicament (*Trin.* 5, 7, 8). Hence, in saying that God undergoes no change, one is denying something of God according to passion.

predicates. In *Trin.* 15, 5, 8 Augustine tries to show that the multiplicity of terms that we use in speaking about God is not incompatible with the simplicity of the being of God. He begins with twelve predicates of God and attempts to reduce them to a smaller number. For example, he argues that "immortal," "incorruptible," and "immutable" can be comprised within "eternal," that "living," "powerful," and "beautiful" can be comprised within "wise," and that "just," "good," and "spirit" can be comprised within "happy." He does not intend to say that these words have the same meaning or that the many terms are synonymous; for, if they had the same meaning or were synonyms, there would be no need to argue that the twelve terms can be reduced to three. What he tries to do is to argue that, since no one can be happy without being just and good and a spirit, in saying "happy" one is implicitly saying all the rest. His presupposition is that God is not merely spoken of in many terms *(multipliciter dicitur),* but is thought of in many senses *(multiplicitur cogitatur)* because the terms have different meanings. Thus our speech about God involves a multiplicity of terms that have a multiplicity of meanings; however, "one and the same reality is expressed, whether God is said to be eternal or immortal or incorruptible or immutable" (*Trin.* 15, 5, 7). Augustine does not go on to attempt to reduce "eternal," "wise," and "happy" to one term in the sense that their meanings can be implicitly expressed in one of the three terms, but claims that one and the same reality in the nature of God can be eternity and wisdom or happiness and wisdom (*Trin.* 15, 7, 9). Hence, though our speech and our thoughts about God are multiple, the being of God is simple, for what the different terms with their different meanings refer to is one and the same reality. Thus the doctrine of divine simplicity is not a doctrine about our speech about God or about our thoughts about God, but about the being of God.

PROPERTIES AND ACCIDENTS

La Croix construes "the use of the word 'property' . . . in such a way that a thing, x, has the property of being P (the property of being a P) if and only if the statement that x is P (that x is a P) is true."[9] He goes on

---

9. La Croix, "Augustine on the Simplicity of God," 455.

to distinguish between contingent and necessary properties. "A property, P, will be said to be a *contingent* property with respect to a thing, x, if and only if x can begin to possess P or cease to possess P. A property, P, will be said to be a *necessary* property with respect to a thing, x, if and only if x possesses P and x cannot begin to possess P or cease to possess P, that is, if and only if x has P but P is not a contingent property with respect to x."[10] Though Plantinga is speaking of Aquinas's doctrine that there are no accidents in God, he interprets this claim—which Augustine as well as Aquinas makes —to mean that God has no contingent properties. "Presumably this must be understood as the claim that God has no accidental properties. All of God's properties are essential to him; each property he has is one he couldn't possibly have lacked."[11] Though La Croix does not—as Plantinga does—explicitly identify "accident" with "contingent property," both authors use "property" in the wide contemporary sense. In this wide contemporary sense of "property" anything predicated of a subject according to any of the ten Aristotelian predicaments counts as a property. Thus, "being a horse" or "being a man" will be a property just as much as "being large" or "being yellow" or "being a father." Moreover, in the wide contemporary sense of "property" there are negative as well as positive properties; that is, "not being a horse" or "not being a father" are just as much properties as their complements. Furthermore, "being blind" is just as much a property as is "being sighted."[12]

La Croix attempts to interpret Augustine's account of divine simplicity "as the claim that a thing, x, is simple if and only if x does not have any nonrelative properties that are contingent (or if and only if all of the contingent properties possessed by x are relative)."[13] He argues that Augustine's account of divine simplicity and immutability is incoherent because he does not provide any criterion for distinguishing relative and nonrelative properties of God.

10. Ibid.
11. Plantinga, *Does God Have a Nature?*, 39.
12. Ibid., 19–20, 40–42.
13. La Croix, "Augustine on the Simplicity of God," 463. La Croix gives two other interpretations of Augustine's account of divine simplicity that he rejects. The first is that "a thing, x, is simple if and only if x does not have any contingent properties" (456). The second is that "a thing, x, is simple if and only if it is possible for x not to possess any contingent properties" (457). He rejects both accounts, for God does have some contingent properties and indeed must have some contingent properties.

Augustine does claim that there is no accident in God because there is nothing in God that is able to be changed or lost or that is capable of increase or decrease.[14] Furthermore, he does say that a nature is said to be simple that does not have something that it can lose or because there is no difference between what it is and what it has.[15] However, Augustine also maintains that there are predicates that begin to be said of God at some time that were not previously said of God (*Trin.* 5, 16, 17). Hence, it would seem that Augustine would admit that there are contingent properties of God if "contingent property" is taken in La Croix's sense and that he would nonetheless deny that there is any accident in God. What then does Augustine mean by an accident? He says that one usually means by "accident" "only that which can be lost by some change of that reality to which it pertains" (*Trin.* 5, 4, 5). However, he also includes within "accidents" what can increase or decrease without being lost. He gives the example of the life of the soul, which increases or decreases insofar as the soul becomes more or less wise. Moreover, he mentions "inseparable accidents," which cannot be lost as long as the thing to which they pertain exists, but which can be lost insofar as the thing itself ceases to exist.[16] He uses the example of the blackness of a crow's feather, which, though inseparable from the feather, can nonetheless cease to exist when the feather or the crow perishes. An accident, then, for Augustine is something that inheres in a subject and that can

14. "Nihil itaque accidens in Deo, quia nihil mutabile aut amissibile. Quodsi et illud dici accidens placet, quod licit non amittatur, minuitur tamen vel augetur . . . nec tale aliquid in Deo fit, quia omnino incommutabilis est" (*Trin.* 5, 4, 5).

15. "[P]ropter hoc itaque natura dicitur simplex, cui non sit aliquid habere quod vel possit amittere; vel aliud sit habens, aliud quod habet" (*civ. Dei*, 11, 10). La Croix's translation is: "A nature is said to be simple on the grounds that it cannot lose any of the properties that it possesses; that is, there is no distinction to be made between what that nature is and the properties that it has" (La Croix, "Augustine on the Simplicity of God," 455). His translation introduces the term "properties," which is not in the Latin and which suggests that he—like Plantinga—would identify "accident" with "contingent property." However, since properties occur in statements, his translation would seem to imply that no statement of the form "God is P" could be a contingent statement—despite the fact that Augustine does argue that some predicates begin to be true of God in time that were not previously true of God (*Trin.* 5, 16, 17).

16. In speaking of "inseparable accidents" Augustine seems to confuse the predicament and the predicable. "L'accident-prédicable et l'accident prédicament ne sont toujours nettement distingués" (BA 15, p. 40). Hendrikx suggests that such lacks of precision may be due in part to the translation of the *Categories* by Marius Victorinus that Augustine used (ibid.).

be lost by a change of that reality to which it pertains, or something that inheres in a subject and that, though not lost, is capable of increase or decrease, or something that inheres in a subject and that, though inseparable from that subject, is nonetheless lost through the destruction of that subject.

Hence, a being that has no accidents is intrinsically unchangeable since it cannot lose or gain anything, increase or decrease, or cease to exist. "Other things which are called essences or substances possess accidents by which there occurs in them a great or at least some change, but such a thing cannot happen to God. Therefore, he alone is immutable substance or essence" (*Trin.* 5, 2, 3). In saying that there are no accidents in God, Augustine is not saying that there are no statements about God that begin to be true or cease to be true of God. Rather he is saying something about the being of God and about how we are to think of God. For example, Augustine says that God produces changeable things; however, he does so without any change of himself.[17] Indeed God alone may—Augustine suggests—be said to cause something in the truest sense (*Trin.* 5, 8, 9). A statement such as "God created Adam" is one that affirms a property of God that God at one time did not have; in the contemporary sense of "property" such a statement or *dictio* ascribes a contingent property to God. However, though such a statement does say something about God, the being of God is not changed, for he is altogether immutable. It is one thing for there to be a change in the truth value of a statement about God; it is quite another thing for there to be a change in God.[18] The Augustinian doctrine of divine immutability—along with the doctrine that there are no accidents in God—does not exclude statements about God whose truth value changes or exclude the ascription of contingent properties to God.

---

17. "[S]ine ulla sui mutatione mutabilia facientem" (*Trin.* 5, 1, 2).

18. Plantinga interprets Aquinas's claim that God has no accidents to mean that God has no contingent properties. He then claims, "In essence Aquinas . . . rejects the claim that God has accidental properties by denying that such items as *having created Adam* or *knowing that Adam sinned* are properties. . . . It seems plainly mistaken to say that the proposition God created Adam characterizes Adam but not God or says something about the former but not the latter." Plantinga, *Does God Have a Nature?* 42–43. Augustine and Aquinas, however, do not identify "accident" and "contingent property." When Augustine denies that there are accidents in God, he is saying something about the being that God is; yet he clearly maintains that there are true propositions about God that begin to be true in time and that, consequently, assert contingent properties of God.

Augustine says that nothing is said of God according to accident *(secundum accidens* or *accidentaliter)*. It might seem that this claim entails that no statement about God can contain a predicate that falls under any of the last nine predicaments. Yet we have just seen that Augustine says that God causes things, and he also argues that God is said to be creator and lord relatively or according to relation. The expression *dici secundum accidens* or *accidentaliter dici* and the corresponding expression *dici secundum substantiam* or *substantialiter dici* have to do not merely with the grammatical form of a statement, but with what the statement means or signifies. Augustine distinguishes what seems to be said according to quality from what is said according to quality. He says that such adjectives as "eternal, immortal, incorruptible, immutable, living, powerful, beautiful, just, and happy" seem to signify qualities in God, while "spirit" seems to signify a substance. However, "whatever in that ineffable and simple nature seems to be said according to qualities, must be understood according to substance or essence" (*Trin.* 15, 5, 8). The adjectival expressions seem to signify qualities, but they must be understood to signify the substance. "Far be it from us that God be said to be spirit according to substance and good according to quality" (*Trin.* 15, 5, 8). So too, Augustine says that, "when we say, 'He is a man,' we designate the substance" (*Trin.* 5, 7, 8). Hence, the claim that nothing is said of God according to accident means that nothing predicated of God signifies or designates an accident in God or that nothing predicated of God should be understood to signify or designate an accident in God.

Hence, at the level of speech about God *(dicere)*, many statements about God may seem to signify or designate an accident in God, but at the level of thought about God *(cogitare)* they must not be so understood, because in the being of God *(esse)* there is no accident, that is, no reality in God that can be lost or gained or that can increase or decrease.

If we turn to the individual predicaments, the situation may become clearer. Augustine says that four of the predicaments are said of God in not a proper but a figurative sense, or metaphorically. He provides examples from Scripture for each of these predicaments. God is said to be seated above the cherubim according to the predicament of posture *(situs);* he is said to be clothed with the abyss according to the predicament of possession *(habitus)*. So too, in saying that God's years shall not fail, one is speaking according to the predicament of time *(tempus)*, and if one says, "If I ascend to heaven, you are there," one is speaking according to the predicament of place *(locus)*.[19] I take it that Augustine regards such scriptural statements as true, but not as to be understood in a literal or proper sense. Unfortunately he does not further elucidate the issue, though we may be able to suggest what he had in mind. In a literal sense it would seem that only an animal with a certain organized set of limbs could be said to have a posture. Predication according to posture *(situs)* says something about the relation of the parts of the animal. Thus, though predication according to posture may involve some sort of relation, it also presupposes extended and differentiated parts, and an immaterial being, such as God, cannot have such extended and differentiated parts. So too, predication according to possession *(habitus)* says something about how a man, or possibly an animal, is dressed or equipped. Thus, though it may express a relation to clothing or equipment, it once again presupposes an organized and extended being so that God cannot be literally said to be anything according to possession. Predication according to place says something about the relation of a body to surrounding things; thus, though it does not directly say anything about the being of what is in a place, it does imply that the being in place is extended or has some dimensions so that God cannot be literally said to be in some place. Hence, these three predicaments presuppose extension and differentiated parts in that of which they are literally and properly predicated. Finally, because God is eternal, he is not temporal in the sense that he exists at one time after another.[20]

It might seem surprising that Augustine does not say that predicates ascribing greatness to God are also to be understood in a figurative or metaphorical sense. However, he speaks of the magnitude or greatness of God as a greatness of power or of quality and seems to understand

---

19. Augustine takes his examples from Ps 79, 2; 103, 6; 101, 28; and 138, 8 respectively.

20. "Non aliud anni Dei, et aliud ipse: sed anni Dei, aeternitas Dei est: aeternitas ipsa Dei substantia est, quae nihil habet mutabile; ibi nihil praeteritum, quasi jam non sit; nihil est futurum, quasi nondum sit. Non est ibi nisi, *Est;* non est ibi, *Fuit* et *Erit;* quia et quod fuit, jam non est; et quod erit nondum est; sed quidquid ibi est, nonnisi est" (*en. Ps.* 9, 11).

such greatness in a literal rather than a metaphorical sense.[21] As for *passio,* Augustine says that God is not changed and does not undergo anything with respect to his substance by which he is God (*Trin.* 5, 8, 9). Thus nothing is said of God according to *passio,* that is, as signifying a change caused in him by something else. However, since affirmation and negation are according to the same predicament, there will be true negations about God according to *passio,* such as God is not changed by events in the world. Similarly, there will be true negations according to posture, possession, time, place, and quantity, at least if quantity is understood in the sense of three-dimensional extension. Since God is said to cause or change other things without any change in himself, affirmation—as well as negation—according to action—about God does not indicate any accident in God. Thus, in saying that nothing is said of God according to accident, that is, as signifying an accident in God, Augustine intends to exclude from the being that God is any quality distinct from the being that God is and any relation that implies a change in the being that God is.

RELATIVE AND NONRELATIVE PREDICATES ACCORDING TO AUGUSTINE

In *Trin.* 5, 16, 17, Augustine draws a conclusion that might seem to provide a rule for distinguishing relative and nonrelative predicates of God. He says, "Therefore, whatever God begins to be said to be in time that he was not previously said to be, is clearly said relatively, nonetheless, not according to an accident of God because something happens to him, but according to an accident of that to which God begins to be said to be relatively."[22] In one sense, of course, anything said of God is presumably said of God in time. Even "God is eternal" was once not said of God and was subsequently said of God, for human acts of speaking are presumably all temporal. If what Augustine is saying is

---

21. "In iis enim quae non mole magna sunt, hoc est majus esse quod est melius esse. Melior autem fit spiritus alicujus creaturae, cum adhaeret Creatori, quam si non adhaereat, et ideo etiam major quia melior" (*Trin.* 6, 7, 9); "non enim mole magnus est, sed virtute" (*Trin.* 6, 7, 8).

22. "Quod ergo temporaliter dici incipit Deus quod antea non dicebatur, manifestum est relative dici: non tamen secundum accidens Dei quod ei aliquid acciderit, sed plane secundum accidens ejus ad quod dici aliquid Deus incipit relative" (*Trin.* 5, 16, 17).

to be significant, he must be understood to mean that statements that begin to be true of God at some time and that were not previously true of God are said of God relatively. That is, he is not concerned with the temporality of acts of speaking, but with the temporality of the truth of the proposition about God or with the temporality of the conditions of the truth of the proposition about God. Thus, he is not concerned with what God begins to be said to be falsely at some time. Nor, as we shall see, is the rule concerned with what God is said *not* to be in time.

Rather Augustine is concerned with the temporality of the conditions of the truth of affirmative propositions about God. The examples he uses are instructive. God began to be said to be lord of the people of Israel at t_2 though he was not said to be lord of the people at t_1, a time at which the people of Israel did not exist. A condition of the truth of the proposition that God is lord of Israel is that the people of Israel exist, and since Israel came into existence as a people at a certain time in history, there was a time when the proposition "God is lord of Israel" was not true of God. Hence, Augustine is claiming that predications that are true of God at one time and that were not previously true of God are said of God relatively.

Augustine's rule deals only with what is said of God. He is not providing a general rule for distinguishing between relative and nonrelative predicates in every case. Moreover, the rule that he states says that all predicates of a certain type are relative; it does not, of course, follow that all relative predicates are predicates of that type, that is, ones that begin to be said truly of God in time. Indeed Augustine's Trinitarian doctrine leads him to hold that there are relative predicates of God that are eternally true of God, such as, the Son is begotten of the Father.[23]

If one prescinds from the eternal relations of the three persons within God, one might ask whether there are predicates that do not begin to be true of God in time and yet express a relation to some creature or creatures. Curiously Augustine seems to leave this possibility open. For, in choosing the proposition "God is lord of Israel" as an example of what begins to be said truly of God in time, Augustine deliberately

---

23. "In Deo autem nihil quidem secundum accidens dicitur, quia nihil in eo mutabile est; nec tamen omne quod dicitur, secundum substantiam dicitur. Dicitur enim ad aliquid, sicut Pater ad Filium, et Filius ad Patrem, quod non est accidens: quia et ille semper Pater, et ille semper Filius" (*Trin.* 5, 5, 6).

avoids the example of Israel in the sense of an individual or the proposition "God is my lord" (*Trin.* 5, 16, 17). He hesitates about such propositions as examples of what God begins to be said to be in time because of the obscure question of the soul.[24] In typically Platonic fashion he interprets the referent of personal names and pronouns as the soul or mind.[25] Moreover, he was never able to determine to his satisfaction the question of the origin of the soul, and at least in his earlier years he seems to have held that the soul existed prior to its incarnation in the body and that incarnation involved a falling into and breaking apart into times.[26] While he does not here endorse that position, he chooses "lord of the people of Israel" as an example of what God begins to be said to be in time rather than "my lord," since, if individual souls—or the soul of a people—always existed or existed before there were times, then God did not begin to be said to be their lord in time.[27]

Furthermore, Augustine raises the objection that God alone is eternal, and times are not eternal because of their variety and changeableness. Yet times did not begin to be in time, for there was no time before times

---

24. The obscure question of the soul concerns the origin of the soul. From the time of his earliest dialogue to the *retr.*, Augustine was never able to settle to his satisfaction the question of the soul's origin. See *b. vita* 1, 1 and 5, and *retr.* 1, 1, 3. In *lib. arb.* 3, 20, 56–58, he presents four hypotheses regarding the origin of the soul: "Harum autem quatuor de anima sententiarum, utrum de propagine veniant, an in singulis quibusque nascentibus novae fiant, an in corpora nascentium jam alicubi existentes vel mittantur divinitus, vel sua sponte labantur, nullam temere affirmare oportebit" (*lib. arb.* 3, 21, 59). Augustine's statement, in *retr.* 1, 1, 3, that he did not then know, i.e., at the time of the *c. Acad.*, and does not now know, i.e., at the time of the *retr.*, the answer to the question of the origin of the soul does allow for the possibility "that there was a time when he *thought* he knew, but only later considered himself to have been mistaken in that view" (O'Connell, *Early Theory*, 150). For an argument showing that Augustine did surrender his earlier Plotinian view of the origin and fall of the soul, see O'Connell, "Augustine's Rejection of the Fall of the Soul."

25. "Homo interior cognovit haec per exterioris ministerium. Ego interior cognovi haec, ego animus per sensus corporis mei" (*conf.* 10, 6, 9); "unus ego animus" (*conf.* 10, 7, 11); "Ego sum qui memini, ego animus" (*conf.* 10, 16, 25).

26. ". . . at ego in tempora dissilui. . . ." (*conf.* 11, 29, 39) ". . . in multa defluximus" (*conf.* 10, 29, 40). "In those early works, I submit, the implications are unquestionably Plotinian; here, I suggest, the continuity is substantially preserved. Augustine is still saying . . . that man in time is a soul, fallen through a sin of 'pride'" (O'Connell, *St. Augustine's Confessions*, 143).

27. "Aut si et hoc propter obscuram quaestionem animae videtur incertum, quid ut esset Dominus populi Israel? quia etsi jam erat animae natura, quam ille populus habebat, quod modo non quaerimus; tamen ille populus nondum erat, et quando esse coepit apparet" (*Trin.* 5, 16, 17).

began, and thus it did not happen to God in time that he is lord. For he was lord of times, which certainly did not begin to be in time.[28] Augustine provides no answer to this objection, though he insists that no creature is eternal and that God cannot be eternally lord unless there is some eternal creature.[29] Hence, though God did not begin to be said to be lord of times at t_2 while at t_1, some previous time, he was not said to be lord of times, he did begin to be lord of times when time began to be or from the first moment of time.[30] His rule might be amended to read: Whatever God begins to be said to be at some time or begins to be said to be in time that he was not previously said to be is clearly said relatively.

Thus, there are according to Augustine statements *(dictiones)* that are temporally true of God. Such statements that are temporally true of God predicate of God contingent properties in the contemporary sense of "property." However, such statements do not, according to Augustine, signify an accident in God, but rather an accident in some creature with respect to which God begins to be said relatively.[31] That is, the change that is requisite for the truth of such statements cannot occur in God's being, but must be understood to occur in the creature. Since the being that God is, is utterly unchangeable, the change requisite for the truth of the statement must be in the creature with respect to which God is said to be relatively. At the level of *dictio* or speech something is said to happen to God. However, at the level of *cogitatio* we have to understand the change as occurring in the creature, not in the being *(esse)* of God.

Augustine provides some examples to show that various things can be spoken of relatively without any change in those things. He says that a coin can become a price or a pledge of something without any change

---

28. "Et quisquis exstiterit qui aeternum quidem Deum solum dicat, tempora autem non esse aeterna propter varietatem et mutabilitatem, sed tempora tamen non in tempore esse coepisse (non enim erat tempus antequam inciperent tempora, et ideo non in tempore accidit Deo ut Dommus esset, quia ipsorum temporum Dominus erat, quae utique non in tempore esse coeperunt)" (*Trin.* 5, 16, 17).

29. "Ecce Dominum esse non sempiternum habet, ne cogamur etiam sempiternam creaturam dicere, quia ille sempiterne non dominaretur, nisi etiam ista sempiterne famularetur. Sicut autem non potent esse servus qui non habet dominum, sic nec dominus qui non habet servum" (*Trin.* 5, 16, 17).

30. "Omnia tempora tu fecisti et ante omnia tempora tu es nec aliquo tempore non erat tempus" (*conf.* 10, 13, 16). Augustine clearly holds that time is a creature and thus there was no time before there were creatures.

31. See above, note 22.

in the coin, or an animal can become a beast of burden without any change in the animal.³² The point he is making can be illustrated by such propositions as "Lake Michigan is to my left" and "Lake Michigan is to my right." The truth value of such propositions changes with my turning from my desk to my typewriter, but though with the mere swivel of my chair the great lake is truly said to be in a different relation to me, there is surely no reason to suppose that the lake itself is changed, although my position has. Similarly, when God begins to be said to be my refuge, the new relative property ascribed to God need not signify a change in God. Indeed, given his immutability, it cannot. The change requisite for the truth of the proposition rather lies in me who take refuge in him.³³

Augustine's rule is worded affirmatively, that is, it deals with what God begins to be said *to be* in time. Does it also deal with what God begins to be said *not to be* in time? Augustine has claimed that affirmation and negation are according to the same predicament.³⁴ Hence, if a true affirmative proposition, such as "God is lord of Israel" is an affirmation according to relation, then "God is not lord of Israel" is a false negation according to relation. And prior to the existence of the people of Israel, it was a true negation according to relation. Thus, what God begins to be said to be or not to be at some time is said according to relation, that is, is an affirmation or negation according to relation. Moreover, the truth or falsity of a statement does not affect whether or not the statement is or is not according to relation.

On the other hand, the conditions requisite for the truth of an affirmation according to relation will differ from the conditions of the

---

32. "Nummus autem cum dicitur pretium, relative dicitur, nec tamen mutatus est cum esse coepit pretium; neque cum dicitur pignus, et si qua similia. Si ergo nummus potest nulla sui mutatione toties dici relative, ut neque cum incipit dici, neque cum desinit, aliquid in ejus natura vel forma, qua nummus est, mutationis fiat, quanto facilius de illa incommutabili Dei substantia debemus accipere, ut ita relative aliquid ad creaturam, ut quamvis temporaliter incipiat dici, non tamen ipsi substantiae Dei accidisse aliquid intelligatur, sed illi creaturae ad quam dicitur?" (*Trin.* 5, 16, 17).

33. "Refugium ergo nostrum Deus relative dicitur, ad nos enim refertur, et tunc refugium nostrum fit, cum ad eum refugimus: numquid tunc fit aliquid in ejus natura, quod antequam ad eum refugeremus non erat? In nobis ergo fit aliqua mutatio . . . in illo autem nulla" (*Trin.* 5, 16, 17).

34. "Et omnino nullum praedicamenti genus est, secundum quod aliquid aiere volumus, nisi ut secundum idipsum praedicamentum negare convincamur, si praeponere negativam particulam voluerimus" (*Trin.* 5, 7, 8).

truth of a negation according to relation. A temporally true affirmation about God according to relation will require as a condition of its truth some creature. Thus, "God is lord of Israel" requires as a condition of its truth the existence of the people of Israel. However, prior to the existence of the people of Israel, the statement "God is not lord of Israel" does not require as a condition of its truth any positive reality other than God. The nonexistence of the people of Israel, along with the existence of God, suffices as a condition of the truth of the negation. In the contemporary sense of "property," "being lord of Israel" and "not being lord of Israel" are equally properties. Augustine would agree that both the affirmation and the negation are *dictiones* or statements according to relation; however, in terms of what is signified or understood, affirmation and negation differ radically. A negation according to relation does not signify a negative relation but simply denies a relation; it does not signify a negative accident or negative way of being, but denies an accident or way of being.

Hence, Augustine's rule, though directly concerned with relations in the sense of accidents in some creatures, might be modified as follows to provide a rule for distinguishing relative and nonrelative properties of God: "*P* (and its complement) is a relative property of God, if 'God is *P*' requires as a condition of its truth some being other than God, or if 'God is *P*' would require as a condition of its truth some being other than God, were 'God is *P*' true." Thus stated, the rule gives the sufficient conditions for *P* or its complement being a relative property of God in the contemporary sense of property. However, the rule does not state the necessary conditions as well, for, given the eternal relations of the three persons within God, there are in Augustine's view other relative properties of God.[35] However, if one prescinds from the Trinitarian doctrine, then the rule can be taken as stating both the sufficient and necessary conditions for *P* or its complement being a relative property of God. So too, if one again prescinds from the eternal relations within God, one can formulate a rule that provides the sufficient and necessary conditions for a property of God being nonrelative: "*P* (or its complement) will be a nonrelative property of God, if neither 'God is *P*' nor 'God is not *P*' requires as a condition of its truth a being other than

---

35. See above, note 23. Strictly speaking, the subject of the eternal relative properties is not God or the divine nature, but the single persons of the Trinity. Thus, it is not the divine nature that is said relatively to the Son, but the Father.

God and if neither 'God is P' nor 'God is not P' would require any being other than God, were either 'God is P' or 'God is not P' true."

LA CROIX'S PROBLEM AND AUGUSTINE'S SOLUTION

Will Augustine's formulation of the distinction between relative and nonrelative properties of God solve the problems raised by La Croix? The latter presents two formulations of the distinction between relative and nonrelative properties and argues that neither formulation is coherent. He says, "(1) P is relative with respect to x if and only if 'x has P' is a statement that refers to a being not identical to x.[36] (2) P is relative with respect to x if and only if 'x has P' is a statement containing a predicate that refers to a being not identical to x."[37] The difficulty with (1) arises from a proposition such as (3) "The entity worshiped by Augustine is omniscient." For, according to (1) "omniscience" is a nonrelative property in a proposition such as (4) "God is omniscient," but is a relative property in a proposition such as (3), in which God is referred to by "the entity worshiped by Augustine."

Now (1) does not seem to be at all a plausible formulation of the distinction between relative and nonrelative predicates or properties. For any P could always, by means of (1), be shown to be a relative property by the use of a denoting phrase for x that refers to an entity not identical to x, though not every P could be thus shown to be nonrelative, since some Ps themselves refer to entities not identical to x. For example, in (5) "Monica's son was the father of Adeodatus," P cannot be shown, by (1), to be a nonrelative property, by replacing the subject with "Augustine." The basic problem, however, with (1) as a formulation of the distinction between relative and nonrelative properties or predicates is that it allows that something other than the property or predicate may determine whether the property or predicate is relative or nonrelative.

However, (2) might seem a more promising formulation of the distinction, for in this case the distinction between relative and nonrelative properties or predicates seems to lie in the properties or predicates. However, La Croix argues that in (4) "God is omniscient" (or "God has omniscience"), "omniscient" (or "omniscience") is nonrelative because

36. La Croix, "Augustine on the Simplicity of God," 465.
37. Ibid., 466.

no entity not identical to God is referred to by the predicate. However, in (6) "God has the property I am thinking of," "the property I am thinking of" is, according to (2), a relative property. Hence, if the property I am thinking of is omniscience, omniscience turns out to be both a relative and a nonrelative property. Any P can, by means of (2), be shown to be a relative property of x by the use of a phrase to designate P that contains a reference to an entity not identical to x.

If one applies Augustine's criterion for distinguishing between what is said of God relatively and what is said of God nonrelatively, (4) "God is omniscient" is a nonrelative predication about God, for "is omniscient" does not begin to be true of God in time, at least given the claim that God is eternal and immutable—a claim that Augustine and all classical theists have held. On the other hand, (6) "God has the property I am thinking of" is a proposition that begins to be true of God in time. Among the conditions of the truth of (6) are that I exist, that I am thinking, and that I am thinking of a property that is a property of God, namely, omniscience. (6) requires as conditions of its truth a being other than God and that being's act of thinking of a property of God. Before I existed and before I was thinking of a property of God, (6) was not true. It is a proposition that begins to be true of God in time; and hence, according to Augustine's criterion "has the property I am thinking of" is a relative predicate or property of God. However, the change that provides the conditions requisite for the truth of that proposition is not a change in God, but in me, for it is I who begin to think of a property that God has. Hence, the relative property or predicate said of God signifies an accident in me, not in God. That is, for the conditions requisite for the proposition to be true there is no need for God to acquire or to lose something, though there is need for my act of thinking of a property of God.

Propositions that have different conditions requisite for their being true are surely different propositions. For the truth of (4), "God is omniscient," my existence and thinking are not required. For the truth of (6), "God has the property I am thinking of," my existence and thinking are required. Hence, (4) and (6) are different propositions, the first predicating a nonrelative, the second a relative property of God.[38]

---

38. See William J. Wainwright, "Augustine on God's Simplicity: A Reply," *New Scholasticism* 53 (1979): 118–123, and Richard R. La Croix, "Wainwright, Augustine and

In conclusion, I believe that I have shown that Augustine's claim that there are no accidents in God is quite compatible with the claim that there are contingent predicates or properties of God. Augustine's distinction between speech about God, thought about God, and the being of God allows him to hold that there is a multiplicity of terms used in speaking of God and that there is a multiplicity of meanings for those terms, though the being of God is simple. I have shown how Augustine provides the basis for a rule to allow the distinction between relative and nonrelative properties of God and how this rule solves the problems raised by La Croix regarding the supposed incoherence of this distinction. Hence, the objections raised against Augustine's account of divine simplicity have thus far been met.

God's Simplicity," *New Scholasticism* 53 (1979): 124–127. In this interchange, La Croix argues that the statement "Omniscience is the property I am thinking of" is a contingent truth and that the statement "Omniscience is the property I am thinking of, when I am thinking of omniscience" is a necessary truth. Hence, it is either contingently true or necessarily true that the two properties are identical. And if they are identical, then one cannot be relative and the other nonrelative. However, the fact that "Omniscience is the property I am thinking of" is a contingent truth indicates that "omniscience" does not mean "the property I am thinking of." While "omniscience" and "the property I am thinking of" may denote the same property or be identical in their denotation, they are not identical in their meaning or connotation. While the basic problem with (1) is that it allows something other than P to determine whether or not P is relative, the basic problem with (2) and with La Croix's argument that (2) leads to incoherence is that (2) allows something other than the meaning of P to determine whether or not P is relative.

6

AUGUSTINE'S USE OF *SUBSTANTIA* IN SPEAKING ABOUT GOD

In the present article I examine what Augustine meant by his use of "substance" in three sets of expressions. First, various predicates are said of God according to substance. Secondly, God is himself said to be substance. And thirdly, the three persons are said to be of the same substance. In the present article I argue against various claims that Augustine's language in speaking about God is unintelligible and try to show how his use of substance and of the other predicaments or categories in speaking about God is not merely intelligible, but a brilliant contribution to our language about God.

In *Trin.* 5 Saint Augustine begins to speak of God in terms of the Aristotelian categories or predicaments.[1] In another article

---

1. In *conf.* 4, 16, 28, Augustine tells us that he read and understood Aristotle's *Categories* when he was a young man and that he mistakenly applied them to his thinking about God. Yet by the time of the *Trin.* Augustine is using the categories for speaking about God. In fact, according to the editors of the BA edition of the *Trin.*, "C'est ainsi que dans le *De Trinitate* la scholastique a connu son heure de naissance" (BA 15, 16–17). I suspect that the radical difference in attitude toward the categories from the period referred to in *conf.* 4 to that of *Trin.* may well have to do with the fact that Augustine's second encounter with the categories was mediated by Neoplatonism. After all, Augustine certainly found in Plotinus and Porphyry a use of the categories combined with a spiritualism in philosophy. Bréhier points out in the introduction to *Ennead* 6, 1, where Plotinus in chapters 2 to 14 presents a critical commentary on the *Categories* of Aristotle that Simplicius cites in his *Commentary on the Categories* no less than fifteen different commentaries

I tried to show why Augustine claims that nothing is said of God according to accident and how he distinguishes between relative and nonrelative predication about God.[2] In that article I deliberately avoided dealing with Augustine's further claim that God is substance or essence. In the present article what I wish to do is to examine Augustine's use of *substantia* or *essentia* with regard to God. His use of these terms falls into three expressions or three sets of expressions. First, various predicates are said of God *secundum substantiam* or *substantialiter*. Second, God is said to be *substantia* or *essentia*. And third, the Father, the Son, and the Holy Spirit are said to be *ejusdem substantia, unius ejusdem substantiae*, or *una essentia, tres personae*. Though the latter set are theological and, hence, are out of place in a philosophical investigation, it would seem that the sense of such a theological expression must be open to philosophical understanding, even if one does not in faith accept the truth of the theological statement.[3] Or, since other philosophers have argued that Augustine's use of "substance" in speaking about God is devoid of sense, it would seem that it should also be possible within the limits of philosophy to argue the opposite case or at least to reexamine the issue to see whether the case for the intelligibility of what Augustine says is indeed in the dire straits in which it has been said to be.[4]

---

on the *Categories,* many of which were written prior to the time of Augustine. See Plotin, *Ennéades* VI, part 1 (Paris: Les belles lettres, 1963). Moreover, in *Plotin et l'Occident* (Louvain: Spicilegium Sacrum Lovaniense, 1934), 54–56, Paul Henry argues that Victorinus, who had translated the *Categories* into Latin, probably drew his three definitions of substance in his *Adv. Arium* 1, 30 from the *Enneads*. And since Victorinus surely was the source of the translation of the *Enneads* that Augustine knew, it is likely that Augustine's concept of substance by the time *Trin.* was heavily influenced by Plotinian thought.

2. See "Properties of God and the Predicaments in *De Trinitate* V," *The Modern Schoolman* 59 (1981): 1–19.

3. I do not here mean to take sides in the contemporary discussion in theology regarding the necessity for a theologian to have faith in order to do theology. See Thomas Ommen, "The Pre-Understanding of the Theologian," in *Theology and Discovery: Essays in Honor of Karl Rahner,* ed. William Kelly (Milwaukee: Marquette University Press, 1980), 231–261. All I wish to claim is that a statement of the Christian faith must be able to be understood at some level even prior to one's having faith, i.e., it must be possible to understand what a proposition means before one assents to it on faith.

4. See Michael Durrant, *Theology and Intelligibility* (London and Boston: Routledge and Kegan Paul, 1973), where Durrant argues that Augustine's claims that God is substance or essence and that there are three persons in one substance are both without sense. Durrant says that "the Trinitarian formula is an impossible one and hence that the doctrine of the Trinity is an impossible one" (x). He devotes his fourth chapter to an examination of Augustine's use of "substance" in the Trinitarian formulae and concludes that its use in such formulae is not only nonsensical, but "necessarily nonsensical" (125).

DICI SECUNDUM SUBSTANTIAM

At the beginning of book 5 Augustine makes a statement that indicates that he distinguishes between speaking about God *(dicere),* thinking about God *(cogitare),* and the being of God *(esse).*[5] Though it might seem that such expressions are more rhetorical than doctrinal, I have tried to show that the distinction between our language about God, our thought about God, and the being of God is crucial to understanding what Augustine is saying.[6] For example, when he says that nothing is said of God according to accident, he does not mean that there are no contingent predications about God. For something to be said of God according to accident means for Augustine that there is in God, that is, in the being that God is, something that can be lost or increased or decreased by a change in God.[7]

To say that something is said of God according to accident means that what is said signifies an accident in God. Yet, because he is utterly immutable, there can be no accident in God.[8] Similarly, to say something of God according to substance or substantially is to signify or designate the substance of God.[9]

---

5. "Hinc jam exordiens ea dicere, quae dici ut cogitantur vel ab homine aliquo, vel certe a nobis non omni modo possunt: quamvis et ipsa nostra cogitatio, cum de Deo trinitate cogitamus, longe se illi de quo cogitat, imparem sentiat, neque ut est eum capiat" (*Trin.* 5, 1, 1). Even more clearly Augustine says, "Verius enim cogitatur Deus quam dicitur, et verius est quam cogitatur" (*Trin.* 7, 4, 7). Translations from Augustine, unless otherwise indicated, are my own.

6. I have attempted to show in "Properties of God . . ." (see above, note 2) that one must distinguish between the structure of language about the real and the structure of the real if one is to make sense of what the classical theists have said about God. For example, Richard LaCroix has argued that Aquinas cannot consistently maintain that God is omnipresent and not in time; however, he confuses God's being in time with there being temporal predicates said truly of God. La Croix, "Aquinas on God's Omnipresence and Timelessness."

7. "Accidens autem non solet dici, nisi quod aliqua mutatione ejus rei cui accidit amitti potest. . . . Quod si et illud dici accidens placet, quod licet non amittatur, minuitur tamen vel augetur . . . nec tale aliquid in Deo fit, quia omnino incommutabilis manet" (*Trin.* 5, 4, 5).

8. "Quamobrem nihil in eo secundum accidens dicitur, quia nihil ei accidit. . . . In Deo autem nihil quidem secundum accidens dicitur, quia nihil in eo mutabile est; nec tamen omne quod dicitur, secundum substantiam dicitur" (*Trin.* 5, 5, 6).

9. *Trin.* 15, 5, 8. Clearly, for something to be said of God according to substance means that what is said signifies the substance of God. Elsewhere Augustine uses "des-

Augustine realizes that it might seem that to say that God is spirit is to say something according to substance, but that to say that God is good or wise is to say something according to accident. However, such is not the case. Since there can be no accident in God, what seems to be said of God according to accident must be understood to be said of him according to substance, that is, must be understood to signify or designate the substance of God.[10] Predications about God are either *ad se* (with respect to himself, or absolute) or *ad aliquid* (with respect to something, or relative).[11]

Predication according to the categories of substance, quantity, and quality are *ad se;* they do not contain a reference to something other than the subject of which they are predicated. Predication according to the other categories are *ad aliquid* and involve a reference to something other than the subject of which they are predicated—with the exception of the category of *situs,* which involves an internal relatedness of the subject's parts. Augustine's rule for what is said of God according to substance is that whatever is said of him *ad se* is said according to substance; thus, what might seem to be a predication according to quantity or quality is to be understood according to substance, that is, as signifying the substance of God.

The reasons that Augustine gives for this are of two sorts. At times he appeals to God's immutability and the fact that to be said to be something according to accident involves having an accident, that is, having something in respect to which that which has the accident is

---

ignates" or even "shows" *(designare* or *ostendere)* in place of "signifies." See *Trin.* 5, 7, 8: "Velut cum dicimus: Homo est, substantiam designamus." "Quidquid ergo ad se dicuntur, non dicitur alter sine altero, id est quidquid dicuntur quod substantiam ostendat, ambo simul dicuntur" (*Trin.* 6, 2, 3).

10. "Proinde si dicamus, Aeternus, immortalis, incorruptibilis, immutabilis, vivus, sapiens, potens, speciosus, justus, bonus, beatus, spiritus; horum omnium novissimum quod posui quasi tantummodo videtur significare sustantiam, caetera vero hujus substantiae qualitates: sed non ita est in illa ineffabili simpliciqué natura. Quidquid enim secundum qualitates illic dici videtur, secundum substantiam vel essentiam est intelligendum. Absit enim ut spiritus secundum substantiam dicatur Deus, et bonus secundum qualitatem: sed utrumque secundum substantiam" (*Trin.* 15, 5, 8).

11. "Quapropter illud praecipue teneamus, quidquid ad se dicitur praestantissima illa et divina sublimitas, substantialiter dici; quod autem ad aliquid, non substantialiter, sed relative" (*Trin.* 5, 8, 9). "Quod autem proprie singula in eadem Trinitate dicuntur, nullo modo ad se ipsa, sed ad invicem, aut ad creaturam dicuntur; et ideo relative, non substantialiter ea dici manifestum est" (*Trin.* 5, 11, 12).

mutable.[12] At other times he appeals to God's simplicity and argues that to be said to be great, for example, according to accident involves *having* greatness rather than *being* greatness, that is, involves a participation in greatness itself, which must, of course, be greater than that which participates in greatness. Thus there would be something greater than God by which God is great.[13]

Hence, Augustine holds that whatever is said of God with respect to himself, that is, *ad se,* is said according to substance. However, for something to be said according to substance means that it signifies or designates the substance. Hence, if anything is to be said of God according to substance, it would seem that God would have to be a substance.

EST SINE DUBITATIONE SUBSTANTIA

Augustine's claim that God "is without a doubt substance—or if he is better so called—essence, which the Greeks call *ousia*" occurs immediately after he has told his readers that we should understand God as far as possible as "great without quantity, as good without quality, creator without need, presiding without posture, containing all things without possession, whole everywhere without place, eternal without time, making mutable things without any change of himself, and undergoing nothing" (*Trin.* 5, 1, 2). That is, the text asserting that God is a substance or essence follows upon a list of what are clearly the last nine predicaments. Augustine is saying that though God is great, good, creator, presiding, and the rest, he does not have quantity, quality, relation, posture, and so on. Augustine claims that nothing is said of God according to accident; however, God is without a doubt substance or essence. From the context this claim would seem to say that God is an Aristo-

---

12. See above note 8 and also *Trin.* 5, 4, 5: "Nihil itaque accidens in Deo, quia nihil mutabile aut amissibile."

13. In *Trin.* 5, 10, 11, Augustine argues, "Sed illa est vera magnitudo, qua non solum magna est domus quae magna est, et qua magnus est mons quisquis magnus est; sed etiam qua magnum est quidquid aliud magnum dicitur: ut aliud sit ipsa magnitudo, aliud ea quae ab illa magna dicuntur. Quae magnitudo utique primitus magna est, multoque excellentius quam ea quae participatione ejus magna sunt. Deus autem quia non ea magnitudine magnus est quae non est quod est ipse, ut quasi particips ejus sit Deus cum magnus est; alioquin illa erit major magnitudo quam Deus, Deo autem non est aliquid majus: ea igitur magnitudine magnus est qua ipse est eadem magnitudo."

telian substance and that God falls under the category of substance.[14]

Augustine seems, moreover, to use the terms "substance" and "essence" as if they were equivalent. For example, he goes on to say that "other things that are called essences or substances receive accidents, by which there may occur in them either a great change or at least some change. However, nothing of that sort can happen to God, and therefore the substance or essence that is God is alone immutable" (*Trin.* 5, 2, 3). Though God is a substance or essence unlike any other substance or essence insofar as he is a substance or essence with no accidents, he seems, if we are to judge by this text, to be called either substance or essence with equal propriety. Elsewhere, while discussing the Greek usage of "one essence, three substances," that is, *mia ousia, treis hupostaseis,* in speaking of the Trinity, Augustine mentions that speakers of Latin use "one essence, three persons" instead because "in our language, i.e., in Latin, essence and substance are understood to have the same meaning" (*Trin.* 7, 4, 7). Though the Greek Fathers use *hupostasis* where the Latin writers use *persona,* Augustine admits that he cannot find any distinction between *ousia* and *hupostasis* and, hence, says that he does not dare to say "one essence, three substances"—which would be a literal translation of the Greek.[15] And elsewhere Augustine makes it clear that he views *essentia* as the equivalent of the Greek *ousia*.[16]

14. Any doubt that Augustine is thinking in terms of the Aristotelian categories must surely be removed by *Trin.* 5, 7, 8, where Augustine explicitly runs through all ten of the categories to show that an affirmation and its negation are always according to the same category.

For an interesting analysis of Saint Thomas's position denying that God is a substance or is in the genus of substance, see Etienne Gilson, "Quasi Definitio Substantiae," *St. Thomas Aquinas 1274–1974: Commemorative Studies,* ed. Armand A. Maurer (Toronto: Pontifical Institute of Mediaeval Studies, 1974), 1:111–29.

15. See the "Notes complémentaires" in the BA edition, especially "Essence et substance," BA 15, 584, and "Une essence, trois hypostases," BA 15, 585, by M. Mellet and P.-T. Camelot, and "Personne et substance," BA 16, 572, by Paul Agaësse. Augustine claims that he does not understand the difference between *ousia* and *hupostasis,* and his ignorance—regardless of the state of his knowledge of the Greek language—is excusable. For the Council of Nicaea identified *ousia* and *hupostasis* in condemning the Arian claim that the Son is of another *ousia* or *hupostasis* than the Father; yet fifty years later the formula "one *ousia,* three *hupostaseis*" was accepted in the East. Despite his claim that he does not dare speak of three substances, in book 8, he does speak of "substance" as the equivalent of "person." "Ideoque dici tres personas, vel tres substantias, non ut aliqua intelligatur diversitas essentiae, sed ut vel uno aliquo vocabulo responderi possit, cum dicitur quid tres" (*Trin.* 8, 1).

16. *Trin.* 5, 1, 2; see also *Trin.* 5, 8, 9: "Essentiam dico, quae ousia graece dicitur, quam usitatius substantiam vocamus."

One often wishes that Augustine had included among his many volumes a dictionary of philosophical and theological terms or that he would at least have indicated that a term would be used in a variety of different, though connected, senses. However, he has not done so.[17] There are several texts in which Augustine seems to give a definition of *substantia*. In *ep.* 166 to Jerome, in speaking of the soul, he says, "If every substance, or essence or whatever 'that which exists somehow in itself' is better called, is a body, then the soul is a body" (*ep.* 166, 2, 4). Here "that which exists somehow in itself"—about as close to a definition of substance as Augustine comes—signifies an individual thing, the sort of thing that Aristotle called "first substance," though Augustine does not use that term. Similarly, in commenting on Psalm 68, he says, "Substance is understood in another way: that which we are whatever we are."[18] He admits that the term needs explanation because it is unfamiliar, though he insists that the things that the term signifies are quite familiar. "We say 'man' or 'cow' or 'earth' or 'sky'; we say 'sun,' 'moon,' 'stone,' 'sea,' or 'air'; all these are substances, by the very fact that they are. Natures themselves are called substances. God is a certain substance (*quaedam substantia*). For what is no substance is nothing at all. Therefore, substance is to be something (*esse aliquid*)" (*en. Ps.* 68, 5).[19] This

---

17. Joseph Owens, in *The Doctrine of Being in Aristotelian Metaphysics* (Toronto: Pontifical Institute of Mediaeval Studies, 1951), 140–143, presents a history of the translation of *ousia* into English.

18. Augustine is commenting on Ps 68:5, which in the text he had read: "Infixus sum in limo profundi, et non est substantia." That is, "I am caught in the mud of the deep, and there is no substance." For *substantia* the Septuagint has *hupostasis*, which can mean, according to Liddel and Scott, "anything set under, a stand, base, bottom, prop, support, stay." Hence the Greek text means: "I am caught in the mud of the deep, and there is no support [or place to stand]." The Hebrew word in question, *ma'amad*, contains the radical for "stand" and means "a standing or a station." However, the Latin *substantia* has no meaning similar to that of the Greek or Hebrew. Hence, Augustine—always an inventive exegete—places the verse in the mouth of Christ who in becoming man and taking the form of the servant became poor for our sakes. He further takes the second half of the verse as saying that the mud, that is, human nature, was not substance, that is, riches, for he took on our poverty. It is in the light of such an interpretation of *substantia* as "riches"—as in English might speak of a man of substance—that Augustine turns to "another meaning."

19. Augustine's claim that what is not a substance is nothing at all need not be taken to deny the reality of accidents, for he says in the text from *mor.* 2, 2, 2, that nature or substance is what is "something in its kind." Hence, he does not anticipate Descartes's rejection of any real accidents. See René Descartes, *Oeuvres Philosophiques,* ed. Ferdinand Alquié (Paris: Garnier, 1967), 2:875–876: "tout ce qui est réel peut exister séparément de

text may well be using "substance" in the sense of Aristotelian second substance. That is, "substance" here may mean not an individual thing, but the nature of an individual thing, that which is signified by predication according to substance.[20] Similarly in *mor.* 2, 2, 2, Augustine says, "For even nature itself is nothing else than what is understood to be something in its kind. Therefore, as we have referred to what we usually call 'substance' as 'essence' by a new name formed from '*esse*,' so the ancients who did not have these terms, used 'nature' for 'substance' and 'essence.'" There are in any case texts in which it is clear that Augustine is using "substance" in the sense of second substance. For example, in *ep.* 166, 2, 4, he is asking about the substance of the soul, and he says that "the soul is understood—whether it should be called a body or incorporeal—to have a certain nature of its own created with a substance more excellent than all these elements of the earthly mass." Since he has just mentioned the earthy, humid, airy, and ethereal bodies, the soul must have a substance or nature more excellent than these. Hence, Augustine does use "substance" in the sense of Aristotelian first substance and in the sense of second substance; however, he does not use such terminology and does not seem concerned with the differences in meaning, though he is certainly aware of the difference between individual things that have accidents and predicates that designate the substance or are said according to substance.

On the other hand, Augustine also recognizes that *essentia* is the preferable term for speaking about God. In book 7 he distinguishes between *substantia* and *essentia*. The former comes from *subsistere*, as the latter comes from *esse*. However, God cannot be correctly said to subsist, for that term "is correctly understood of those things in which as in subjects there are those things that are said to be in some subject, as color or shape are in a body. For a body subsists and, therefore, is a substance" (*Trin.* 7, 5, 10). Thus Augustine says that "changeable things that are not simple are properly called substances. However, if God sub-

---

tout autre sujet: or ce qui peut ainsi exister séparément est une substance, et non point un accident."

20. *Categories* 5, 2a11–18. Though Augustine uses what we could call "second substance" terms, since what is said according to substance is—at least apart from the case of God—a second substance, he does not use such language. Durrant's translation of *secundum substantiam* as "with respect to second substance" simply confuses the preposition with the ordinal numeral. See Durrant, *Theology and Intelligibility*, 747.

sists so that he can properly be called a substance, there is something in him as in a subject, and he is not simple" (ibid.).[21] Thus God is called *substantia* in an improper sense or *abusive* "so that by means of that more familiar term one might understand *essentia,* which he is truly and properly called." In fact, "perhaps God alone should be truly called *essentia.*"[22] Hence, we must turn our attention to what Augustine understands by the term *essentia.*

We have seen that the context of the assertion that God is without doubt substance or essence along with the discussion of accidents and predication according to the categories would seem to indicate that Augustine's claim should be understood in terms of Aristotelian first and second substance. However, Augustine also reveals a clear preference for the term "essence," which he links to eternity and immutability and to the text from Exodus 3:14, in which God tells Moses that his name is He Who Is.[23]

---

21. Augustine's language is very strong: "It is something abominable *(nefas)* to say that God subsists and is subject to his goodness, and that goodness is not his substance or rather essence, and that God himself is not his goodness, but that it is in him as in a subject" (*Trin.* 7, 5, 10). Hence, it is surprising to find that James F. Anderson, in *St. Augustine and Being: A Metaphysical Essay* (The Hague: M. Nijhoff, 1965), 19 and 21, quotes Augustine as saying, "hoc est Deo esse quod subsistere" (*Trin.* 7, 4, 9), for, though Augustine does use those words, he does so in the protasis of a hypothetical proposition, whose apodosis is not clearly—as I read it—affirmed as true.

Durrant claims that "it is no contingency that anything falling under the category of substance admits of accidents; indeed it is part of the very concept of substance that anything that falls under this category *should* admit of accidents.... The idea of an unchangeable substance, that is the idea of a substance which cannot sensibly be spoken of as being subject to change ... is a nonsensical one, hence to say that God is an unchangeable substance is itself nonsensical. I thus contend that, far from it being the case that St. Augustine has established an important truth, he has engrossed himself in a nonsense" (Durrant, 121–122). Durrant, however, seems to argue that Aristotle has set the sensible meanings of "substance" and that a sense of "substance" that does not conform to Aristotle's is *eo ipso* nonsense. If one were to accept Durrant's argument, one would have to dispose of the whole Neoplatonic tradition in which "substance" has non-Aristotelian senses. Indeed, Augustine's reaction to the *Categories* described in *conf.* 4 bears a striking similarity to Durrant's position. However, at the time referred to in *conf.* 4 Augustine had not yet learned to conceive a spiritual substance—which he acknowledged as the principal cause of his errors (*conf.* 5, 10, 19).

22. "Unde manifestum est Deum abusive substantiam vocari, ut nomine usitatiore intelligatur essentia, quod vere ac proprie dicitur; ita ut fortasse solum Deum dici oporteat essentiam" (*Trin.* 7, 5, 10). In *vera rel.* 11, 23, Augustine says, "summa essentia esse facit omne quod est, unde et essentia dicitur."

23. Texts in which Augustine deals with the name of God given to Moses in Ex 3:14 are abundant. For an excellent study of several of the principal texts, especially *s.* 7, 7;

First of all, Augustine claims that the term *essentia* is derived from *esse*, just as wisdom *(sapientia)* is derived from *sapere*, and knowledge *(scientia)* is derived from *scire*. In *Trin.* 5, 2, 3, immediately after listing these derivations, Augustine asks: "Who is more *(plus est)* than he who said to his servant Moses: 'I am who am,' and 'You shall say to the children of Israel, he who is sent me to you'?" It is clear that Augustine understands the Exodus passage as one in which God gives his name to Moses: "You say: I am. Who? Gaius. Another says, Lucius. Another, Mark. Would you be answering the question if you were not saying your name? This was expected from God. This was asked of him. What are you called? By whom shall I say that I have been sent when they ask? I am. Who? Who am. This is your name? This is all that you are called?" *(en. Ps.* 101, 2, 10). Starting from the *Qui est* and *Ego sum qui sum* of Exodus 3:14, Augustine moves to other closely allied expressions that he seems to take as equivalent to names of God. Thus, for example, in *en. Ps.* 134, 4, he says that, when asked for his name, God "did not say 'omnipotent,' 'merciful,' 'just'—names, which, of course, would be true, if he were to say them. With all the [other] names by which God could be called and named set aside, he answered that he is called *ipsum esse,* and as though this were his name, he said, 'This you shall tell them: Who is, sent me.'" Augustine adds that God "is in a such way that by comparison things that were made are not. If God is not considered, they are, because they are from him. However, if they are compared to him, they are not, because he is *verum esse, incommutabile esse,* and he alone is that."[24] And shortly thereafter Augustine speaks of God as *ipsum proprie*

Jo. ev. tr. 38, 8, 8; *en. Ps.* 101, 10 and 14, see Étienne Gilson, *Philosophie et incarnation selon saint Augustin* (Montréal: Institut des études médiévales, 1947). John C. Murray, S.J., in *The Problem of God, Yesterday and Today* (New Haven: Yale University Press, 1964), discusses what the Ex 3:14 name meant to the ancient singers, the later editor, and the community that listened to both. He argues, "One would risk anachronism if one were to read this sense [the 'I am who am' of the Septuagint version with its metaphysical resonances] back into the situation described in Exodus 3" (8). On the other hand, he argues that this "sense is valid and true; it is in the text. But it was probably heard only later."

24. For Augustine what differentiates a creature from God is that the creature is mutable and that God is utterly immutable. To be truly is, for Augustine, to be immutable; creatures are and are not. "Et inspexi cetera infra te et vidi nec omnino esse, nec omnino non esse. Esse quidem, quoniam abs te sunt; non esse autem, quoniam id quod es non sunt: id enim vere est quod incommutabiliter manet" *(conf.* 7, 11, 17). Furthermore, creatures are mutable and changing merely by being in time. "Praeteritum et futurum invenio in omni motu rerum: in veritate quae manet, praeteritum et futurum non invenio,

esse, which is indeed difficult, he admits, for the human mind to grasp.

Est itself seems to be used as the equivalent of a name for God in several texts, which, as Gilson has remarked, do violence to the language.[25] For in *en. Ps.* 101, 2, 10, immediately after citing Exodus 3:14, Augustine adds: "Behold a great Is, a great Is! What is man compared to this? Compared to that great Is, what is man whatever he is? Who may grasp that To Be? Who can become a sharer in it? Who may gasp after it? Who long for it? Who presume that he can be there?"[26]

Finally, Augustine uses *Idipsum* as an equivalent for the name that God gave to Moses. In commenting on Psalms 121:3, once again immediately after citing Exodus 3:14, Augustine says, "*Ecce Idipsum:* Behold the Selfsame." And Augustine links *Idipsum,* which he found in six places in the Vulgate text of the Psalms, with the one, the immutable, the eternal, the simple.[27] In commenting on Psalms 121:3, which in his text read, "Jerusalem, which is built as a city, whose participation is in the selfsame *(idipsum),*" Augustine tries by means of related words and meanings *(quibusdam vicinitatibus verborum et significationum)* to lead the mind of man to think the Selfsame. "What is the selfsame? That which is always the same way; that which is not now this and then that,

---

sed solum praesens, et hoc incorruptibiliter, quod in creatura non est. Discute rerum mutationes, invenies Fuit et Erit: cogita Deum, invenies Est, ubi Fuit et Erit esse non possit" (*Jo. ev. tr.* 38, 10). And for that reason Augustine can say that eternity is the very substance of God: "Aeternitas, ipsa Dei substantia" (*en. Ps.* 101, 2, 10).

25. Gilson says that at least twice Augustine does "violence to the language in using the verb 'Est' as a substantive" ("Notes sur l'être," 205). Thus in *conf.* 13, 31, 46, he says that through the Holy Spirit, "videmus, quia bonum est, quidquid aliquo modo est: ab illo enim est, qui non aliquo modo est, sed est est." And in *en. Ps.* 134, 4, he says, "Est enim est, sicut bonorum bonum, bonum est." Surely "Magnum ecce Est, magnum Est" (*en. Ps.* 101, 2, 10) belongs in the same group of texts. In *Ennead* 5, 1, 4, Plotinus uses *to estin* as a substantive in a passage that is strikingly similar to what Augustine is saying in the above passages.

26. Augustine's "Ad illud tam magnum Est, homo quid est, quidquid est?" calls to mind two difficult lines: "Et quis homo est quilibet homo, cum sit homo?" (*conf.* 4.1.1), and "Et cum te primum cognovi, tu assumpsisti me ut viderem esse quod viderem et nondum me esse qui viderem" (*conf.* 7, 10, 16). See O'Connell, *St. Augustine's Confessions,* 1–3, for Plotinian metaphysics implicit in such texts. For "to be" is to be eternal and unchanging, and thus Augustine can say that he "as yet is not." But the *nondum* surely implies that at some time he will be. Hence, Augustine can speak of the mission of Christ in the startling phrase: "vocans temporales, faciens aeternos" (*en. Ps.* 101, 10).

27. See Swetnam, "A Note on *In Idipsum,*" 328: "For [Augustine] *idipsum* is a peculiarly apt expression for God, for it emphasizes some of the basic divine attributes: simplicity, unity, immutability, eternity."

What is that which is? What is eternal. For what is always different is not, because it does not remain. It is not altogether not being, but it is not supremely being. And what is that which is but he who, when he sent Moses, said to him, 'I am who I am.'" Thus *Idipsum* is, as Augustine says in *vera rel.* 21, 41, "the immutable and singular nature, in following which one does not err and in attaining which one is without sorrow." Thus in *conf.* 9, 10, 24, in the famous vision at Ostia, Monica and Augustine long to rise up to share in *Idipsum,* in the very eternity of God.

If *Qui Est,* or *Ego Sum Qui Sum,* or *Ipsum esse,* or simply *Est,* or even *Idipsum* are names of God, then *essentia,* which is formed from *esse,* must also come very close to being a name for God. The name, however, that God gives to Moses, as Augustine understands it, is not a proper name in the sense that Marcus Tullius Cicero is a proper name.[28] It would, after all, be a mistake to ask for the connotative meaning of a proper name, since such names—at least generally—have only a denotative meaning, but not a connotative meaning. Yet the name that God gave to Moses certainly is understood by Augustine as having connotative meaning, as having the sort of meaning that can be expressed in a definition. *Qui Est* would seem to be a description that is proper to God, a description that applies only to God.

If *Qui Sum* is a name of God or a definite description of God, then the task before us is to unpack its meaning. In commenting on Psalm 101, Augustine says that when God replies to Moses, "I am who I am," he reveals himself "as Creator to a creature, as God to man, as immortal to a mortal, and as eternal to one that is temporal" (*en. Ps.* 101, 2, 10). Clearly *Qui Sum* is rich in meaning for Augustine, if it says that he is the creator, God, immortal, and eternal. Yet, if there is one aspect of content that Augustine returns to again and again in dealing with the Exodus text, it is divine immutability and eternity.

Thus when Augustine unpacks the significance of *Est,* we find that God is *Est,* because, as he says, "I remain for eternity, because I cannot be changed. For those things that change are not, because they do not last. For what is remains. What, however, is changed was something and

28. As Peter Geach has argued that "the term 'God' is not a proper name but a descriptive term," so *Qui Est* and *essentia* would seem to be descriptions proper to God. See *God and the Soul,* 108. Geach points out that a proper name is not translated from one language to another; however, the term "God" is translated. So too *Qui Est* is translated.

will be something; yet it is not, because it is changeable. Hence, the immutability of God has deigned to make itself known by that word: I am who I am" (*s.* 6, 3, 4). Even more explicitly Augustine ties *Qui Est* with immutability in *s.* 7, 7. "To be is the name of immutability. For all things that are changed cease to be what they were and begin to be what they were not. Only what is not changed has true being, pure being, genuine being." Hence, if God is called *ipsum esse* or simply *est,* because he is eternal and immutable, then *essentia* too, it would seem, must be a name or description proper to God that signifies the divine immutability, eternity, and selfsameness. Thus God is *ipsum esse* or is simply *est;* he is "to be itself" or is "is." In this sense "essence" seems to be a description that is proper to God, since *essentia* signifies immutability, self-sameness, and eternity.

In commenting on Psalms 134 and 101 in *en. Ps.* 134, 6 and *en. Ps.* 101, 2, 10, Augustine acknowledges the difficulty there is for the human mind to grasp the very being of God, *ipsum proprie esse.* Yet Augustine immediately adds, in the latter text, that human frailty should not give up all hope. For God goes on to say that he is the God of Abraham, Isaac, and Jacob. The latter expression tells us what God is on our account *(quid sim propter te);* the former tells us what God is with himself *(quid sim apud me).* And shortly thereafter (*en. Ps.* 101, 2, 14) he offers a similar contrast. For "with a greatness and excellence of wisdom," God said, "I am who I am." But "for our consolation" he went on to say that he was the God of Abraham, Isaac, and Jacob. And, according to Galatians 3:29, we are offspring of Abraham. We are servants, but "on our account our Lord took the form of a servant" (Phil 2:7); he died for us and gave us the example of the resurrection. "Therefore, we hope that we will come to those standing years in which days do not pass by with the sun's circuit, but there remains what is as it is, because that alone truly is." In commenting on Psalm 121:3 (*en. Ps.* 121, 6), Augustine notes that God no sooner has said that he is "Who Is" than he seems to change his name and says that he is the God of Abraham, Isaac, and Jacob. The first name is true, but we do not grasp it; the second is true, and we do grasp it. The first pertains to God; the second to us. Lest anyone should think, however, that only the former name belongs to God eternally, he adds that the latter name is his eternally, "not because Abraham is eternal, Isaac is eternal, and Jacob is eternal, but because God made them eternal afterward without end; for they had a beginning, but they will not have an end." Thus, though eternity is the very substance of God, we are called to share in that eternity. For Augustine adds, "In Abraham, Isaac. and Jacob, think of the whole church; think of the whole offspring of Israel, not merely of that which is from the flesh, but of that which is from faith."

We have seen that Augustine uses *substantia* and *essentia* in speaking of God in a fashion that would seem to indicate that he means to say that God is an Aristotelian substance, albeit an Aristotelian substance unlike any other. However, we have also seen that Augustine insists that God is not properly substance and that perhaps God alone is *essentia,* for he alone is immutable and eternal. And in still a more un-Aristotelian fashion, he links *essentia* with the name of God that God gave to Moses in Exodus 3:14—a name whose meaning takes on for Augustine all the Neoplatonic connotations of self-sameness, immutability, and eternity. Hence, it might seem that Augustine's claim that God is undoubtedly substance or essence borders on metaphysical schizophrenia.[29] For it seems to juxtapose rather than to blend Aristotelian and Neoplatonic concepts of substance or essence.

However, this combination of the Aristotelian and Platonic traditions is not a concoction original with Augustine. Rather in the *libri platonicorum* with which Augustine came into contact in the year before his baptism in Milan, he found ready-made this transformation of the Aristotelian *ousia* into the intelligible, immutable, and eternal being of the Neoplatonists. And to this he linked the *ego sum qui sum* of Exodus 3:14.

In a future study I hope to argue that *Ennead* 3, 7, "Eternity and Time"—upon which Augustine drew for *conf.* 11[30]—seems a most promising source for the Augustinian doctrine of God as immutable and being, that is, as *essentia*—or as he says in *vera rel.* 11, 22 and *civ. Dei* 12, 2—"summa essentia."[31]

---

29. James F. Anderson argues in *St. Augustine and Being,* 4–5, that, though Augustine was influenced in many ways by Neoplatonism, he was not a Neoplatonist in metaphysics. And, if one insists that to be a Neoplatonist in metaphysics, one must place God above being, then Augustine surely was not a Neoplatonist. I find Gilson's position more convincing. See his "Notes sur l'être."

30. See O'Connell, *St. Augustine's Confessions,* 139–144.

31. In *Saint Augustine et le Neó-Platonisme* (Paris, 1896; reprint Frankfurt am Main: Minerva, 1967), 74–81, L. Grandgeorge juxtaposes texts on God from Augustine with

EJUSDEM SUBSTANTIAE

We have seen that whatever is said of God with reference to himself, that is, nonrelatively, is said of God according to substance. We have also seen that Augustine's claim that God is without a doubt substance or essence seems to involve two claims that Augustine himself did not distinguish: First, that God is a substance, that is, that which exists in itself in some way. In this sense it would seem that God is an instance of the category of substance. Second, God is essence or *ipsum esse*. And in this sense *essentia* seems to be a proper description of God.

Augustine also uses "substance" in a third set of expressions in speaking about God. He claims that the Father, the Son, and the Holy Spirit are "of the same substance," or are "of one and the same substance," or are "one substance, three persons."[32] He clearly understands these expressions as translations of the Greek word *homoousion* from the Nicene Creed.[33] In this paper we cannot deal at length with Augustine's language regarding the Trinity. However, since Durrant has argued that Augustine's use of such formulae is nonsensical and since he rests his case upon *Trin.* 5, 8, 9, it would seem to be within the scope of this paper to examine Durrant's claim. In the text in question, Augustine says, "And the force of 'of the same substance' in the Father, the Son, and the Holy Spirit is that whatever is said of each of them with respect to themselves is to be taken, not in the plural in sum, but in the singular. For though the Father is God, the Son is God, and the Holy Spirit is God—which no one doubts is said according to substance—yet we do not say that the supreme Trinity is itself three gods, but one God."[34]

---

parallel texts from the *Enneads*. He concludes somewhat too facilely, "En un mot, Dieu est pour Plotin, ce qu' il est pour saint Augustin, une pure essence."

32. See *Trin.* 5, 8, 9; *c. Max.* 2, 14, 3; *Trin.* 7, 4, 7.

33. See *c. Max.* 2, 14, 3.

34. This translation is mine and differs from Durrant's at several points that are important. First, he translates *vis* as "effect," i.e., "the effect of the same substance and Holy Spirit." *Vis* can mean "power," "force" or "significance," but I know of no translating it as "effect." Second, the Latin is at least open to my translation, according to which the text is speaking of the significance of the expression *ejusdem substantiae*, though it could grammatically refer to the power or force of the divine substance. Third, Durrant (127) translates *dici secundum substantiam* as "to be said with respect to second substance." And that is simply a mistake.

Augustine does not use—to the best of my knowledge—the expression, "second substance." Perhaps he does not use the expression for a good reason, for a "second sub-

The point that Augustine is making in this text is that the expression *ejusdem substantiae* in the case of the three persons of the Trinity signifies not merely specific identity, but numerical identity. In *Trin* 7, 6, 11, Augustine uses *ejusdem naturae* of Abraham, Isaac, and Jacob. Since Abraham is a man, Isaac is a man, and Jacob is a man, the three are "of the same nature" or "of the same substance." There is a nonproblematic use of "of the same substance" in speaking of three individuals who share the same specific nature or substance. The text from *Trin.* 5, 8, 9 is not presenting the meaning of *ejusdem substantiae,* but is pointing out that its use with reference to God implies a different sort of sameness than does its use with reference to three men, dogs, or trees.

We have seen in the first part of this article that Augustine claims that whatever is said of God *ad se,* that is, with reference to himself, is said according to substance, that is, signifies or designates the substance of God. That is, since there are no accidents in the being of God, whatever might seem to be said of him according to accident must be understood to be said of him according to substance. Hence, if one says that the Father is wise, the Son is wise, and the Holy Spirit is wise, the force of the expression "of the same substance" is that there are not three wise gods, but one wise God.[35]

In commenting on Psalm 68, Augustine asks what "of one substance" means. He answers with an example, namely, that, if the Father is gold, the Son too is gold, and the Holy Spirit is also. He formulates this idea in a general rule: "Whatever the Father is because he is God, this the Son is, this the Holy Spirit is" (*en. Ps.* 68, 5).

On the other hand, when God is said to be Father or Son, he is not said to be Father or Son according to substance. Rather God is said to be Father with respect to the Son, just as he is said to be Son with respect to the Father. With reference to himself, however, he is said to

---

stance" term after all signifies the nature or essence that finite individuals share. Yet in God there are not three individuals who share the divine substance or nature, as Abraham, Isaac, and Jacob are three individuals who share the same nature or essence. Indeed, the point of the text we are examining is precisely that there are not three gods, but one God.

35. Durrant's insistence (143) that one must be able to complete "of the same substance" with "namely, _____," where the blank is filled in with an appropriate second substance predicate, overlooks or ignores Augustine's claim that whatever is said of God *ad se* signifies the substance of God and that adjectives, such as "good" and "wise," signify the divine substance just as much as do nouns, such as "spirit" (*Trin.* 15, 5, 8).

be God. Therefore, by that by which he is substance, he is God. And because the Son is of the same substance, the Son is surely God. Moreover, Augustine tells us that if one asks what the Father is, the answer is that he is God, and that if one asks what the Son is the answer is God. But if one asks what is the Father and the Son, the answer is God, not gods. He realizes that such is not the case with Abraham and Isaac. Though Abraham is a man and Isaac is a man, Abraham and Isaac are not a man, but men. In God "there is so great a unity of substance that there is equality, but not plurality" (ibid.). That is, in God sameness of substance involves not merely specific sameness or identity but numerical identity.

There are a number of points worth noting about this text commenting on Psalm 68. First, Augustine distinguishes *ejusdem substantiae* and *unius substantiae*. Abraham and Isaac are said to be "of the same substance" because each of them is a man. The Father and the Son, however, merely "of the same substance," but are "of one substance," for they are not gods, but God. At least in this text *unius substantiae* implies numerical identity of substance; whereas, *ejusdem substantiae* need not imply any more than equality with plurality, that is, specific identity. Second, the above distinction means that "of the same substance" in the sense of specific identity has a legitimate and, I believe, nonproblematic use with regard to individual things in the world that are members of the same species.[36] If Tom, Dick, and Harry are each a man, then they are "of the same substance," though the force of the expression "of the same substance" is not such that Tom, Dick, and Harry are not three men, but one man. Hence, what Augustine says in *Trin.* 5, 8, 9 about the force of "of the same substance" must be understood as signifying in the case of the Trinity "equality, without plurality," or numerical, not merely specific, identity.

Third, since nothing is said of God according to accident, any pred-

---

36. In *an. et or.* 4, 13, 19, Augustine uses *unius substantiae* to mean sameness of nature and uses the expression apart from any Trinitarian theology. He writes to Vicentius Victor, who claimed that the soul is not spirit, but body. Victor based his argument on the distinct mention of spirit along with soul and body in 1 Thes 5:23. Augustine responds: "If, however, you claim that the soul is a body although body was mentioned distinctly, allow that it is also spirit, though spirit was mentioned distinctly. For the soul ought to seem to you to be spirit much more than body, since you admit that spirit and soul are of one substance. Therefore, how is the soul body, where there is a diverse nature of it and body, and how is the soul not spirit, since it and spirit have one and the same nature?"

ication about God that might seem to signify a quality in God must be understood to signify his substance. Hence, "omnipotent," "wise," or "good" must be understood to signify the substance of God, not qualities of God. Hence, if the Father is omnipotent and wise and good, the Son too is omnipotent and wise and good. However, there are not three omnipotent, wise, and good gods, but one. Finally, Augustine seems to provide a rule for predication about the three persons that provides a definition of *ejusdem substantiae,* for he says "Whatever the Father is because he is God, this the Son is, this the Holy Spirit is." And he goes on to indicate that in the Trinity the force of that expression is such that there are not three gods, but one God.

CONCLUSION

In this article I have examined Augustine's use of *substantia* in speaking of God. We have seen that his use of *substantia* with respect to God falls into three sets of expressions. First, whatever is said of God *ad se,* that is, with respect to himself and not relatively, is said of God according to substance, that is, signifies the substance of God. Second, God is substance or essence. We have seen that, despite Augustine's seeming to equate the two expressions and to take them in an Aristotelian sense, he clearly prefers *essentia* to *substantia.* It seems highly likely that his facile movement from an Aristotelian *ousia* to a Neoplatonic immutable and selfsame *Ipsum esse* was facilitated by his coming into contact with the Aristotelian categories for the second time through the works of Porphyry. After all, as early as the *c. Acad.* he is able to suppose that the doctrines of Plato and Aristotle were really the same and to suggest that Plotinus seems a reincarnation of Plato.[37] Finally, we turned to the Trin-

37. In *c. Acad.* 3, 19, 42, Augustine says, "[T]here have been acute and clever men who taught in their disputations that Aristotle and Plato in such wise agree with one another that those who are unskilled or examine the matter cursorily think they disagree." The translation is John O'Meara from *Against the Academics,* 149. That Plato and Aristotle taught the same doctrine was apparently a commonplace among Neoplatonists, and O'Meara even cites a title of a lost work of Porphyry's on the oneness of the doctrine of Plato and Aristotle; see 161. "Not long after this ... Plato's doctrine, which in philosophy is the purest and most clear ... shone forth especially in Plotinus. This Platonic philosopher is regarded as being so like Plato, that one would think that they lived at the same time. The interval of time between them is, however, so great that one should rather think that Plato had come to life again in Plotinus" (*c. Acad.* 3, 18, 41; O'Meara, *Against the Academics,* 148).

itarian usage of *ejusdem substantiae* and saw that the expression has perfectly legitimate usage with regard to individuals in the world that are specifically the same. However, in the case of the Trinity the expression has the stronger sense of "equality without plurality," or of not merely specific, but numerical, sameness. Though the Trinity is certainly such that "our thought . . . feels itself unequal to that of which it thinks and does not grasp it as it is," nonetheless, what Augustine says in speaking about God certainly falls far short of nonsense (*Trin.* 5, 1, 1).

7

DIVINE IMMUTABILITY IN AUGUSTINE

Divine immutability is one of the hallmarks of classical theism; yet the idea of an immutable God has often met with resistance from Christian thinkers who find that such a God is religiously unavailable. In the present article I examine what Augustine meant by divine immutability and his grounds for holding that God was immutable. I also argue that at least some objections to divine immutability can be met and that there are good reasons for maintaining such a doctrine. In it, as in several other articles, I referred to Augustine's materialism prior to his discovery of the books of the Platonists, but I would have done better to refer to his corporealism, which he held in common with both the Stoics and the Manichees. For even after his conversion, Augustine maintained that matter is the principle of mutability and is found in everything except God. I also said that Augustine "mistakenly" thought that Manichaeism was a Christian heresy. Scholarly opinion has now, however, come to agree with Augustine and no longer views Manichaeism as a distinct world religion.

The immutability of God has in recent years come under discussion for a number of reasons. It has seemed to some that an immutable God cannot be genuinely concerned about and involved with his creatures.[1] It has seemed to others that God's eternal and

---

1. In "A New Look at the Immutability of God," in *God Knowable and Unknowable*, edited by Robert J. Roth, S.J. (New York: Fordham University Press,

immutable knowledge destroys human freedom.[2] This article does not aim directly at settling such questions; rather its aim is to examine Augustine's reasons for insisting upon the absolute immutability of God's being.[3] Generally the doctrine of divine immutability is thought to stem from Platonism, and it is sometimes regarded as a philosophical accretion that is not at all essential to the Judaeo-Christian concept of God.[4] I shall argue that there are good reasons for believing that Augustine's position regarding divine immutability is as much the result of his dissatisfaction with Manichaeism as the result of his contact with Neoplatonism.[5] Of

---

1973), 43–72, W. Norris Clarke, S.J., says that the traditional or Thomistic position is challenged from two sources: "process philosophy, in terms of the speculative exigencies of its own metaphysics of reality, and existential religious consciousness." Of the two Father Clarke finds the objections from the second source of much more concern.

2. Robert Ayers, for example, argues along such lines in "A Viable Theodicy for Christian Apologetics," *The Modern Schoolman* 52 (1975): 391–403, here 395. He maintains that "even a relative freedom of man cannot be maintained. If God knows with absolute certainty the totality of one's existence from eternity, then his life is complete before he himself has actualized it in time." See Richard Swinburne, *The Coherence of Theism* (Oxford: Clarendon Press, 1977), 175–76, for an attempt to limit God's knowledge to the past and present. For an attempt to deal with this sort of challenge to classical theism, see "Omniscience, Omnipotence, and Divine Transcendence," *New Scholasticism* 53 (1979): 277–294, where I draw heavily upon Bernard Lonergan's writings in order to locate the mystery where, I believe, it belongs, namely, in God's eternity.

3. One of the tasks of this article will be to unpack what Augustine means by the immutability in God. However, the topic of immutability runs through so much of Augustine's treatment of God that I shall have to limit my discussion in this article to the immutability of God's being or essence and leave for another time an investigation of God's immutable knowledge and will. Nonetheless, God's essence, knowledge, and willing are one and the same immutable reality. "Nam sicut omnino tu es, tu scis solus, qui es incommutabiliter, et scis incommutabiliter, et vis incommutabiliter. Et essentia tua scit et vult incommutabiliter, et scientia tua est et vult incommutabiliter, et voluntas tua est et scit incommutabiliter" (*conf.* 13, 16, 19). Despite all of his emphasis upon divine immutability, one could hardly maintain that the God of the *conf.* is a religiously unavailable metaphysical abstraction. Augustine's use of imagery makes his God much more humanly approachable than his theory might seem to allow. Here, as in so many areas, Augustine eludes facile categorization. For the importance of imagery in Augustine and in metaphysics generally, see O'Connell, *Imagination and Metaphysics*.

4. For example, in *Aquinas to Whitehead: Seven Centuries of Metaphysics of Religion* (Milwaukee: Marquette University Press, 1976), Charles Hartshorne traces divine immutability to Plato and argues for growth in God's knowledge. Though Hartshorne does not say so in this lecture, I recall him telling a group of faculty later that his God was, of course, not a creator in the traditional sense—a point that, one would think, should give pause to some Catholic process thinkers.

5. In *Aquinas to Whitehead,* Hartshorne traces process thought with regard to God's knowledge back to the Socinians, who were concerned with defending human freedom against the harsher versions of the Calvinist doctrine of predestination. Though the Manichees were not a Christian sect, Augustine thought that they were. And though

course, if this suggestion has merit, there are implications for the direction that contemporary discussion of the issue might take.

THE MEANING AND SCOPE OF DIVINE IMMUTABILITY

Before examining how and why Augustine came to hold that God is immutable, it is necessary to clarify what he means by the term "immutable." First of all, "immutable," as a negation or denial of change, is an element of negative or apophatic theology. For Augustine's God is better known by not knowing.[6] Moreover, the term excludes from God not merely the fact of change, but the possibility of change.[7] Third, the Latin verb *mutari* literally means "to be changed." Though the force

---

they are perhaps less desirable intellectual ancestors, they did, nonetheless, admit change in the divine nature long before Laelius and Faustus Socinus. Augustine, of course, was convinced that God's immutability was found in the Scriptures and was a matter of faith. In *nat. b.*, 24, Augustine cites against the Manichees texts from both Testaments: "Mutabis ea, et mutabuntur; tu autem idem ipse es" (Ps 101:27–28); "In se ipsa manens innovat omnia" (Ws 7:27); Paul refers to God as "invisibili incorruptibili soli Deo" (1 Tim 1:17); and James says, "Omne datum optimum et omne donum perfectum desursum est descendens a patre luminum, apud quem non est commutatio nec momenti obscuratio" (Jas 1:17). Augustine sees this doctrine as a matter of faith that can nonetheless be known apart from faith. He tells us that those who have less capacious intellects and cannot grasp this doctrine should believe the divine authority and thus merit to understand. However, he warns that those who understand this matter without having been instructed in the Scriptures should not think that he has merely drawn this doctrine from his own mind and that it is not contained in Scripture (see *nat. b.*, 24).

6. See *ord.* 2, 16, 44. That is, God is better known by our knowing what he is not. Or at least knowing what God is not is a major step forward in knowing God. "Nunc si non potestis comprehendere quid sit Deus, vel hoc comprehendite quod non sit Deus; multum profeceritis, si non aliud quam est, de Deo senseritis. Nondum potes pervenire ad quid sit, perveni ad quid non sit" (*Jo. Eu. tr.* 23, 9). Or, as he puts it elsewhere: "Quod enim, sicuti est, cogitare non possumus, utique nescimus, sed quicquid cogitanti occurrerit abicimus, respuimus, improbamus, non hoc esse quod quaerimus novimus, quamvis illud nondum, quale sit, noverimus" (*ep.* 130, 14, 27). To this Augustine adds, "Est ergo in nobis quaedam, ut ita dicam, docta ignorantia, sed docta spiritu Dei qui adiuvat infirmitatem nostram" (ibid. 130, 15, 28). See Vladimir Lossky, "Les elements de 'Théologie négative' dans la pensée de saint Augustin," in *Augustinus magister* (Paris: Études augustiniennes, 1954), 1:575–581, where the author argues that Nicholas of Cusa derived the expression "docta ignorantia," from Augustine rather than Pseudo-Dionysius. Translations from Augustine are my own, except for the *conf.,* where I have used John K. Ryan's translation, though at times with modifications (Garden City, N.Y.: Image Books, 1960).

7. Augustine makes this point explicitly: "Aliud est enim non mutari cum possit mutari, aliud autem prorsus non posse mutari" (*nat. b.* 39). See also *Trin.* 5, 2, 3: "Quod enim mutatur, non servat ipsum esse; et quod mutari potest, etiamsi non mutetur, potest quod fuerat non esse, ac per hoc solum quod non tantum non mutatur, verum etiam mutari omnino non potest, sine scrupulo occurrit quod verissime dicatur esse."

of the passive voice is often lost in the English translation, the Latin means that God cannot be acted upon or modified by some thing else. He is, after all, "changing everything, while remaining unchangeable," and he "makes changeable things without any change of himself and is acted upon in no way."[8] In the latter text Augustine is dealing with the Aristotelian categories of *actio* and *passio*. He explicitly excludes from God any *passio*, or being acted upon, though he goes on to say that perhaps God alone can be truly said to make *(facere)*. "In the case of making perhaps it is said truly of God alone, for God alone makes and is not made *(facit, et ipse non fit)* and is not acted upon in his substance by which he is God."[9] Hence, it is, first of all, passivity that is ruled out by immutability. Augustine says, "We are not permitted to believe that God is affected in one way when he rests and in another way when he works, since he must not be said to be affected, as if something comes to be in his nature that was not previously there. For one who is affected is acted upon, as everything that undergoes something is mutable" (*civ. Dei* 12, 17). God cannot be changed or acted upon or undergo anything, though he can certainly change and act upon and make things. Indeed, perhaps he alone can be truly said to act.[10]

When Augustine speaks of God's immutability, he frequently adds other terms, such as incorruptible and inviolable—much stronger terms that clearly emphasize that God cannot be acted upon, be corrupted, or suffer violence.[11] However, though "everything that undergoes something is mutable," it need not follow that everything mutable undergoes something. That is, could there not be a change that does not involve being acted upon or undergoing something, such as a mere increase in

---

8. "Immutabilis, mutans omnia" (*conf.* 1, 4, 4); "sine ulla sui mutatione mutabilia facientem, nihilque patientem" (*Trin.* 5, 1, 2). As early as that difficult work, *imm. an.* 3, 3–4, Augustine is struggling with the problem of a cause of changing things, which itself remains unchanged.

9. "Quod autem ad faciendum attinet, fortassis de solo Deo verissime dicatur; solus enim Deus facit et ipse non fit, neque patitur quantum ad ejus substantiam pertinet qua Deus est" (*Trin.* 5, 8, 9).

10. If God alone could be truly said to act, then of course nothing else could act upon him, simply because nothing else could truly act. There are moments when Augustine seems to verge upon such a pantheistic denial of all created causality. In commenting on *conf.* 13, 31, 46, O'Connell says in *St. Augustine's Confessions*, 178, "Here our human agency seems to have vanished altogether. God has become the only actor on the scene." However, Augustine generally steers well clear of such a position.

11. See *conf.* 7, 1, 1.

perfection without any loss or passivity? It seems clear that for Augustine even such change in God is ruled out.

Besides such texts that rule out any form of passivity from the divine substance, there are other texts that exclude any addition or development or betterment from God. Thus in *Jo. ev. tr.*, in comparing the soul's life with God's life, Augustine says, "God neither increases nor decreases, but is ever in himself and is as he is—not now one way, later another, and before still another."[12] And in other texts he insists that God's knowledge and will are immutable, though God knows and wills mutable things.[13] There is, furthermore, another series of texts in which Augustine rules out any literal signification of predicates that might seem to attribute emotions or change of mind to God.[14] Finally, there is still another cluster of texts in which immutability clearly is tied to the Neoplatonic themes of true being, selfsameness, and eternity.[15] For all temporal things are mutable, and God alone who truly is, is not distended in time. In him there is no "was" and no "will be," but only "is."[16] We shall return to some of these aspects of immutability in the final section of this article.

12. *Jo. ev. tr.* 19, 11; see also *Trin.* 5, 4, 5.
13. See *civ. Dei* 11, 21; *conf.* 12, 15, 18.
14. For example, "Ubi legitur quod paeniteat eum, mutatio rerum significatur, immutabili praescientia manente divina" (*civ. Dei* 17, 7, 3), or, "Cum Deus irasci dicitur, non eius significatur perturbatio, qualis est in animo irascentis hominis, sed ex humanis motibus translato vocabulo, vindicta eius, quae non nisi justa est, irae nomen accepit" (*ench.* 33, 10).
15. Speaking of the name that God revealed to Moses, Augustine says, "Esse, nomen est incommutabilitatis. Omnia enim quae mutantur, desinunt esse quod erant, et incipiunt esse quod non erant. Esse verum, esse sincerum, esse germanum, non habet nisi qui non mutatur" (*s.* 7, 7). "Quod incommutabile est, aeternum est; semper enim eiusmodi est. Quod autem commutabile est tempori obnoxium est: non enim semper eiusdem modi est, et ideo aeternum non recte dicitur. Quod enim mutatur, non manet: quod non manet, non est aeternum" (*div. quaes.* 19). "Est enim, et vere est, et eo ipso quod vere est, sine initio et sine termino est" (*en. Ps.* 134, 6).
16. "Si enim recte discernuntur aeternitas et tempus, quod tempus sine aliqua mobili mutabilitate non est, in aeternitate autem nulla mutatio est; quis non videat quod tempora non fuissent, nisi creatura fieret, quae aliquid aliqua motione mutaret" (*civ. Dei* 11, 6). "Non tempore augetur, aut loco distenditur, aut aliqua materia concluditur aut terminatur, sed manet apud se et in se ipso plena et perfecta aeternitas, quam nec comprehendere humana cogitatio potest, nec lingua narrare" (*s.* 225, 2). "Praeteritum et futurum invenio in omni motu rerum: in veritate quae manet, praeteritum et futurum non invenio, sed solum praesens, et hoc incorruptibiliter, quod in creatura non est. Discute rerum mutationes, invenies Fuit et Erit: cogita Deum, invenies Est, ubi Fuit et Erit esse non possit" (*Jo. Ev. tr.* 38, 10).

For the moment, however, it is important to distinguish two sorts of change. There is a first sort of change, in which something is intrinsically modified; there is another sort of change by extrinsic denomination, where something new is said of something without that thing being intrinsically changed.[17] Divine immutability does not mean that we cannot truly say new things about God. That something new begins to be truly said of God need not entail a change in God's substance, since the newness can be on the part of some creature with respect to which God is said to begin to be something. Augustine explicitly allows for the fact that some predicates begin to be said of God in time, not because God begins to be in a new way, but because of a change in some creature with respect to which God is said to be.[18] Thus, God came to be the Lord of Israel, only when that patriarch came to be. Unless one keeps this distinction in mind and realizes that language is not a perfect mirror of being, much of what Augustine has to say about God will be simply unintelligible.

IMMUTABILITY IN THE *CONFESSIONS*

Before looking at arguments Augustine uses to establish the immutability of God, let us look at his account, especially in the *conf.*, of how he came to realize that God is immutable. In the opening paragraphs of

---

17. Peter Geach has described the two sorts of change in *Logic Matters* (Berkeley and Los Angeles: University of California Press, 1972), 321ff., and *God and the Soul* (London: Routledge and Kegan Paul, 1969), pp. 71f. His example of "Cambridge change" is Socrates' becoming shorter than Theatetus as the latter grows up; there is no real change in Socrates, despite the fact that he has different predicates at different times. Some contemporary authors seem to think that everything said of God is a property of God, such that temporal predicates of God necessarily mean that he is in time and that he changes. Such a position simply denies that anything is said of God—and presumably of anything else—by extrinsic denomination. Or, in other words, such a position fails to distinguish between being that is divided into the ten categories and being that is signified by true propositions. See Richard LaCroix's two articles that make this mistake: "Augustine on the Simplicity of God," *New Scholasticism* 51 (1977): 453–469 and "Aquinas on God's Omnipresence and Timelessness," *Philosophy and Phenomenological Research* 42 (1982): 391–399.

18. In *Trin.* 5, 16, 17, Augustine says, "Quod ergo temporaliter dici incipit Deus quod antea non dicebatur, manifestum est relative dici: non tamen secundum accidens Dei quod ei aliquid acciderit, sed plane secundum accidens eius ad quod dici aliquid Deus incipit relative." See my attempt to unpack the meaning of that claim in "Properties of God and the Predicaments in *De Trinitate* V," *The Modern Schoolman* 59 (1981): 1–19.

book 1 Augustine addresses God with a long list of paradoxical expressions: "most hidden and most present, most fair and most strong, most stable and most ungraspable, unchangeable and changing all things, never new and never old" (*conf.* 1, 1, 1). Though he does not explicitly deal with God's immutability until book 4, he says some things that are pertinent to this topic in book 3, where he speaks of his encounter with the *Hortensius* of Cicero, his recourse to the Scriptures, and his entering the ranks of the Manichees.

In some sense these three constitute a "conversion"—and indeed a turning toward the better.[19] In order to understand his later conversion in 386–387, it is essential to understand what had happened thirteen or fourteen years earlier in 373, when he began to burn with the love of wisdom as the result of reading Cicero.[20] For, though he was aflame with love of wisdom, he could not find satisfaction with Cicero's work or that of other philosophers—for the name of Christ was not present there.[21] Because he desired wisdom with the name of Christ he turned to the Scriptures, but there he met with—he thought—an anthropomorphism and a moral degeneracy that led him to look elsewhere for wisdom.[22] And the Manichees promised a wisdom in which the name of Christ was present and which avoided the grossness of the reading of Scripture

---

19. See Masai, "Les conversions de saint Augustin," 5–10, on his conversion to Manichaeism shortly after reading the *Hortensius*. See also Le Blond, *Les conversions de saint Augustin*.

20. The point is that any conversion is a change from one state to another. To understand its significance one has to know the *terminus a quo* and the *terminus ad quem*. In this case one has to know what Augustine was or thought he was in the years prior to 386–387 in order to know what he became in 386–387. Following Masai's suggestion, I am inclined to hold that he always thought of himself as a Christian and perhaps even as a catechumen in the *Catholica*. Thus, Masai agrees, though only verbally, with the infamous line of Prosper Alfaric that "moralement comme intellectuellement c'est au Néoplatonisme qu'il s'est converti, plutôt qu' à l'Evangile"; Masai, "Les conversions de saint Augustin," 11; quoted from Prosper Alfaric, *L'évolution intellectuelle de saint Augustin* (Paris: E. Nourry, 1918), 399.

21. "Hoc solum me in tanta flagrantia refrangebat quod nomen Christi non erat ibi.... et quidquid sine hoc nomine fuisset, quamvis literatum et expolitum et veridicum, non me totum rapiebat" (*conf.* 3, 4, 8).

22. Apart from the matter of literary style, there seem to have been at least two sorts of difficulties that Augustine encountered in the Scriptures. The one was theoretical and concerned an anthropomorphism stemming from the Genesis statement that man is made in God's image. The other was moral and stemmed from his somewhat prudish reaction to the behavior of the Patriarchs. See Brown, *Augustine of Hippo*, 50.

that Augustine found in the *Catholica*. Hence, he unwisely—it turned out—sought wisdom in what he regarded as a Christian sect.[23]

There are a number of things about this conversion that, I believe, are important for our purposes. First, in embracing Manichaeism Augustine thought he was choosing the most intelligent way to be a Christian. He had resolved to seek wisdom, but not a wisdom from which the name of Christ was absent, as we have seen. Second, this conversion seems to have been precipitated by what he later referred to as the *superstitio* that he found in the *Catholica*. This point seems well established with reference to the "yoke" of faith, but it seems quite plausible that the term referred to the whole anti-intellectual tone of the African Church.[24] After all, without a concept of God and the soul as spiritual substances, the African Church, it would seem, could offer only an anthropomorphic interpretation of the scriptural claim that man was made in the image of God.[25] Surely, within such an atmosphere the questioning mind of Augustine suffered under the yoke of authority.[26] Not every Christian finds comfort in Tertullian's "credo quia absurdum"; yet he remained the dominant intellect of the African Church.[27]

---

23. Masai provides a number of texts from Augustine that reveal that his judgment that the Manichees were a Christian sect was quite reasonable. See Masai, "Les conversions de saint Augustin," 5–10, as well as *util. cred.* 16, 30; *conf.* 3, 3; and *c. Faust.* 20, 2–3.

24. Augustine uses the term *superstitio* on several occasions. He tells us in *b. vita* 1, 4, that "superstitio quaedam puerilis" deterred him from critical investigation. O'Connell says in *Early Theory,* 231, "The superstition he refers to ... is ... not Manichaeism, but the sort of intransigent, obscurantist Catholicism he had experienced as a youth." So too in *util. cred.* 1. 2, Augustine explains that he and his friends would never have fallen in with the Manichees, "nisi quod nos superstitione terreri et fidem nobis ante rationem imperari dicerent." Hence, he and his friends spurned the old wives' tales *(aniles fabulas)*. So too *ord.* 1, 8, 23, where superstition is linked with Monica's piety. See also Alfaric, *L'évolution intellectuelle,* 70.

25. See Verbeke, *L'évolution de la doctrine,* and Masai, "Les conversions de saint Augustin," for substantiation of the view that prior to Augustine (and, of course, the Neoplatonic group in Milan) the Western Church was simply without a concept of God as a spiritual substance.

26. His latter reluctance to respond to the Manichees' question about what God was doing before he made the world with the derisory reply that he was making hell for those who ask such questions may very well indicate both the sort of answer all too often given in the African Church and Augustine's dissatisfaction with such a handling of substantive questions. See *conf.* 11, 12, 14. After all, his own flight to Manichaeism was also a flight from "a certain childish superstition," which he encountered in the Church in Africa and which deterred him from critical investigation (*b. vita* 1, 4).

27. Tertullian did not use these precise words, though what he did say comes very close to them. In *De carne Christi* 5, he says, "Natus est Dei Filius; non pudet, quia

Finally, a corporeal being is, inevitably, subject to change. Indeed, as we shall see, it is God's simplicity that accounts for his utter immutability; yet no bodies are or can be simple.[28]

The topic of immutability is once again raised late in book 4, where Augustine points to the source of his intellectual difficulties and explains how at the age of twenty he understood on his own Aristotle's *Categories,* but mistakenly thought that God, whom he now knows to be "marvelously simple and immutable," was subject to his greatness or beauty so that they were in God as in a subject, just as greatness and beauty are in bodies. For God is his greatness and his beauty, whereas, a body is not great or beautiful by being a body, for it would still be a body even if it were smaller or less beautiful. Augustine then thought that everything was comprehended by the Aristotelian categories and thought of God as subject to accidents, as a body, and as changeable or mutable.[29] And in the following years as a Manichee, Augustine held that God was a bodily being that was extended infinitely on all sides except on the side where he was limited by the evil substance.[30] God was also, for Augustine the Manichee, subject to change and was indeed attacked, injured, and even corrupted in his substance.[31]

---

pudendum est: et mortuus est Dei Filius; prorsus credibile est, quia ineptum est: et sepultus, resurrexit; certum est, quia impossibile." Gilson points out the *ineptum* really does mean "absurd," but then softens the sense. Actually the last part of the sentence makes the strongest point. See Etienne Gilson, *History of Christian Philosophy in the Middle Ages* (New York: Random House, 1955), 45.

28. "Ac per hoc multiplex esse convincitur natura corporis, simplex autem nullo modo" (*Trin.* 6, 6, 8).

29. See *conf.* 4, 16, 28.

30. *Conf.* 5, 10, 20. See *c. ep. Man.* 21, 23, where Augustine uses an image of a cross-shaped loaf of bread to describe the Manichaean God: "Tamquam si unus panis—sic enim, quod dicitur, facilius videri potest—in quadras quattuor decussatim formetur, in quibus tres sunt candidae, una nigra; modo de tribus candidis tolle distinctionem et fac illas et sursum versus et deorsum versus et undique retro infinitas: sic ab eis esse creditur terra lucis. Illam vero nigram quadram fac deorsum versus et retro infinitam, supra se autem immensam inanitatem habere: sic opinantur esse terram tenebrarum."

31. Peter Brown points out that what Augustine continued to find intolerable in the Manichaean position was the passivity of the good. He points out how Augustine the bishop drives home this point against Fortunatus; see Brown, *Augustine of Hippo,* 51–53, where he refers to *c. Fort.* 33–37, as well as *c. Jul. imp.* 1, 97. In *c. ep. Man.* 21, 24, he uses language with a sexual ring to describe the masculine aggressivity of the evil principle as compared to the feminine passivity of the good: "Quam deinde melior ipsius terrae tenebrarum figura ostenditur, si quidem illa findit, haec finditur; illa inseritur, haec interpatet. . . . Maluerunt penetrari terram lucis quam penetrare."

Later at Rome, as Augustine became more and more disillusioned with the myths of the Manichees, he was drawn to skepticism and regarded the Academic philosophers as wiser than the rest. Though he lived with a Manichaean and found his closest friends among them, he was no longer a defender of the Manichaean doctrine with anything like his former ardor and even restrained his host from his beliefs in the myths contained in their books. He tells us that he also despaired of finding the truth within the Church, and he goes on to explain—while addressing God—the grounds for this despair. "To me it seemed a most base thing to believe that you have the shape of our human flesh and are bounded by the outward lines of our members" (*conf.* 5, 10, 19). Augustine clearly believed that the *Catholica* taught that God had the shape of a human body. Only later under the influence of Ambrose in Milan did Augustine begin to realize that the "spirituals" in the Church did not think of God anthropomorphically. In his earliest work, Augustine paints for us the scene as he listens to Ambrose preach and it begins to dawn on him that when Ambrose speaks of God he is not thinking of a body: "For I noticed often in the sermons of our priest . . . that one should think of no body at all when one thinks of God or of the soul; for that is the one thing closest to God" (*b. vita* 1, 4). Hence, he was filled with joy to find "that 'man was made in your image' was understood by your spiritual sons, whom you had regenerated by grace in our Catholic Mother, not as though they believed and thought of you as limited by the shape of the human body—although what a spiritual substance would be like I did not surmise even in a weak and obscure manner—I blushed joyfully because I had barked for so many years, not against the Catholic faith, but against the fantasies of a carnal imagination" (*conf.* 6, 3, 4). It is not everyone, but only the "spirituals" in the Church who have this nonbodily understanding of God. Among the "spiritual sons" of the Church there were, it seems, such Neoplatonic Christians as Ambrose, Victorinus, and Simplicianus.[32]

In the opening lines of book 7, Augustine recounts his intellectual state in 385 at the age of thirty-one, that is, about a year before his conversion. He tells us that he "could conceive of no substantial being except

---

32. In "Spirituals and Spiritual Interpretation in St. Augustine," *AS* 15 (1984): 65–81, I argue that the "spirituals" in the Church are precisely those who were able to rise to a spiritual understanding of God and the soul.

such as those that I was wont to see with my own eyes" (*conf.* 7, 1, 1). However, he congratulates himself on the fact that from the time he was first acquainted with philosophy, he did not think of God as "being in the shape of a human body."[33] He rejoices that the *Catholica* does not hold the anthropomorphic view he once believed that it held.[34] Indeed, later in disputing with the Manichees, he admits that there are some "little ones" in the Church who think of God as having a human shape, though he admits that no Manichee holds such a view.[35]

---

33. The time when he first began to learn of wisdom would seem to be when at the age of 19 he read the *Hortensius*, a lost work of Cicero, which marked a turning point in Augustine's life. He tells us, "Et surgere iam coeperam, ut ad te redirem. . . . Amor autem sapientiae, nomen graecum habet philosophiam, quo me accendebant illae litterae" (*conf.* 3, 4, 7–8).

34. In *b. vita* 1, 4, Augustine tells us that, as he listened to Ambrose preach, "animadverti enim et saepe in sacerdotis notri . . . sermonibus . . . cum de deo cogitaretur, nihil omnino corporis esse cogitandum, neque cum de anima; nam id est unum in rebus proximum Deo." His surprise and bewilderment echo through the centuries, for Augustine and the whole Church of the West seem to have been without a concept of God as a spiritual being. See Masai, "Les conversions de saint Augustin," 19n34: "La vérité est qu'avant Augustin, il est vain de chercher dans l'Afrique chrétienne un spiritualisme." It is hard for us to imagine the implicit materialism of the African Church, but Tertullian was still its master. And Augustine's plaintive cries about his inability to conceive a spiritual substance seem to echo his crisp formulae, such as, "Omne quod est, corpus est sui generis; nihil est incorporale, nisi quod non est" (*De carne Christi* 11) and "Nihil enim si non corpus" (*De anima* 7). See *conf.* 5, 10, 19: "Et quoniam cum de Deo meo cogitare vellem, cogitare nisi moles corporum non noveram, neque enim videbatur mihi esse quicquam, quod tale non esset," to which Augustine adds, "ea maxima, et prope sola causa erat inevitabilis erroris mei."

Given the materialism of the African Church, it is easy to see why Augustine was so vexed by man's being made in the image of God. In *conf.* 3, 7, 12 he tells us that he was "absolutely ignorant" of what in us makes us an image of God and according to what we are called images of God. Among the questions that troubled him were: "Is God confined within a corporeal form? Does he have hair and nails?" It is only from the perspective of a decade later that he is able to address God in terms of Neoplatonic omnipresence and see the solution in terms of the soul. "But you, most high and most near at hand, most secret and most present . . . who are everywhere whole and entire, who are never confined in place, and who surely are not in our corporeal shape, you have made man to your own image. And behold, from head to foot he is contained in space!" (*conf.* 6, 3, 4).

35. To us it might seem almost incredible that Augustine could have thought that the *Catholica* held such an anthropomorphic view of God. However, in *mor.* 1, 10, 17, Augustine admits that there are "pueri quidem . . . non tempore, sed virtute atque prudentia" who think of God with a human form and suppose that he is so: "humana forma Deum cogitent, atque ita se habere suspicentur." On the other hand, Augustine admits that among the Manichaeans "nemo quidem reperitur qui Dei substantiam humani corporis figuratione describat"—and he insists that no opinion is more abject than that. I

Augustine says of himself at that time, "I believed with all my soul that you are incorruptible, and inviolable, and immutable." He does not know what is the source of this conviction or how he has come by it, but he tells us, "I clearly saw and was certain that what can be corrupted is inferior to what cannot be corrupted, and what cannot be violated I unhesitatingly placed above what is violable, and what suffers no change I saw to be better than what can be changed" (*conf.* 7, 1, 1). Augustine says that he *saw* this truth; however, at that time he did not as yet understand that it was God's illumination of his mind that allowed him to see it and grasp it with certitude. Shortly thereafter he speaks of his discovery "that the incorruptible is better than the corruptible," which led him to affirm that God is incorruptible, for no soul can "conceive anything better than you [God], who are the supreme and best good" (*conf.* 7, 4, 6). Again he tells us that "it is of the utmost truth and certainty that the incorruptible is preferable to the corruptible." And he tells us that where he saw the preferability of the incorruptible to the corruptible, "there I ought to seek you," that is, within himself. Still later he continues to say that it was by faith that he knew God's "substance is unchangeable" (*conf.* 7, 7, 11), though he saw that the incorruptible is superior to the corruptible.

Hence, in the opening paragraphs of book 7 Augustine sees with certitude—we have here almost the prime analogate of divine illumination, though he does not as yet know it—that the immutable, inviolable, and incorruptible is better than the mutable, violable, and corruptible. However, at that same time he was still unable to conceive of anything but bodies. He could not but think of God "as something corporeal, existent in space and place, either infused into the world or even diffused outside the world throughout infinite space" (*conf.* 7, 1, 1).[36] Hence, though he

---

have argued that Augustine's use of the Pauline expressions *animales* or *carnales*, as opposed to *spirituales*, refers to those in the Church who cannot rise to an understanding of God as incorporeal; see my "Spirituals and Spiritual Interpretation," see note 32 above. See also Maurice Jourjon, "The Image of God according to Irenaeus," *Theology Digest* 32: (1985): 253–255, digested from "L'homme image de Dieu selon Irenée de Lyon," *Christus* 31:24 (1984): 501–508. The digest says that it is the whole man that is God's image, and notes, "Augustine would reject such a view because he would see it as making God to be like human beings existing with flesh and bones. . . ." Indeed!

36. The Stoic influence on this stage of Augustine's conception of God has been noted by O'Connell. See his *Early Theory,* 97–98. See also Verbeke, "Augustin et le stoicisme."

believed God was immutable, he could not conceive of God as nonspatial, for whatever he so conceived "seemed to me to be nothing, absolutely nothing, not even so much as an empty space" (*conf.* 7, 1, 1). He thought of God, he tells us, as "a great corporeal substance, existent everywhere throughout infinite space, which penetrates the whole worldmass, and spreads beyond it on every side throughout immense, limitless space" (*conf.* 7, 1, 2). Only later did he realize that on this theory a larger part of the world would have more of God and a smaller part less of God and that "an elephant's body would receive more of you [God] than would a sparrow's" (*conf.* 7, 1, 2). That is, Augustine had not yet come to the Neoplatonic grasp of a spiritual substance that is whole everywhere, such as he will find in the books of the Platonists (*conf.* 7, 9, 14). Yet before he knows where and how he knows it, that is, before he knows that he should seek God within and before he knows about the intelligible light in which the Truth is seen, he saw that the immutable is superior to the mutable, and that truth allows him definitively to reject Manichaeism.

Given this insight, he is able to confront the Manichees with a dilemma. Either the nation of darkness could do God some injury or it could not. If it could, then God would be violable, corruptible, and mutable—which Augustine sees cannot be. But if the nation of darkness could not do God any injury, then their whole myth of particles of light being captured in darkness is false. Hence, the Manichees must either acknowledge that God is violable or admit the falsity of their cosmic myth (*conf.* 7, 2, 3). But this means that Augustine saw that immutability was superior to mutability before he read the books of the Platonists, even though without them he could not conceive of a incorporeal and eternal being.[37] Hence, it seems that he saw the superiority of the immutable to the mutable prior to his direct contact with the books of the Platonists and prior to coming to the central insight of Platonism, namely, a concept of a spiritual substance, without which he could not conceive an immutable being.

---

37. See Masai, "Les Conversions de saint Augustine," 22–23: "Avec Verbeke, il faut admettre que chez Augustin l'évolution doctrinale de *pneuma* a atteint son terme; mais il convient d'ajouter que, de l'aveu même de l'évêque d'Hippone, jamais l'idée de l'immatérialité de l'esprit n'avait été soupçonnée par lui avant le contact avec les chrétiens plotinisants de l'église de Milan."

ARGUMENTS FOR DIVINE IMMUTABILITY

We have seen Augustine's account of how he came to hold that God is immutable. The opening paragraphs of *conf.* 7 indicate that he came to believe that God is immutable before he came into direct contact with the *libri Platonicorum* and before he was able to conceive of an incorporeal substance. He tells us that he believed that God was immutable because he clearly saw and was certain that the immutable was superior to the mutable. Since he believed that there is nothing superior to God, he concluded that God was immutable. Here the superiority of the immutable to the mutable seems to rest upon an immediate vision of the truth.[38] If, however, that is the case, then it would seem that there is no need or room for further argument. For either one sees such a truth or one doesn't.

On the other hand, there are other texts where Augustine presents arguments for the immutability of God as if it were a matter of mediate knowledge. How can this be? I believe the answer runs along the following lines. At the stage of his intellectual development described in the beginning of *conf.* 7, Augustine could not conceive a spiritual and incorruptible substance. For the ability to do so is something he owed to his contact with the books of Platonists.[39] For bodily substances are obviously all mutable; hence, without the concept of an incorporeal substance he could not conceive an immutable one. Thus, Augustine became certain of the fact that God is immutable before he could understand what an incorporeal and immutable substance was. Once he had read the books of the Platonists and had come to a grasp of God as incorporeal and immutable, he could offer reasons for holding that God is immutable and articulate what an immutable substance was.

---

38. Indeed, in *conf.* 7, 17, 23, in describing the mind's ascent to God, he says "erexit se ad intelligentiam suam et abduxit cogitationem a consuetudine . . . ut inveniret quo lumine aspergeretur, cum sine ulla dubitatione clamaret incommutabile praeferendum esse mutabili, unde nosset ipsum incommutabile . . . et pervenit ad id quod est in ictu trepidantis aspectus."

39. According to A. Solignac, the first influence of Ambrose's preaching upon Augustine would seem to date from the end of 384. See *conf.* 5, 14, 24–25. A. Solignac dates the second period of Ambrose's influence (*conf.* 6, 4, 6) late in 385; see Solignac's "Essai de Chronologie" in BA 13, 204–205. Nonetheless, Augustine was explicit that at this point he was still unable to conceive a spiritual substance, even though he had already noticed that Ambrose apparently did not think of a body when he spoke about God (See *b. vita* 1, 4).

There are a number of texts in which Augustine deals with God's immutability at some length. For example, in *civ. Dei,* Augustine explicitly gives God's simplicity as the ground for his immutability. In contrast with angelic creatures that can change and be deprived of their goodness, God is simple and immutable. "There is, therefore, but one good that is simple and for this reason immutable, namely, God. By this good all created goods have been created, but they are not simple and for this reason are mutable" (*civ. Dei* 11, 10, 1). The situation is, of course, further complicated by the fact that God is Father, Son, and Holy Spirit. Yet God's being a Trinity does not mean that he is not simple. Augustine explains that what is born of the simple good is equally simple and is the same as that *(et hoc est quod illud)* from which he is born.[40] The Father is someone other than the Son, but not something other than the Son *("alius" dixi, non "aliud")*. Each person of the Trinity is equally simple and equally immutable and eternal. "But [God's nature] is thus said to be simple, because it is what it has, except for what each person is said in relation to another. For the Father has a Son, but he is not the Son. In that which he is said to be with reference to himself and not to another, he is that which he has. Thus he is said in reference to himself to be alive by, of course, having life, and he is that same life" (*civ. Dei* 11, 10, 1). Thus predication about God is either relative or absolute. Relative predication will express either the relation of the persons within the Trinity or the relation of God to some creature. Since God has no accidents, every nonrelative predication about God will be a predication that signifies the divine essence or substance. There are no qualities in God, and whatever seems to signify a quality must be understood to signify his essence.[41] Augustine goes on to restate the meaning of simplicity. "For this reason then a nature is said to

40. The expression would seem to be equivalent to *ejusdem substantiae,* in which case the force of the expression is: "is numerically the same substance as." See *Trin.* 5, 8, 9: "tantamque vim esse ejusdem substantiae in Patre et Filio et Spiritu sancto, ut quidquid de singulis ad se ipsos dicitur, non pluraliter in summa, sed singulariter accipiatur."

41. In *Trin.* 15, 5, 8, Augustine says, "Quidquid enim secundum qualitates illic dici videtur, secundum substantiam vel essentiam est intelligendum. Absit enim ut spiritus secundum substantiam dicatur Deus, et bonus secundum qualitatem: sed utrumque secundum substantiam." For God to be said to be good according to quality would mean that God's goodness inhered in his substance as an accident in its subject. That is, "dici secundum qualitatem" has to do with the being of God, not with the structure of language. What is said of God relatively is either the relation of one person to another or the relation of God to some creature.

be simple, because it does not have something that it is able to lose or because there is no difference between what it is and what it has" (*civ. Dei* 11, 10, 2). Augustine elsewhere defines an accident as that which can be lost or increased or decreased.[42] His definition of simplicity here certainly excludes accidents, though it is more general. Augustine supplies a series of examples: a jug that has liquid, a body that has color, the air that has light and warmth, the soul that has wisdom. "None of these is what it has" (ibid.). Obviously, the jug is not the liquid, the body its color, the air light or warmth, or the soul wisdom. "For this reason," he continues, "they can be deprived of the things they have and be turned and changed into other habits or qualities." Thus the jug is emptied, the body discolors, the air darkens and cools, and the soul loses wisdom.

However, even a quality that cannot be lost is incompatible with simplicity. Augustine points out that even an incorruptible body, such as is promised to the saints at the resurrection, "has the inamissible quality of incorruption, but since the corporeal substance remains, it is not its incorruption" (ibid.). He argues that the incorruption is whole in the individual parts of the body and not greater in one part and lesser in another. After all, one part is not more incorrupt than another. But the body itself is greater in the whole than in any part. Though some parts of the body are larger or smaller, they are not more or less incorrupt. "Thus the body which is not whole in every part of itself is other than the incorruption which is whole in every part of it" (ibid.).

So too Augustine points out that the soul that will be forever wise once it has "been freed into eternity" will, nonetheless, be wise by participating in immutable wisdom; the soul is not such wisdom as it will have. He also tells us that even if the air were always filled with light, the air would still not be the light. Despite the great difference between air and the soul, there is still a parallel that allows one to speak of the incorporeal soul as illumined by the incorporeal light of the wisdom of God, as the bodily air is illumined by the bodily light.[43]

---

42. "Accidens autem non solet dici, nisi quod aliqua mutatione ejus rei cui accidit amitti potest" (*Trin.* 5, 4, 5). Augustine's consideration of the incorruptibility of risen bodies and the wisdom of the blessed shows that it is ontological composition that he means to exclude from God, not merely the possibility of loss.

43. Augustine notes that he does not say this "quasi aer sit anima, quod putaverunt quidam qui non potuerunt incorpoream cogitare naturam." In BA 35, 66–67, Bardy suggests that he is most likely thinking not merely of the pre-Socratics, but also of such Christian theologians as Tertullian.

Augustine puts the matter in yet another way: "Accordingly, those things which are principally and truly divine are called 'simple,' because in them quality is not different from substance, and they are not divine or wise or blessed by participation in other things" (*civ. Dei* 11, 10, 3).[44] Thus, though in Scripture the Spirit of wisdom is said to be multiple, because he has many things in himself, he is what he has and all that he has is one *(unus)*. That is, the plurality of divine attributes is in no way incompatible with divine simplicity or unity, since each of the attributes signifies the one divine substance. Furthermore, God has within himself "all the invisible and immutable ideas *(rationes)* of even the visible and mutable things which were made by him" (ibid.). For God did not produce them without knowing what he was doing. And despite this multiplicity of ideas in God's mind, his wisdom is one. Finally, Augustine points out, "An amazing, but true thought comes to mind from this: This world could not be known by us unless it existed; but unless it were known by God, it could not exist" (ibid.). That is, God's knowledge is not caused by the things that he knows; rather his knowledge is their cause. Hence, there can be no change in God's knowledge because of his simplicity.

We have seen that Augustine argues that God is immutable because he is simple. We have seen that his being simple means that he is what he has, that every nonrelative predication signifies his substance, and that in him quality and substance are not different. But what then is the reason for holding that God is simple? In *Trin.* 5, 10, 11, Augustine offers an answer in terms of participation. He is speaking of things that are great by participation in greatness, for example, a great house, a great mountain, or a great soul; in these, he tells us, "greatness is other than that which is great by that greatness, and greatness is obviously not the same thing as a great house." Indeed, true greatness is not the greatness by which anything great is great, for in such cases the greatness is other than the things that are called great by reason of it. "That [true] greatness is surely originally great and is more excellently than those things which are great by participating in it. God, however, is not great by that greatness which is not what he is so that God would

---

44. In "Augustine on the Simplicity of God," Richard La Croix has argued that Augustine's account of divine simplicity is unintelligible. I have tried to show that it is not; see my "Properties of God." See also Wilma G. von Jess, "La simplicidad de Dios en el pensamiento agustiniano," *Augustinus* 19 (1974): 45–52.

participate in it to be great; otherwise that greatness would be greater than God. But nothing is greater than God. Therefore, he is great by that greatness in virtue of which he is that same greatness" (*Trin.* 5, 10, 11). Thus, if God were not identical with his greatness, then he would be great by participating in greatness. But that would mean that God is great by reason of something other than himself. Hence, he would not be originally great or supremely great; his greatness would be derivative and less than that which is original greatness. By similar arguments, it would follow that God would not be originally and supremely wise or good or happy. Hence, the argument from participation leads us to see that, if God is to be supremely good, great, and wise, he must be his goodness, his greatness, and his wisdom, that is, he must be identical with his attributes.[45]

THE INFLUENCE OF THE *PLATONICI*

If Augustine became certain that God was immutable prior to his contact with the *libri Platonicorum,* there is still no doubt that his reading these books and learning from them enabled him to conceive of God as incorporeal, immutable, and eternal. When he speaks of the things that he found in those books, he explicitly mentions immutability and eternity: "For that your only-begotten Son coeternal with you remains immutably before all times and above all times . . . is there" (*conf.* 7, 9, 14). Shortly thereafter he tells us that after reading and being instructed by these books, he saw "the invisible things of God" (Rom 1:18). "Driven back, I perceived what that was, which I was not permitted to contemplate because of my mind's darkness. I was made certain that you are, that you are infinite, although not diffused through spaces, either finite or infinite, that you who are always the very same truly are, in no part and by no motion other or otherwise, and that all other

---

45. Though I have not found anything quite to this effect in Augustine, I suspect that he would agree with Aquinas's principle, "Semper enim quod participat aliquid, et quod est mobile, et quod est imperfectum, praeexigit ante se aliquid quod est per essentiam suam tale, et quod est immobile et perfectum" (*Summa theologiae* I, q. 79, a. 4 cor). This principle is, after all, the foundation of the Fourth Way—the most Platonic of the Thomistic proofs. It is also the Aristotelian dictum: "Propter quod unumquodque tale, et illud magis" (*Posterior Analytics* I, 1, 72a29–30; see *Summa theologiae* I, q. 16, a. 1, arg. 3).

things are from you by this one most solid proof that they are" (*conf.* 7, 20, 26). Though the darkness of his mind does not allow him to remain in the contemplation of the *invisibilia Dei* that he saw, he perceived and is able to articulate what he could not contemplate. He has come to a grasp of God as infinite, but not spatially so, as being truly *(vere esse)*, as ever the very same *(semper idem ipse)*, as in no part and by no motion other or otherwise *(alter aut aliter)*. Other things are for the sole reason that they are from God.

That Augustine learned from the books of the Platonists how to conceive of God and the soul as incorporeal beings seems beyond doubt. That it was through Augustine that the whole Western Church came to an idea of God and the soul as spiritual seems equally beyond doubt.[46] Moreover, as Augustine's inability to conceive of a spiritual being was "the greatest and almost the sole cause of [his] inevitable error" (*conf.* 5, 10, 19), so what freed him from this same error was the ability to conceive of God as a substance that is whole everywhere, as infinite but not spatially so, as above us, not as oil is above water or the sky above the earth, but because he made us. As incorporeal, God obviously does not have the three spatial dimensions of length, breadth, and depth; he is not extended through stretches of space. However, just as Augustine learned from the Platonists that God cannot be spatially extended, so he also learned from the *Enneads* that God cannot be distended through time.[47]

---

46. See Masai, "Les Conversions of saint Augustin," where the author attributes to Augustine the definitive adoption of a spiritualist philosophy in the West. The beginnings lie in Marius Victorinus's translation of the *Enneads* and his conversion to Christianity. "Ses disciples milanais continuèrent son oeuvre et surent gagner au catholicisme, ainsi renouvelé philosophiquement, le génie qui devait lui assurer la victoire définitive. C'est dans cette perspective que se découvre la position historique d'Augustin, on voit qu'elle est absolument centrale: la conversion de 386 qui, sur le plan philosophique, peut se définir comme le passage du matérialisme stoïcien et manichéen au spiritualisme, à l'idéalisme néoplatonicien, a entraîné à sa suite la conversion philosophique de l'Occident" (29).

47. In *"Vocans Temporales, Faciens Aeternos,"* I proposed the hypothesis that, just as prior to Augustine the Western Church was without a concept of God as a spiritual substance, so it was without a concept of God's eternity as *tota simul*. The concepts "incorporeal" and "eternal" are, it seems to me, closely related. The former entails the denial of length, breadth, and depth; the latter before and after. A spiritual substance is whole wherever it is; an eternal substance is whole whenever it is. As the former is everywhere, the latter is everywhen.

For a careful presentation of Plotinus's and Aquinas's views of time, see John F. Cal-

Augustine's definition of time in *conf.* 11 as a "distention of the mind" is clearly derived from *Ennead* 3, 7, as is his concept of eternity.[48] That Augustine viewed the distention of time as parallel to the distention of bodies in three dimensions is reflected in his saying of God: "He is not increased by time or distended by place" (*s.* 225, 2). Places distend as much as does time. Just as God has no bodily parts and cannot change spatially, since he is wholly present everywhere, so too he has no temporal parts and cannot change temporally, since he is wholly present everywhen.[49]

It is worth noting that once again the disciples of Mani stand in the background. As they prodded the young Augustine and many others in the African Church with questions about man's being made in God's image (*conf.* 3, 7, 12), so they delighted in asking of the same simple folk what the God of Genesis was doing before he created heaven and earth (*conf.* 11, 10, 12 and 12, 14). If Augustine needed the concept of incorporeality to articulate a response to the problem of God's image, he needed a concept of eternity to handle the problem of the time before God made heaven and earth.[50]

I have elsewhere argued that if Augustine was the first thinker in the West to develop the concept of God as an incorporeal being that is whole everywhere, then it would seem that he would also have to be the

---

lahan, *Four Views of Time in Ancient Philosophy* (Cambridge: Harvard University Press, 1948), 88–187. For Augustine's dependence on Plotinus's account of time and eternity in *Ennead* 3, 7, see O'Connell, *St. Augustine's Confessions*, 139–144. Commenting on Augustine's "Ecce distentio vita mea" (*conf.* 11, 29, 39), O'Connell says, "That definition is Plotinus' classic *diastasis*. It comes from the very treatise (*Enn* III, 7) that has served as Augustine's model, here and in the *De Musica,* for reflecting on the soul's fall from a contemplative eternity into the distraction, dissipation, dispersion of time and the manifold life of action" (142).

48. This would seem to be the inevitable conclusion given the parallel between space and time. Both are seen as distensions or extensions or even swellings that are to be denied of God. Time is something we have fallen into and from which need to be freed. See my *"Vocans Temporales,"* 36–58.

49. Soon after his conversion he mentions "hoc quiddam grande et breve": "Est natura per locos et tempora mutabilis, ut corpus. Et est natura per locos nullo modo, sed tantum per tempora etiam ipsa mutabilis, ut anima. Et est natura quae nec per locos, nec per tempora mutari potest: hoc Deus est. Quod hic insinuavi quoquo modo mutabile, creatura dicitur; quod immutabile, Creator" (*ep.* 19, 2).

50. Hence, the Neoplatonic concept of eternity as *tota simul* was necessary for dealing with the full scope of the Manichaean objections to the God of Genesis. Without a concept of nontemporal existence the Augustinian answer that there was no time when God did nothing would not have been possible. See *conf.* 11, 13, 15–16.

first to articulate the concept of eternity, the concept of a God who is whole everywhen.[51] Augustine says that God is eternal because he is immutable.[52] So too being temporal involves not merely the possibility of change, but change. The being of creatures is a ceasing to be, a tending to nonbeing, even a dying.[53] Creatures are all both being and nonbeing; compared with God they are not; apart from such comparison they are.[54] To be temporal involves becoming ever other. Hence, the God whose very name is "IS," who is the Selfsame, is He whose essence is eternity.[55]

51. Though the definition of eternity as "interminabilis vitae tota simul et perfecta possessio" stems from Boethius, he found all the elements ready at hand in Augustine, who in turn found them in Plotinus. See Boethius, *De consolatione philosophiae* 5, prosa 6.

52. "Quod incommutabile est, aeternum est; semper enim eiusdem modi est. Quod autem commutabile est, tempori obnoxium est: non enim semper eiusdem modi est, et ideo aeternum non recte dicitur. Quod enim mutatur, non manet: quod non manet, non est aeternum" (*div. quaes.* 19).

53. In "Notes sur l'être," 212, E. Gilson suggests that except for *tempus* Augustine did not have a word for the world of becoming, since *esse* meant for him immutable being. "Si ergo praesens, ut tempus sit, ideo fit, quia in praeteritum transit, quomodo et hoc esse dicimus, cui causa, ut sit, illa est, quia non erit, ut scilicet non vere dicamus tempus esse, nisi quia tendit non esse" (*conf.* 11, 14, 17). "Quidquid enim mutari potest, mutatum non est quod erat; si non est quod erat, mors quaedam ibi facta est." (*Jo. ev. tr.* 38, 10).

54. "Et inspexi cetera infra te et vidi nec omnino esse nec omnino non esse: esse quidem, quoniam abs te sunt, non esse autem, quoniam id quod es non sunt. Id enim vere est, quod incommutabiliter manet" (*conf.* 7, 11, 17). "Ita enim ille est, ut in ejus comparatione ea quae facta sunt, non sint. Illo non comparato, sunt; quoniam ab illo sunt; illi autem comparata, non sunt, quia verum esse, incommutabile esse est, quod ille solus est" (*en. Ps.* 134, 4).

55. "Non aliud anni Dei, et aliud ipse: sed anni Dei, aeternitas Dei est: aeternitas ipsa Dei substantia est, quae nihil habet mutabile" (*en. Ps.* 101, 10).

3

Creation & Beginnings

8

THE MOTIVE FOR CREATION ACCORDING TO AUGUSTINE

Several texts in lib. arb. *seem to entail in a Leibnizian sort of fashion that the world is the best possible one that God could have created and that God had to create such a world. These texts led me to an investigation of the motive for creation in Augustine's thought. Despite the presence of the so-called voluntarist and Platonist texts, I came to the conclusion that for Augustine the divine will was necessitated by its own goodness in a way that is foreign to later philosophy and theology. At the time I wrote this article, I had not worked my way through the anti-Pelagian works with Augustine's later understanding of human freedom under divine grace. Had I done so, I could perhaps have come to a better understanding of God's freedom in a Platonist context. Despite that, I think that the main contentions of the article remain valid.*

To the question, "Why did God create heaven and earth?" Augustine replied at times, "Because he willed to," and at other times, "Because he is good." Gilson labels the first sort of answer as voluntarism and the second as Platonism. He says that it "is an easy matter" to reconcile the voluntarism of the first sort of texts with the Platonism of the second sort "since God is the Good and God's will is God: 'so that it might be shown that the thing which was made befits the goodness on account of which it was made."'[1] Boyer admits that the second response, if taken alone, would lead to a deterministic optimism of the Plotinian or Leibnizian sort: "If the goodness of things accounts for their creation, God could not but create them and could not create a world other than the best possible."[2] He claims, however, that Augustine explicitly rejects this interpretation, "first of all, because it would place the goodness of things above the will of God, secondly because it would lead to saying that the world could not be other than it is." Boyer adds, "The goodness of God—and consequently that of creatures, a gift of the divine goodness—explains that God can create if he wills. But nothing determines his will to will this save his will itself.... Although the world is good, God would have been able not to create it, but because the world is good God was able to create it."[3]

Gilson and Boyer are certainly right in holding that according to Augustine nothing apart from God determines his will to create. It is not, however, nearly so clear that the goodness of God did not necessitate his creating the world and his creating a world with every step on the scale of being filled. I began this article in the hope of being able to reconcile what Gilson has called the voluntarist and the Platonist texts. However, in the process of writing it I have come to the conclusion that the conflict between the two sorts of texts disappears only at a price, namely, at the price of admitting an optimistic determinism of the divine will. Hence, I agree with the conclusion of Robert-Henri Cousineau that "if there is any problem, it is not voluntarism but a certain determinism."[4]

There are two classical texts cited in favor of the voluntarist view.[5] First, in *Gn. adv. Man.*, Augustine says that the Manichees who ask

---

1. Gilson, *Christian Philosophy*, 375n17. Gilson quoted from *civ. Dei* 11.24.
2. Boyer, *L'idée de la verité*, 177. The translation is mine.
3. Ibid., 177–178.
4. Robert-Henri Cousineau, "Creation and Freedom: An Augustinian Problem: 'Quia voluit'? and/or 'Quia bonus'?" *Recherches augustiniennes* 2 (1963): 253–271; here 255. Cousineau cautiously qualifies his conclusion and suggests that Augustine may have held both positions at once, though *aufgehoben* in Hegelian fashion (see 270–271). I find the evidence in favor of a determinism much stronger than Cousineau did.
5. See also *c. Prisc.*1, 3: "Cum enim dicitur, Deus ex nihilo fecit; nihil aliud dicitur, nisi non erat unde faceret, et tamen quia voluit fecit." I do not see that this text stresses what Cousineau claims, "When we say that God created out of nothing, we stress the fact that he created because he willed to do so" ("Creation and Freedom," 254).

why God created heaven and earth should first learn the power of the human will if they want to know the will of God.⁶

For they seek to know the causes of the will of God though the will of God is itself the cause of all things that exist. For if the will of God has a cause, there is something that precedes the will of God—and this we may not believe. Hence, one who says, "Why did God make heaven and earth?" should be told, "Because he willed to." For the will of God is the cause of heaven and earth, and the will of God, therefore, is greater than heaven and earth. But one who says, "Why did God will to create heaven and earth?" is looking for something greater than the will of God, though nothing greater can be found.⁷

Here "because he willed to," at least when taken alone, gives the impression that creation is almost a matter of divine whim for which further explanation neither need be sought nor can be found. The second voluntarist text is from *De diversis quaestionibus octoginta tribus* (hereafter *div. quaes.*): "One who asks why God willed to make the world is seeking the cause of the will of God. But every cause is efficient. And everything efficient is greater than that which is effected. But nothing is greater than the will of God. Therefore, one should not seek its cause."⁸ Once again the divine will is given as the ultimate explanation of creation. Both of these texts insist that the divine will is the cause of the world and that there is no cause—at least no efficient cause—of the divine will, though Augustine adds here that every cause is efficient.⁹

---

6. That is, by knowing the power of the human will one can get some idea of the power of the divine will, though the human will, unlike the divine will, cannot do whatever it wills. See *en. Ps.* 134.12, where Augustine contrasts the will of the omnipotent God with the limited human will, which is unable in so many cases to do what it wills.

7. *Gn. adv. Man.* 1.2.4. In *L'intelligence de la foi en la trinité selon s. Augustin: Genèse de sa théologie trinitaire iusqu'en 391* (Paris: Études augustiniennes, 1966), 272, Olivier du Roy points out with regard to this passage that Augustine identifies the will of God with the Holy Spirit. He says, "des le premier texte où Augustin parle du motif de la création, il opère la synthèse des deux motifs dans l'idée d'une volonté qui est amour personnel et qu'on ne comprend qu'en y participant." He claims that by so doing Augustine solves the problem of the *quia voluit* and *quia bonus* texts since the will is the personal love of the Spirit. I believe that du Roy is right that Augustine does make this identification, but I fail to see how this removes the problem of a determinism of the divine will.

8. *Div. quaes.* 28. I have translated *efficiens* as "efficient" though it does not seem likely that Augustine was speaking of an efficient cause as one of the four Aristotelian causes. If he were, he would be denying that there were any other sorts of causes.

9. See *civ. Dei* 5, 9, 4, where Augustine distinguishes three kinds of causes: fortuitous, natural, and voluntary. Augustine there says that only voluntary causes are efficient causes.

In contrast with the few texts in Augustine that might be read as supportive of a voluntarist view of the motive for creation, there are many texts in which the cause of God's creating is said to be his goodness or the goodness of creatures. Let me cite a few of them. In *Trin.*, Augustine says, "For what in accord with its kind and in its measure does not have a likeness to God? For God made all things very good, for no other reason than that he himself is supremely good?" (*Trin.* 11, 5, 8).[10] And in *ep.* 166 he says, "But if one seeks the cause of creating, no quicker or better response is given than that every creature of God is good. And what is more appropriate than that the good God should make good things, which no one but God can make?" (*ep.* 166, 5, 15). Finally, in *civ. Dei* he says, "In the words, 'God saw that it was good,' it is sufficiently shown that God made what has been made by no necessity, by no need of any benefit, but by goodness alone *(nulla necessitate, nulla suae cuiusquam utilitatis indigentia, sed sola bonitate)*, that is, because it is good. And so these words are said after it was made so that it might be shown that the thing which is made befits the goodness on account of which it was made" (*civ. Dei* 11, 24).

In these texts God is said to have created because he is good or because creatures are good or to have created by his goodness. Is there a conflict between these texts and the voluntarist texts? Since, as Gilson correctly points out, God is the Good and his will and his goodness are identical, it might seem that there is no conflict. The problem can, however, be brought more sharply into focus if we look at the implications of God's goodness for Augustine. In the last text cited, Augustine says that God creates not because he is lacking some advantage that he attains by creating. His creating is not caused by something other than his goodness, which is God himself. He creates because he wills to create and his goodness leads him to so will. However, what is denied in the above text by the phrase *nulla necessitate*? To say simply that all necessity is denied may be a bit precipitous.

Augustine throws further light on what he understood by "necessity" in commenting on the words of the Psalmist, "The Lord has made all that he willed in heaven and on earth, in the sea and in all the abysses" (Ps 134:6). He says, "He is not forced to make all the things which

---

10. See also *civ. Dei* 11, 22 and *doc. chr.* 1, 32, 35. Saint Thomas interprets the latter text as speaking of God's goodness as the final cause (*Summa theologiae* I, q. 5, a. 4 ad 3um).

he made; 'he made everything he willed.' His will is the cause of all the things which he has made" (*en. Ps.* 134, 10). That is, he contrasts "being forced, or coerced": *coactus* with "willing." Because his will is the cause of what he made, he was not forced or coerced. In explanation of this point Augustine turns to concrete examples of human making, such as the making of a house or clothing. We build houses because unless we do so, we will have no shelter. We make clothing because unless we do so, we will walk around naked. Here necessity forces *(necessitas cogit)* us; we do not act by free will *(libera voluntate)*. So too we plant crops by necessity because, unless we do so, we will not have food. God, on the other hand, made by his goodness *(bonitate)* all that he made. He did not need anything he made; hence, "he made everything that he willed." If we interpret the two phrases *nulla necessitate, nulla suae cuiusdam utilitatis indigentia* from the *civ. Dei* text in the light of the comments on Psalm 134, *necessitas* means "need," that is, a need of something else. To make whatever one wills means that one does not need what one makes.[11] The second phrase would seem to be simply a paraphrase of the first. If that is correct, Augustine is ruling out a need in God for something he makes or an advantage he derives from what he makes; it is not clear that he is ruling out by that phrase an internal necessity grounded in the goodness of God.

If one looks at the texts on the theme of the Good as not being envious or grudging, the problem becomes more acute.[12] Let me cite a few. In *Gn. litt.* Augustine says, "But if he could not make good things, there would be no power; if, however, he could and did not, there would be great enviousness *(invidentia)*. Hence, because he is almighty and good, he made all things very good" (*Gn. litt.* 4, 16, 27).[13] Other

11. This is supported by *Trin.* 5, 1, 2, where Augustine deals with the application of the Aristotelian categories to God. There he says that God is creator without need *(sine indigentia creatorem)*. The position of the phrase in the list of the categories indicates that he is excluding from God a relation of dependence upon creatures.
12. Du Roy has collected the principal texts in which Augustine mentions this theme as well as its sources in Plato and Plotinus. See du Roy, *L'intelligence de la foi en la trinité*, in the appendix, "Bonus invidit nullo bono," 474–475.
13. In the BA 48, p. 644, Agaësse and Solignac note, "Cette argumentation est une rétorsion, peut-être voulue, du célèbre dilemme d'Epicure: 'Deus aut vult tollere mala et non potest, aut potest et non vult. . . . ; si vult et non potest, imbecillis est, quod in Deum non cadit; si potest et non vult, invidus, quod aeque alienum est a Deo' . . . Augustin inverse exactement le sens de l'argument pour en tirer une conclusion diamétralement opposée."

texts on this theme are: "But there is nothing of enviousness in that nature to prevent its offering itself to the soul to enjoy" (*imm. an.* 6, 11), and "God, however, supremely good and supremely just, is envious toward no beauty that is brought about, whether it be by the condemnation of the soul or by its return or its abiding" (*mus.* 6. 17, 56). Also, "Thus from the highest to the lowest that goodness is envious toward no beauty which could be from him alone" (*vera rel.* 39, 72). And again, "Yet none of these things would come to be from the Father through the Son nor would they be preserved within their limits if God were not supremely good. He is envious toward no nature which he could make to be good" (*vera rel.* 55, 113).[14]

All these texts stress that God's goodness means that he begrudges no nature the being and goodness it could have. Augustine is particularly insistent against the Manichees that the divine goodness would be lacking, that is, God would be envious, if he had not produced an *omnia,* a universe containing all things, not just the higher things.[15]

There are, moreover, several surprising texts that seem to imply that God had to create the best world. In discussing why God made souls he knew would sin, Augustine insists that one should say neither that they should not have been made nor that they should have been made otherwise than they were made. In *lib. arb.* he says, "For you should know that God as the maker of all good things has already made anything better that occurs to you with true reason. It is not true reason, but envious weakness to will that nothing else lower be made when you think that something better should have been made. . . . Hence, there can be something in the nature of reality that you do not think of with your reason. But there cannot fail to be what you think of with true reason. For you cannot think of something better in creation that has escaped the artisan of creation" (*lib. arb.* 3, 5, 13).

Augustine explains that when the human soul judges correctly that one thing would be better than another, it judges correctly because it sees what it says and it sees it in the divine ideas, to which it is tied

---

14. These four texts bear a marked similarity to Plotinus, *Ennead* 2, 9, 9; 5, 4, 1; and 5.5.12.

15. See O'Connell, *Imagination and Metaphysics,* 26–27, for his unpacking the Augustinian notion of judgment and the conclusion "that it was 'very good' that God created an *Omnia,* the panoply of 'All Things' which he produced as an ordered hierarchy of realities, lower as well as higher."

or connected by its nature.[16] "Hence, let it believe that God has made what it knows by true reason ought to have been made by him, even if it does not see this among the things made. For even if it could not see the sky with the eyes and yet inferred by true reason that something of the sort ought to have been made, it ought to believe that it has been made, even if it did not see it with the eyes. For it would not see that it should have been made except in these reasons by which all things were made. But what is not there no one can see with true thought, and it is not true" (*lib. arb.* 3, 5, 13). This is an extraordinary text. If one sees correctly, that is, with true reason, that X should have been made, then he can be sure that X already has been made, even if he cannot by observation check that it has been made. One sees what he sees correctly in the divine ideas, and the divine ideas are the patterns in God's mind in accord with which God produces whatever he produces.[17] The text does not imply that something apart from God, for example, the goodness of X, causes God to create it. But what we know in the divine ideas, God obviously knows as well. If we can be certain that he has created X because we see X in his ideas, it would seem that, given this knowledge of his, he could not but create X.

If the ideas are his knowledge according to which he creates, then it would follow that if we see something in his ideas, we can be sure that it already exists. There remains the question whether he has some other sort of knowledge according to which he could create things other than those that he does create. Does God have knowledge of things that could be, but are not, have not been, and will not be?[18] The question is—as far as I can see—not one that arose for Augustine in any explicit sense. And it is perhaps dangerous and unfair to ask from him answers to questions that arose only later. Nonetheless, if the Augustinian God

---

16. "Humana quippe anima naturaliter divinis ex quibus pendet connexa rationibus, cum dicit: 'melius hoc fieret quam illud', si verum dicit et videt quod dicit, in illis quibus connexa est rationibus videt" (*lib. arb.* 3, 5, 13).

17. Augustine is clear that these *rationes* are the divine ideas; see *div. quaes.* 46, 2.

18. This sort of question is raised by Coelestin Zimara, S.M.B., in "Das Ineinanderspiel von Gottes Vorwissen and Wollen nach Augustinus," *Freiburger Zeitschrift für Philosophie and Theologie* 6 (1959): 271–299, 371–334. However, such questions and the distinctions implied are simply not found in Augustine. In BA 6, 532, F. J. Thonnard suggests in his note, "Optimisme augustinien," that the Augustinian God ("étant infiniment bon et sage produit toujours ce qui est meilleur, mais dans le plan actuel de sa Providence, qu'il s'est librement fixé: cela n'exclut pas la possibilité d'un autre plan, où il serait crée un monde absolument meilleur que le notre."

knows only what he creates, then he could not create anything other than what he does create.[19] And thus he would not be free in the sense that he could have created other things than he did create.[20]

There is another striking passage later in *lib. arb.*: "If someone should say, 'It was still not difficult or troublesome for almighty God that all the things whatsoever that he made should have their order in such a way that no creature ends in wretchedness. For an omnipotent God was not unable to do this, and a good one was not envious.' I will answer that the order of creatures from the highest to the lowest proceeds in just steps so that he is envious who says, 'This should not be so.' He is envious too who says, 'This should be so'" (*lib. arb.* 3, 9, 24). Augustine is arguing that God's being good, that is, not *invidus*, entails that the order of creatures proceeds from the highest to the lowest by degrees or steps that are just. God is not grudging so that he refuses to create what is lower on the scale of being. One who says that something should be other, that is, better than it is, is envious or grudging. Here the divine goodness seems to entail that no level of being be empty. Unfortunately it sometimes seems that sinful souls that end in misery form one of those levels of being.[21] But if every step on the ladder of being

---

19. Zimara rightly, I believe, concludes that Augustine held that there was in God what will later be called a freedom of spontaneity as opposed to a freedom of choice. He says that one should not forget "dass hier weder für das freie Wollen Gottes noch für das der Engel and Menschen der präzise vervollstandigte Begriff einer Wahlfreiheit gilt, den spätere Philosophie and Theologie ausprägen wird. Augustinus sieht Willensfreiheit, zumal bei Gott, bereits in dem, was man Spontaneität (Aktivitat aus Selbstbestimmung dazu) nennen kann" (Zimara, "Das Ineinanderspiel," 391). Indeed, it seems that it was not until approximately the time of Abelard's condemnation by the Council of Sens (1140) for having taught that God could not have done other or better than he did in creating that the concept of divine freedom was given such scholastic precision. And Abelard—interestingly enough—backed up his position by citing many of the same texts from Augustine that I have pointed to in this article.

20. Boyer supports his claim that Augustine clearly states that the world could be other than it is only by *lib. arb.* 3, 9, 26. He argues that Augustine says that the perfection necessary to the world can be found in quite different conditions: "soit, par exemple que les âmes pèchent et qu'elles soient chatiées, soit qu'elles ne pèchent pas et qu'elles soient recompensées." Augustine's point in that passage is that it is the existence of souls that is necessary to the perfection of the universe. Whether these souls sin and suffer misery or do not sin and enjoy beatitude, the universe is always full and perfect by reason of all natures ("semper naturis omnibus universitas plena et perfecta est"). That is, the creation of souls was necessary to the perfection of the universe, and that perfection is not destroyed whether souls sin and are justly punished or do not sin.

21. For texts on the ordering even of sins, see H.-I. Marrou, *St. Augustine and His Influence through the Ages* (New York: Harper and Brothers, 1957), 142–143. See also G.

must be filled, then it would seem once again that God is not free not to create some kind of creatures, that is, to leave a step of the ladder of being without creatures. Indeed, Augustine claims that justice demands that God create an *omnia*. "By the justice . . . of God . . . it was brought about that all things not only are, but that they are so that they could not be in any way better."[22]

Given such texts, does it not seem that God could not but create the world and could not but create the best possible world? De Blic says that Augustine leaves undecided "whether the spontaneous and gratuitous will to pour forth its riches is of the essence of the sovereign good or whether it must be thought of as a free determination that is somehow contingent."[23] However, both de Blic and du Roy note that Augustine twice applies the same argument from God's lack of envy and impotence to the generation of the Son. In the first text Augustine says, "Of course, on this point the matter comes to this: God the Father either was not able or was not willing to generate a Son equal to himself. If he was unable, he was weak; if he was unwilling, he is found to be envious. But each of these is false. Therefore, the Son is a true equal to God the Father" (*c. Max.* 2, 7). In the second texts he says, "Since he could not generate one better than himself (for nothing is better than God), God had to generate as an equal him to whom he gave birth. For if he willed and could not, he is weak; if he could and would not, he is envious. From this it follows that he generated a Son equal [to himself]" (*div. quaes.* 50). The transferal of the argument to the generation of the Son implies that the creation of the world and the generation of the Son are equally necessary. God creates necessarily—not in the sense that he is coerced or creates out of some need, but in the sense that he could not be both good and able to create and yet not create. On this point de Blic says, "Since the act of creating would be essential to the Sovereign Good, it would owe to its spontaneity its being able to be called fully free. This terminology is no longer familiar today either to theologians or to philosophers; it was that of Saint Augustine."[24] De

---

Folliet, "Etiam Peccata (De doctr. christ. III, xxiii, 33)," *Revue des études augustiniennes* 5 (1959): 450.

22. "Iustitia . . . Dei . . . factum est ut non modo sint omnia, sed ita sint ut omnino melius esse non possint" (*quan.* 33, 73). See *Enneads* 3, 2, 15; 3, 3,3; and 6, 8, 17.

23. Jacques de Blic, "Platonisme et christianisme dans la conception augustinienne du Dieu createur," *Recherches de science religieuse* 30 (1940): 172–190, here, 180.

24. De Blic, "Platonisme et christianisme," 180.

Blic points to *Ennead* 6, 8, 3–4 as the source of this view and adds, "There is much more here than terminology: it is the determinism of the divine will."[25]

What then is one to make of all this? In order to come to some conclusion, let us return to the commentary on Psalm 134. There Augustine asks whether we have something that we do with free will, and he answers that when we praise God in love, we act with free will. We do this with free will when we love what we praise, "not out of necessity, but because it pleases us." He adds that God is pleasing to the holy and just even when he scourges *(flagellans)* and tortures *(torquens)* them. "This is to love freely, not with an eye on receiving a reward, for your supreme reward will be God himself, whom you freely love. And you ought to love him so that you do not cease to desire as a reward him who alone can satisfy you" (*en. Ps.* 134, 11). Our loving God with free will *(libera voluntate)* is a gratuitous love in the sense that we do not love him for the sake of a reward other than God; we love him freely because he pleases us or because he is our delight. So too God's creating out of goodness or with free will is creation out of gratuitous love, and gratuitous love is simply goodness acting with no need of anything or for any advantage he might attain, but simply because it pleases him. On the other hand, the Augustinian God, it seems, could not be both good and powerful and yet not create the world—and create an *omnia*, a panoply of things "so that they could not be in any way better."[26]

25. Ibid.
26. See above, note 22.

9

PROBLEMS WITH "THE BEGINNING" IN AUGUSTINE'S SIXTH COMMENTARY ON GENESIS

In the beginning of Contra adversarium legis et prophetarum *(hereafter* c. adv. leg.*), Augustine returned to the Book of Genesis for the sixth time in order to answer questions that the people of Hippo found in a book by an anonymous heretic, most probably someone in the Marcionite tradition. The present article focuses upon the anonymous author's questions about what God was doing before he made heaven and earth, questions with which Augustine had dealt with in* conf. 11. *The questions posed by the heretical author forced Augustine to provide a more extensive replies to various problems about the beginning, and his replies reveal not merely his patience as a teacher and pastor, but his ability to argue with great subtlety.*

In 419 or 420 some Carthaginian Christians came upon an anonymous volume that was being read aloud in a square near the harbor and attracting an interested crowd of people. These concerned Christians sent the volume to Augustine and begged him to write a refutation of the work without delay. Hence, the bishop of Hippo wrote the two books of his *c. adv. leg.*—one of Augustine's less well known works that has not yet been published in an English translation, but a work, I believe, well worth more attention.¹ This article will first sum up the scholarly opinion with regard to the identity of the heresy that the work represents. Then it will turn to a series of questions concerning the beginning in which God created heaven and earth. Finally, it will briefly sum up what Augustine says in this work on the topic of human goodness.

THE IDENTITY OF THE HERESY OF THE ANONYMOUS AUTHOR

The anonymous author of the work held "that God did not make this world and that the God of the Mosaic Law and of the Prophets pertaining to that same Law is not the true God, but an evil demon."² That is, he held that the God who created this world was not the true God, but an evil demon, in fact, the worst of demons.³ The volume brought to Augustine contained, along with the work of the anonymous heretic, another work that Augustine identified as that of the Manichee Adimantus and, perhaps, also the beginning of another work that he could not identify.⁴ Augustine, nonetheless, recognized that the anonymous author was not a Manichee. In his preliminary attempt to identify the heresy to which the author belongs, he says, "But this fellow, whose name I did not find in this book, detests the God who made the world. Although the Manichees do not accept, but speak irreverently against the Book of Genesis, they admit that the good God made the world, even if he made it from another nature and material."⁵ So too, toward

---

1. The work is translated into French in *Oeuvres complétes de Saint Augustin* 14 (Bar-le-Duc, 1864) and into Spanish in *Obras completas de San Agustin* 38 (Madrid, 1990). My English translation has subsequently appeared in the Works of Saint Augustine I, 18 (Hyde Park, N.Y.: New City Press, 1994).
2. *Retr.* 2, 84 (58): "opinatur quod istum mundum non Deus fecerit, nec Deus legis quae data est per Moysen et prophetarum ad eandem legem pertinentium verus sit Deus sed pessimus daemon."
3. *C. adv. leg.* 2, 2, 4: "Quid, quod Deum Israel audet infelix dicere non solum daemonem, verum etiam ceteris daemonibus peiorem?"
4. See *c. adv. leg.* 2, 12, 42. The Latin text leaves it unclear whether there was one work that Augustine first says he could not identify and then goes on to identify a few lines latter as that of Adimantus or whether there were the beginnings of two works, the one unidentified and the other that of Adminatus.
5. *C. adv. leg.* 1, 1, 1: "Iste autem, cuius nomen in eodem libro non comperi, detestatur Deum mundi fabricatorem; cum Manichaei, quamvis librum Geneseos non accipiant atque blasphemant, Deum tamen bonum fabricasse mundum etsi ex aliena natura atque materia confiteantur." On the Manichees, see also *haer.* 46, 4: "Proinde mundum

the end of the second book, Augustine concludes with regard to the anonymous author, "I do not think he is a Manichee."[6] In one passage Augustine suggests that the author may have been a follower of Marcion.[7] In another he mentions other heretics opposed to the books of the Old Testament and the God of the Law and the Prophets, who made this world, such as Basilides, Carpocrates, Cerdon, Apelles, and Patricius, as well as Marcion, and draws the very general conclusion, "This fellow belongs to some heresy of theirs."[8]

Augustine twice mentions "a certain Fabricius" whom the anonymous heretic claimed "to have discovered at Rome as a teacher of the truth" and whose disciple he professed to be.[9] A. Harnack has made the plausible suggestion that this Fabricius may very well have been the Patricius whom Augustine mentions in *De haeresibus* (hereafter *haer.*) 61 as the founder of the Patricians.[10] Very little, however, is known of Patricius and the Patricians apart from the few sentences that Augustine took from Filastrius of Brescia for his entry on them in *haer.*[11] Harnack's suggestion, therefore, that the anonymous heretic was a follower of Patricius, even if correct, does not help one to set the thought of the anonymous author in a context. Hence, it seems better to consider him simply as a Neomarcionite, as Harnack does, though others have viewed him as a Manichee, a Gnostic, or some combination of these.[12] The evidence seems to indicate that the anonymous heretic was, if not a

---

a natura boni, hoc est, a natura Dei, factum confitentur quidem, sed de commixitione boni et maii quae facta est quando inter se utraque natura pugnavit."

6. Ibid. 2, 12, 40: "non eum puto esse Manichaeum."

7. *Retr.* 2, 58 (85): "liber quidam cuiusdam heretici sive marcionistae sive cuiuslibet eorum quorum error opinatur, quod istum mundum non Deus fecerit."

8. See *c. adv. leg.* 2, 12, 40: "De aliqua istorum haeresi est iste."

9. See ibid. 2, 2, 3 and 2, 12, 41: "Hanc ei videlicet erroris machinationem nescio quis Fabricius fabricavit, quem velut magistrum veritatis Romae se invenisse gloriatur," and "Sed cuiuslibet sit haeretici erroris vel ipse vel Fabricius nescio quis, cuius se gloriatur esse discipulum."

10. See A. von Harnack, *Marcion: Das Evanqelium vom fremden Gott,* 2nd ed. (Leipzig: J. C. Hinrichs, 1924; repr. Darmstadt: Wissenschaftliche Buchgesellschaft, 1985), Beilage X, 424*–433*.

11. In *haer.* 61, Augustine rather slavishly follows Filastrius and mentions that the Patricians say that it was not God, but the devil who created the substance of human flesh and that some Patricians have followed the logic of their belief to the point of committing suicide. See Philastrius, *Divuversarium hereseon liber* 62.

12. See T. Raveaux, "Aduersarium legis et prophetarum (Contra—)," in *Augustinus-Lexikon,* vol. I, 1/2, 107–122, for a summary of the scholarly opinion.

Marcionite, at least someone in the Marcionite tradition who regarded the creator God of the Old Testament as an evil demon, in contrast with the previously unknown God of peace and goodness who was unexpectedly and utterly gratuitously revealed by Jesus.

Augustine cites the anonymous author frequently, and two citations provide especially clear evidence for locating him in the Marcionite tradition.[13] In the first passage, which bears the title "The discernment of the spirits of wickedness and goodness," the anonymous heretic says,

> Let us, brother, withdraw from the wickedness of the past error and look to Christ, the true and sovereign God, not to the prince of this age and maker of this world in which we are on pilgrimage from our home. Let us, I say, look to that pious and meek one who called us the light of the world, revealing that we are his kinship, not the one who, according to the Jewish Scriptures, assigned to us an earthly beginning and indicated, thereby, our end in the earth. Let us look to him who called us brothers and urged us to be vigilant and wise concerning what is divine, not to the one who did not even permit us to have a discerning mind.[14]

In the second passage, which Harnack says is taken verbatim from Marcion, the anonymous author says, "The father of peace and love is distinct from the author of war and fury; the former is Christ; the latter the God of the Law and the Prophets."[15] Since the heresy of the anonymous author is clearly opposed to the creator God of the Old Testament, it is not surprising that in his answer to the author of this work Augustine spends a great deal of time on the goodness of creation and on human beings. Augustine has, moreover, reordered the statements of the anonymous heretic in accord with the order of the biblical books for the pur-

---

13. Harnack claims that the first of these most probably reflects the *Antitheses* of Marcion and that the second is taken verbatim from Marcion. See Harnack, *Das Evanqelium*, 426* and 433*.

14. *C. adv. leg.* 2, 11, 36: "Quare, igitur, frater, inquit, recedentes ab iniquitate praeteriti erroris intendamus Christum verum ac summum Deum, non huius seculi principem et mundi factorem, in quo nos peregrinari saepissime declaratum est. Intendamus, inquam, illum pium ac mitem, qui nos suae cognationis ostendens mundi lumen vocauit; non illum, qui secundum scripturas Iudaicas terrenum nobis initium assignans in terra nobis finem indixit. Qui nos fratres appellans vigilare ac divina sapere persuasit; non illum, qui nec dignoscentiae quidem sensum habere permisit."

15. Ibid. 1, 12, 38: "Dicens autem alium esse pacis et caritatis patrem, alium belli et furioris auctorem, illum volens intelligi Christum, hunc autem legis et prophetarum Deum."

pose of refuting them.[16] Hence, the beginning of the first book on the *c. adv. leg.* constitutes a commentary on the beginning chapters of Genesis, Augustine's sixth commentary on the hexaemeron.[17] Much of what Augustine writes against the anonymous heretic in this work reflects his previous commentaries on Genesis, especially his anti-Manichaean works. The anonymous heretic, however, does present him with several new objections to the goodness of creation and to the God who created this world. In this article, I want to focus upon a series of problems that the anonymous heretic raises concerning the beginning in which God created heaven and earth and that led Augustine to defend both the goodness of the created world and the goodness of the Creator.

WHEN GOD BEGAN TO BE OR WHEN HE
BEGAN TO BE BORED?

With regard to the first verse of Genesis, the heretic asks regarding the beginning in which God created the world, "From what beginning? When God himself began to be, or when he was bored from being idle?" The question is an interesting one that Augustine had faced from the Manichees in a slightly different form as early as his first commentary on Genesis, *Gn. adv. Man.*, written in 388 or 389, shortly after his return to Africa. The Manichees had posed the objection in two forms. The first ran as follows: "In what beginning? If God made heaven and earth in some beginning of time, what was he doing before he made heaven and earth?"[18] The second asked, "And why did he suddenly decide to make what he had not previously made through eternal time?"[19] E. Peters has tagged these two forms of the question as the *quid antequam* (what before?) form and the *cur non antea* (why not before?) form.[20] He traces the

---

16. See *c. adv. leg.* 2, 10, 35, where Augustine acknowledges that he has reordered the citations of the anonymous author.
17. See Gilles Pelland, *Cinq études d'Augustin sur le début de la Genèse* (Paris and Tournai: Desclée; Montréal: Bellarmin, 1972), which lists *Gn. adv. Man., Gn. litt. imp.,* the last three books of the *conf., Gn. litt.,* and books 11 and 12 of *civ. Dei.*
18. *Gn. adv. Man.* 1, 2, 3: "Quaerunt, in quo principio; et dicunt: Si in principio aliquo temporis fecit Deus coelum et terram, quid agebat antequam faceret coelum et terram?"
19. Ibid. 1, 2, 3: "et quid ei subito placuit facere, quod nunquam antea fecerat per tempora aeterna?"
20. E. Peters, "What Was God Doing before He Created the Heavens and the Earth?" *Augustiniana* 34 (1984): 53–74.

source of the *cur non antea* form of the question to the Epicureans and that of the *quid antequam* form to the Gnostics.[21] Peters suggests that "a Gnostic—probably not Marcion, but possibly Valentinus or Ptolemaeus or one of their followers—would have found that by turning the *cur non antea* Epicurean question into a *quid antequam* form he could indict the Old Testament creation story and the Christian doctrine of Christ as Logos and at the same time imply a secret knowledge of exactly what that 'God' was doing before he created the heavens and the earth."[22] Peters examines the question in Augustine solely in the context of his conflict with the Manichees; though the question clearly does arise in *c. adv. leg.*, the anonymous heretic is, in Augustine's eyes, quite clearly not a Manichee.

The anonymous heretic takes the beginning as either God's beginning to be or as his beginning to be bored with his idleness. The question implies answers to both forms of the question: to the *quid antequam* form of the question, it suggests that God did not exist before the beginning, and to the *cur non antea* form of the question, it suggests that God had not, prior to the beginning, become bored with his idleness. For the heretic, the question clearly implies that God has a beginning, either a beginning of his existence or a beginning of his boredom. As we shall see in the following section, the author maintains the principle that whatever has a beginning has an end. Hence, his form of the question presents the dilemma: either God himself began to be, or God began to be bored. If God himself had a beginning, then he will have an end. But if he began to be bored, then he was not sufficient unto himself, but in need of what he created, at least for the purposes of relieving his boredom.

In his reply to the Manichaean questions in his earliest commentary on Genesis, Augustine first offered two interpretations of "the beginning." The first is that "God made heaven and earth in the beginning, not in the beginning of time, but in Christ, since he was the Word with the Father, through whom and in whom all things were made."[23]

21. Ibid., pp. 66–67.
22. Ibid., 72.
23. *Gn. adv. Man.* 1, 2, 3: "His respondemus, Deum in principio fecisse coelum et terram, non in principio temporis, sed in Christo, cum Verbum esset apud Patrem, per quod facta et in quo facta sunt omnia." Augustine appeals to Jn 8:25, where Jesus states that he is "Principium, quia et loquor uobis."

However, one can also take "the beginning" to mean "the beginning of time." In that case, "we ought, of course, to realize that before the beginning of time there was no time."[24] Hence, Augustine points out that "we cannot claim that there was some time when God had not yet made anything."[25] This answer of Augustine presupposes a concept of God's timelessness or eternity as *tota simul*—a concept that Augustine learned from the Neoplatonists and that he seems to have been the first to hold among Western Christian thinkers.[26]

With regard to the *cur non antea* form of the question, Augustine points out that it implies the existence of past times during which God was idle. "But when they say, 'Why did he suddenly decide [to make heaven and earth],' they speak as if some times went by during which God produced nothing."[27] On the other hand, if the Manichees drop "suddenly" from their objection and ask why God made heaven and earth, Augustine replies that he did so because he willed to do so.[28] And if they push the question further and ask why he willed to do so, Augustine replies that, in asking for a cause of God's will, they are asking for something greater than God's will, though there is nothing greater for them to find.[29]

In his answer to the anonymous heretic, Augustine points out that God neither began to be nor began to be bored by his inactivity.[30] There was, Augustine states, no point at which God did not exist. But he also indicates that the divine boredom suggested by the heretic implies a highly anthropomorphic view of a god who becomes sluggish through inactivity, labors hard when he does something, lacked a throne before

24. Ibid.: "Sed etsi in principio temporis Deum fecisse coelum et terram credamus, debemus utique intelligere quod ante principium temporis non erat tempus."
25. Ibid.: "Non ergo possumus dicere fuisse aliquod tempus quando Deus nondum aliquid fecerat."
26. See D. Balás, "Eternity and Time in Gregory of Nyssa's *Contra Eunomium*," esp. 147, where Balás argues for Gregory's priority over Augustine as the first Christian thinker to hold a non-temporal eternity.
27. *Gn. adv. Man.* 1, 2, 3: "Cum autem dicitur, quid ei placuit subito, sic dicitur, quasi aliqua tempora transierint, quibus Deus nihil operatus est."
28. Ibid. 1, 2, 4: "Qui dicit, Quare fecit Deus coelum et terram? respondendum est ei, Quia voluit."
29. Ibid.: "Voluntas enim Dei causa est coeli et terrae, et ideo maior est voluntas Dei quam coelum et terra. Qui autem dicit, quare voluit facere coelum et terram? majus aliquid quaerit quam est voluntas Dei: nihil autem majus invenire potest."
30. *C. adv. leg.* 1, 2, 2: "nec Deus esse coepit nec eum vacationis suae taeduit."

heaven was made, and seated himself on the heavenly throne, like a tired traveler, once it had been made.³¹ "After all," Augustine adds, "he is able to abide in himself with perfect happiness."³² His perfect happiness rules out any need on the part of God and, hence, eliminates the need for anything to relieve his boredom.

Having rejected the erroneous interpretation suggested by the anonymous heretic, Augustine tells his readers that they should understand the beginning either as the point at which creatures began to be or as Christ, the power and wisdom of God, in which God created all things.³³ Thus, Augustine's positive interpretation of *in principio* in this later work does not represent a notable advance over his earliest commentary on Genesis, though the form of the question about the beginning posed by the anonymous author required a new refutation.

THERE IS NO BEGINNING WITHOUT AN END

The anonymous heretic appealed to a principle that Augustine encountered earlier in his conflict with the Manichees, namely, "that there is no beginning without an end."³⁴ The principle seems to have been almost a commonplace among the ancients.³⁵ Even a Christian thinker such as Nemesius in the fourth century followed the Platonists in hold-

---

31. Ibid.: "qui neque aliquando non fuit nec cessando torpuit nec operando laboravit nec sine caelo sedis indiguit nec facto caelo sedem tamquam finitis erroribus peregrinus invenit."

32. Ibid.: "Potens est enim beatissime manere in semetipso."

33. Ibid.: "Aut ergo sic intellegendum quod scriptum est: *In principio fecit Deus caelum et terram,* ut principium sit, ex quo esse coeperunt; non enim Deo coaeterna semper fuerunt, sed facta initium, ex quo esse coeperunt, acceperunt. Aut certe quia in principio sibi coaeterno fecit Deus caelum et terram, hoc est in unigenito filio."

34. Ibid. 1, 2, 3: "iste ... putavit esse dicendum ac definiendum, nullum esse sine fine principium." For a discussion of this principle, see T. Raveaux, *Augustinus: Contra Adversarium Legis et Prophetarum. Analyse des Inhalts and Untersuchung des geistesgeschichtlichen Hintergrunds* (Würzburg: Augustinus Verlag, 1987), pp. 14–19.

35. Among the philosophers, see Plato, *Republic* 8, 546A and Aristotle, *De caelo* 1, 10, 279b21 and 289a12–13, where he explicitly states that whatever begins to be comes to an end. So too, in *ep.* 166, 5, 14, Augustine rejects with regard to the human soul the claim that "omne, quod in tempore coepit esse, inmortale esse non posse,"—a claim that is supported by Sallust's statement that "omnia orta occidunt et aucta senescunt" (*Bellum Iugurthinum* 2, 3). Augustine simply points out, "coepit esse in tempore inmortalitas carnis Christi, quae tamen 'iam non moritur et mors ei ultra non dominabitur'" (Rom 6:9).

ing a corollary of the principle, namely, that the soul's preexistence was a condition of its immortality.[36]

The anonymous heretic uses the principle to imply that if the creator had a beginning, he will himself have an end, but he also uses the principle to prove that the work of the creator, which, according to the Law and the Prophets, had a beginning, is destined to perish completely. T. Raveaux sees in the words of the anonymous heretic an indication that he regarded the work of the creator God as doomed to extinction and as completely divorced from the work of the Savior.[37] On the other hand, according to the anonymous author, human souls can have a kinship with Christ, who has no beginning and, therefore, no end. Hence, it would seem that they can through their union with Christ be exempted from the extinction that the principle entails for things that have a beginning.

There is, on the other hand, no evidence that the anonymous heretic held that human souls were particles of God so that they were literally divine, as the Manichees claimed and the Priscillianists at least allegedly claimed.[38] Certainly, Augustine found no grounds to confront the anonymous heretic with that accusation, though he does mention an incorrect interpretation of Genesis 2:7, in accord with which God is said to breathe the breath of life into the man he had formed.[39] Augustine does cite the words of the anonymous author by which he indicates that Christ showed "that we are of his kinship" and "called us brothers." Hence, we should not look to "the one who, according to the Jewish Scriptures, assigned to us an earthly beginning and indicated,

---

36. See G. Verbeke, "L'immortalité de l'âme dans le 'De Anima' d'Avicenne. Une synthése de l'Aristotélisme et du Néoplatonisme," *Pensamiento* 25 (1969): 271–290.

37. See T. Raveaux, *Augustinus: Contra Adversarium Legis et Prophetarum,* pp. 14–19.

38. See *c. Prisc.* I, 1, where Augustine uses his standard argument to refute the Manichees to refute the Priscillianists. Whether Priscillian actually held that human souls were particles of God is difficult to determine, since the accusations against him seems to rest upon the work of his fierce opponent, Ithacus of Ossonuba, who accused him of Manichaeism as well as sorcery, sexual orgies, and various doctrinal errors. See Henry Chadwick, *Priscillian of Avila: The Occult and the Charismatic in the Early Church* (Oxford: Oxford University Press, 1976), for the best study of Priscillian in English.

39. See *c. adv. leg.* 1, 14, 22, where Augustine mentions that some interpret Gn 2:7 as referring to the ensoulment of the man God made, while others take it as referring to the bestowal of the Holy Spirit. Augustine himself leaves both of these possibilities open, while insisting, "animam tamen non esse partem Dei nec de substantia et natura eius creatam siue prolatam, sed ex nihilo factam dubitare fas non est."

thereby, our end in the earth."⁴⁰ Despite our very limited knowledge of the teaching of the anonymous heretic, his position seems thoroughly in accord with the Marcionist doctrine that Christ did not redeem us, or buy us back, from the creator God, because we had never belonged to Christ. Rather, he freely and unexpectedly made us his own brothers. And our union with him, it would seem, exempts us from implications of the principle that there is no beginning without an end, so that our souls can enjoy an immortality with Christ, despite their temporal beginning. Since Augustine does hold that many things in the created world have a beginning and also an end, he needs to explain, not that some of God's creatures will cease to be, but how they can be good, despite the fact that they cease to be. He also needs to explain that some of God's creatures that have come to be will not cease to be, for example, human souls.

With regard to the latter point, Augustine offers two arguments against the universality of the principle that there is no beginning without an end. First, he points out that the anonymous author must not have not noticed that numbers begin with one and have no end, since another number can also be added on, at least in thought.⁴¹ Second, he reminds his readers that, if the heretic is a Christian, "he certainly promises himself a happy life in Christ, which will have its beginning when this wretched life has its end."⁴² But then Augustine has the poor fellow hooked on a dilemma, for that happy life will either have or not have an end. "If he says that it will, how will he dare to call himself a Christian? If he says that it will not, what has happened to his bold claim that there is no beginning without an end?"⁴³

Having presented these strong arguments that not everything that has a beginning comes to an end, Augustine must still show that things that come to be and perish are, nonetheless, good. Furthermore, the anonymous author has yet another objection concerning the beginning.

---

40. *C. adv. leg.* 2, 11, 36, cited above in note 14.

41. Ibid. 2, 2, 3: "nec ipsum potuit attendere numerum, cuius initium est ab uno et finis in nullo. Nullus quippe numerus quamlibet magnus vel dicitur vel si iam dici non potest cogitatur, cui non addi possit ut maior sit."

42. Ibid.: "vitam sibi promittit in Christo utique beatam, cuius tunc poterit esse principium, cum vitae huius miserae finis fuerit."

43. Ibid.: "Si dixerit habituram, quomodo se audebit dicere christianum? Si dixerit non habituram, ubi est quod ausus est dicere nullum esse sine fine principium?"

WHY DID GOD NOT MAKE THE WORLD FROM THE START

The anonymous heretic poses a distinct version of the *cur non antea* form of the question about the beginning. In order to impugn the goodness of the world and also the goodness of the creator, the heretic asks, "If this world is something good, why did [God] not make it back at the start, since that would have been better?"[44] The anonymous author here uses "start": *initium* instead of "beginning": *principium*. Though the two Latin words need not differ in meaning any more than the two English words, it is likely that the anonymous heretic is consciously distinguishing the two. The Manichees, as well as other Gnostics, distinguished the starting time *(initium)* from the present middle time *(medium)* and the end time *(finis)*.[45] If that is what he means, the anonymous heretic is asking why God did not make the world in the starting time, that is, before this present age, while also implying that he has secret knowledge of this starting time.

Augustine takes the anonymous heretic as implying that "God should have made the world something better than it is" or that "this world should not have been made, because it is not equal to its maker."[46] Augustine may have suggested an answer insofar as he takes the heretic to imply that the world should have been equal to God, that is, equal in duration, since Augustine could, after all, argue that it is impossible for a creature to be equal to God in any respect. But he offers no immediate answer to the objection that if the world were something good, it would have been better if God had made it back at the start.

He does, however, point out that God created the world at the start, not at God's start, but at the world's.[47] Or, if "the start" in the heretic's

---

44. Ibid. 1, 3, 4: "Si mundus iste bonus aliquid est, cur non olim ex initio ab eo factum est, quod melius fuit?"

45. See, for example, *c. Fel.* 1, 6, 9 and 2, 1, 1: "Felix dixit: . . . et quia venit Manichaeus et per suam praedicationem docuit nos initium, medium et finem; docuit nos de fabrica mundi, quare facta est et unde facta est, et qui fecerunt" and "ista enim epistula fundamenti est, quod et sanctitas tua bene scit, quod et ego dixi, quia ipsa continet initium, medium et finem."

46. *C. adv. leg.* 1, 3, 4: "Quasi se ipso aliquid melius Deus fecerit mundum aut ideo non debuit hoc bonum fieri, quia non aequale facienti."

47. Ibid.: "Immo vero olim ex initio factum est; ex initio suo, non Dei, cui nullum est initium."

question can mean the same thing as "the beginning" in Genesis 1:1, Augustine can and does turn the heretic's earlier question against him and asks, "From what start then? That in which God himself began to be, or that from which he was bored with being idle?"[48] Augustine argues that by the question "Why did he not make it back at the start?" the author can imply that God should have made the world from the start of his own existence. But then, of course, as Augustine points out, God himself would have a start and would, by the heretic's principle, also have an end. Hence, Augustine infers the alternative, namely, that God made the world "from the beginning of his making, that is, when there began to be what he made."[49]

But then Augustine has again caught the heretic on a dilemma: "Either, then, their God never made any good or, according to this fellow, he made whatever good he made from the start of his existence. And we must fear that he will have an end, because he has a start."[50] Augustine acknowledges that the anonymous author may mean something else by "the start" than he means by "the beginning," so that he has no problem with God having a start, provided that he does not have a beginning. In any case, Augustine points out, he must admit, in accord with the first verse of the Gospel according to John, that on his interpretation the Word has a beginning and, therefore, must have an end. Hence, Augustine adds, even the Manichees will pronounce him insane.[51]

Augustine still faces two questions from the anonymous heretic, one implicit, the other explicit. The implicit question asks how anything destined to perish can be good; the explicit question asks why God did not make the world better by making it earlier. With regard to the implicit question, Augustine presents the standard answer he earlier gave to his Manichaean opponents, namely, that in creating all things, the *omnia*, that is, the full panoply of creatures from the highest to the low-

---

48. Ibid.: "Ex initio igitur quo? eiusne quo idem Deus esse coepit an ex eo quo vacuum esse taeduit?"

49. Ibid.: "Ac per hoc ex initio fecit illo ex quo fecit, id est, ex quo coepit esse quod fecit."

50. Ibid.: "Aut ergo Deus ipsorum nihil boni umquam fecit; aut secundum istum, quodcumque boni fecit, ex illo initio fecit, ex quo ipse est; et habenti initium metuendus est finis."

51. Ibid. 1, 3, 5: "Dicat hic si placet etiam illam definitivam suam, ubi audit: *In principio erat verbum,* dicat etiam hic, si audet: Nullum est principium sine fine, ut ab ipsis etiam Manichaeis . . . iudicetur insanus."

est, God created something not merely good, but something very good. "But he who is supremely good made all things, unequal to one another, but still good. . . . They had to be not only unequal to him by whom they were created, but unequal to one another, and thus they form a universe. For if they were equal, they would be one kind of good and not all kinds. But they are now all kinds of goods, because some are better than others."[52] Augustine finds in the variety of good things, some better than others, which is required to form a universe, a beauty that would be lacking if there were only one kind of good thing.[53] To prove that things that perish are good, Augustine points out that, though the heretic finds fault with God's creatures that he sees are destined to perish, "he could not complete this very speech of his, in which he finds so much pleasure that he has committed it to writing and memory, except by sounds attached to each of his words that come to be and pass away. Thus he could not display the beauty of his discourse, by which he wants to persuade us that whatever comes to be and dies cannot be good, save by syllables that come to be and die."[54] Augustine's aesthetic defense of the beauty of mortal things might seem to leave him open to the sort of ridicule Voltaire poured out upon the Leibnizian optimism in *Candide*, except for the fact that he admits that "the mind that can perceive this beauty is greater than human."[55]

Augustine then takes up the explicit objection about why God did not make the world as far in the past as God himself goes back. "This

---

52. Ibid. 1, 4, 6: "Sed summe bonus fecit omnia, sibi quidem imparia, sed tamen bona. Quae non solum illi, a quo sunt condita, sed nec inter se esse oportet aequalia, et ideo sunt omnia. Nam si essent aequalia, unum genus bonorum esset, non omnia. Nunc vero ideo sunt omnia bona, quia sunt aliis alia meliora."

53. Ibid.: "et bonitas inferiorum addit laudibus meliorum: Et in rerum bonarum inaequalitate ipsa est iucunda gradatio, ubi minorum comparatio ampliorum est commendatio." See O'Connell, *Imagination and Metaphysics,* pp. 28–33, for Augustine's use of this sort of aesthetic defense of the goodness of an *omnia*.

54. Ibid.: "eumdem sermonem suum, qui usque adeo illi placuit, ut eum litteris memoriaeque mandaret, nisi vocibus ad sua quaeque verba pertinentibus et incipientibus tamen et deficientibus implere non posset, ita pulchritudinem disputationis, qua vult persuadere quidquid oritur et moritur bonum esse non posse, nisi orientibus et morientibus syllabis non potuit explicare."

55. Ibid.: "Sed maior quam humanus est sensus quo talis pulchritudo sentitur." Augustine makes the same point in *vera rel.* 22, 42–43, where he drawing an analogy between the passing syllables of a poem and order of temporal things. There he adds that not only can no human being perceive the whole order of the passing ages, but that we ourselves have become part of them by reason of our fall.

fellow complains," he says, "asking why God did not make these good things back as far as God goes back."[56] Augustine's response is that God did not make these creatures out of any need for them, since he could exist without them and remain perfectly happy, everlasting and without beginning.[57] Since God had no need for them, the only cause for their existence is the goodness of God.[58] The answer might seem unsatisfactory, but in the context it is a good answer. Augustine has, after all, shown that creatures that come to be and perish are, nonetheless, good and that all good creatures come from God, both those that come to be and perish and those that come to be and last immortally. Furthermore, he has shown that God has no need of any creature; hence, the only cause of a creature's coming to be is God's will or God's goodness. The two, namely, God's will or God's goodness, are not alternatives, but complementary. Elsewhere, Augustine contrasts our making things out of need or necessity with God's making by his free will and out of his goodness, "God created out of his goodness; he did not need anything he made; therefore, he made all things whatsoever that he willed."[59] We, on the other hand, do with free will what we do without any need or necessity. We do with free will what we do with love.[60]

A POSTSCRIPT ON HUMAN GOODNESS

In drawing this article to a close, I want to point out a passage in *c. adv. leg.* in which Augustine addresses the topic of human goodness. He points to many aspects of goodness that are to be found in all human beings, even in fallen, sinful, and heretical human beings. The anonymous heretic objected that the Creator seemed surprised to find

---

56. Ibid. 1, 7, 10: "Et unde iste calumniatur, cur non ista bona tam olim, quam olim est ipse, fecerit Deus."

57. Ibid.: "hinc potius intelligendum est, quod non ea fecerit eorum indigus, sine quibus esse in sua perfecta beatitudine potuit esse sine initio sempiternus."

58. Ibid.: "Ideo quippe istorum faciendorum causa sola Dei bonitas fuit, quia necessitas eius ulla non fuit."

59. *En. Ps.* 134, 10: "Deus bonitate fecit, nullo quod fecit eguit; Ideo omnia quaecumque uoluit, fecit." See my "The Motive for Creation according to St. Augustine," *The Modern Schoolman* 65 (1988): 245–253.

60. Ibid.: "Ea enim quae diximus, ex necessitate facimus; quia si non faceremus, egentes et inopes remaneremus. Invenimus aliquid quod libera voluntate faciamus? Invenimus plane, cum ipsum Deum amando laudamus. Hoc enim libera uoluntate facis, quando amas quod laudas; non enim ex necessitate, sed quia placet."

that the light he made was good.⁶¹ Augustine pointed out that God did not learn that his creatures were good after he made them, but rather made them because he saw they were good in the light that he himself is.⁶² Even the wicked who, as he foresaw, would reject the Law and the Prophets pose no difficulty, for even they are good "insofar as they are human beings, insofar as they are composed of a body and a rational soul, insofar as the members of their bodies have their distinct functions and cooperate harmoniously in their different ways toward a peaceful unity involving a wonderful order. They are good insofar as the soul presides and rules over them by its natural excellence, insofar as it fills and enlivens the five senses of the flesh with their different powers that work together with one another, insofar as it can, unlike the soul of a beast, have wisdom and understanding by its mind and reason."⁶³ If there is all that goodness in even sinful and heretical human beings, the work of the creator, the God of the Law and the Prophets, is, for Augustine of Hippo, very good indeed.

61. *C. adv. leg.* 1, 7, 10: "Sed iste vaniloquus blasphemator . . . videte quid dixerit: *Adeo antea nescivit,* inquit, *lux quid esset, ut modo eam primum videns optimam iudicaret.*"

62. Ibid.: "Quid autem Deus vidit a se factum, quod non in luce, quod ipse est, prius vidit esse faciendum?"

63. Ibid.: 1, 6, 9: "quia et ipsos, in quantum homines sunt, in quantum corpore atque anima rationali constant, in quantum membra corporis eorum suis distinguuntur officiis et concordissima differentia in unitatem suae pacis mirabili ordinatione consentiunt, in quantum anima eis naturali excellentia praestat atque imperat, in quantum sensus carnis quinque partitos implet ac vegetat dissimili potentia, sociali convenientia, in quantum etiam mente atque ratione, quod bestialis anima non potest, sapere atque intellegere potest, vidit Deus quia boni sunt, et ideo creavit."

10

AUGUSTINE'S VIEW OF THE ORIGINAL HUMAN CONDITION IN *DE GENESI CONTRA MANICHAEOS*

Augustine wrote his first commentary on Genesis in 388–389, several years before his ordination to the priesthood. In it he offers his readers a fascinating insight into his early understanding of the state of the first human beings in paradise. Although the future bishop of Hippo wanted to give a literal interpretation of the biblical text, he found that he was unable and had to resort to a highly figurative interpretation of it. Deeply influenced by the thought of Plotinus, which he came to know in the Church of Milan, Augustine presents us with a highly spiritualized account of the first parents of the human race—an account that jarred with the biblical account and with much of later Christian theology. Gn. adv. Man. does, however, provide a valuable insight into how Augustine's thought developed by showing us his first attempt at biblical exegesis, which must surely have mystified the more down-to-earth Christians of the African Church.

For many years and in many books Robert O'Connell has argued that Saint Augustine held at least up to and including the time of his *conf.* a view of man as a fallen soul, that is, as a soul that has come to be in body and in time as a result of sin.[1]

---

1. In *Origin of the Soul*, O'Connell says, "My interpretation of Augustine's theory of the human condition compelled me to conclude that his early works

Other scholars have remained unconvinced by O'Connell's thesis. For example, after examining the evidence, Gerard O'Daly concludes that Augustine did not believe in the soul's preexistence.² Similarly, in a recent paper, Frederick Van Fleteren claims that O'Connell has led the world of Augustinian scholars into a cul-de-sac with his emphasis upon the theme of the fall of the soul.³ O'Daly does not deal extensively with *Gn. adv. Man.* In fact he dismisses the work with the claim, "In the early works—*de Genesi contra Manichaeos* and *de libero arbitrio*—Augustine is only marginally concerned with the problem of the soul's origin."⁴ Yet *Gn. adv. Man.* is one of the principal early works upon which O'Connell relies for his interpretation of Augustine.⁵

The question obviously cannot be settled by a single study of a single work. On the other hand, given the fact that patristic commentaries on the creation narrative in Genesis 1–3 provided the *locus classicus* for expounding one's view of human existence, it would seem worthwhile to investigate Augustine's view of the original human condition in his first commentary on the Genesis account of creation, a work that deserves much more attention than it has previously received.

SOME PRENOTES

Several prenotes can help to focus such an investigation. First, *Gn. adv. Man.* presents a highly figurative interpretation of the beginning chapters of Genesis. This is especially true of book 2. There Augustine notes at the start that the text of Genesis is beginning to deal with human beings in greater detail and that "the whole narrative unfolds, not

---

enshrined a view of man as 'fallen soul' [and] that this view of our journey through 'this' life persisted in his *Confessions*" (2). O'Connell adds that this view that he originally presented as an hypothesis he now regards as verified by his study of the later works. See J. Patout Burns, "St. Augustine: The Original Condition of Humanity," in *Studia Patristica* 22, ed. E. A. Livingstone (Leuven: Peeters, 1989), 219–222, for a defense of O'Connell's thesis.

2. Gerard O'Daly, *Augustine's Philosophy of Mind* (Berkeley and Los Angeles: University of California Press, 1987), 16–17, especially n48, and 199–202. O'Daly argues that the passages in which Augustine speaks of the soul's return and recollection are metaphorical or figurative and should not be taken in any literal sense (see 199–202).

3. Frederick Van Fleteren, "A Reply to O'Connell," *AS* 21 (1990): 127–137.

4. See O'Daly, *Augustine's Philosophy of Mind*, 17. It is hard to square this with the beginning of his earliest work, *beata v.*, where Augustine emphasizes the question of the soul and is clearly troubled by its origin.

5. See O'Connell, *Early Theory*, 155–179.

clearly, but in figures."⁶ Augustine tells us that he would have preferred to give a literal interpretation of the text, "to understand it just as the letter sounds," as he puts it.⁷ However, he found that he could not understand the text in its literal sense in a pious manner that is worthy of God. That is, he had recourse to a figurative interpretation of Genesis because he could not take the text in its literal sense and avoid impiety or blasphemy toward God. Hence, his spiritual interpretation of the text is something he regards not as optional, but as necessary, not something in addition to the literal sense, but the only way of interpreting the text that accords with the Christian faith.⁸ As far as Augustine can see at this point, the literal sense of the text often involves absurdity, blasphemy, or impiety; hence, he has to understand the text in a nonliteral sense.⁹ The figurative interpretation of the text does not deny a literal sense of the text; however, it does imply that the literal sense is one that involves absurdity, blasphemy, or impiety.¹⁰ Or, to put the point in another way, the absurd, blasphemous, or impious literal sense certainly cannot be the sense of the text intended by God.¹¹

An example may help to clarify this point. After the account of the six days of creation followed by the Sabbath rest, Genesis 2:5 says, "There was, then, made the day on which day God made heaven and earth, and all the green of the field and every food of the field before they were on

---

6. *Gn. adv. Man.* 2, 1, 1: "Deinde incipit de homine diligentius narrari. Quae omnis narratio non aperte, sed figurate explicatur."
7. See ibid. 2, 2, 3: "Secundum litteram accipere, id est non aliter intelligere quam littera sonat."
8. See ibid.: "Sane quisquis voluerit omnia quae dicta sunt, secundam litteram accipere . . . et potuerit evitare blasphemias, et omnia congruentia fidei catholicae praedicare, non solum ei non est invidendum, sed praecipuus multumque laudabilis intellector habendus est. Si autem nullus exitus datur, ut pie et digne Deo quae scripta sunt intelligantur, nisi figurate atque in aenigmatibus proposita ista credamus."
9. This claim is supported by Augustine's later judgment. See *Gn. litt.* 8, 2, 5: "Et quia non mihi tunc occurrebant omnia quemadmodum proprie possent accipi magisque non posse videbantur aut vix posse atque difficile, ne retardarer, quid figurate significarent, ea quae ad litteram invenire non potui, quanta valui breuitate ac perspicuitate explicavi."
10. See the introduction to *Gn. litt.* in BA 48, 38, where Agaësse and Solignac suggest that in *Gn. adv. Man.*, we have allegory in the modern sense that denies or excludes a literal sense.
11. For more on "the absurdity criterion" for recourse to a figurative understanding of the text, see Jean Pépin, "A propos de l'histoire de l'exégèse allégorique: l'absurdité, signe de allégorie," *Studia Patristica* in *Texte und Untersuchungen* 63 (1955): 395–415.

earth."¹² Yet according to Genesis 1:1 God made heaven and earth in the beginning, and he made the green of the field and food on the third day. What then can this day mean? Moreover, why does Genesis 2:5 mention the green of the field and food and not mention so many other things? And how could God have made the green of the field before it was on earth? A literal reading of the passage—"just as the letter sounds"—leads to absurdity. Hence, Augustine understands the passage so that this day signifies the whole of time and so that the green of the field signifies "an invisible creature like the soul," while "the field is this world." So too, "before they were on the earth" means "before the soul sinned."¹³

Second, Augustine uses phrases such as "an invisible creature like the soul" or "the spiritual and invisible creature" or "before the soul sinned" in a way that is disconcertingly vague as to the number of souls.¹⁴ So too, he says that the fountain of truth watered the invisible creature before sin, that is, that "the soul was watered by such a fountain."¹⁵ Moreover, he tells us that the fountain watering the whole face of the earth signifies "the flood of truth satisfying the soul before sin."¹⁶ Once Augustine speaks of the soul's having been ordered in the middle position in reality beneath God and above bodies. Twice he speaks of Adam and Eve in that middle position.¹⁷ So too, he says that "that nature that God made from nothing, after it sinned, has to do penance for sins."¹⁸

---

12. *Gn. adv. Man.* 2, 3, 4: "Factus est ergo dies, quo die Deus caelum et terram, et omne viride agri, antequam essent super terram, et omne pabulum agri."
13. Ibid. 2, 3, 4–5: "viride agri invisibilem creaturam vult intellegi sicut est anima. Ager enim solet in Scripturis figurate mundus appellari. Nam et ipse Dominus: 'Ager est hic,' inquit, 'mundus.' Deinde quod addidit: 'antequam essent super terram,' intellegitur antequam anima peccaret."
14. Ibid.: "invisibilem creaturam . . . sicut est anima . . . spiritalem atque invisibilem creaturam . . . antequam anima peccaret."
15. Ibid. 2, 4, 5–5, 6: "Ante peccatum vero, cum viride agri et pabulum fecisset Deus, quo nomine invisibilem creaturam significari diximus, irrigabat eam fonte interiore. . . . anima tali fonte irrigabatur."
16. Ibid. 2, 6, 7: "et nomine fontis ascendentis et irrigantis omnem faciem terrae, inundatio veritatis animam satians ante peccatum."
17. Ibid. 2, 11, 12: "ut intellegat anima, in meditullio quodam rerum se esse ordinatam, ut quamvis subiectam sibi habeat omnem naturam corpoream, supra se esse intellegat naturam Dei." Ibid. 3, 15, 22: "illa medietate, per quam Deo subiecti erant, et corpora subiecta habebant." Ibid. 2, 16, 24: "ad seipsos, qui in medio rerum infra Deum et supra corpora ordinati erant."
18. Ibid. 2, 19, 43: "eam naturam quam Deus fecit de nihilo, postquam peccavit cogi ad poenitentiam peccatorum."

Finally, if "all the green" signifies "an invisible creature like the soul" and "the field" signifies "this world," it is difficult to avoid the implication that "all the green of the field" is "the soul of this world." Recall that in his early writings Augustine spoke of "the soul that is either in us or everywhere."[19] So too, he speaks of the highest essence giving form to body through soul so that "body subsists through soul, and it is by the very fact that it is ensouled, either universally, as the world, or particularly, as each living thing within the world."[20] The point of this second prenote can perhaps best be summed up in the words of a ninth-century treatise on the soul by Ratramus of Corbie in which he quotes Maccarius Scotus: "Hence, I set this forth, brother, in order that you may know what Augustine held. He did not hold one soul; he did not hold many souls. He held what he stated in the second place, that is, that the soul is one and many."[21] Maccarius was referring to *quan.* 32, 69, a text virtually contemporary with *Gn. adv. Man.* There Augustine indicates that he cannot say that the soul is simply one or that it is simply many; rather he implies that it is one and many at the same time.[22] I suggest that this view of the soul as one and many underlies Augustine claims about "that death that all of us who have been born from Adam have begun to owe to nature" and about "the penal mortality that we have merited by sinning."[23] For it was soul that sinned in Adam and Eve; it was nature that sinned. And "no nature is harmed save by its own sins."[24] Hence, there is in Augustine's doctrine of a universal soul, with which individual souls are somehow one, an ontological basis for

---

19. *Ord.* 2, 11, 30: "ad Deum intellegendum vel ipsam quae aut in nobis aut usque quaque est animam."

20. *Imm. an.* 15, 24: "Per animam ergo corpus subsistit et eo ipso est, quo animatur, sive universaliter, ut mundus; sive particulariter, ut unumquodque animal intra mundum." For further evidence that Augustine held such a view, see Vernon J. Bourke, "St. Augustine and the Cosmic Soul," *Giornale de Metafisica* 9 (1954): 431–440; revised in his *Wisdom from St. Augustine* (Houston: Center for Thomistic Studies, 1984), 78–90. Also see my "The World-Soul and Time in St. Augustine," *AS* 14 (1983): 75–92.

21. Ratrame de Corbie, *Liber de anima ad Odonem Bellovacensem,* texte inédit publié par D. C. Lambot, O.S.B. Analecta Mediaevalia Namurcensia 2 (Namur: Godenne; Lille: Liard, 1951), 17. I owe this reference to Vernon Bourke's study mentioned above.

22. See *Quan.* 32, 69.

23. *Gn. adv. Man.* 2, 21, 32: "Nam illa mors, quam omnes qui ex Adam nati sumus, coepimus debere naturae," and 2, 26, 38: "propter mortalitatem, quam peccando meruimus."

24. Ibid. 2, 29, 43: "nulli naturae nocere peccata nisi sua."

the claim that we all sinned in Adam.[25] Indeed, there is good reason to think that the Plotinian doctrine of an all-soul in which individual human souls were all once one and with which they remain one underlies Augustine's view of our relation to Adam as early as *Gn. adv. Man.* If that is the case, then in Adam's sin, or when the soul sinned, we by sinning merited death. If that is the case, then the original human condition was once ours, and in Adam we all fell.

BODIES OR NOT?

The first book of *Gn. adv. Man.* says little about the original human condition until Augustine deals with Genesis 1:26. When he comes to the man's being made to the image and likeness of God, Augustine insists that the "all who understand the Scriptures spiritually" or "the spiritual faithful" know that it is the interior man "where reason and intellect are found" that is made to God's image.[26] Augustine argues that we may understand the union of male and female before the sin in a spiritual sense and hold that carnal fecundity came about only after the sin. Thus, a chaste union of male and female before the Fall would fill the earth with "spiritual offspring of intelligible and immortal joys"![27] Augustine says, "We should believe that it was this way," and continues in words that seem open to more than one meaning, "because they were

---

25. The Plotinian roots of this position that the soul is both one and many can be found in *Ennead* 4, 2, 2 and the preceding argumentation. See Philippe Delhaye, *Une controverse sur l'âme universelle au IXe siécle*. Analecta Mediaevalia Namurcensia 1 (Namur: Centre d'études médiévales, 1950), 15, where in the historical introduction to the doctrine of Ratramus of Corbie, Delhaye says, "Saint Augustin ne pense point pour autant que les âmes humaines participent à la substance de cette âme cosmique. . . . D'autre part, les âmes forment un tout qui, réalisé en une fois dans le premier homme, se déploie au cours des temps: cette unité est réelle, elle n'est pas seulement une vue de l'esprit et c'est elle qui explique la participation de chacun au péché originel. 'Tous ont péché par la mauvaise volonté d'un seul, car à ce moment tous étaient cet homme' *(omnes ille unus fuerunt)*." See *nupt. et conc.* II, 5.

26. *Gn. adv. Man.* 1, 17, 27–28: "Sed omnes qui spiritualiter intelligunt Scripturas . . . noverint in catholica disciplina spirituales fideles non credere Deum forma corporea definitum; et quod homo ad imaginem Dei factus dicitur, secundum interiorem hominem dici, ubi est ratio et intellectus."

27. Ibid. 1, 19, 30: "Erat enim prius casta conjunctio masculi et feminae; hujus ad regendum, illius ad obtemperandum accommodata: et spirituales fetus intelligibilium et immortalium gaudiorum replens terram."

not yet children of this world before they sinned. For the children of this world generate and are generated, as the Lord says, when he shows that this carnal generation should, in comparison with the future life that is promised us, be despised."[28] Augustine will later explicitly reject this view and claim that he had not at this point seen that children could have been born even if parents did not die.[29]

Augustine continues this figurative interpretation of the sexes in the second book and views the making of the woman from the man's rib as "the knowledge by which we understand that there is one thing in us that rules by reason, another that obeys reason."[30] Augustine concedes the possibility that a visible woman was made from the body of the man in accord with history, but insists that whether these are figurative expressions or figurative deeds, they are clearly mysteries and sacraments.[31] So too, "bone from my bones, and flesh from my flesh" signifies fortitude and temperance. "For we are taught that these two virtues pertain to the lower part of the soul that rational prudence rules."[32]

Just as Augustine permits and urges a spiritual interpretation of the sexes and of their union and offspring, so he suggests a spiritual interpretation of man's domination over the other animals as his rule over the affections and emotions of his soul.[33] However, the first book does not contain very much that is terribly problematic about Augustine's view of the original human condition. Human bodies are mentioned,

---

28. Ibid.: "Quod ideo sic credendum est, quia nondum erant filii saeculi hujus antequam peccarent. Filii enim saeculi hujus generant et generantur, sicut Dominus dicit, cum in comparatione futurae vitae quae nobis promittitur, carnalem istam generationem contemnendam esse demonstrat" (Lk 2:34–36). The term *saeculum*, for instance, might be translated either as "world" or as "age." So too, "this carnal generation" might refer to the act of generating or to the stretch of time in the flesh as opposed to the life to come. I suspect that Augustine meant us to read more rather than less in the text.

29. See *retr.* 1, 10, 2; see also *s. Dom. mon.* I, xv, 40, where Augustine says, "Hoc et de patre et de matre et de ceteris vinculis sanguinis intellegendum est, ut in eis oderimus quod genus humanum nascendo et moriendo sortitum est." He rejects this doctrine in *retr.* 1, 19, 5.

30. *Gn. adv. Man.* 2, 12, 16: "Ipsa enim cognitio, qua intellegitur in nobis aliud esse quod ratione dominetur, aliud quod rationi obtemperet; ipsa ergo cognitio veluti effectio mulieris est de costa viri, propter coniunctionem significandam."

31. Ibid. 2, 12, 17.

32. Ibid. 2, 13, 18: "Hae namque duae virtutes, ad inferiorem animi partem, quam prudentia rationalis regit."

33. See ibid. 1, 20, 31.

though little is said of them apart from the fact that before sin men were not mortal and did not generate carnally.[34]

We have already seen how Augustine interprets Genesis 2:5 so that "the green of the field" signifies "the invisible creature like the soul," which was not on earth "before the soul sinned."[35] Genesis also says that God had not as yet made it rain upon the earth and that even now God produces the green of the field by raining, that is, "he makes souls become green again by his word by which he waters them from the clouds, that is, from the writings of the prophets and apostles."[36] Augustine explains that these writings are correctly termed clouds, because "these words that sound by striking the air and pass become like clouds when the obscurity of allegories are added like a fog drawn over them, and when they are pressed by study, the rain of truth, so to speak, is poured out upon those who understand well. But this was not the case before the soul sinned."[37] For prior to the sin "*There was no man to labor on [the earth]* (Gn 2:5). For man laboring on the earth rain from the clouds was necessary.... But before the sin, when God had made the green of the field and food, by which expression we have said the invisible creature is signified, he watered it with an interior fountain, speaking to its intellect, so that it did not receive words from the outside like rain from the clouds we mentioned, but was satisfied by its own source, that is, by the truth flowing from its interior."[38] The text is at least open to the interpretation that before the sin man did not yet exist, that is, there was only

---

34. See my "The Image and Likeness of God in St. Augustine's *De Genesi ad litteram liber imperfectus*," *Augustinianum* 30 (1990): 441–451, where I argue that this first attempt at a literal interpretation was brought to an abrupt halt by Gn 1:27: "male and female he created them."

35. *Gn. adv. Man.* 2, 3, 4–5.

36. Ibid. 2, 4, 5: "Facit animas revirescere per verbum suum; sed de nubibus eas irrigat, id est de Scripturis Prophetarum et Apostolorum."

37. Ibid.: "Verba ista quae sonant et percusso aere transeunt, addita etiam obscuritate allegoriarum quasi aliqua caligine obducta, velut nubes fiunt: quae dum tractando exprimuntur, bene intelligentibus tanquam imber veritatis infunditur. Sed hoc nondum erat antequam anima peccaret."

38. Ibid.: "'Nec erat homo qui operaretur in ea.' Laboranti enim homini in terra imber de nubibus est necessarius. Ante peccatum vero, cum viride agri et pabulum fecisset Deus, quo nomine invisibilem creaturam significari diximus, irrigabat eam fonte interiore, loquens in intellectum ejus: ut non extrinsecus verba exciperet, tanquam ex supradictis nubibus pluviam; sed fonte suo, hoc est de intimis suis manente veritate, satiaretur."

the spiritual creature, to whose intellect God spoke directly and from within. Thus the invisible creature did not receive words externally.

Genesis speaks of a single fountain that watered the whole face of the earth, and Augustine understands this as referring to the interior fountain of truth that watered the soul before it sinned through pride.[39] His description of the soul's pride, based on Sirach 10:14 and 10:9–10, as its thrusting forth its interior and as "swelling into exterior things through pride" suggests that the soul's pride is precisely its becoming embodied.[40] He asks, "For what is pride but the abandonment of the inward place of consciousness and the wish to appear externally what one is not?"[41] The text is open to a variety of meanings. Pride is often described as wanting to appear to be what one is not, that is, to seem to be more than one is. But the soul that abandons its interiority and wants to be seen externally as a body wants to be what it is not, namely, a body. Furthermore, that swelling into bodily form is not merely becoming what the soul is not, but is a becoming what is not, a fall from the being of a soul to something less. The soul is not a body; yet, when puffed up with pride, it swells into external things, that is, bodies, by desiring to appear externally in bodies what it in reality is not.[42] What is particularly striking about the *Gn. adv. Man.* text is the suggestion that the soul's embodiment is the natural result of its pride. And once the soul had swollen into exterior things through pride, "it began not to be watered by the interior fountain. . . . And, hence, laboring now on earth, it had need of the rain from the clouds, that is, teaching in human words, so that it might in this way again become green from that dryness and become the green of the field."[43] After this account of

---

39. Ibid. 2, 5, 6: "Iste, credo, fons ante peccatum ascendebat de terra, et irrigebat omnem faciem terrae, quia interior erat, et nubium non desiderabat auxilium."

40. Ibid.: "In exteriora per superbiam tumescens."

41. Ibid.: "Quid est enim superbia aliud, nisi deserto secretario conscientiae foris videri velle quod non est?"

42. Elsewhere Augustine refers to body as "a swelling": *tumor,* which reflects the Plotinian *onkos* and has at least some of the negative connotations of the English cognates. See *quan.* 14, 24. For further references see my "Love of Neighbor in St. Augustine," in *Atti III* of *Congresso internazionale su s. Agostino nel xvi centenario della conversione* (Rome: Augustinianum, 1987), 81–102, here 87–88n16.

43. *Gn. adv. Man.* 2, 5, 6: "Coepit non irrigari fonte intimo. . . . Et ideo laborans jam in terra necessariam habet pluviam de nubibus, id est doctrinam de humanis verbis, ut etiam hoc modo possit ab illa ariditate revirescere, et iterum fieri viride agri."

the soul's sin of pride as its swelling into exterior things, Genesis next turns, Augustine tells us, to "what we are specifically taught about human beings—matter that especially concerns us."[44] Genesis 2:7 declares that "God formed man from the mud of the earth." The Manichees objected to God's having made man from mud: "Did he lack a better and heavenly matter out of which to make man so that he formed him from earthly filth in such a fragile and mortal condition?"[45] Augustine replies that "the human body began to be something wasting away, frail, and destined to die after sin."[46] Augustine mentions that "some of ours" interpret Genesis 2:7 as referring to the formation of the body, while Genesis 1:26 refers to the making of the interior man, which is made to the image and likeness of God.[47]

In dealing with the breathing into the man of the breathe of life, Augustine sees two possibilities. The first is that there was as yet only the body, and the soul was then joined to the body—"whether the soul had already been made, but was in the mouth of God, that is, in his truth or wisdom . . . or whether the soul was made at that moment."[48] The second possibility is that by that breath awareness is given to the man who had already been made. In either case the first human had a body prior to sin, though not a body that was wasting away, frail and destined to die. Later Augustine again makes it clear that Adam and Eve had bodies, for after their sin "God changed their bodies into this mortality of the flesh."[49]

---

44. *Gn. adv. Man.* 2, 7, 8: "Nunc videamus . . . quid de homine specialiter intimetur, quod ad nos maxime pertinet."

45. Ibid.: "an defuerit ei melior et caelestis materia, unde hominem faceret, ut de labe terrena tam fragilem mortalemque formaret?"

46. Ibid.: "Dicimus enim tabidum et fragile et morti destinatum corpus humanum post peccatum esse coepisse."

47. I have suggested elsewhere that the *nonnulli nostri* in question include Origen. See "Origen and St. Augustine's First Commentaries on Genesis," in *Origenianum Quintum* (Leuven: Peeters, 1992), 179–185.

48. *Gn. adv. Man.* 2, 8, 10: "sive quae iam facta erat, sed tamquam in ore Dei erat, id est in eius veritate vel sapientia . . . sive anima tunc facta est." For the Origenian background of the first alternative, see my "Origen and St. Augustine's First Commentaries on Genesis." If, as I argue, Augustine was already under the influence of Origen's thought at this early date, it is possible that Augustine owed to Origen the view that the soul originally existed not merely without a corruptible body, but without any body whatsoever.

49. Ibid. 2, 21, 32: "Et Deus corpora eorum in istam mortalitatem carnis mutavit."

PARADISE AND HEAVENLY BODIES

Yet Adam and Eve did not have bodies anything like the bodies subject to failure and death that we know. What sort of bodies were these? And in what sort of paradise were they? Augustine tells us that paradise signifies human beatitude and that its trees signify our spiritual joys. The tree in the middle of paradise signifies the wisdom by which the soul knows its mid-rank position below God and above bodies.[50] So too, the rivers of paradise signify the cardinal virtues.[51] Man was placed in paradise to work and guard it, but his only work was to keep the commandment of God.[52] With regard to the devil's temptation of Eve, Augustine warns us not to be surprised that the devil could speak to the woman, though he was not in paradise and she was. "For either she was not in paradise in terms of place, but rather in terms of the state of beatitude, or even if there is such a place called paradise in which Adam and the woman dwelled, should we interpret the devil's approach in a bodily sense?"[53] And Augustine answers, "No, indeed; he approached them spiritually."[54] Hence, despite the fact that Adam and Eve had bodies, the bodies they had need not have been in a bodily paradise or in any bodily place.

Augustine interprets their nakedness as simplicity—something they became ashamed of after their sin. Hence, having lost their simplicity, they made aprons for themselves from fig leaves. "The fig leaves signify itching if one can speak this way in the case of incorporeal beings."[55] One of the most striking features of these heavenly bodies is their utter transparency such that thoughts could not be concealed and that lying was impossible. "For we should not believe that in those heavenly bodies thoughts could be concealed as they are concealed in these. Rather as some stirrings of our minds, are apparent on the countenance and especially in the eyes, so, I believe, in the clarity and simplicity of

---

50. Ibid. 2, 9, 12.   51. Ibid. 2, 10, 13–14.
52. Ibid. 2, 11, 15.
53. Ibid. 2, 14, 20: "non enim aut illa secundum locum erat in paradiso, sed potius secundum beatitudinis affectum: aut etiamsi locus est talis qui paradisus vocetur, in quo corporaliter Adam et mulier habitabant, etiam diaboli accessum corporaliter intellegere debemus?"
54. Ibid.: "Non utique, sed spiritaliter."
55. Ibid. 2, 15, 24: "Folia vero fici pruritum quemdam significant, si hoc bene in rebus incorporeis dicitur."

heavenly bodies no stirrings of the mind at all could be concealed."[56] Augustine argues that those who, though they could conceal lies in this life beneath the tunics of skin, hate them and burn with a love of the truth will be changed into angelic form. He interprets this future transformation as the time when "there is nothing hidden that will not be revealed" (Mt 10:26). Hence, the angelic form into which the saints will be transformed is similar to the celestial bodies of Adam and Eve insofar as neither kind of body permitted the concealment of any thoughts. That is, their heavenly bodies were, in Augustine's view, highly spiritualized bodies that were much more like the bodies of angels than the mortal bodies we now inhabit.[57]

Now man is situated in the dryness of sins and needs teaching in human words. It was for the sake of that rain from human words that "our Lord, having deigned to assume the cloud of our flesh, poured forth the abundant rain of the holy Gospel. He promised that, if anyone should drink of its water, he will return to the inner fountain and thus not seek rain from the outside. Rather, he says, 'There will come to be in him a fountain of water springing up unto eternal life.'"[58]

Now while laboring on the earth man needs teaching in such human words, but such knowledge in human words will be destroyed. Augustine compares our present knowledge to seeing in an enigma, for we now seek our food in a cloud. He contrasts this knowledge with the face-to-face vision we will have, according to 1 Corinthians 13:8 and 12. Then we will see face to face, "when the whole face of our earth will be watered by the interior fountain of water springing up."[59] Here Augustine links the interior fountain that will water the whole face of our earth with the water springing up unto eternal life that Christ promised in John 4:14. But equally significant is the fact that this fountain of

56. Ibid. 2, 21, 32: "Neque enim in illis corporibus caelestibus sic latere posse cogitationes credendum est, quemadmodum in his corporibus latent; sed sicut nonnulli motus animorum apparent in vultu, et maxime in oculis, sic in illa perspicuitate ac simplicitate caelestium corporum omnes omnino motus animi latere non arbitror."
57. See ibid.
58. Ibid. 2, 5, 6: "Dominus noster nubilum carnis nostrae dignatus assumere, imbrem sancti Evangelii largissimum infudit, promittens etiam quod si quis biberit de aqua ejus, rediet ad illum intimum fontem, ut forensicus non quaerat pluviam. Dicit enim: 'Fiet in eo fons aquae salientis in vitam aeternam'" (Jn 4:14).
59. Ibid.: "Quando universa facies terrae nostrae interiore fonte aquae salientis irrigabitur."

living water, namely Christ, once watered the whole face of the earth before the soul sinned and became a man who labored on the earth and needed the rain from human words. The implication is that before its fall into body the soul enjoyed the same direct knowledge of God that it will enjoy hereafter.

PLOTINUS IN THE BACKGROUND?

There are at least two characteristics of the life in paradise described in *Gn. adv. Man.* that do not square well with the biblical narrative. While Genesis has man placed in paradise to work and keep it, Augustine insists that the only work was to keep God's command. "That praiseworthy work was not toilsome. For work in paradise is different from the work on earth to which he was condemned after sin."[60] And while Genesis describes the serpent lying to Eve and Eve misleading Adam, Augustine claims that thoughts could not be hidden in such heavenly bodies, so that deception of the sort we can now practice was impossible.

These incongruities, I suggest, become understandable if they are viewed against their Plotinian background. In *Ennead* 5, 8, 4, "On the Intelligible Beauty," Plotinus describes the soul's life in heaven and emphasizes its freedom from toil and weariness: "For it is 'the easy life' there, and truth is their mother and nurse and being and food.... They do not grow weary of contemplation there, or so filled with it as to cease contemplating. Life holds no weariness for anyone when it is pure, and how should that which leads the best life grow weary?"[61] But in the same passage he also stresses the transparency of all to everyone: "[F]or all things are there transparent, and there is nothing dark or opaque; everything and all things are clear to the inmost part to everything; for light is transparent to light. Each there has everything in itself and sees all things in every other, so that all are everywhere and each and every one is all."[62] O'Connell has already argued that *Ennead* 5, 8 was one of

---

60. Ibid. 2, 11, 15: "operatio illa laudabilior laboriosa non erat. Alia est namque in paradiso operatio, et alia in terra, quo post peccatum damnatus est."

61. *Plotinus* with an English translation by A. H. Armstrong (Cambridge, Mass.: Harvard University Press, 1984), 5:249–251.

62. See O'Connell, *Early Theory*, 9.

the treatises that Augustine probably read.[63] He has also pointed to the parallel between *Ennead* 4, 3, 18 and *Gn. adv. Man.* 2, 4, 5; 2, 20, 30; and 2, 21, 32.[64]

CONCLUSION

In the first prenote I argued that Augustine regarded the figurative interpretation of Genesis that he gives in *Gn. adv. Man.* not as optional, but as necessary if one is to read the text in accord with Christian faith. In the second prenote I argued that the Plotinian view of the identity of the many souls with the one soul seems to underlie Augustine's talk of the soul having sinned and our having merited death by sinning. That is, we too were once in Adam and sinned in him.

In the body of the article we saw that at times Augustine speaks of the soul or the spiritual creature before it sinned and that at times he speaks of Adam and Eve as having bodies, although highly spiritualized ones. In accord with the first manner of speaking, Augustine describes the soul's pride as its swelling into exterior things and worries about the propriety of mentioning the itching fig leaves in the case of incorporeal beings. In accord with the second manner of speaking, Augustine clearly refers to Adam and Eve as having bodies, though their bodies seem to have been more nonbodily than bodily. For example, the difference of the sexes is interpreted figuratively, and there was no carnal union and reproduction before their sin. Despite their having bodies they were not necessarily in paradise in terms of place, and their bodies were such that their minds were completely transparent to each other. Human speech was unnecessary, and God spoke directly to their intellect.

Did Augustine, then, in *Gn. adv. Man.* hold that the first humans were originally souls that became embodied as the result of sin? Or did he hold that they were embodied even before sin, though not in frail and fragile and mortal bodies like ours, so that they received mortal bodies after sinning? He at least suggests the first view, though he more clearly articulates the latter. He seems to waver between speaking of them in their original state as being souls and as having bodies, though

63. See ibid.
64. Ibid., 163–164.

heavenly ones. Such a tension is very much what one might expect from an attempt to understand the very earthy biblical narrative in the light of a highly spiritualized Neoplatonic philosophy. And that, of course, it just what Augustine was doing.[65]

65. Fr. O'Connell has recently shared with me his review of my translation of Augustine's *Gn. adv. Man.*, in which he points to another way of reconciling the tensions I find in Augustine's thought in this area. I am now, I believe, much closer to O'Connell's position than when I wrote the introduction to the translation, though I still find tensions in Augustine's thought that I have not been able to resolve to my satisfaction.

4

The Soul & Time

II

AUGUSTINE ON THE INCORPOREALITY OF THE SOUL IN LETTER 166

Seldom does Augustine construct an argument that one would even today recognize as philosophical. In ep. 166, however, the bishop of Hippo wanted to prove to Jerome that he did know at least a few things about the soul, even though he was pleading for Jerome's help on the question of the soul's origin, that is, whether post-Adamic human souls were individually created by God, were somehow generated by the parents, or preexisted their embodiment and either fell or were sent into bodies. In this article I unpacked Augustine's argument that aimed to establish that the soul is incorporeal and pointed out some of its presuppositions and problems. The article shows that Augustine derived his argument from Plotinus and indicates some serious problems with it.

In *ep.* 166, written to Saint Jerome in 415, Saint Augustine presents an argument to show that the soul is incorporeal. The purpose of this article is to examine and evaluate that argument. Though the argument is an interesting one for a variety of reasons, it has received little, if any, critical attention.[1] Part of the

---

1. For example, Gilson mentions the argument from *ep.* 166 in dealing with the question of the relation of the soul and body. See *Christian Philosophy*, 48. Gilson regards the proof in *Trin.* 10 as the basic argument for the incorporeality of the soul. "In addition to this basic proof, Augustine has proposed less impor-

reason for the lack of attention paid to the argument may be the fact that it is based on the sense of touch, so that the argument, if sound, would prove that the souls of animals are incorporeal, though animals do not, of course, have minds and would, therefore, be unable to understand that their souls are incorporeal.[2] Though such a position might strike one as somewhat odd, one ought to bear in mind that Augustine did not—to the best of my knowledge—argue from the soul's incorporeality to its immortality.[3] Moreover, at least in his early years he seems to have held the existence of a world soul and to have expressed some uncertainty about whether there is one soul or whether there are many souls or whether soul is both one soul *and* many.[4] On such a view, if

---

tant arguments" (ibid., 272n11). Here Gilson refers to Jean F. Nourrisson's list of the less important arguments in *La Philosophie de s. Augustin* (Paris: Didier et Cie, 1865), 1:19–82. On pages 177–179 Nourrisson cites in full, but without any commentary or explanation, the argument from *ep.*166 after the eighth argument that he has explicitly numbered.

2. In the last lines of the argument, Augustine says that the nature of the soul cannot be thought *(cogitari)* in the imagination that deals with bodily images, but is understood by the mind *(mente intelligi)* and felt by life *(vita sentiri)*. Since in *imm. an.*, 16, 25, Augustine uses "irrational soul" and "life" interchangeably, one could translate *vita sentiri* as "felt or perceived by the irrational soul." In *De Immortalitate Animae of Augustine: Text, Translation and Commentary* (Amsterdam: B. R. Grüner, 1977), 156, C. W. Wolfskeel says that Augustine has in this passage begun to adduce arguments for the immateriality and immortality of irrational souls.

3. Despite Wolfskeel's claim to the contrary, I have been able to find no Augustinian argument for the immortality of the soul that is based on the immateriality or incorporeality of the soul. See Nourrisson, *Philosophie,* 224ff., and Gilson, *Christian Philosophy,* 51–55, where in dealing with the arguments for immortality in Augustine these authors do not mention any argument from the incorporeality of the soul. Furthermore, Augustine does not argue for the immateriality of the soul, since the soul has a kind of materiality rooted in its mutability (see Gilson, *Christian Philosophy,* 209, and *conf.* 12, 6, 6).

4. That Augustine, in his early writings at least, held that there is a world soul seems clear from such texts as the following from *imm. an.* 15, 24: "Per animam ergo corpus subsistit, et eo ipso est quo animatur, sive universaliter, ut mundus, sive particulariter, ut unumquodque animal intra mundum. . . . Nec invenitur aliquid quod sit inter summam vitam, quae sapientia et veritas est incommutabilis, et id quod ultimum vivificatur, id est corpus, nisi vivificans anima." For the question of whether the soul is one or many, see *quan.* 32, 68, where Augustine says, "Your mind must first be trained . . . to give you the insight and perspicacity to understand most clearly whether what certain very learned men say is actually true, namely, that the soul can in no way be divided in itself; but that this is possible by reason of the body." For this text I have used the translation by Joseph M. Colleran, *The Greatness of the Soul and The Teacher* (Westminster, Md.: Newman, 1964). See *Ennead* 4, 1, where Plotinus holds that the world soul is indivisible, but "in breathing life into bodies, is virtually multiplied into many souls, although it retains its fundamental unity" (Colleran, *Greatness,* 212n86). So too Augustine says in *quan.* 32, 69, "As to the number of souls, however,—seeing that you thought this relevant to the

any soul were incorporeal, then all souls or the soul of all would also be so.

Moreover, another version of the argument for the incorporeality of the soul from the sense of touch is found in Augustine's early work, *De immortalite animae* (hereafter *imm. an.*). The argument appears in the final paragraph of the work (*imm. an.* 16, 25) and is used to show that the soul cannot become a body. However, *imm. an.* is a work that even Augustine found confusing when he reviewed it for his *retr.* "It is first of all so confused because of the complexity and brevity of the arguments that it wearies even my mind when it is read and I scarcely understand it myself" (*retr.* 1, 5, 1). With such a commendation from its author, it is not surprising that a subsidiary argument in the final paragraph has not been the object of much philosophical attention.[5]

Despite the fact that the argument has been ignored to a large extent, there are grounds for viewing it as an argument that Augustine regarded as a strong one, if not the strongest one that he had at his disposal. For, if we turn to *ep.* 166, we find Augustine pleading—humbly and cautiously in view of previous tumultuous outbursts of rage from Bethlehem—for Jerome's help regarding the difficult question of the soul.[6] What Augustine wants to learn from Jerome is the answer to the

---

problem in hand—I do not know what answer to give you." Augustine seems to find the idea that the soul is "one and many at the same time" less difficult to accept than there being one soul only or there being simply many. Colleran once again finds a Plotinian background for such views in *Enneads* 3, 5, 1 and 4, 9, 1 (Colleran, *Greatness,* 212n88).

5. Augustine also tells us that he wrote this work after the *sol.* just after he had returned to Milan in the spring of 387. He seems to have envisioned it as an outline for a third book of the *sol.* Moreover, it was published without his approval, as he tells us in *retr.* 1, 5, 1. Of the argument in 16, 25, John Mourant, in *Augustine on Immortality* (Villanova: Augustinian Institute, 1969), 8–9, merely says, "Nor can the irrational soul be transformed into a body. Rather it permeates the body in its entirety and gives it life. Thus the whole argument closes on the purely psychological problem of the relation of the soul to the body." Though one might with difficulty, I believe, make a case for Mourant's claim that *imm. an.* 16, 25 is primarily concerned with the relation of the soul to the body, I believe that a much stronger case can be made to show that Augustine is arguing that the soul—even the irrational soul—is not a body. However, whether or not this is the case with *imm. an.*, it is clear that in *ep.* 166 he is arguing for the incorporeality of the soul.

6. For a brief, but vivid account of the correspondence between Jerome and Augustine, see O'Connell, "Augustine's Rejection," 11ff. As background to *ep.* 166, O'Connell admits that "it is hard to overcome the temptation to reproduce, round by ferocious round, (to profit from a metaphor Jerome introduces into the discussion) the battle that ensues between these two strong personalities." Given the history of misunderstandings in

question: Where does the soul—even of an infant—contract the guilt of sin that requires baptism? In order to show that he is not totally ignorant—and certainly not to instruct Jerome!—Augustine states what he holds most firmly regarding the soul either by faith or by knowledge: First, that the soul of man is immortal; second, that the soul is not a part of God; third, that the soul is incorporeal; and fourth, that the soul fell into sin by its own free will and cannot be freed therefrom except by the grace of Christ.

The argument that the soul is incorporeal is developed at considerable length; in the PL edition it runs nearly a full column. Unlike the arguments for the first and fourth claims, which involve appeals to scriptural texts and theological argumentation, the second and third claims are developed in a style of argumentation that is clearly philosophical. Augustine devotes the equivalent of a third of a column in the PL edition to the argument that the soul is not a part of God. He is aware that in *ep.* 165 Jerome mentioned to Marcellinus, as a fifth hypothesis regarding the origin of the soul (besides the four that Augustine had listed in *lib. arb.* 3, 20, 56–59), the view that the soul is a part of God.[7]

At the time of *lib. arb.* Augustine was still battling against the Manichees. He tells us in *ep.* 166 that he had then not even heard of the Priscillianists, whose views he knew by 415 were quite similar to those of the Manichees.[8] Hence, when he listed the four possibly true opinions regarding the origin of the soul, he did not in *lib. arb.* list the view that the soul is a part of God not only because the view was clearly heretical, but also because it concerned the soul's nature, not its embodiment (*ep.* 166, 3, 7). Thus Augustine is gently pointing out that Jerome's fifth

---

the correspondence between the two saints and Augustine's sincere pleas for information, he would surely have tried to produce for Jerome his strongest and clearest argument.

7. The four opinions "on the soul's incarnation" are that "the rest are propagated from the one given to the first man," that "new souls are produced even now for each individual," and that "already existing somewhere, they are either divinely sent, or fall of their own accord into bodies" (*ep.* 166, 3, 7). The translation of this letter used throughout this article is my own, though I have checked it against the translation by Sr. Wilfrid Parsons in *St. Augustine: Letters 165–203*, Ancient Christian Writers 12 (New York: Cima Publishing, 1955).

8. For Augustine's relation to the Priscillianist heresy, see Laureano Robles, "San Agustín y la cuestión priscilianista sobre el origen del alma," and Luis Arias, "El priscilianismo en san Agustín," *Augustinus* 25 (1980): 51–69 and 71–82.

hypothesis is not comparable with the other four and is out of place. Yet he does not ignore this hypothesis, but lists it second among the things that he wants Jerome to know that he holds most firmly either by faith or by knowledge. Hence, while Augustine rejects the view that the soul is a part of God as a hypothesis regarding the soul's origin, he tactfully gives it a position of emphasis among the things he knows about the soul.

Augustine also thought it important in writing to Jerome not only to indicate that he held that the soul is incorporeal, but also to provide his reasons—purely philosophical reasons—for holding this position. Since at least in the West there was no concept of God's or the soul's spirituality until the time of Augustine, though in the East there had been such a concept at least from the time of Origen, Augustine certainly knew that there was no need to hold a spiritualist view of God and the soul in order to be a good member of the *Catholica*.[9] Yet once he had himself accepted the spiritualist doctrine of the Milanese Church, he was well aware of the intellectual power of this view. For until he had accepted the Plotinian spiritual version of Christianity, he was unable to deal effectively with the problem of evil and to interpret the Scriptures in a nonliteral sense.[10] As Masai says, Augustine's return to Monica's religion "was not a return, in the first sense . . . because Christianity had never been abandoned. It was no more a return in another sense . . . because the Christian theology and philosophy that Augustine professed as of 386 had never been his before, because the Church of Milan was the first to teach these doctrines and because neither in Africa nor in any part of the West had any Christian known them before."[11] Hence, having experienced the power of the Plotinian spiritualism and conscious of having risen above the materialism common throughout the West, Augustine would surely want to make it clear to Jerome that he was not entirely ignorant of the nature of the soul as that had been understood

---

9. Masai, "Les conversions de saint Augustin." According to Masai not only the African Church, but the whole Western Church was without a spiritual view of the soul and of God until Augustine's conversion to the spiritualist doctrines of Ambrose and the Church of Milan. Recall that Augustine moved away from the version of the faith that he had learned from Monica and in the Church of Thagaste largely because the African Church was unable to deal with his questions about man's being made in the image of God (*conf.* 3, 7, 12). See also Verbeke, *L'évolution de la doctrine*.

10. *Conf.* 5, 10, 19 and 5, 14, 25.

11. Masai, "Les conversions de saint Augustin," 13–14. The translation is mine.

in the East for over a century. In view of the history of the correspondence with Jerome, in view of Augustine's desire to learn from Jerome and to accommodate himself to Jerome's views, and in view of the fact that the West had clung to a Stoic materialism long after the Greek Church had come under the influence of a spiritualism, it would seem that Augustine would not merely include his philosophical reasons for holding the incorporeality of the soul in his letter to Jerome, but would also present his strongest and clearest reasons for that view.

AN ANALYSIS OF THE ARGUMENT

Having seen some reasons for believing that the argument in *ep.* 166 should not be regarded as an unimportant argument for the incorporeality of the soul, let us now turn to an examination of that argument. The general structure of the argument is as follows: Everything that is a body is spread out in space with smaller parts occupying smaller places and with larger parts occupying larger places. That is, all bodies are larger in larger places and smaller in smaller places, and no body is whole in a part of itself. But the soul is whole in the whole body and is whole in each part of the body. Therefore, the soul is not a body.

Augustine admits that those who are slower can be convinced of the incorporeality of the soul only with difficulty; he, however, is convinced of it. A preliminary step to the argument is to define "body" so as to avoid a merely verbal dispute. "If every substance, or essence, or—if that which exists somehow in itself is more suitably called anything else—is a body, then the soul is a body. So too if one prefers to call only that nature incorporeal which is immutable in the highest degree and whole everywhere, the soul is a body, because it is not such a thing. But if only that is a body which is at rest or in motion through space with length, breadth and height so that it occupies a larger place with a larger part of itself and a smaller place with a smaller part and is smaller in a part than in the whole, then the soul is not a body."[12] Such a clarification of the meaning of "body" is necessary in view of the fact that Tertullian held that everything that exists is a body and that nothing is

---

12. The Cartesian character of body for Augustine has been noted. See Gilson, *Christian Philosophy,* 271n8, and Colleran, *Greatness,* 197–198.

incorporeal except that which does not exist.[13] Augustine certainly does not want to imply that the soul is nonexistent when he says that it is incorporeal. Furthermore, Vincentius Victor, the former Rogatist, held that only God is incorporeal, and Augustine certainly does not want to imply that the soul is God or a part of God.[14] Such views, and not spiritualist ones, were, it must be remembered, prevalent throughout the West until Augustine.

It is the minor premise in the above syllogism, of course, that carries the burden of the argument. Augustine formulates the argument that the soul is whole in the whole body and is whole in each part of the body in a series of statements that I shall number for the sake of clarity.

(1) The soul is stretched out through the entire body that it animates, not by a local diffusion, but by a certain vital intention.

Augustine presupposes that the soul is the principle of life, that which by its presence makes the body a living body. As he says in *quan.* 33, 70, "The soul by its presence gives life to this earth- and death-bound body. It makes of it a unified organism and maintains it as such, keeping it from disintegrating and wasting away."[15] In (8) below, Augustine says that the other parts of the body, that is, those in which there is no modification of the body of which the soul is unaware, are living by reason of the soul's presence.

Augustine contrasts "local diffusion" with "vital intention" as modes of the soul's presence in the body. He illustrates presence by local diffusion with the example of blood spread out through the body (*quan.*, 30,

---

13. Verbeke, *L'évolutions de la doctrine,* 445, provides a series of texts from Tertullian. "Omne, quod est, corpus est sui generis, nihil incorporale, nisi quod non est" (*De carne Christi* 11). "Cum ipsa substantia corpus sit rei cuiusque" (*Adversus Hermogenem* 35). "Nihil enim nisi corpus" (*De anima* 7). For Tertullian even God is a body, though he is a spirit. "Quis negabit Deum corpus esse, etsi Deus spiritus est?" (*Adversus Praxean* 7). In *Gn. litt.* 10, 25, 41, Augustine suggests that Tertullian's principal purpose in claiming that the soul is a body was to preserve its reality and to prevent that it be thought merely an abstraction.

14. Vincentius Victor, against whom Augustine wrote the four books *an. et or.,* held that God was not a body, but thought that the soul was a sort of bodily thing. See *an. et or.* 4, 12, 18.

15. Though both Aristotle (*De anima* 2, 2) and Plotinus (*Ennead* 4, 4, 18) speak of the soul as the principle of life, the action by which the soul vivifies the body in a Platonic context is radically different from the soul's vivification of the body in an Aristotelian context.

61). Or, in the *conf.*—to use a better known example of local diffusion—in speaking of God as he had once conceived him, Augustine says, "The sun penetrates the air, not by breaking it up or cutting it apart, but by completely filling it. Just so, I thought that bodies . . . are all subject to your passage and penetrable in all their parts . . . so that they receive your presence. . . . In that theory, a larger part of the earth would hold a larger part of you, a lesser part, a smaller portion" (*conf.* 7, 1, 2). What Augustine means by "local diffusion" is fairly clear; his meaning for "vital intention" is less so.

That "intention" is linked with the incorporeality of the soul is clear from *conf.* 7, 1, 2, where Augustine says that he did "not see that this same intention, by which [the soul] was forming those very images was no such corporeal substance. Yet it could not form them unless it were some great thing." In *imm. an.* 10, 17, he says, "For, who in examining himself well has not experienced that he understands something so much the more purely, the more he is able to remove and withdraw the intention of the mind from the senses of the body." And in *De musica* (hereafter *mus.*) 6, 5, 9, Augustine makes the following puzzling claim: "For I do not think that this body is animated by the soul except by the intention of the maker. Nor do I think it suffers anything from it, but acts concerning it and in it as subjected by God to its domination."[16]

Thus Augustine speaks of the intention by which we form bodily images as well as of the intention of the mind being withdrawn from the senses of the body. In the first text "intention" seems to be an activity that produces mental imagery; in the second "intention" seems to mean much the same thing as "attention." However, the *mus.* text—though more obscure—is more closely tied to sensation and, hence, to our topic. Though its meaning is open to several interpretations, there are a number of things that are clear: First, Augustine is dealing with the relation between body and soul in the context of sensation. Second, he is insistent that the soul undergoes or suffers nothing from the body. Third, he says that the soul acts concerning and in the body as in something that has been subjected to the soul by God. What he means by saying that the body is animated by the soul only "intentione facientis"

---

16. "Ego enim ab anima hoc corpus animari non puto nisi intentione facientis. Nec ab ipso quidquam illam pati arbitror, sed facere de illo et in illo tamquam subjecto divinitus dominationi suae" (*mus.* 5, 6, 9).

is more problematic. Some interpret *facientis* as referring to God, so that the phrase is translated "only through the intention of its maker."[17] F.-J. Thonnard allows for this as a possible translation, but points out that if it is by the will or intention of God that the soul animates the body, the will of God is that the soul organize the body.[18] He prefers to translate the key phrase "dans un but d'activite"(for the purpose of action). He comments that the soul is united to the body "as to its natural field of action."[19] Jean Rohmer translates the phrase "par l'intentionalite de ses actes" (by the intentionality of its acts).[20] However, it seems better to follows Thonnard's interpretation; the soul is present to the body as to its natural field of action, and it is present there for the purpose of action. The relevant actions of the soul in this context are the vivification of the body and becoming aware of the changes in the body.[21]

(2) For the whole soul is at the same time present through all the body's parts and is not smaller in the smaller parts and larger in the larger.

(2) and (3) further explain (1). The three together represent the thesis to be proved, that is, the minor premise in the syllogism. (2) states what Augustine means by the soul's not being present in the body by local diffusion. What is crucial in (2) is not that the whole soul is in the whole body, but that the whole soul is in each part of the body. For—to use an example—the whole car can be in the whole garage without any implication of the car's being incorporeal. But the whole car cannot be in each part of the garage if the car is corporeal—as all cars, of course, are.

Though it might seem obvious that the whole soul is in the whole body, since otherwise we would not, as Evodius says in *quan.* 30, 61, know where we are, yet it does not seem that Augustine saw any inconsistency in maintaining that the whole soul is in the whole body and is also outside the body. For, Evodius asks, after the argument has

---

17. Colleran, *Greatness,* 219n123.   18. BA 7, 380 and 517n78.
19. Ibid., 517n78.
20. In "L'intentionalité des sensations chez saint Augustin," in *Augustinus magister* (Paris: Études augustiniennes, 1954), 1:494, Jean Rohmer presents an interpretation of the intentionality of sensation in Augustine that supposedly explains how he can circumvent the post-Cartesian problem regarding the immediate awareness of the objects of sensation.
21. In *quan.* 33, 71, Augustine uses the interesting expression *Intendit se anima in tactum.* Here there is an *intentio animae* that involves the soul's presence to all the living parts of the body, or at least to all the parts in which there is the sense of touch.

led them to see that the soul does not see where the eyes are, but rather sees only things at a distance from the eyes: "Can it not be established by such arguments that our souls are not in our bodies? And if such is the case, is it not true that I do not know where I am? For who can take away from me the fact that I myself am my soul?" (*quan.* 30, 61). Augustine bids Evodius not to lose his head. This consideration calls us to enter into ourselves and separates us from the body to the extent that this is possible. Moreover, "although it may seem absurd, there have been some very learned men who held that view, and I think there are some even now." With the further warning that the question is a most delicate one, Augustine steers the discussion back on its course.

W. Thimme has suggested that the passage from *quan.* represents a step beyond the view in *imm. an.* into the philosophy of enthusiasm.[22] However, even if that interpretation were correct, by the time of *ep.* 166 Augustine once again holds that the soul is whole in the whole body and in each of its parts. The fact of the matter seems to be that in the case of an incorporeal being, such as the soul, it is whole wherever it is, and it is wherever it acts. The wholeness of the soul is obviously not the wholeness of a body, the togetherness and continuity of spatially spread out parts. Rather it is the wholeness of self-identity and simplicity.[23] If there is no inconsistency in saying that the soul is whole in each of two spatially distinct parts of the body, then there need be no inconsistency in maintaining that the soul is whole in the body and also whole outside the body. Indeed the stages in the ascent of the soul in *quan.* seem to involve the soul's being purified from the body by returning into itself and turning toward God. For example, in *quan.* 33, 75, he says, "This spirit

---

22. In *Augustins geistige Entwicklung in den ersten Jahren nach seiner 'Bekehrung,' 386–391* (Berlin: Trowitzsch und Sohn, 1908), 18, Wilhelm Thimme says, "Wir sehen, seit De im. an., hat Augustin noch einen Schritt weiter in die Philosophie des Überschwanges hinein getan. Damals schien ihm die ganze Seele in jedem Körperteil gegenwärtig zu sein, nun ist er so weit, es fur mindestens sehr probabel zu halten, dass die Seele sich uberhaupt nicht im Körper befinde."

23. In *Ennead* 4, 7, 7, where Plotinus discusses how the sensation of a pain in the toe occurs—a text with which Augustine was apparently familiar at least from the time of *imm. an.*—he concludes that "it is necessary to admit that the sensing being is such that it is identical to itself in every place of the body. Now only a being different from the body is able to do that." Furthermore, in *Trin.* 6, 6, 8, in explaining how the divine substance is both simple and multiple, Augustine uses an abbreviated version of the argument in *ep.* 166 to show that the soul is more simple than the body, though apart from such a comparison it is multiple. Thus the soul is more simple than the body precisely because it is incorporeal.

is not really 'renewed' in anyone unless his heart is first made clean, that is to say, unless he first controls his thoughts and drains off from them all dregs of attachment to corruptible things."[24] What is all too easy to lose sight of in such a text is the fact that one's own body is one of the corruptible things from which he needs to become detached.

(3) Rather it is in one place more intent, in another more remiss, and it is whole in all the parts and is whole in each part of the body.

This third statement expands on the presence of the soul to the body by vital intention. It also makes it explicit that the soul is whole not merely in the whole body, but in the individual parts of the body. Though the whole soul is present in each and every part of the body it animates, the presence of the soul varies in intensity from one part to another. Thus, in *mus.* 6, 5, 10, Augustine says, "when the soul senses in the body, it does not suffer something from it, but acts more attentively in the modification of the body, and these actions . . . do not escape the soul's notice; and this is all that is meant by sensing."[25] Thus sensation involves a heightened attention of the soul to the modifications that occur in parts of the body.

(4) For in no other way does the whole soul nonetheless sense what it senses not in the whole body.[26]

The first three statements formulate and explain the thesis to be proved. (4) claims that if (1) through (3) are not true, then the whole soul does not sense what occurs in only a part of the body. The argument proceeds by *modus tollens:* The whole soul does sense what occurs in only a part of the body. For example,

(5) For when at a small point in the living flesh something is touched, although that place is not the place of the whole body, but hardly seems to be in the body at all, it does not, nevertheless, escape the notice of the whole soul.

24. In *Early Theory,* 190, O'Connell says, "And yet, virtually every page of the Cassiciacum Dialogues is studded with that emphasis the Augustine of the *Retractationes* later goes to such lengths to correct: the 'flight' from both body and sense."

25. See Gilson, *Christian Philosophy,* 61–63 and the notes for further texts illustrating the *attentius agere* involved in Augustine's account of sensation.

26. In a note in the PL edition the editors point out that some manuscripts read "quod in corpore non toto fit tamen." (4) would then read: "For in no other way does the whole soul nonetheless sense what does not occur in the whole body." The parallel texts in *imm. an.* 16, 25 and *Trin.* 6, 6, 8 favor the latter reading.

In *quan.* 30, 59, Augustine defines sensation as "corporis passio per seipsam non latens animam (a modification of the body of itself not escaping the notice of the soul). The Plotinian sources for this definition are well known.[27] There is one significant difference between the above definition and what Augustine says in (5), for in the latter the bodily modification does not escape the notice of the whole soul—"animam tamen totam non latet." Since the fact that an occurrence in a small part of the body does not of itself escape the notice of the soul merely means that the soul senses that occurrence, what is crucial is that the occurrence does not escape the whole soul's notice.

Statements (6) through (10) attempt to argue that the whole soul, not merely the part of the soul in the affected part of the body, becomes aware of the modification in that part of the body.

(6) Nor does that which is sensed run through all the parts of the body, but is sensed only there where it occurs.

With this statement Augustine is rejecting the Stoic account of the transmission of what is sensed from the part of the soul in the part of the body affected through other parts of the soul in the other parts of the body to the ruling part of the soul. His reason for rejecting that account is that the soul is aware of a pain there where the injury to the body occurs.

In the *imm. an.* 16, 25, version of the argument, Augustine says, "For it is not believable that the soul is informed by a messenger that does not sense that which it reports. For the impression which occurs does not run through the continuous mass so that it cannot escape the notice of the other parts of the soul which are elsewhere." Augustine most probably has in mind Plotinus's argument against the Stoic account of sensation in *Ennead* 4, 7, 7: "How does this occur? By transmission, [the Stoics] say; the psychical breath *(pneuma)* around the toe suffers first; then it hands it on to that part next to it, and that part to another, until it comes to the ruling part of the soul." Plotinus's objection to such an account is that the ruling part of the soul does not feel the pain in the toe, but is at most aware of the pain in the part next to it.

27. *Ennead* 4, 4, 19, for example, includes the expression μὴ λαθεῖν, which is preserved in Augustine's Latin as *non latere* and accounts for the awkward English "does not escape the notice of." See Colleran, *Greatness*, 209.

He concludes, "If then it is impossible that the sensation of the pain in the toe take place by transmission and that in the material mass of the body there be knowledge of one thing when another is affected—for every magnitude has distinct parts—it must be admitted that the sensing being is such that it is identical with itself in every part of the body. Now only a being different from the body is able to do that."[28] Plotinus and Augustine are appealing to what one is directly aware of when one experiences a pain in a toe or some other part of the body. That is, they are not giving a causal account of sensation that would involve the role of the nervous system. They are rather giving a descriptive or phenomenological account of what we are directly aware of in experiencing a pain.[29] C. W. Wolfskeel, on the other hand, says that this theory, "in which the nervous system does not play a part, is very strange, taking into consideration that it had already been discovered in the fourth century before Christ."[30] Augustine's knowledge of physiology was, of course, somewhat primitive. Yet in *Gn. litt.* 7, 12, 20, he mentions what physicians not merely say, but even claim to have proved, namely, that from the brain to the senses there are thin tubes *(tenues fistulae)* and that the senses are directed by the brain through the *medulla cervicis* and the spinal cord so that certain very fine streams *(tenuissimi quidem rivuli)* that constitute the sense of touch are spread out from there through all the members of the body. In this view the senses are clearly messengers from which the soul receives whatever awareness it has of corporeal things.[31]

28. *Ennead* 4, 7, 7. The translation is my own, though I have consulted Bréhier's translation.

29. One wonders what account Augustine would have given of the experience of amputees who feel pains in the amputated limb. The phenomenon of phantom limbs led Descartes to give an account of sensation involving a mechanical transmission of motion to the seat of consciousness in the brain, where alone the sensation of pain occurs. See *Principia Philosophiae* 4, 196, in *Oeuvres de Descartes,* vol. 8, ed. Charles Adam and Paul Tannery (Paris: J. Vrin, 1964).

30. Wolfskeel, *De Immortalitate,* 191n304, where he refers to Friedrich Solmsen in "Griechische Philosophie und die Entdeckung der Nerven," in *Antike Medizin* 221 (Darmstadt: Wissenschaftliche Buchgesellschaft, 1971).

31. "Cum igitur his quasi nuntiis accipiat anima quidquid eam corporalium non latet" (*Gn. litt.* 7, 14, 20). In *De Immortalitate,* 3–4, Wolfskeel claims that *imm. an.* 16, 25, presents "a totally different view of the process of perception" from that in 14, 23. "The presumption, that the senses could announce something to the rational soul is entirely rejected here." In *De Immortalitate,* 156, he also refers the reader to Plotinian texts that contain this view of perception: *Enneads* 4, 6, 2; 4, 4, 19, and 4, 7, 7.

However, it does seem possible to give an account of the experience of touching something in which one does not deal with the physiology of the nervous system, but merely describes that of which one is immediately aware when one is touching. Certainly one is not aware of the function of the nervous system when one has a sensation, and one does become immediately aware of a pain in an extremity. However, the difficulty with the account of the experience of touching found in *ep.* 166 and in the closing paragraph of *imm. an.* is that, were such an account correct, there would be no need for the nervous system at all.[32]

Once Augustine has ruled out the transmission of the sensation from one part of the body to another according to the Stoic view, in which the *pneuma* in one part becomes aware of the change in another part of the body, he has to explain how the whole soul is immediately aware of what happens in a part of the body.

(7) Therefore, how does that which does not occur in the whole body immediately come to the whole soul, unless it is because the whole soul is there where it occurs and yet does not abandon the other parts in order that the whole soul might be there?

That is, Augustine claims that the whole soul could not become aware of what happens in only a part of the body if the whole soul were not present there where something occurred. Yet though the whole soul is present in that part of the body in which something occurs, the soul is also present in the other parts of the body.

(8) For the other parts of the body are also living by the soul's presence where no such thing has occurred.

For, as the principle of life the soul is present in all the parts of the living body, and the soul does not leave the other parts of the body in order to be whole in the part in which the pain is felt. On the other hand, if something were to occur in one or more of those other parts of the body, the soul would notice each such occurrence.

32. Since the soul is whole in each part of the body, there would seem to be no need for any system of nerves to carry any report from one part of the body to a center of consciousness. The fact that there would apparently be no need for the nervous system does not, however, mean that the sense organs themselves are unnecessary. In the present theory the senses can still be called messengers from which the soul receives whatever of bodily things does not escape its notice.

Incorporeality of the Soul 211

(9) But, if something were to occur there and if each were to occur at the same time, each would at the same time not escape the notice of the whole soul.

That is, if one were to stub his toe and burn his hand at the same time, the whole soul would at the same time become aware of both events. And in order to be aware of both events in the different parts of the body, the whole soul would have to be both in the toe and in the hand at the same time. However, such a simultaneous total presence in both places is precisely what no body can achieve.

Clearly the crux of Augustine's argument is to show that the whole soul is present not merely in the whole body, but in each part of the body. In *imm. an.* 16, 25, he formulates the argument as follows: "For the whole soul senses a modification of a part of the body, though not in the whole body. For when something hurts in the foot, the eye turns, the tongue speaks, the hand moves. This would not happen, unless whatever of the soul is in those parts also sensed in the foot. And it cannot sense what happened there unless it is present there." In this text, Augustine is first of all claiming that when I feel a pain in my toe, it is my soul that feels a pain in my toe. Second, he claims that when my soul feels a pain in my toe, it does not feel the pain in the whole body. This point seems obvious since we would not talk about the pain as being in the toe if we felt it elsewhere or everywhere in the body. Third, when my soul feels a pain in my toe, it is my whole soul that feels the pain in my toe. As evidence that it is my whole soul that feels the pain in my toe, Augustine points to the fact that other parts of my body react immediately. For I look to see what is the matter, I utter expressions of surprise or hurt, and I reach out to remove the source of the pain. Some such scenario is likely to occur when one stubs a toe or cuts a finger. Since these other parts of the body react immediately to the pain felt in the toe, Augustine claims, fourth, that whatever of the soul is in these other parts of the body, that is, in the parts of the body other than the toe, that react to the pain in the toe is also aware of the pain in the toe. Fifth, Augustine holds that the soul cannot sense, that is, become directly aware, of an occurrence in a part of the body unless it is present in that part of the body. But we have seen that whatever of the soul is in parts of the body other than the toe, such as, the eye, the tongue, and the hand, is also aware of the pain in the toe. Therefore, whatever of the soul is in parts of the body other than the toe is also present in the toe.

And if that is so, then the soul is not stretched out in space as a body is. Hence, the soul is not a body.

The argument from *imm. an.*, if sound, would seem to establish at most that whatever of the soul is in some other parts of the body, namely, those that react to the pain in the toe, is also present in the toe. It does not show that whatever of the soul is in other parts of the body, namely, those that do not react to the pain in the toe, is also present in the toe. However, to have shown that whatever of the soul is in the hand or the eye or the tongue is also in the toe is certainly to have shown that the soul is not stretched out in space as is a body. Moreover, if one couples with this argument the further argument from *ep.* 166, namely, that should something occur in a finger at the same time that there is a pain in the toe, the soul would become aware of each of the occurrences, then one could conclude that whatever of the soul is in such parts of the body as the eye, the tongue, and the hand is also both in the toe and the finger. These arguments, if sound, then establish that the presence of the soul to the body is not presence by local diffusion. Since the sense of touch is present throughout the body so that one could be aware of an occurrence in any part of the body and since other parts of the body could react to the occurrence in any part of the body, it would seem to follow that the whole soul is present not merely in the whole body, but in each part of the body.

(10) Moreover, the whole soul could not be at the same time both in all the parts and in each of the parts of its body, if it were diffused through those parts just as we see that bodies, diffused through stretches of space, occupy smaller spaces with their smaller parts and larger spaces with their larger parts.

Hence, if the whole soul is whole in several parts of the body at the same time, then the soul is not a body in the ordinary sense.

(11) Hence, if the soul is to be called a body, it is certainly not a body such as the earthly or the humid or the airy or the fiery. For all such bodies are larger in larger places and smaller in smaller places, and none of them is present whole in some part of itself. But as are the parts of places, so are they occupied by parts of bodies.

And Augustine's conclusion then follows:

(12) Hence, whether the soul should be called a body or incorporeal, it is understood to have a certain nature of its own, created with a substance more

excellent than all these elements of the worldly mass. It cannot be thought in some imagination of bodily images which we perceive through the senses of the flesh, but is understood by the mind and felt by life.

CRITIQUE AND CONCLUSION

Augustine's argument for the incorporeality of the soul rests upon a number of assumptions, some of which are indeed questionable. First of all, the argument assumes that the soul is a substance or "that which has being somehow in itself." And the proof that the soul is incorporeal is meant to provide an answer to the question: What kind of a substance is the soul? Or, what is the nature of the soul? That is, if one should say that the soul is an airy or fiery substance, one would, in Augustine's view, be giving the correct sort of answer, though not, of course, the correct answer. For, the soul is not an airy or fiery substance, but an incorporeal or nonbodily substance.

Second, Augustine assumes that in the case of man the soul is the person or is that to which personal pronouns refer. Thus Evodius can say, "For who can take away from me the fact that I myself am my soul?" (*quan.* 30, 61). Moreover, the soul is that which vivifies the body and that which is not unaware of occurrences in the body. While it may sound acceptable to say that the whole soul senses a pain in the toe, it is surely odd or worse to say that the whole of me is in my toe, even if the whole of me is also at the same time in each of the other parts of my body.

The fact that the argument assumes that the soul is a substance and that the human soul is the person reduces the significance of the conclusion of the argument, since personal survival of the death of the body is at least possible if the soul is a personal substance, regardless of whether or not it is incorporeal. Moreover, since the argument rests upon the sense of touch, it establishes, if sound, that the souls of animals are incorporeal substances—or perhaps parts of an incorporeal substance.

The presence of the whole soul in each part of the living body along with the substantiality of the soul seems to do away with any need for the nervous system or for any specific structure for the sensory organs. The soul's sensing is merely its heightened attention to bodily changes. The act of sensing is not as with Aquinas an *operatio conjuncti* where the structure of the sensory organs plays an intrinsic role in the activity, but is an action of the soul alone by which it becomes aware of bodily changes. Perhaps no clearer indication of this view of sensation as an activity of the soul alone can be found than Augustine's statement that God senses everything.[33] For to the extent that sensation is an activity of the soul alone, to that extent it can be attributed to God as properly as can intellection.

Augustine's proof depends upon an account of sensation, specifically, of touching or feeling pain, that explicitly rejects any neural transmission of the sensation from the affected part of the body to the brain or seat of consciousness. Because there cannot, according to Augustine and Plotinus, be a transmission of the sensation from the affected part of the body to the ruling part of the soul, the soul must be present in each part of the body. However, there is some sort of transmission in which the nervous system does play an essential role. Hence, the desired conclusion does not follow. Moreover, the Augustinian account of sensation seems to reject any role for the body as an organ of touch as opposed to an object of the soul's awareness. Here an Aristotelian view of the senses as informed organs might have provided Augustine with a needed alternative to a Stoic mechanicism and a Plotinian spiritualism.

Finally, though Augustine's argument in *ep.* 166 is not sound, nonetheless, one ought in fairness to him to distinguish between the concept of the soul as incorporeal and the proof that the soul is incorporeal. After all, what troubled Augustine intellectually prior to 386 was not the lack of a proof, but his inability to conceive a spiritual substance. And he admits that this inability was "the greatest and perhaps sole cause of my inevitable error."[34] Once he had come to the conception of a spiritual substance, he was able to free himself from the errors of Manichaeism. Furthermore, the Augustinian conception of incorporeality

---

33. *Trin.* 15, 5, 7: "at illa vita quae Deus est, sentit atque intelligit omnia: et sentit mente, non corpore, quia spiritus est Deus. Non autem . . . per corpus sentit Deus . . . simplex illa natura sicut intelligit sentit, sicut sentit intelligit; idemque sensus qui intellectus est illi." Though Augustine's claim that God senses might—incorrectly, I suspect—be interpreted in a benign fashion to accord with Aquinas, there remain problems with such a move, for there is no indication that *sentit* should be interpreted metaphorically, while *intelligit* is understood properly. The expressions *sentit mente, non corpore* and *non per corpus sentit Deus* seem to imply that there is a purely mental form of sensation or a sensing that does not involve having a body.

34. *Conf.* 5, 11, 19; also see *conf.* 5, 14, 25.

was the decisive step in the conversion of the West to a spiritualism, as Verbeke and Masai have argued, and that concept became a central part of the Christian view of man, even in the more Aristotelian philosophy of Aquinas. For Aquinas finds in man an image of God—at least in a secondary sense—"insofar as man's soul is whole in his whole body and also whole in each part of it, as God is in relation to the world" (*Summa theologiae* I, q. 93, a. 3).

12

THE WORLD-SOUL AND TIME IN AUGUSTINE

Augustine's definition of time in conf. *11 has been a source of much philosophical reflection and debate among philosophers and theologians. In this article I argued that Augustine offered a definition of time and that, given the concept of a world-soul, it is possible to see how the definition of time as a* distentio *of the soul need not entail the sort of subjective and private view of time that Bertrand Russell found utterly unacceptable. The basic thesis of the article met with approval by Kurt Flasch in his study of time in Augustine,* Was ist Zeit? Augustinus von Hippo, das XI. Buch der Confessiones *(Frankfurt am Main: V. Klostermann, 1993), and I returned to the topic in* Paradoxes of Time in Saint Augustine *(Milwaukee: Marquette University Press, 1996). I still believe that Augustine gave us a definition of time in* conf. *11 and that the concept of a world-soul with which individual souls are somehow one is necessary to save his view of time from the subjectivism to which Bertrand Russell so strongly objected. I had not, however, paid sufficient attention to some aspects of the Plotinian doctrine of the fall of the soul, which I now believe had a deeper influence on Augustine at the time of the* conf. *than I had previously thought. For example, the fall of the soul that Augustine got from Plotinus had cosmogonic implications, which left me wondering whether creation and the fall of the soul coincided. In his* Saint Augustine and the Fall of the Soul: Beyond

O'Connell and his Critics *(Washington, D.C.: The Catholic University of America Press, 2006)*, Ronnie J. Rombs has distinguished cosmogonic, metaphysical, and moral senses of the fall of the soul in Augustine. As late as conf. there are, I believe, some of the conceptual trappings of a cosmogonic fall in the link between time and the world-soul.

In *quan.* 32, 69, Saint Augustine turns to Evodius's question regarding the number of souls. He admits that he does not know what to say in answer. "I would be more inclined to say that the question should not be brought up at all or at least that you should postpone it for the time being rather than that I should say that number and multitude have no connection with quantity, or that I am presently equal to the task of solving such an involved problem for you" (*quan.* 32, 69). However, before turning to what he calls a more profitable and less burdensome topic, namely, the seven degrees of the greatness of soul, Augustine presents his reader with his grounds for shelving the question. "For if I should tell you that there is only one soul, you will be at sea because of the fact that in one it is happy, in another unhappy; and one and the same thing cannot be both happy and unhappy at the same time. If I should say that it is one and many at the same time, you will smile, and I would not find it easy to make you suppress your smile. But if I say simply that it is many, I shall have to laugh at myself, and it will be harder for me to suffer my own disapprobation than yours" (*quant.* 32, 69).

The first suggestion, that there is but one soul, seems to be rejected as self-contradictory. But the second suggestion, namely, that there is one soul and also many souls or that the soul is one and many, may offer Evodius grounds for laughter; nonetheless, Augustine clearly finds it preferable to the thesis that there is simply a multiplicity of souls. The implication seems to be that individual souls are one with the world-soul.[1] Indeed, just prior to this section, Augustine tells Evodius, "Your mind must first be trained ... to give you the insight and perspicacity to understand most clearly whether what certain very learned men say

---

1. In *Early Theory*, 122, Robert O'Connell says that "the *De Quantitate Animae* shows Augustine exploiting the very technique Plotinus uses in *Ennead* V, 1: the soul must be reminded that all the beauty and order of the sensible world is really, were she only awakened to it, her production. The implication is that the individual soul is one with the World-Soul which accomplishes these marvels—a thought that might disturb his friend Evodius."

is actually true: namely, that the soul can in no way be divided in itself, but that this is possible by reason of the body" (*quan.* 32, 68). Colleran comments, "The reference is probably to Plotinus, who held there is a 'world soul' which is indivisible, but which, in breathing life into bodies, is virtually multiplied into many individual souls, although it retains its fundamental unity" (see *Ennead* 4.1).[2] By themselves such texts would be at most curious; however, there are several other texts from the early writings that indicate that Augustine held a doctrine of a world-soul or universal soul with which individual souls are somehow identical.

This article will, first of all, present the evidence that Augustine at least in his early writings held such a doctrine, which he seems to have derived from Plotinus.[3] This first part of the article seems to be relatively noncontroversial. However, I hope in the second part to go on to show that this doctrine that the soul is both one and many, or that there is one soul with which individual souls are identical, continues to be—if not an explicit doctrine—at least an implicit but influential piece of Augustine's conceptual scheme that is operative in his discussion of the heaven of heaven and time in the *conf.*

---

2. Colleran, *Greatness*, 212n86. Though Augustine's immediate concern is whether the soul of a worm is divided when the worm is cut in half, the problem seems general. If, in other words, individual souls are somehow one with the all-soul, what accounts for their multiplicity? Unlike in Aquinas, according to whom souls are individuated by the quantified matter they inform, for Augustine souls, it would seem, are individuated, i.e., made individual, by their activity upon and attention to a body. See *ep.* 166, 2, 4, where Augustine speaks of the whole soul as present in the whole body and in each part of the body by a certain vital intention, "quadam vitali intentione."

3. Under "Neoplatonic Theories First Adopted, Then Rejected," Eugène Portalié mentions in *A Guide to the Thought of Saint Augustine*, trans. Ralph J. Bastian (Chicago: Regnery, 1960), 104, the doctrine of a universal soul. "The Platonic explanation of the world led him to adopt at first the famous thesis that there existed a universal soul which made the world an immense living being." Gilson sees the question of a world-soul as one that kept recurring for Augustine throughout his long career, though he was not able to settle it to his satisfaction. See Gilson, *Christian Philosophy,* 209. Though I believe a strong case could be made that Augustine derived the doctrine of a world-soul from Plotinus, I neither argue that he did nor wish to exclude the possibility of other sources. Augustine attributed the doctrine of a world-soul to Plato and Plotinus. In *civ. Dei* 10, 2, he says, "Plotinus, in explaining the thought of Plato, often and forcefully affirmed that not even that soul, which they believe is the soul of the universe, receives its happiness from another source than our soul does." In *civ. Dei* 13, 16, 2–17, 1, the doctrine is attributed to Plato and the Platonists, and their pride in refusing to accept the possibility of a resurrected body suggests that it is Porphyry he is thinking of. See J. J. O'Meara, *Charter of Christendom: The Significance of the City of God* (New York: Macmillan, 1961), 80–82.

SAINT AUGUSTINE AND THE WORLD-SOUL

In *imm. an.* 15, 24, Augustine is discussing the priority of soul over body in terms of the soul's nearness to the eternal reasons. That nearness, he tells us, is not in terms of place, but in terms of the order of nature. "This order means that the highest essence gives form to body through soul, by which it [body] is to the extent that it is. Therefore, body subsists through soul, and it is by the very fact that it is animated, either universally, as the world, or particularly, as each animal within the world."[4] It is through soul that God gives form to body, and the world as a whole—as well as each animal within the world—is ensouled. Of this passage he says in his *retr.*, "All this was said with utter rashness."[5]

Further on in the same section of *imm. an.*, Augustine says, "Nor is there found something that is between the highest life, which is immutable wisdom and truth, and that which is last vivified, i.e., body, except vivifying soul." That is, between God and lifeless body there is nothing but soul that gives life to body. Such a claim is odd for a number of reasons.

First of all, Augustine does not distinguish between animal and human souls, as we might expect him to do.[6] Second, this sort of hierarchy of being does not seem to have room for created spiritual beings that do not animate bodies. And, third, there is no indication that *anima vivificans* is to be understood as plural. Though it may, of course, refer to a kind of being, nonetheless, occurring as it does immediately after

---

4. The translation is mine. I have translated *species* as "form," though the term is open to a variety of meanings. It can also mean "idea" in the Platonic sense, "appearance" or "figure," or even "beauty." In his notes to the *conf.*, A. Solignac says in BA 14, 598–599, "En tant qu'elle informe les corps, la species leur confère aussi la beauté; la signification du mot semble alors dériver de Plotin: 'nous disons que les choses sont belles parce qu'elles participent à une idée (εἶδος); car toute chose privée de forme et destinée à recevoir forme et idée (μορφὴ καὶ εἶδος) reste laide et hors de la raison divine tant qu'elle est privée de raison et d'idée' (*Ennead* 1, 6, 2)."

5. *Retr.* 1, 5, 3. "Illud quoque temere dictum est"; after quoting the passage, he concludes, "hoc totum prorsus temere dictum est."

6. In the immediately following section, Augustine speaks of irrational soul or life and offers a proof of the incorporeality of soul from the sense of touch. Is Augustine suggesting not merely that human or rational souls are somehow one, but that all souls are somehow one and are differentiated only by the function they exercise? Moreover, at least in his early works, Augustine held that the human soul was equal to the angel in nature, though not in function. See *quan.* 34, 78, and *lib. arb.* 3, 11, 32.

a reference to the world-soul, the term suggests that this soul is one and is also many.

In a slightly earlier work, *ord.*, Augustine speaks of "the soul which is either in us or everywhere."[7] He offers a definition of reason as "the motion of the mind able to distinguish and connect those things that are learned." And then he goes on to say, "Only the most exceptional kind of man is able to use it as a guide to understand God or that soul which is either in us or everywhere, precisely because it is difficult for one who has plunged into the concerns of these senses to return into himself" (*ord.* 2, 11, 30). The close linkage between self-knowledge and knowledge of God is a familiar theme in Augustine.[8] However, the return into oneself is tied in this passage to the soul that is everywhere. The Latin brackets the relative clause, *quae aut in nobis aut usque quaque est*, with *ipsam* and *animam* and thus emphasizes the oneness of soul—whether it is the soul in us or the soul everywhere. The suggestion is that the return into oneself is at the same time a return into the soul that is everywhere. It is interesting that Augustine found no need to comment on this passage in his *retr.*

In *mus.* 6, 14, 44, Augustine once again makes a claim that implies the existence of a soul of the world: "Love of this world is more of a struggle *(laboriosior)*. For what the soul seeks in it, namely, permanence and eternity, it does not find, because the lowest beauty reaches its completion through things passing away. And that which in it imitates permanence comes from the highest God through soul, since form *(species)* which is mutable only in time is prior to that which is mutable in both time and place."[9] The passage bears a close resemblance to that from *imm. an.* In both texts form is given to body by God through soul. In both passages Augustine is dealing with the order of nature by which soul is prior to body, that is, closer to God. The *retr.* is highly instructive. There Augustine points out that if the lowest beauty is taken to

---

7. The Fathers of the Church series translation by Robert Russell translates *animam quae . . . usque quaque est* as "world-soul." Since it may be that Augustine continues to maintain the existence of a soul that is present everywhere after he begins to doubt whether this soul animates the world, i.e., makes it one huge animal, it seems best to avoid such an interpretation.

8. In *sol.* 1, 2, 7, Augustine says that he desires to know only God and the soul. So too philosophy has to do with but two questions, God and the soul (*ord.* 2, 18, 47).

9. The translations from *mus.* and the *retr.* are mine, though I have relied upon G. Bardy's translation in BA 12 for the latter work.

refer only to the bodies of men and beasts, there is no problem; indeed, clear reason, he says, defends the passage. "For what imitates permanence in that beauty is that bodies remain the same in their organization to the extent that they do remain; that, however, is communicated to them through soul by the highest God. For soul maintains this organization so that it does not dissolve and flow away, as we see happens in bodies of animals when the soul departs" (*retr.* 1, 11, 4). However, if the lowest beauty is taken to be present in all bodies, then the expression implies that the world itself is an animal, "so that what imitates permanence in it [the world] is communicated to it through soul by the highest God." Though, Augustine notes, many philosophers, including Plato, have held that the world is an animal, he himself claims to "have been unable to discover this by certain reason or know that the authority of Scripture proves it." For this reason he has labeled "rash" what he said in *imm. an.*—"not because I assert it is false, but because I do not grasp that it is true that the world is an animal." *Retr.* 1, 11, 4, indicates that what Augustine considered rash about his statement in *imm. an.* was precisely the claim that the world is an animal. Even at the time of the *retr.* Augustine does not say that this view is incorrect; he only maintains that he does not have sufficient grounds either from reason or from Scripture to assert that it is true. The fact that by the time of the *retr.*—some forty years after the early writings—he regards the position as rash does not, of course, mean that he did not once hold the view. Rather it would seem to indicate that he did once hold such a position—at least during the years immediately after his baptism.

However, the situation may be a bit more complicated. For the *retr.* passage continues: "Even if the world is not an animal, that there is, nonetheless, a spiritual and living power which serves God in his holy angels to adorn and to administer the world is correctly believed even by those by whom it is not understood. By the term 'holy angels,' I am now referring to every holy spiritual creature established in the secret and hidden ministry of God, but Scripture does not usually refer to angelic spirits by the term 'souls.'"[10] This living spiritual power, though

10. In BA 12, 339, Bardy translates *et a quibus non intelligitur, rectissime creditur* as "et les anges n'en pénètrent pas le secret: du moins on peut le croire avec la plus grande probabilité." His translation, though not impossible, seems needlessly contrived. It has to supply "le secret" as subject of *intelligitur*, to take *angelis*—a full line away—as ante-

not a soul of the world, nonetheless adorns and administers the world and, in so doing, serves God in every holy and spiritual creature. This spiritual power includes the holy angels and souls; it is one power in many—very much like "that soul which is either in us or everywhere." In fact, in adorning and administering the world, this spiritual power performs functions that Augustine elsewhere attributed to souls, though it does not animate the world, we may assume, since he has just called into question the idea that the world is an animal.[11]

Hence, it seems that Augustine at one time early in his career held that there was a soul of the world such that the world is an animal. He later regarded the claim that the world is an animal as rash, that is, not as false, but as without sufficient foundation in either reason or Scripture. But even after he surrendered his previous claim that the world is an animal, he still—even to the end of his life—maintained a single living spiritual power that adorns and administers the world under God in angels and holy souls. That is, he maintained to the end a living spiritual power that is both one and many, a spiritual creature with which individual souls and angels are one. Since what Augustine explicitly labels rash is that the world is an animal and since he at the same time continues to maintain that one correctly believes or even knows that there is one living spiritual power in angels and souls that adorns and administers the world, may it not be the case that the rashness bears upon the animating function that makes the world an animal rather than upon the existence of a soul or spiritual creature with which the many souls and angels are identical?[12]

---

cedent of *quibus*, to weaken the sense of *rectissime creditur*, and to ignore the parallelism between *intelligitur* and *creditur*.

11. See, for example, *lib. arb.* 3, 11, 32, where Augustine says that God made souls that they might adorn the universe, not in order that they might sin. To those holy souls that never sinned, the whole world is subject, and without them the universe could not exist.

12. In *cons. Ev.* 1, 23, 35, which was written in 400 A.D., Augustine says, "Whether, however, this whole bodily mass, that is called the world, has a soul of its own, or something like a soul *(vel quasi animam)*, i.e., rational life, by which it is governed as each animal is, is a large and deep question. Nor should that opinion be affirmed unless it is discovered to be true, nor rejected unless discovered to be false." This work dates from a time shortly after the *conf.* and reveals Augustine's ambivalent attitude toward the idea of a world-soul as well as a suggestion of a *quasi* soul that governs the world and that nonetheless perhaps does not animate it.

There is another text that is noteworthy because of its relatively late date, namely, *Gn. litt. imp.* 4, 17. This work was begun around 393 and was never completed, though

Though Augustine may have become uncertain with regard to the world-animating function of the soul that is everywhere, he clearly distances himself from the Plotinian position that regarded the all-soul as divine. "I, of course, have no doubt that we should firmly hold that the world is not our God, whether it has a soul or not. For, if there is such a soul, he who made it is our God. However, if there is no such soul, the world can be the God of no one, much less our God" (*retr.* 1, 11, 4). Though there is some evidence that Augustine may have held that the soul was divine in his Cassiciacum period, he soon moved away from that position and clearly rejects it here.[13] What I want to suggest in the next part of this article is that the idea of a world-soul or of an all-soul with which individual souls are identical remained operative in Augustine's conceptual scheme as late as the *conf.*

THE HEAVEN OF HEAVEN AND TIME

There is, of course, no explicit doctrine in the *conf.* of a soul of the world. However, in the *retr.* he finds but two points regarding the *conf.* that need comment, and the first of them bears upon our subject: "In the fourth book, when I was confessing the unhappiness of my soul over the death of a friend and said that our soul had somehow become one from two, I said, 'Perhaps because of this I feared to die, lest he whom I had loved so much should wholly die.' This seems to me a light rhetorical exercise rather than serious confession, although the silliness is tempered by the addition of 'perhaps'" (*retr.* 2, 6, 2). The silliness is directly attributed to the idea that should Augustine die, his friend would wholly die—an idea that a Christian bishop might find silly for

---

Augustine added some touches around 426. In commenting on the spirit that was borne over the waters, he offers a second interpretation of *spiritus Dei:* "Potest autem et aliter intelligi, ut spiritum Dei, vitalem creaturam, qua universus iste visibilis mundus atque omnia corpora continentur et moventur, intelligamus, cui Deus omnipotens tribuit vim quamdam sibi serviendi ad operandum in quae gignuntur." This living creature by which this whole visible world and all bodies are contained and moved sounds very much like a world-soul. And this text dates from at most a few years before the *conf.*

13. In *Early Theory,* 122, O'Connell says, "The first strong indication that Augustine means the soul's 'divinity' in more than a transferred sense is his willingness to accept the doctrine of a World-Soul and his connected readiness to proclaim the individual soul's radical identity with this World-Soul," but also see the whole of chapter 4, "The Soul's Divinity at Cassiciacum."

a variety of reasons. However, the text need not be taken as repudiating the oneness of the two souls. After all, Augustine said much the same thing in *c. Acad.* 2, 3, 9, where he excuses his expression "my Lucilianus," and says, "In saying so, however, what else have I said but that he belongs to you and to all of us who are one?"[14] And Augustine apparently found nothing objectionable in that line when he reviewed all his writings.

If, as O'Connell suggests, the idea that Augustine's soul and that of his friend "were but one soul in two bodies" (*conf.* 4, 6, 11) "meant something to him at the time of writing the Confessions,"[15] then surely many of the things that Augustine has to say about the "heaven of heaven" in book 12 tend to confirm that he believed that individual souls were one with the world-soul or all-soul. The heaven mentioned in the first verse of the Book of Genesis is "some kind of intellectual creature" (*conf.* 12, 9, 9) that was created before any mention of days and is what Psalms 113:3 calls "the heaven of heaven"—a heaven to which the heaven of this earth is but earth. Though this intellectual creature is not coeternal with God, "it is yet a partaker of your eternity, and because of its most sweet and happy contemplation of you, it checks its own mutability. Without any lapse from its first creation, it has clung fast to you and is thus set beyond all the turns and changes of time" (*conf.* 12, 9, 9).[16] In contrast to this intellectual creature that has never ceased to contemplate its God, Augustine says of himself, "I fell away [literally, I flowed down: *defluxi*] to these material things . . . I went astray. . . . But now, see, I return." (*conf.* 12, 10, 10). The heaven of heaven is the house of God that, unlike souls who have fallen, has not wandered off in a foreign land *(peregrinata non est)*.[17] The heaven of heaven is "a pure mind

---

14. The translation is from *St. Augustine: Against the Academics,* Ancient Christian Writers 12, translated and annotated by John J. O'Meara (Westminster, Md.: Newman Press, 1950), 73.

15. In *St. Augustine's Confessions,* 56, O'Connell continues, "If our individual souls are in fact 'one' with the World-Soul, then the death of a friend quite literally liberates, and separates us from, a part of our very 'soul.'"

16. Unless otherwise noted, translations from the *conf.* is from *The Confessions of St. Augustine,* trans. John K. Ryan (Garden City, N.Y.: Image, 1960).

17. I have here modified Ryan's translation. *Peregrinari* means "to journey in a foreign land, to be abroad, to be away from home." It calls to mind the soul's being away from the fatherland whence we have come and to which we flee (see *Ennead* 1, 6, 8) as well as the parable of the prodigal son—themes that Augustine ties together explicitly in *conf.* 1, 18, 28. See O'Connell, *St. Augustine's Confessions,* 44.

most harmoniously one by the established peace of holy spirits, citizens of your city in heavenly places above these present heavens" (*conf.* 12, 11, 12). It is "the intellectual heaven where it belongs to intellect to know all at once" (*conf.* 12, 13, 16). It is "a certain sublime creature" (*conf.* 12, 15, 19). It is "that wisdom which is created, namely, an intellectual nature" (*conf.* 12, 15, 20). It is "the rational and intellectual mind of your chaste city" (*conf.* 12, 15, 20). Moreover, this heaven of heaven "surpasses all distention and all turning tracts of time" (*conf.* 12, 15, 22).

Though some of the terms that Augustine uses to refer to the heaven of heaven imply a plurality of spiritual creatures referred to collectively, for example, "house," "city," or "Jerusalem," other terms that he uses are strangely and explicitly singular, for example, "some intellectual creature": *aliqua creatura intellectualis,* "a certain sublime creature": *sublimem quamdam . . . creaturam,* or "that creature": *creatura illa*.[18] And still others seem to suggest the sort of unity or identity of a plurality that characterizes the relation of individual souls to the world-soul, for example, "a pure mind most harmoniously one by the established peace of holy spirits, citizens of your city": *mentem puram concordissime unam stabilimento pacis sanctorum spirituam, civium civitatis tuae,* and "the rational and intellectual mind of your chaste city": *mens rationalis et intellectualis castae civitatis tuae.* If Augustine were attempting to suggest to an audience not wholly receptive of his Plotinian Christianity that we fallen souls who "have flowed down into many things": *defluximus in multa* (*conf.* 10, 29, 40) and "have leapt apart into times": *dissilui in tempora* (*conf.* 11, 29, 39) were once one with that sublime creature that never fell, he could hardly have chosen his language more aptly.[19]

---

18. Ryan, as well as Pine-Coffin, translates *aliqua creatura intellectualis* as "some kind of intellectual creature." Sheed and Warner prefer "an intellectual creature," while Watts uses "some intellectual creature" and Thehorel and Bouissou "quelque créature intellectuelle."

19. The translations of the last two quotations are more literal translations of the text than Ryan's; in the last one I have followed O'Connell, *St. Augustine's Confessions,* 143, where he provides a survey of other attempts to deal with the difficult wording. Even so balanced a scholar as A. Solignac, after asking whether it is necessary to hypostatize this mind in the manner of the Plotinian Nous and admitting that the Plotinian doctrine underlies Augustine's expression, concludes, "Le sens de *mentem puram* est donc un sens *collectif,* du moins tout autant qu'un sens *substantiel:* on aurait ainsi un synthèse, assez hybride d'ailleurs, de vues plotiniennes et de vues proprement chrétiennes" (BA 14, 594).

H. A. Armstrong finds in the heaven of heaven the Plotinian conception of Nous. "What we have here, in fact, is a wonderful Christian transposition of the Plotinian

If what Augustine says about the heaven of heaven is open to his holding that there is a world-soul with which individual souls are one, then his definition of time as a distention of mind-soul not merely is open to this idea, but requires such a doctrine both in order to avoid inconsistency with what Augustine says about time elsewhere and to avoid the claim that his view of time is utterly subjective.[20] For, besides defining time as a distention of soul, Augustine speaks of time as the mode of existence characteristic of any creature, so that time is independent of any human mind-soul.[21] That is, much of what Augustine says about time seems to imply that time is objective and real, though his definition of time, if it is taken to refer to an individual mind or soul, seems to imply that time is subjective and unreal.[22] Aside from

---

doctrine of Nous applied to the Created Wisdom, the Heavenly City, the company of blessed spirits." See "Spiritual or Intelligible Matter in Plotinus and St. Augustine," in *Augustinus magister* (Paris: Études Augustiniennes, 1954), 1:277–283, here 280. After citing the texts in the *conf.* and *Gn. litt.*, Armstrong turns to a consideration of the Plotinian elements in the description. "First of all, who except a Christian steeped in the thought of Plotinus would pass so naturally, in a single sentence, from speaking of the *spiritalis creatura*, the company of angels, as *coelum* and *domus Dei* to speaking of it as *mens* (*Conf.* XII, 11 and 15); and where except in Plotinus can we find the conception of a Mind transcending the material world which is both one and many, a community of minds or spirits formed by and united in a single contemplation?" (ibid.).

20. The problems of the consistency of what Augustine says about time and of the subjective character of time appear in R. A. Markus's comments upon Augustine's treatment of time. Markus says that "Augustine rejected the conception of time according to which time has a substantial reality of its own, and he adopted a theory according to which time is the field of temporal relations between temporal events." There does not seem to be anything subjective or mind-dependent in such a conception of time; however, as Markus says, Augustine goes "further in his reflections on time." He finds that neither past nor future is real. "But if only the present is real, then reality shrinks to a dimensionless point at which the future is becoming the past. Augustine resolved the whole problem by locating time in the mind and adopting at the end of this discussion, though with hesitation, a definition of time as 'extension *[distentio]*, I am not sure of what, probably of the mind itself' (*Confessions* XI, 26, 33)." R. A. Markus, "Augustine, St.," in *The Encyclopedia of Philosophy*, ed. Paul Edwards (New York: Macmillan, 1967), 1:204. It is not clear how locating time in the mind solves any problem, though such a move clearly makes time mind-dependent and subjective.

21. In "Notes sur l'être," 212, Etienne Gilson argues that, because of his identification of being with *vere esse* and because of the ambiguity of *existere* at that period, Augustine had no other term for the world of becoming than *tempus*. If time is the mode of existence characteristic of any creature, then time would not seem to be mind-dependent.

22. C. W. K. Mundle, in "Time, Consciousness of," in *The Encyclopedia of Philosophy*, 8:136, says of Augustine, "He proceeded logically to the conclusions that when a person perceives or measures time, what he is attending to is 'something that remains fixed in his memory' and therefore that time is not 'something objective.'" He adds,

the consistency of the various things that Augustine says about time, there is also the question of the truth of what he says, and if "[m]emory, perception, and expectation . . . made up all that there is of time," as Russell interprets him, then Augustine's account of what time is cannot be correct.[23]

That Augustine's definition of time as *distentio animi* owes much to Plotinus's *Ennead* 3, 7, "On Eternity and Time," is commonly acknowledged.[24] However, despite the many points of similarity between the account of time in *Ennead* 3, 7 and that in book 11 of the *conf.*, there are also clear and crucial elements of difference. For, in Plotinus's view the existence of time results from the separation of the universal soul from the Intelligence, while for Augustine God creates time in creating the world. Perhaps two quotations from A. Solignac's note on eternity and time in Plotinus and Augustine will help make clear not merely the radical difference between the two thinkers, but also the reasons for regarding the second half of this paper as presenting a very tentative hypothesis. Solignac first claims, "Chez Augustin, il ne saurait être question d'une création du monde objectif par une Ame universelle: c'est Dieu qui crée le temps, nous l'avons vu, tout comme il crée le monde."[25] His second claim is: "Le point de vue d'Augustin semble plus étroit que celui de Plotin; celui-ci met le temps dans l'Ame universelle et peut ainsi donner une signification au temps des choses (see *Ennead*, III, vii, 12, 24–25)."[26] With regard to the first claim, Solignac is certainly correct that for Augustine God is the creator of time as he is the creator of the world. However, "une creation du monde objectif par une Ame universelle" is ambiguous and can be understood in the light of Augustine's earlier statements, namely, that it is through or by the soul

---

"Idealists may be happy to accept Augustine's conclusion that time is unreal (subjective)." I have not been able to discover the translation Mundle is using, but "something objective" seems more an interpretation than a translation.

23. Bertrand Russell, *Human Knowledge: Its Scope and Limits* (New York: Simon and Schuster, 1948), 212.

24. In L. Grandgeorge, *Saint Augustin et le Néo-Platonisme*, 76–79, there are four pages of texts from *Ennead* 3, 7 in one column juxtaposed with texts from Augustine in another. Solignac's note, "La conception du temps chez Augustin," in BA 14, 581–591, presents an excellent introduction to Augustine's treatment of eternity and time, evidence of his dependence upon Plotinus, and a brief bibliography to the question.

25. BA 14, 588.
26. Ibid., 590.

that *summa essentia* gives form to body or that the highest God gives form to the material world.[27] In both of these early texts Augustine is speaking of God's giving form to the world through the world-soul, as we have seen. God creates the world and time, but he does so through or by soul. The world-soul of Plotinus has become in Augustine a creature that God uses to form, administer, and order the world, but—and this is the point I wish to argue—even as late as the *conf.* the idea of the world-soul with which individual souls are identical remains an operative element in Augustine's conceptual scheme. For, when he speaks of time as a *distentio animi,* as a distention of the mind-soul, he is—I suggest—still thinking in terms of individual souls being one with the world-soul, with that soul by which God gave form to this world. If this hypothesis is correct, then Solignac's second claim is incorrect, for time as a distention of mind soul is "un temps des choses," an objective and not merely a subjective time.

Thus, what Augustine says at the end of his account of time, namely, "What takes place in the whole psalm takes place also in each of its parts and in each of its syllables. The same thing holds for a longer action, of which perhaps the psalm is a small part. The same thing holds for a man's entire life, the parts of which are all the man's actions. The same thing holds throughout the whole age of the sons of men, the parts of which are the lives of all men" (*conf.* 11, 28, 38), is not merely a stretching out of the present consciousness to embrace all of one's life and the addition of all lives to make up all time, but a stretching out of all of creation, which is formed by the world-soul. However, that Augustine is thinking in these terms is at most a hypothesis. What sort of evidence can one offer that the hypothesis is correct?

First of all, since it seems beyond doubt that Augustine was quite familiar with *Ennead* 3, 7, he would have been aware of Plotinus's concern at the end of 3, 7, 13 with time's being split up. "Is time, then, also in us? It is in every soul of this kind, and in the same form in every one of them, and all are one. So time will not be split up, any more than eternity, which, in a differing way, is in all the [eternal] beings of the same form" (*Ennead* 2, 7, 13, lines 66–69).[28] Whereas Augustine ap-

---

27. See *imm. an.* 15, 24, and *mus.* 6, 5, 13.
28. Plotinus, *Enneads,* trans. A. H. Armstrong (Cambridge, Mass.: Harvard University Press, 1967), 3:355. I have used Armstrong's translation of the *Enneads* throughout this article.

proaches the nature of time from the individual soul that is distended and moves from there to "the whole age of the sons of men," Plotinus begins with the distention of the universal soul and moves to the individual souls that are one with Soul. Thus for Plotinus time as a *diastasis* of Soul is objective and one. "How, then, is time everywhere? Because Soul, too, is not absent from any part of the universe, just as the soul in us is not absent from any part of us" (*Ennead* 3, 7, 13, lines 47–48). The final section of *Ennead* 3, 7 is explicitly concerned with time's being everywhere and with its not being fragmented in individual souls. Could Augustine, who was very familiar with this *Ennead* and who is otherwise so sensitive to the nuances of Plotinus's thought, have failed to spot Plotinus's concern with the unity and objectivity of time and also have failed to realize that the Plotinian solution rested upon the doctrine of the universal soul with which individual souls are one?

Second, what Augustine says about time apart from the definition of time as *distentio animi* requires that time be objective in a way that would be impossible if time were merely a distention of individual souls that are simply many. For, even in book 11 of the *conf.*, Augustine develops his account of time at least partially in response to the stock Manichaean objection that asked what God was doing before he made heaven and earth. He insists that the question deserves a serious answer, and his answer is that time is a creature and that, consequently, there was no time when God made nothing.[29] Hence, God does not precede time in time. "You have made all times, and you are before all times, and not at any time was there no time. At no time, therefore, did you do nothing, since you made time itself" (*conf.* 11, 13, 16–11, 14, 17). Furthermore, God is the maker of all times, and time began to be along with heaven and earth.[30] Times pass by means of the changing motions of a creature, or times began to run by means of the motions of a creature that was made.[31] There

---

29. Augustine was not satisfied with the response that was perhaps typical within the unsophisticated and even anti-intellectual Church of Africa, namely, that God was preparing hell for those who asked such questions. See *conf.* 11, 12, 14, and O'Connell, *St. Augustine's Confessions*, 138, for the link to "the conservative, anti-intellectual Catholics of his day."

30. "Quomodo enim erat tempus quod Deus non fecerat, cum omnium temporum ipse sit fabricator? Et si tempus cum coelo et terra esse coepit, non potest inveniri tempus quo Deus nondum fecerat coelum et terram" (*Gn. adv. Man.* 1 2, 3).

31. "Ubi enim nulla creatura est, cuius mutabilibus motibus tempora peraguntur, tempora omnino esse non possunt" (*civ. Dei* 15, 20). "Factae itaque creaturae motibus

is time by means of which the future succeeds the past through the present in virtue of the motion of a creature—either spiritual or corporeal.[32] Hence, it seems clear that time began with the existence of the motion of a creature—no matter whether that creature was spiritual or corporeal.[33] Such time would not seem to be dependent upon the existence of individual souls; rather it would seem to be objective and independent of human consciousness.[34] Hence, Augustine's definition of time as *distentio animi* seems inconsistent with what he says elsewhere. One way in which one might try to render the various claims that Augustine makes consistent lies in distinguishing various kinds of time.[35] Thus, one might view the definition of time as distention of mind-soul as a definition of human or psychological time as opposed to physical time. On the other hand, when Augustine speaks of time as beginning with God's creating heaven and earth, one might regard him as speaking of physical or objective time. In *Gn. litt.* 5, 5, 12, he provides what would seem to be a definition of such time: "the motion of a creature from one state to another, with things following according to the ordering of God administering

---

coeperunt currere tempora: unde ante creaturam frustra tempora requiruntur, quasi invenire ante tempora tempora" (*Gn. litt.* 5, 5, 12).

32. "Motus enim si nullus esset vel spiritualis vel corporalis creaturae, quo per praesens praeteritis futura succederent, nullum esset tempus omnino" (*Gn. litt.* 5, 5, 12).

33. The heaven of heaven and unformed matter are both creatures, but neither of them is in time. The former "suffers no change in time" (*conf.* 12, 11, 13), and the latter "could not exhibit temporal change . . . because without variety of motions there are no times, and there is no variety where there is no form" (*conf.* 12, 11, 14). Formless matter, however, was not prior in time to formed matter, "since the forms of things give rise to times" (*conf.* 12, 29, 40).

34. Since Augustine held that God created everything at the same time *(simul)*, there was no time at which there were not human souls. See *Gn. litt.* 4, 23, 52. Nonetheless, what Augustine says about time apart from his definition of time as *distentio animi* does not imply that time is mind-dependent, even if other creatures are not temporally prior to human souls.

35. In BA 14, 591, Solignac speaks of time as having "une valeur *existentiale* (au sens heideggerien du mot), par laquelle il est un des aspects fondamenteaux de l'existence humaine, ambivalent d'ailleurs comme cette existence elle-même." But he also speaks of "un temps des choses" as well as of "le temps et l'histoire de l'univers" (590–591) and tries to show that through presence to the world by soul Augustine can give some sense to "un temps des choses." Robert Jordan, in "Time and Contingency in St. Augustine," *Review of Metaphysics* 8 (1954–55): 394–414, contrasts Augustine's psychological view of time in book 11 with a physical view of time in book 12. He says that the passages in book 12 "present not a different version of time but the that-without-which there could be no time. Or, in other words, they reveal the foundation in reality of what is described in the eleventh Book in psychological or spiritual terms" (406).

all that he has created": *creaturae motus ex alio in aliud, consequentibus rebus secundum ordinationem administrantis Dei cuncta quae creavit*. If one claims that Augustine distinguished two kinds of time, then one can maintain that time as a distention of soul is subjective, but that time as the motion of creatures is objective and independent of minds.

There are, however, several difficulties with this solution to the problem. For Augustine's language, first of all, indicates that in book 11 he intends to define time and not one kind of time as opposed to another. Thus, his celebrated question, "What, then, is time? If no one asks me, I know; if I want to explain it to someone who asks me, I do not know" (*conf.* 11, 23, 30), seems to be aiming at a definition of time.[36] He tells his readers that he desires "to know the power and the nature of time, by which we measure bodily movements" (*conf.* 11, 23, 30). He does not "ask what it is that is called a day, but rather what is time by which we would measure the sun's circuit" (*conf.* 11, 23, 30). And as he approaches his definition, he comes to see "that time is a kind of distention": *tempus quamdam esse distentionem* (*conf.* 11, 23, 30). Thus Augustine's language offers no indication that he means *distentio animi* as a definition of a kind of time; rather his language indicates that he thought he was defining time *sans phrase*.

Second, the definition of time is developed at least partially in response to the Manichaean question about what God was doing before he made heaven and earth, and Augustine's answer is that there was no time when God was doing nothing, since time began when God created heaven and earth. But were Augustine to have in this context defined psychological time or human time as distinct from physical time, then the Manichaean objection would stand with respect to physical time. That is, within the context of the Manichaean objection a distinction between two kinds of time and a definition of psychological as opposed

---

36. Augustine's question and expression of puzzlement reflects the opening lines of *Ennead* 3, 7, 1, where Plotinus says much more prosaically than Augustine that "we think that we have a clear and distinct experience of them [eternity and time] in our souls, as we are always speaking of them and using their names on every occasion. Of course, when we try to concentrate on them and, so to speak, to get close to them, we find again that our thought runs into difficulties." Since Augustine is clearly indebted to Plotinus for his definition of time and since Plotinus is not defining a kind of time, e.g., human time, it would seem very likely that Augustine is not distinguishing several kinds of time and defining psychological or human time in book 11.

to physical time would have been singularly inept.[37] For even if prior to creation there were no psychological time, the Manichaean objection would recur with regard to physical time.

Finally, both Plotinus and Augustine approach the nature of time from the nature of eternity, and the definition of time as *diastasis* or distention is developed in contrast with eternity, which is all at once.[38] Were Augustine in that context to have distinguished two kinds of time and were he to have defined but one kind of time, his contrast between eternity and time would be askew. Hence, there seems to be no evidence that Augustine intended to distinguish several kinds of time and to define only human or psychological time, and there are good reasons to believe that he meant his definition to be a definition of time, not of a kind of time.

If, then, *distentio animi* is a definition of time, one might—as generally seems to have been done—understand the *animus* that is stretched out or distended to be the individual mind-soul.[39] Such an understanding of Augustine's definition of time not merely is not consistent with what else he says about time, as I have tried to argue; such an understanding also has to face the very serious objections that Bertrand Russell has raised, namely, that Augustine "substitute[d] subjective time for

---

37. C. W. K. Mundle, in "Time, Consciousness of," 137, says that Augustine "ended by, in effect, defining 'past' in terms of human memories and 'future' in terms of human expectations." He then adds, "These conclusions suited Augustine, for his purpose in discussing time was to show that it is meaningless to ask what God was doing before he made heaven and earth." Mundle is right insofar as he claims that making time dependent upon individual human souls would allow Augustine to answer the Manichees; however, Augustine did not need such an idealistic position in order to answer them.

38. After noting the similar beginnings, O'Connell goes on to say, "As Augustine does, Plotinus treats first of eternity, and only then approaches the nature of time. At that stage he proceeds to evaluate successively the varied notions other philosophers proposed before him: again, Augustine's procedure" (O'Connell, *St. Augustine's Confessions*, 139). So too, after coming to Augustine's "Ecce distentio vita mea," O'Connell adds, "That definition is Plotinus' classic διάστασις. It comes from the very treatise (*Enn.* III, 7) that has served as Augustine's model, here and in the *De Musica,* for reflecting on the soul's fall from a contemplative eternity into the distraction, dissipation, dispersion of time and the manifold life of action" (*St. Augustine's Confessions,* 142).

39. In "Time," in *The Encyclopedia of Philosophy* (ed. John Edwards [New York: Macmillan, 1967]), 8:126, J. J. C. Smart says that Augustine's formulation of the question "What is time?" gives the impression that he is looking for a definition: "This looks like a request for a definition, and yet no definition is forthcoming." All other sources that I have been able to consult regard *distentio animi* as a definition, and I know of no one who interprets *animus* as anything other than the individual soul.

the time of history and physics." If time is nothing more than memory, perception, and expectation of individual humans, then Russell is surely right in saying that "obviously this won't do. All [Augustine's] memories and all his expectations occurred at about the time of the fall of Rome, whereas mine occur at about the time of the fall of industrial civilization, which formed no part of the bishop of Hippo's expectations. Subjective time might suffice for a solipsist of the moment, but not for a man who believes in a real past and future, even if only his own."[40] If one interprets Augustine's definition of time in terms of the distention of individual souls, then it would seem that there could be no common temporal frame of reference within which we can date all real events; rather there would seem to be as many distinct temporal series as there are distinct distended souls.[41] And—worse yet—these many independent temporal series would be private in the same way that Augustinian minds are private. Hence, an idealistic interpretation of Augustine's definition of time avoids a plurality of kinds of time, but destroys the possibility of an objective or public time, such as history and physics presuppose.

Therefore, I conclude that if Augustine's definition of time as *distentio animi* is to be consistent with what else he says about time and if that definition is to escape the charges that it makes time subjective and private to individual souls, the *animus* that is distended must be the world-soul by which God gave form to the world and with which individual souls are somehow one. Thus far I have tried to argue that Augustine could have understood his definition of time in such a fashion and that he needed such an understanding of time if he were to be consistent and to be able to avoid the sort of objections that Russell pointed out. Of course, one might admit that what Augustine says is

---

40. Russell, *Human Knowledge*, 212. In "Time and Contingency in St. Augustine," 395, Robert Jordan speaks of "the quite staggering irrelevance" of what Russell has to say. If one understands time to be a distention of individual souls, it seems to me that what Russell says is both relevant and devastating.

41. Only a philosopher as free from respect for common sense as Francis H. Bradley can admit a plurality of temporal series. In *Appearance and Reality* (Oxford: Clarendon Press, 1930), 186, Bradley says, "For there is no valid objection to the existence of any number of independent time-series. In these the internal events would be interrelated temporally, but each series, as a series and as a whole, would have no temporal connexion with anything outside." If time for Augustine were a distention of individual souls, then he would have, it would seem, the multiplicity of temporal series that Bradley speaks of.

open to his holding the existence of a world-soul and that his definition of time requires that he hold such a view and yet maintain that Augustine unfortunately did not hold such a view since there is no textual evidence that he saw time as a distention of both individual and world-soul.

SOME TEXTUAL EVIDENCE?

There is one text in *conf.* 11 that, though it may not put the question beyond reasonable doubt, certainly provides some confirmation for the hypotheses that Augustine held as late as the *conf.* a doctrine of the world-soul with which individual souls are somehow one and that his definition of time is to be understood as a distention of the world-soul with which human souls are one. And if O'Connell is correct in claiming that one of Augustine's audiences for the *conf.* was the conservative African Catholic Church for whom a Plotinian understanding of the faith may have been a bit too much, one can understand why Augustine at most implies and suggests a doctrine of the world-soul.[42] The text in question begins at the end of *conf.* 11, 30, 40, where Augustine says in addressing God that "times are not coeternal with you, nor is any creature such, even if there were a creature above time."[43] And he immediately takes up this creature whose existence has been suggested as he begins the next section, "What, O Lord, my God, is that bosom of your deep secret, and how far have the consequences of my sins cast me forth from there?"[44] The *sinus alti secreti tui*, from which the consequences of Augustine's sins have cast him forth, would seem to be the heaven of heaven that he speaks of in book 12 or perhaps the bosom of Abraham mentioned in book 11, where Augustine speaks of Nebridius's death and of the place where he now lives.[45] In any case this creature

---

42. See O'Connell, *St. Augustine's Confessions,* 18–21, and *Early Theory,* 232–235, for evidence of the conservative and even anti-intellectual atmosphere of the Church in Africa.

43. In a footnote to this text Solignac mentions that Augustine will deal with the duration proper to angelic existence in *civ. Dei* 12, 16, but then adds that "ici il songe plutôt à l'univers des esprits, au *coelum coeli* dont va parler le livre XII" (BA 14, 341).

44. I have replaced Ryan's translation with my own more literal version in the above sentence.

45. For Solignac's suggestion that Augustine is thinking of the heaven of heaven, see note 43 above. For the bosom of Abraham, see *conf.* 11, 3, 6: "Now he [Nebridius] lives

The World-Soul and Time 235

above times is a mind-soul from which sin has separated Augustine and, one presumes, every fallen soul. The text continues, "Heal my eyes, and let me share in the joy of your light. Surely, if there is a mind possessed of such great knowledge, so that to it are known all things past and future, just as I know one well-known psalm, then supremely marvelous is that mind and wondrous and fearsome. From it whatever there is of ages past and of ages to come is no more hidden than there are hidden from me as I sing that psalm what and how much preceded from its beginning and what and how much remains to the end."

There are a number of things to note with regard to such a text. First, there is no hint that *iste animus* can be understood as referring to a plurality, such as the company of angels, or "l'univers des esprits," as Solignac suggests. Second, though Augustine twice makes reference to the existence of that mind in a hypothetical clause, he employs the same sort of hypothetical expression with regard to the heaven of heaven, the existence of which he does not seem to doubt.[46] Third, Augustine uses *non lateat*—the same expression he uses in his definition of sensation—to express that mind's awareness of ages past and to come, just as he uses *non latet* to express his awareness of the part of the psalm he has already sung and the part as yet unsung.[47] The connotation of

---

in Abraham's bosom. Whatever is that abode signified by the word 'bosom,' in it lives Nebridius. . . . There he lives. What other place is there for such a soul? . . . [H]e puts his spiritual mouth to your fountain, and in accordance with his desire drinks in wisdom, as much as he can, endlessly happy." See also Solignac's note, "Le sein d'Abraham," BA 14, 549–550.

In "Time and Contingency in St. Augustine," 262–263, Jordan seems to interpret this marvelous mind as God. The translation that he is using, from *The Basic Writings of St. Augustine*, 2 vols., ed. Whitney J. Oates (New York: Random House, 1948), refers to that mind with "Him," though it is clearly a creature.

46. See *conf.* 12, 11, 12, where of the heaven of heaven Augustine says, "O happy creature, if there be such, for cleaving to your happiness." The hypothetical mode of expression is, I suggest, more a matter of gently insinuating a Plotinian idea into the mind of an audience not entirely receptive of such intellectualizing than an expression of doubt upon Augustine's part.

47. See *quan.* 24, 46, for Augustine's definition of sensation "corporis passio per seipsam non latens animam." In *Greatness*, 209n73, Colleran comments, "The *non latere* of Augustine quite certainly derives from the μὴ λαθεῖν of Plotinus." Colleran refers to *Ennead* 4, 4, 19. Since, however, in both sensation and knowledge something does not escape *(non latet)* the soul's awareness, the mere use of that expression does not necessarily imply that this *animus* senses all past and future ages; see *quan.* 30, 58. However, the awareness of *iste animus* is compared with Augustine's awareness of the psalm he is singing, and the expression *sensus distenditur* seems to suggest that the *attentio* of the

the language and the comparison with Augustine's own awareness of the psalm he is singing seems to imply that the awareness of that mind with respect to ages past and to come is sensory awareness—the sort of awareness of what happens in the world that a world-soul would have if the world were a single animal.

Furthermore, when Augustine goes on to distinguish God's immutable and eternal knowledge from the mutable knowledge of *iste animus,* he says that nothing happens to God, the creator of minds, "as emotions are changed or senses filled up *(sensus distenditur)* by expectation of words to come and memory of those past in one who sings well-known psalms or hears a familiar psalm." Though it might seem that Augustine is merely saying that God's eternal knowledge is not like ours, in the context *sensus distenditur* seems to refer to the awareness of *iste animus.* For Augustine introduces that passage with the following: "But far be it that you, creator of the universe, creator of souls and bodies, far be it that in such wise [like *iste animus*] you should know future and past. Far, far more wonderfully, far more deeply do you know them! It is not as emotions are changed or senses filled up." Hence, this wondrous creaturely mind, if there is such, is one whose sensory awareness is distended by memory of the past and expectation of the future and is one whose awareness nothing past or future escapes *(non latet).* And that mind is the *sinus* from which the consequences of sin have cast forth individual souls. If that *sinus* is the heaven of heaven, as Solignac suggests, then it would seem to be the universal soul—"that rational and intellectual mind of God's chaste city" *(conf.* 12, 15, 20)—from which sinful souls have fallen and to which they return. All that is missing from Augustine's earlier doctrine of a world-soul is, it seems, the life-giving function of this soul in virtue of which the world is one huge animal, and that claim is, of course, what Augustine explicitly backed away from in the *retr.*

Hence, I conclude that there is good reason for believing that as late as the time of his writing the *conf.,* when he was already a Christian bishop, Augustine still held, if not as an explicit doctrine, at least as an implicit but operative element of his conceptual scheme, the idea of a universal or world-soul with which individual souls are one, from

---

world-soul is stretched out or distended, just as our attention lasts. See *conf.* I, 28, 37: "sed tamen perdurat attentio, per quam pergat abesse quod aderit."

which individuals souls have fallen, and in virtue of which his definition of time as *distentio animi* can escape charges of inconsistency with what he says elsewhere about time as well as charges that such a definition of time is purely subjective and hopelessly idealistic. For, time, if my very tentatively suggested hypothesis is correct, is for Augustine, as it was for Plotinus, primarily a distention of that soul by which form is given to the world and with which we are all somehow one.[48]

48. I have repeatedly said that I regard the second half of this article as a very tentative hypothesis. The hypothesis could, I believe, receive further confirmation from a careful comparison of *Ennead* 3, 7 and *conf.* 11. O'Connell has shown Augustine's indebtedness to *Ennead* 3, 7, 11 for the element of *curiositas* in the soul's triple sin. See *Early Theory,* 175–181. But it is in that very section that Plotinus says that "Soul, making the world of sense in imitation of that other world . . . put itself into time, which it made instead of eternity." And just before this, he says, "[W]e made a long stretch of our journey and constructed time as an image of eternity." Armstrong notes, "'We,' because it is soul which moves and produces time, and we are souls, parts of universal soul and already present in it as it moves out from eternity" (*Plotinus,* 3:338).

Further confirmation might also be provided through a careful study of Augustine's use of *distentio, attentio, intentio,* and *extentio,* all of which terms are associated both with Augustine's discussion of time and with his account of sensation and the soul's relation to its body. However, there are also difficulties to be met. For example, if the world-soul is distended in the creation of the world, is not soul's fall into time the same as the creation of the world? Or, in Christian terms, do not creation and original sin coincide?

13

VOCANS TEMPORALES, FACIENS AETERNOS

Augustine on Liberation from Time

Augustine's description of the Word of God as coming to call temporal beings and make them eternal aroused my interest, especially given the facts that Augustine thought of God's eternity as timeless and that temporality seems so intimately tied to human existence. The article points to texts in which Augustine seems clearly to have thought that the Word of God came to free us from all temporal duration, not merely from time in some particular sense. Augustine admittedly viewed time ambivalently, that is, as good insofar as it was a creature, but as evil insofar as tied to nonbeing and sin. Plotinus, however, had linked the origin of time to the fall of the soul such that the fall of the soul was not merely a matter of personal sin, but cosmogonic. The theme of liberation from time in Augustine carries with it some of that Plotinian conceptual framework, which does not fit with his insistence upon the goodness of the created world. I now regard my hypothesis that Augustine was the first in the Latin West to conceive of God's eternity as timeless as more than merely a hypothesis.

In several texts Augustine speaks of the Word of God as becoming man in order to make men eternal or to free men from time. Though this theme may well be a relatively minor one in

Augustine's treatment of the purpose of the Incarnation, it is one that is interesting both in itself and also, I believe, in terms of what it reveals about Augustine's Plotinian understanding of the Christian faith.[1] In this article I shall first set forth the texts that I have found in which Augustine deals with this liberation of men from time by the Word. Then, after pointing out some problems with this theme, I shall try to show how this theme is intimately tied to several other themes in Augustine's thought that bear a decidedly Plotinian stamp, especially the fall of the soul, the heaven of heavens, and the definition of time. Finally, I shall argue that, though Augustine's claim that the Word came as man to free man from time can be understood in a quite orthodox sense, some of the oddities surrounding this idea are quite likely due to the Plotinian conceptual framework within which the theme is articulated.

LIBERATION FROM TIME

In his *en. Ps.* 101, when commenting on verse 25, Augustine describes the mission of the Word in language that is both striking and puzzling: "O Verbum ante tempora, per quod facta sunt tempora, natum et in tempore, cum sit vita aeterna, vocans temporales, faciens aeternos" (*en. Ps.* 101, 10).[2] The final words, "vocans temporales, faciens

---

[1]. This theme of liberation of man from time by the Word become man—perhaps a minor one in Augustine's soteriology—has nonetheless received very little attention. For example, in his *Le dogme de la rédemption chez saint Augustin* (Paris: J. Gabalda, 1933), Jean Rivière makes no mention of it. Nor is there any reference to it in Victorino Capánaga, O.R.S.A., "La deificación en la soteriología agustiniana," in *Augustinus magister* (Paris: Études augustiniennes, 1954–55), 2:745–754. Even in Eugene TeSelle's excellent work, *Augustine the Theologian* (New York: Herder and Herder, 1970), there is no mention of this theme. The only explicit discussion of it that I have found occurs in the note by M.-F. Berrouard, "Le Christ et la libération du temps," BA 72, 850–851. This note refers to several other works on time in Augustine. Among these are Le Blond, *Les conversions de saint Augustin*, 246–275; Jean Guitton, *Le temps et l'éternité chez Plotin et saint Augustin*, 3rd rev. ed. (Paris: J. Vrin, 1959); Marrou, *L'ambivalence du temps de l'histoire chez saint Augustin;* Maurice Huftier, *Le tragique de la condition chrétienne chez saint Augustin* (Paris: Desclée, 1964). There is one work that treats the theme in Aquinas and in his commentators: Carl J. Peter, *Participated Eternity in the Vision of God: A Study of the Opinion of Thomas Aquinas and his Commentators on the Duration of the Acts of Glory* (Rome: Gregorian University Press, 1964); Peter gives one reference to Saint Augustine (*civ. Dei* 9, 21) where he speaks of the angels enjoying "participata aeternitate."

[2]. I have quoted for the most part from the PL, though I have also used the BA edition. I have consulted and at times paraphrased John K. Ryan's translation of the *Confessions*.

aeternos," seems an unusual way to describe the Word's salvific role. For we think of temporality as being intimately tied to human existence—so intimately tied to human existence that it would not seem to be human existence if it were no longer temporal.³

However, "eternal" is open to at least two possible interpretations: in one sense, it might mean simply that the Word makes those beings continue to live without end.⁴ And there are texts in Augustine that can

---

3. According to Augustine, even though we shall remain mutable, yet, insofar as we participate in God's eternity, we will not change in any respect. There will be, he claims, no yesterday and no tomorrow, but only the lasting today in which nothing passes.

On the one hand, since God's eternity is his substance or nature, our participation in his eternity is our participation in the divine nature, and this latter theme is much more common in Augustine. For example, "deos facturus qui homines erant, homo factus est qui Deus erat" (s. 192, 1). And in another sermon he speaks of "vocans illum ad divinitatem" (s. 341A, 1), a phrase that recalls "vocans temporales, faciens aeternos." On the other hand, divine eternity interpreted as timelessness—as Augustine and Plotinus do interpret it—seems particularly opaque to the human mind, and human participation in such timeless existence seems to imply a startling transformation of the sort of existence that we know. If Descartes were correct, the situation, of course, would be worse than startling. Of eternity being *simul et semel*, he says, "Hoc concipi non potest. Est quidem simul et semel, quatenus Dei naturae nunquam quid additur aut ab ea quid detrahitur. Sed non est simul et semel, quatenus simul existit: nam cum possimus in ea distinguere partes jam post mundi creationem, quidni illud etiam possemus facere ante eam, cum eadem duratio sit?" (*Manuscript de Göttingen*, in *Oeuvres de Descartes*, 5:148–149).

Most contemporary philosophers find nonbodily survival of death a very difficult concept with which to deal. Augustine's nontemporal survival—albeit with a resurrected body—is surely even more problematic. On the other hand, there are some texts in which Augustine seems to imply that we shall cease to be human beings. See *Jo. Ev. tr.* 1, 4, where he says, "ne simus homines." However, he interprets this in the line of adopted sonship. Thus, in *s.* 166, 4, 4, he says, "Noli succensere. Non enim ita tibi dicitur ut homo non sis, ut pecus sis: sed ut sis inter eos quibus dedit potestatem filios Dei fieri (Jn 1:12). Deus enim deum te vult facere: non natura, sicut est ille quem genuit; sed dono suo et adoptione."

4. Though the expression "eternal life" is used fairly frequently in the Scriptures, especially in the Johannine writings, there does not seem to be present in the Scriptures anything like the timelessness that is found in Plotinus and Augustine. Even the eternity of God seems to mean no more than that God has neither beginning nor end. In *L'éternité dans la vie quotidienne: Essai sur les sources et la structure du concept d'éternité* (Bruges: Desclée de Brouwer, 1964), 146–147, Jacques Durandeaux sums up the biblical doctrine of eternity. "L'éternité est prise, dans la Bible, comme temps qui ne finit pas." He finds 184 occurrences of the term in the Vulgate and breaks them down into various categories, e.g., eternity as attribute of God, as abode of God, as unchangeable, definitive, and transcendent value, as solidity, as the afterlife, as the renewed world of the parousia, and as the abode of man. Theological manuals seem to rely very heavily on Boethius's definition, "interminabilis vitae tota simul et perfecta possessio," and note that the concept of eternity excludes (1) beginning and end and (2) all succession. See I.

be read as saying no more than that "being made eternal" means that the soul will continue to exist forever. For example, in commenting on Psalms 134, Augustine is discussing that name that God disclosed to Moses when he sent Moses to lead the people of Israel out of Egypt, namely, "I am who I am." Augustine points out that it was not necessary for God to say that this name was his eternally, for it was understood even without his saying it. However, God goes on to tell Moses that he is the God of Abraham, Isaac and Jacob: "ne ibi suboriretur humana sollicitudo, quia hoc temporale est, non sempiternum, securos nos fecit, quia de temporalibus ad aeternam vitam nos perducit. Hoc, inquit, mihi nomen est in aeternum, non quia aeternus Abraham et aeternus Jacob, sed quia Deus illos facit aeternos postea sine fine: habuerunt quippe initium, sed finem non habebunt" (*en. Ps.* 134:6).[5] Here the idea that the Word came to make men eternal might seem to mean only that, though human beings had a beginning in time, they will continue to live forever.[6] "Making the patriarchs eternal" seems equivalent to leading them to eternal or unending life, albeit the Word leads them to it from temporal things (*a temporalibus*). This weaker interpretation of "eternal" is possibly present also in *Sermones* (hereafter *s.*) 229L, where Augustine says, "Ascendat ergo nobis Christus, et tangamus eum, si credimus in eum, quia Filius Dei est, aeternus, coaeternus, non ex quo natus est de virgine, sed aeternus. Nam et nos aeternos facturus est, non quia semper fuimus, sed quia semper erimus." However, there are other texts in which it becomes clear that "becoming eternal" means more than life without end.

M. Dalmau, "De Deo Uno et Trino," in *Sacrae Theologiae Summa* (Madrid: Biblioteca de autores cristianos, 1958), 2:97–98.

5. In *Trin.* 5, 16, 17, Augustine indicates that what begins to be truly said of God from a certain time is predicated of God relatively, i.e., according to accident. However, the accident in question is not in God, but in some creature with respect to which God begins to be said to be. Thus God began to be called the God of the Patriarchs not by reason of a change in himself, but by reason of a change in the Patriarchs. Before they existed, however, God could not be truly said to be their God. Hence, though there was no time when it could not have been truly said of God that he is "Who is," God is truly said to be the God of Abraham only from a certain point in time when Abraham lived. See my "Properties of God and the Predicaments in *De Trinitate* V," *The Modern Schoolman* 59 (1981): 1–19.

6. In *civ. Dei* 11, 11, Augustine seems to equate the eternal life of the angels with endless existence: "Neque enim sicut vita, quamdiucumque fuerit, ita aeterna vita veraciter dici poterit, si finem habitura sit; si quidem vita tantummodo vivendo, aeterna vero finem non habendo nominata est."

Perhaps the most striking of these texts implying a transformation of our mode of duration is one in which Augustine describes the Word's mission as freeing man from time. "Venit humilis creator noster, creatus inter nos: qui facit nos, qui factus est propter nos: Deus ante tempora, homo et in tempore, ut hominem liberaret a tempore" (*s.* 340A).[7] This liberation from time cannot mean simply existence for all time to come; rather it has to mean freedom from that "distention" of our lives into past, present, and future that is the very nature of time, as Augustine has defined it in book 11 of the *conf.*[8] That he means to say that the soul is freed from time Augustine makes quite clear in his *Jo. Ev. tr.:* "Denique ubi venit plentitudo temporis, venit et ille qui nos liberaret a tempore. Liberati enim a tempore, venturi sumus ad aeternitatem illam ubi non est tempus, nec dicitur ibi: Quando veniet hora; dies est enim sempiternus, qui nec praeceditur hesterno nec excluditur crastino" (*Jo. Ev. tr.* 31, 5). In this world, Augustine says, days pass, and no day remains. Moments are driven away as we speak. We have aged since this morning; "ita nihil stat, nihil fixum manet in tempore. Amare itaque debemus per quem facta sunt tempora, ut liberemur a tempore et figamur in aeternitate, ubi jam nulla est mutabilitas temporum" (ibid.).[9] Hence, the liberation from time through the Word become man is not merely the attainment of an endless, though temporal, existence, but a participation in the timeless existence that is God's.

Thus Augustine speaks of men and women as "futuri participes aeternitatis Dei" (*en. Ps.* 101, 11), and he interprets *generatio generationum* as that generation "quae de omnibus generationibus colligitur, et in

---

7. The following line from the sermon just quoted says that there came to heal our swelling a great physician. And the swelling or tumor suggests the sin of pride, by which the soul fell into multiplicity, into body, and into times. See *s.* 123, 1, where Augustine talks of "tumor superbiae."

8. See "The World-Soul and Time in Saint Augustine," *AS* 14 (1983): 77–94, where I argue that the definition of time as *distentio animi* is not a definition of one kind of time, but a definition of time.

9. Augustine holds that we become what we love. Thus, in *s.* 121, 1, he says, "Amando Deum, efficimur dii: ergo amando mundum, dicimur mundus." Similarly, if one wishes to remain eternally, he must love the eternal Word. "Omnis enim anima sequitur quod amat. . . . Verbum autem Domini manet in aeternum. Ecce quod ames, si vis manere in aeternum." So too, "Tenete potius dilectionem Dei, ut quomodo Deus est aeternus, sic et vos maneatis in aeternum: quia talis est quisque qualis ejus dilectio est. Terram diligis? terra eris. Deum diligis? quid dicam? Deus eris? Non audeo dicere ex me. Scripturas audiamus" (*ep. Jo.* 2, 14).

unam redigitur; ipsa particeps erit aeternitatis tuae. Ceterae generationes implendis temporibus generantur, ex quibus illa in aeternum regeneratur; mutata vivificabitur, erit idonea portare te, vires accipiens a te." Of God's years, he adds, "aeternitas illa in illa erit generatione." And in *conf.* 4, 16, 31, Augustine uses the startling phrase "domus nostra, aeternitas tua."[10]

PROBLEMS WITH LIBERATION FROM TIME

One can hardly do better in broaching this topic than borrow from the title of Henri-Irénée Marrou's excellent work, *L'ambivalence du temps de l'histoire chez saint Augustin.* For time, as Augustine treats it, is precisely ambivalent or bivalent. As a creature of God or the mode of existence of creatures of God, time is something good; on the other hand, there is a whole negative side to the topic of time that led Augustine to speak of this life as a deadly life or a living death (*conf.* 1, 6, 7) and to speak of our days as evil (*s.* 167, 1, 1 and 2, 3).

First of all, time is a creature. As early as *ep.* 18, Augustine offers his correspondent "hoc quiddam grande et breve," namely, "Est natura per locos et tempora mutabilis, ut corpus. Et est natura per locos nullo modo, sed tantum per tempora etiam ipsa mutabilis, ut anima. Et est natura quae nec per locos, nec per tempora mutari potest: hoc Deus est. Quod hic insinuavi quoquo modo mutabile, creatura dicitur; quod immutabile, creator. Cum autem omne quod esse dicimus, in quantum manet dicamus, et in quantum unum est, omnis porro pulchritudinis forma unitas sit" (*ep.* 18, 2). Thus it would seem that a creature as such

---

10. There are several other texts that bear at least indirectly upon this theme. For example, in *ench.* 56, Augustine says that the Church is the house in which the Trinity dwells. "Quae tota hic accipienda est, non solum ex parte qua peregrinatur in terris, verum etiam ex illa quae in coelis semper, ex quo condita est, cohaesit Deo, nec ullum malum sui casus experta est. Haec in sanctis Angelis persistit, et suae parti peregrinanti sicut oportet opituletur; quia utraque una erit consortio aeternitatis." In *doc. chr.* 1, 34, 38, Augustine speaks of Christ who came to free our nature from "temporalibus." "Ex quo intelligitur quam nulla res in via tenere nos debeat, quando nec ipse Dominus in quantum via nostra esse dignatus est, tenere nos voluit, sed transire; ne rebus temporalibus, quamvis ab illo pro salute nostra susceptis et gestis, haereamus infirmiter, sed per eas potius curramus alacriter, ut ad eum ipsum, qui nostram naturam a temporalibus liberavit, et collocavit ad dexteram Patris, provehi atque pervehi mereamur." Thus even the temporal reality of the humanity of Christ, it would seem, is not to be clung to. And in *s.* 38, 3, 5, he speaks of our life growing "ut fiat aeterna."

is mutable, and it would also seem that it is temporal precisely because it is mutable. "In quantum igitur mutabiles sumus, in tantum ab aeternitate distamus" (*Trin.* 4, 18, 24).

Time began to be along with heaven and earth; hence, there can be found no time when God had not yet made heaven and earth (*Gn. adv. Man.* 1, 2, 3). "Factae itaque creaturae motibus coeperunt currere tempora: unde ante creaturam frustra tempora requiruntur, quasi invenire ante tempora tempora. Motus enim si nullus esset vel spiritualis vel corporalis creaturae, quo per praesens praeteritis futura succederent, nullum esset tempus omnino. Moveri autem creatura non utique posset, si non esset. Potius ergo tempus a creatura, quam creatura coepit a tempore; utrumque autem ex Deo" (*Gn. litt.* 5, 5, 12). Augustine immediately adds that we should not understand "time begins from creation" as though time were not a creature (ibid.). God is "creator temporum et ordinator" (*civ. Dei* 11, 6). Now since time is a creature of God or a mode of being of every created nature, it is difficult to see how time is not something good. "Iuste sane creator laudatur in omnibus quae fecit omnia bona valde" (*Gn. litt.* 7, 26, 37). God, the highest good, has made all other goods. Everything that he has made from nothing is mutable, but everything that he made from nothing is nonetheless good—whether a great good or a small good. "Omnis autem natura, in quantum natura est, bonum est" (*nat. b.* 1).

Thus time is a creature that began when motion began in creatures. It might seem that there were creatures prior to time—that is, creatures that, though mutable, did not exercise their mutability, such as the heaven of heaven and unformed matter. However, these creatures did not precede time temporally, but in origin (*conf.* 12, 29, 40). Hence, these creatures existed at no time before times began to run. On the other hand, time, though a creature, is not a nature. Augustine asks how we can say that the present *is* if in order to be time it must turn into the past, for the cause of its being is that it will not be, so that we do not truly say that time is except insofar as it tends toward nonbeing (*conf.* 11, 14, 17). The very being of time seems to be its tending toward nonbeing, and the tendency toward nonbeing is to fail, *deficere,* to cease to be and to be good. Not without reason does Augustine speak of our human existence as "mortalem vitam an mortem vitalem" (*conf.* 1, 6, 7). That this life is as much death as life is not meant, I believe, as a mere rhetorical flourish. For Augustine finds death in every change—even in desired change and in the growth of little children. "Sed vide quia cum accedit una, altera moritur. Veniente pueritia, moritur infantia; veniente adolescentia, moritur pueritia; veniente juventute, moritur adolescentia; veniente senectute, moritur juventus; veniente morte, moritur omnis aetas. Quot optas gradus aetatis, tot simul optas et mortes aetatum. Non sunt ergo ista" (*en. Ps.* 127, 15). Augustine speaks in a similar fashion of his own infancy dying into childhood in the *conf.* 1, 6, 9. Even more explicitly in his *Jo. Ev. tr.*, he says, "Res enim quaelibet, prorsus qualicumque excellentia, si mutabilis est, non vere est; non enim est ibi verum esse, ubi est et non esse. Quidquid enim mutari potest, mutatum non est quod erat; si non est quod erat, mors quaedam ibi facta est; peremptum est aliquid ibi quod erat, et non est" (*Io. Ev. tr.* 38, 10). Augustine gives examples of blackness having died on a gray head, of beauty having died in a worn old body, of strength having died in a weakened one, of rest having died in one who is walking, and of walking having died in one who has stopped. "Quidquid mutatur et est quod non erat, video ibi quamdam vitam in eo quod est, et mortem in eo quod fuit" (ibid.).

The shortness and fleeting character of human existence is a favorite topic of his sermons. "A prima infantia usque ad decrepitam senectutem, breve spatium est. Quod tam diu vixerat, quid ei profuisset, si Adam hodie mortuus esset? Quid diu est, ubi finis est? Hesternum diem nemo revocat: hodiernus crastino urgetur, ut transeat. . . . Et modo cum loquimur, utique transimus. Verba currunt, et horae volant: sic aetas nostra, sic actus nostri, sic honores nostri, sic miseria nostra, sic ista felicitas nostra. Totum transit" (*s.* 124, 20). We cannot hold on to a day or an hour. Even if one utters a word of one syllable, such as *est,* "certe una syllaba est, et momentum unum est, et tres litteras syllaba habet: in ipso ictu ad secundam hujus verbi litteram non pervenis, nisi prima finita fuerit; tertia non sonabit, nisi cum et secunda transierit. . . . Momentis transvolantibus cuncta rapiuntur, torrens rerum fluit. . . . Isti ergo dies non sunt: ante abeunt pene, quam veniant; et cum venerint, stare non possunt"(*en. Ps.* 38, 7). Our children are born not to live with us, but rather to push us on and take our place. Their birth over which we rejoice marks our passing, and children as much as say to their parents, "Eia, cogitate ire hinc, agamus et nos mimum nostrum. Mimus est enim generis humani tota vita tentationis" (*en. Ps.* 127, 15).

Thus there seems to be a positive sense to time insofar as time is simply the mode of created existence. In this sense Gilson speaks of Augustine's not having a word other than "time" to speak of the existence of creatures.[11] But there is also the negative sense of time in accord with which time involves a tendency to nonbeing and death.[12] With refer-

[11]. In "Notes sur l'être," 212, E. Gilson says, "En somme, sauf peut-être tempus, Augustin n'a pas eu de nom pour le monde de la genèsis. Ce qui s'oppose chez lui à l'*esse* de l'*essentia* véritable, c'est cette approximation de l'être dont il repète qu'elle est 'plus ou moins' et que, sans être vraiment néant, elle n'est pas 'vraiment.'" So too, in *Le tragique*, 201–202, M. Huftier speaks of time and eternity as characterizing respectively creature and Creator: "Exactement, temps et éternité désignent deux modes d'être différents et hétérogenes, caractérisant respectivement la créature et le créateur: d'un côté l'être, l'immobile permanence; nécessité, immutabilité, éternité, sont les caractéristiques de Dieu, les conditions du *vere esse;* de l'autre, on a un temps lié à la création mobile et changeante—et qui, d'ailleurs, est né avec elle—: les créatures sont à la fois et ne sont pas. Dieu et la creature, l'éternité et le temps, c'est la condition de ce qui est par rapport à ce qui passe et ne tient pas."

[12]. In "Notes sur l'être," 233n43, Gilson remarks that Marrou has correctly emphasized the pessimistic notion of time in Augustine—a notion that has been strangely neglected by recent commentators: "L'excuse de ces commentateurs est que, chez saint Augustin lui-même, le temps n'est jamais là que comme ce qui doit être transcendé. Les techniques de rédemption du temps bouchent la vue. Elles occupent d'autant plus de place que, dans une doctrine où Dieu est l'éternité même, le mieux qu'on puisse dire du temps est qu'il est un moindre bien, et comme une tache sur la pureté de l'être, que la vie chrétienne a pour objet d'effacer."

Along the same lines, Marrou (*L'ambivalence,* 68), speaks of time as having become intimately bound up with "le péché, la dégradation et la mort" from the moment of the fall. For Augustine "l'insertion dans le temps nous condamne à cet effritement de l'être, à ce lent glissement vers la destruction, vers la mort" (ibid., 46).

However, Le Blond claims that the time of the Christian is transformed, restored, and saved. "Mais cette considération entraine au dela du temps du pécheur; pour apprécier la pensée d'Augustin sur le temps, le plus important n'est pas d'analyser la durée pécheresse en posant à la stabilité mysterieuse du premier homme, mais d'étudier sa transformation, sa solidification en l'homme racheté; c'est le temps restauré, sauvé par le Christ, aussi bien dans l'individu que dans l'histoire humaine, le temps du chrétien" (*Les Conversions de saint Augustin,* 271). Despite Le Blond's claim, as far as I can see of what Augustine is saying, time is not transformed or restored or saved. Christ has come not to save time, but to save or free man from time. Time will be transformed—not into a Christian time, but into eternity. (One is tempted to think of time as *aufgehoben* into eternity in the threefold Hegelian sense.)

In *en. Ps.* 38, 9, Augustine says, "Non enim sic Christo induti sumus, ut ex Adam jam nihil portemus. Videte veterascentem Adam, et innovari Christum in nobis." He ties this to the Pauline outer man that is being corrupted, while the inner man is renewed (2 Cor 4:16). However, he explicitly links time and our heritage from Adam. "Ergo ad peccatum, ad mortalitatem, ad praetervolantia tempora, ad gemitum et laborem et sudorem, ad aetates succedentes, non manentes, ab infantia usque ad senectutem sine sensu transeuntes, ad haec attendentes, videamus hic veterem hominem, veterem diem, vetus canticum, Vetus Testamentum." However, the new man, day, song, and covenant are found in the inner man. We pass from the old to the new as the old is corrupted until we come to the resurrection. We are, that is, being renewed now in the inner man; however,

ence to the language of liberation from time, the difference is important, for it does make better sense to think of the Word having become man to free man from some evil or deficiency than it does to think of our being freed from the mode of existence of creatures.[13] In the positive sense time is the consequence of there being creatures; in the negative sense time would seem to be the consequence of sin.[14]

Marrou makes a distinction between the time of history, that is, the time since the fall, and a cosmic time that began with creation. He explicitly deals only with the ambivalence of the time since the fall, the time that bears the wounds of sin.[15] However, that there is such a distinction in Augustine, or even the basis for drawing such a distinc-

---

time is still part of our heritage from Adam. "Ecce trahit adhuc Adam, et sic festinat ad Christum . . . veteres dies ex Adam" (ibid.). The coming of Christ has made a difference; however, time is transformed only *in spe,* not *in re,* until we come to God's eternity where time will be no more.

13. There is, of course, in Augustine the theme of God having become man in order to make men gods, sharers in his divine nature, in eternity. Some of Augustine's language, e.g., "ne simus homines" (see note 3 above) may seem to threaten our survival as humans, but in no case does he speak of the Word freeing us from our being creatures, for our eternity will be a participated eternity.

14. Thus Le Blond says, "C'est donc au péché que l'homme est redevable de sa dispersion dans le temps" (270). For the Neoplatonists, Marrou says, "l'insertion de l'âme humaine dans le devenir était le mal fondamental dont ils aspiraient à s'affrachir, et à bon droit, car enfermés dans le cercle de la nature déchue, ils ne pouvaient connaître ni concevoir d'autre temps que le temps du péché, du vieillissement et de la mort" (*L'ambivalence,* 73). Marrou recognizes in Augustine traces of such Plotinian views. However, I suspect that Marrou is not correct in implying that Augustine has conceived another time than the time of sin, aging, and death. Man's liberation from time is not, as I read Augustine, a liberation from a kind of time, but from time.

15. In *L'ambivalence,* 65–66, Marrou says that historical time, the time since the fall, is only an aspect of time. "Il semble bien qu'il faille concevoir ce qu'on pourrait appeler un temps cosmique, le temps dans lequel se déploie l'oeuvre de la Création divine: c'est celui que postulent les hypothèses du savant moderne, qu'il soit géologue ou biologiste." Similarly J. Chaix-Ruy, in "La cité de Dieu et la structure du temps," in *Augustinus magister* (Paris: Études augustinienne, 1954–55), 2:928, distinguishes an essential time before the fall from the existential time after the fall marked by the sin of the angels and the sin of man. However, he notes, "et voici que nous abordons un problème que saint Augustin n'a touché qu'avec d'infinies précautions, en s'excusant presque de le traiter." So too Marrou passes over the participation of man in this cosmic time before the fall (67). Perhaps Marrou and Chaix-Ruy—neither of whom offers any textual evidence for cosmic or essential time—wisely avoid much discussion of such time. For, given the Plotinian background, there was no way for Augustine to fit it into his account. It is interesting to note that Gabriel Marcel seems to hold what I read Augustine as holding: "il n'y a peut-être pas de sens à parler de temps avant la chute. Le temps est relatif au monde—peut-être n'y a-t-il un *monde* que apres la chute" (*Presence et immortalité* [Paris: Flammarion, 1959], 88).

tion, is not altogether clear. In fact, to the extent to which Augustine relies upon a Plotinian view of time and eternity—and he surely did rely upon such a view rather heavily—to that extent there seems to be less room for such a distinction. For in Plotinus the cosmos came to be as a result of the all-soul falling from contemplation of the eternal into the restless activity from which time results.[16] However, for the moment let us return to Augustine.

THE SOUL'S FALL INTO TIME

If the mission of the Word in becoming man is to free man from time, then it would seem that being in time or being distended in time is a state of sinfulness or of separation from God.[17] After all, Augustine is quite explicit that if man had not sinned, there would have been no reason for the Word to have come as man.[18] Without wounds and disease there is no need of a physician.[19] Hence, it would seem that the theme of a salvific liberation from time implies that time or being in time is, like death, ignorance, and concupiscence, the result of sin.[20]

---

16. In "The World-Soul and Time," I argued that Augustine seems to have held as late as the *conf.* that there was an all-soul of which individual souls were somehow parts and that he avoids a subjective account of time by making time the distention of the all-soul—as Plotinus does. However, it is by this universal soul that the world is formed insofar as that soul falls from contemplation of the eternal into busy activity concerning the world. Thus Augustine seems to tie the beginning of time to the fall of the soul. In *Les conversions,* 263n88, J.-M. Le Blond appeals to the line "In te anima mea tempora metior" to show "Certes l'âme dans laquelle Augustin mesure le temps n'est pas l'âme du monde." But he admits that Augustine's account of time is otherwise quite close to Plotinus's. If, on the other hand, soul is both one and many, as *quan.* 32, 69, suggests, the text Le Blond cites need not count against my argument.

17. An examination of the meanings of *liberare* and *liberatio* in a Latin dictionary indicates that that from which one is freed is something bad or negative, e.g., slavery, an obligation, a debt, a difficulty, fear, taxes. The limited survey of Augustine's use of these terms that I have been able to make would seem to support this idea. For example, Augustine speaks of "liberatio ab omnibus peccatis . . . ab omnibus malis, et ab omni corruptione mortalitatis" (*c. Jul.* 4, 13, 40), and he contrasts *liberatio* with *damnatio* (*ench.* 99).

18. "Si homo non perisset, Filius hominis non venisset" (*s.* 174, 2, 2). "Quare venit in mundum? *Peccatores salvos facere* (1 Tm 1:15). Alia causa non fuit quare venerit in mundum" (*s.* 174, 7, 8).

19. "Nulla causa fuit veniendi Christo Domino, nisi peccatores salvos facere. Tolle morbos, tolle vulnera, et nulla causa est medicinae. Si venit de caelo magnus medicus, magnus per totum orbem terrae iacebat aegrotus. Ipse aegrotus genus humanum est" (*s.* 171, 1).

20. In *pecc. merit.* 1, 16, 21, Augustine speaks of Adam as losing his *stabilitas aetatis,* as beginning to die on that day on which he sinned. "Non enim stat vel temporis

Augustine, moreover, does tie time to sin, and in doing so he is following Plotinus. Robert O'Connell has put this point quite well: "The soul's sin, therefore, involves a loss of spiritual unity in both authors [Plotinus and Augustine], a 'swelling outwards' into the spatialized world of body, a *distentio animi* into the dispersion of time. . . . In both authors, the fall from eternity to time is a fall from the superior occupation of immobile contemplation to the essentially degraded sphere of action."[21] Augustine speaks of the soul's fall into time in a number of texts. First, there is a passage at the end of book 11 of the *conf.* Augustine has come to his definition of time as a *distentio animi:* "Ecce distentio est vita mea" (*conf.* 11, 29, 39). However, God's right hand has taken him (Augustine) up in the Son of Man, who is mediator between the One (God) and the many (we humans), who are dissipated in many ways upon many things, so that Augustine (and, of course, all of us) might be gathered together again from his (and our) former *(veteribus)* days to follow the One.[22] Augustine wants to forget the things that are behind,

---

puncto, sed sine intermissione labitur, quidquid continua mutatione sensim currit in finem, non perficientem, sed consumentem." Hence, he adds, every man needs to be freed from the condemnation of sin *(damnatio peccati)*. Thus Adam's loss of *stabilitas* and his insertion—along with all mankind—into the consuming stream of time is part of the *damnatio peccati* from which we need liberation. This is an important point since most treatments of time in Saint Augustine deal with it as a question in metaphysics—a question about the nature of the created world—and not as a question about sin and the need for salvation. If time is an effect of sin—something from which Christ has come to free us—then it would not seem possible to have a philosophy of time as opposed to a theology of time. In *Les conversions,* 270, Le Blond says, "C'est donc au péché que l'homme est redevable de sa dispersion dans le temps." He maintains that one is obliged to conclude "que notre temps a été bouleversé par le péché dans sa contexture la plus intime et que toute étude purement philosophique de la durée est condamnée à demeurer superficielle." On the other hand, in *L'ambivalence,* 64–65, Marrou cautions, "N'en concluons pas trop hâtivement que le temps lui-même, *in se,* est nécessairement lié au péché . . . nous parlons ici simplement du temps historique, le temps d'après la Chute et ce n'est là, bien entendu, qu'un aspect de la temporalité." However, Marrou's cosmic time before the fall is, it seems to me, not solidly grounded in the Augustinian text (see note 16 above).

21. O'Connell, *Early Theory,* 181.

22. Marrou calls attention to the significance of *vetus* for the ancients. "Ici la notion précieuse à retrouver est celle de vieillissement: saint Augustin ne s'étonne pas de lire en son Psautier . . . : *Ecce veteres posuisti dies meos.* . . . car, à ses yeux l'insertion dans le temps nous condamne à cet effritement de l'être, à ce lent glissement vers la destruction, vers la mort. Nous avons peine, nous modernes, à nous représenter avec exactitude ce qui pouvait signifier pour un Grec ou un Latin le terme de 'vieux, ancien,' *palaios, vetus:* c'était pour eux ce qui, ayant été réel, actif, était maintenant et à jamais depassé, aboli, rejeté au néant par l'inflexible déroulement de la chaîne des âges" (*L'ambivalence,* 45–46).

to be not distended, but extended, not to things that shall be and shall pass away, but to those things that are before.[23] Though God is eternal, Augustine tells us, "At ego in tempora dissilui, quorum ordinem nescio, et tumultuosis varietatibus dilaniantur cogitationes meas, intima viscera animae meae, donec in te confluam purgatus et liquidus igne amoris tui" (*conf.* 11, 29, 39). And *conf.* 10, 29, 40 makes the Plotinian connotations even more clear: "Per continentiam quippe colligimur et redigimur in unum, a quo in multa defluximus." Though Ryan prefers to translate *defluximus* as "we have dissipated our being," it is literally "we have flowed down."[24]

Indeed, the verb is the same one that Augustine used in *ep.* 7, which is his clearest endorsement of the Platonic theory of reminiscence and of the soul's fall into the body and this world. He tells us there that some make false charges against that most excellent Socratic discovery that learning is recollection. They claim that memory is of past things and that what we come to know by the intellect are realities that last forever, cannot perish or be past. Of these objectors, Augustine says, "non attendunt illam visionem esse praeteritam, qua haec aliquando vidimus mente; a quibus quia defluximus, et aliter alia videre coepimus, ea nos reminiscendo revisere, id est, per memoriam" (*ep.* 7, 2). Surely Augustine here is saying that we have flowed down from a vision of the intelligibles to body and bodily vision of sensible things. So too, in *vera rel.* 29, 45, Augustine says, "Sed quia in temporalia devenimus, et eorum amore ab aeternis impedimur, quaedam temporalis medicina, quae non scientes, sed credentes ad salutem vocat, non naturae et excellentiae, sed ipsius temporis ordine prior est." If, then, Augustine seriously believed that the soul fell into body and time, from a contemplation of eternal reality into a life of restless busyness and action, by a desire to be on its own, to be independent—all of which Augustine seems to have derived from Plotinus—then the *liberatio a tempore* would seem to have to be

---

23. The language here calls to mind the language of that most Plotinian and most Christian passage in the *conf.*, namely, the vision at Ostia. And perhaps there is more than a superficial similarity of language, for Paul Henry, in *La vision d'Ostie: Sa place dans la vie et l'oeuvre de saint Augustin* (Paris: J. Vrin, 1938), 114, has said, "La vie éternelle n'est que la vision d'Ostie prolongée sans fin."

24. For the justification of this translation over others, see O'Connell, *St. Augustine's Confessions*, 143. See O'Connell's whole chapter on book 11 of the *conf.* for the fall of the soul into time.

understood within the same conceptual scheme. And that conceptual scheme entails that time came about through the fall of the soul. If that is so, one can see why Augustine so readily sees time as something from which we need liberation. It also says a great deal about why love of temporal things is seen as so misguided.[25]

Turning to Augustine's discussion of the heaven of heaven will, I believe, confirm this hypothesis that Augustine does have the Plotinian notion of time's origin in mind as he speaks of the Word freeing man from time.

THE HEAVEN OF HEAVEN

In commenting on Psalms 101:26–28, immediately after the "vocans temporales, faciens aeternos" text, Augustine reads that "et opera manuum tuarum sunt coeli. Ipsi peribunt; tu autem permanes" (*en. Ps.* 101, 12–14). He distinguishes the perishable heavens near the earth through which the birds of the air fly from the higher heavens of the heavens, and he seems to suggest that these heavens are the angels and the saints of God. This mention of the "coeli coelorum superiores"—interpreted as the angels and saints—suggests the long discussion in *conf.* 12 of the heaven of heaven, which, in turn, will throw considerable light upon our liberation from time.

In *conf.* 12, Augustine begins to comment on the beginning of the Book of Genesis, and the very first verse of that book says that God created heaven and earth *in principio*. Augustine interprets this to mean that God created heaven and earth in the Word. However, since there is explicit mention of the creation of the heaven or sky on the second day, Augustine wonders what this heaven mentioned in the first verse might be. He decides that this heaven made before all mention of days must be that heaven of heaven which is the Lord's, according to Psalms 113:15. So too the earth mentioned in this first verse is understood in a

---

25. For example, in *vera rel.* 46, 88, Augustine says, "Non enim sic quidem ab homine homo diligendus est, ut diligantur carnales fratres vel filii vel conjuges vel quique cognati vel affines aut cives. Nam et dilectio ista temporalis est." And in the next section he adds, "Oderimus ergo temporales necesitudines, si aeternitatis charitate flagramus." Note too the first definition of sin in *lib. arb.* 1, 16, 34: "neglectis rebus aeternis, quibus per seipsam mens fruitur, et per seipsam percepit, et quas amans amittere not potest, temporalia . . . sectari."

special Neoplatonic sense as referring to formless matter, in which also there is no time.

This heaven of heaven that is the Lord's and that was made before time is, Augustine tells us, an intellectual creature, by no means coeternal with the Trinity, but nonetheless participating in God's eternity.[26] This rational mind of the house of God freely checks its mutability by its beatifying contemplation of God without any fall. From the time it was made it has clung to God and surpasses all turning changes of time (*conf.* 12, 9, 9). But Augustine then turns in prayer to the Truth, the light of his heart, from whom he has flowed down *(defluxi)* to his own darkness, where he remembers God and hears God's voice calling him to return.[27]

That creature, the heaven of heaven, is not coeternal with God, for it has been made. But God is its delight, and it has never asserted its mutability. It clings to God who is ever present, and "non habens futurum quod expectet nec in praeteritum traiciens quod meminerit," it is unchanged "nec in tempora ulla distenditur" (*conf.* 12, 11, 12). This happy creature he describes as the house of God "contemplantem delectationem tuam sine ulle defectu egrediendi in aliud, mentem puram concordissime unam stabilimento pacis sanctorum spirituum, civium

---

26. See *conf.* 12, 12, 15. "Duo reperio, quae fecisti carentia temporibus, cum tibi neutrum coaeternum sit: unum, quod ita formatum est, ut sine ullo defectu contemplationis, sine ullo intervallo mutationis, quamvis mutabile, tamen non mutatum, tua aeternitate atque incommutabilitate perfruatur; alterum, quod ita informe erat, ut ex qua forma in quam formam vel motionis vel stationis mutaretur, quo tempori subderetur, non haberet."

27. In *Conversions*, 269, Le Blond equates the heaven of heaven with the angels alone, and in *Christian Philosophy*, 197–198, Gilson makes the same move. Augustine seems rather to have held that the souls of men are quite literally angels fallen into bodies and times. See O'Connell, *Early Theory*, 183: "The main contention of this chapter is exactly this: during the years A.D. 389–391, Augustine said, and meant to say, that we were 'fallen souls.'" Augustine's view of the angels is easily missed if one reads him through Thomistic glasses. For example, in *civ. Dei* 11, 13, 3, he defines man as a mortal rational animal and an angel as an immortal rational animal. Of all that he has created there is nothing closer to God than the human soul, which is equal to an angel (*quan.* 77–78). In the resurrection we will be changed from men so that we are equal to the angels (*en. Ps.* 126, 3). Our body will be changed for the better, i.e., into a spiritual body, when we are made equal to the angels (Mt 22:30), fit for the heavenly dwelling (*Gn. litt.* 6, 24, 35). However, it is not merely our destiny that will be one with the angels. *Conf.* 12 seems to say that our origin was one with theirs in the heaven of heaven from which we have fallen and to which we return.

civitatis tuae in caelestibus super ista caelestia" (*conf.* 12, 11, 12).²⁸ The human soul was once at home in this heavenly city from which it fell. Now the soul is traveling abroad far from its home—"cuius peregrinatio longinqua facta est."²⁹ God is its life—God who is eternal and above all times. Augustine prays that the soul may understand how far God is above all times "quando tua domus, quae peregrinata non est, quamvis non sit tibi coaeternus, tamen indesinenter et indeficienter tibi cohaerendo nullam patitur vicissitudinem temporum" (*conf.* 12, 11, 13). This heaven of heavens, to which Augustine devotes so much of book 12 of the *conf.*, is "coelum intellectuale, ubi est intellectus nosse simul, non ex parte, non in aenigmate, non per speculum, sed ex toto, in manifestatione, facie ad faciem; non modo hoc, modo illud, sed, quod dictum est, nosse simul sine ulla vicissitudine temporum" (*conf.* 12, 13, 16).³⁰ Augustine faces the objections of those who, though not disputing the truth of what he says, claim that Scripture does not mean what he says it means; that is, they do not find in the text of Scripture all the Plotinian philosophy that Augustine finds there.³¹ He speaks of a certain sublime creature that cleaves to God, and "in nullam tamen temporum

---

28. Note how Augustine moves from the singular "mind" to the plural "spirits" and "citizens." I suspect that there underlies this apparent waffling a twofold problem: One, a metaphysical problem concerning the principle of individuation for Augustinian-Plotinian souls; it would seem that they are individuated by the bodies they govern. Two, a textual problem in Plotinus, who has the same one-and-many position as well as some similarities to this that Augustine found in the language of some scriptural texts.

29. *Peregrinatio* is usually translated as "pilgrimage," and perhaps that is not at all a bad translation. However, the Latin literally means a wandering away from one's homeland or fatherland. Hence, one who is a *peregrinus* is a stranger, one away from home, from where he belongs, one suffering from nostalgia—like Odysseus or the prodigal son.

30. In "Spiritual or Intelligible Matter in Plotinus and St. Augustine," 280, A. Hilary Armstrong says, "First of all, who except a Christian steeped in the thought of Plotinus would pass so naturally, in a single sentence, from speaking of the *spiritalis creatura*, the company of angels, as *coelum* and *domus Dei* to speaking of it as *mens* (*Conf.* XII, 11 and 15); and where except in Plotinus can we find the conception of a Mind transcending the material world which is both one and many, a community of minds or spirits formed by and united in a single contemplation? St. Augustine's insistence, too, that the spiritual creation is prior to and not subject to time is exactly in accord with the thought of Plotinus."

31. In *St. Augustine's Confessions*, 20, in dealing with the audiences to which the *conf.* were directed, O'Connell mentions these scriptural exegetes under the rubric "conservative" Catholics, who were quite skeptical about accepting Augustine's Plotinian understanding of the Christian faith.

varietatem et vicissitudinem ab illo se resolvat et defluat, sed in eius solius veracissima contemplatione requiescat" (*conf.* 12, 15, 19). This is the house of God "spiritalis et particeps aeternitatis tuae, quia sine labe in aeternum" (ibid.).

There is no time before it, for it is a created wisdom, before which nothing was created: "intellectualis naturae scilicet, quae contemplatione luminis lumen est . . . mens rationalis et intellectualis castae civitatis tuae, matris nostrae, quae sursum est et libera est et aeterna in caelis" (conf. 12, 15, 20). Although there is no time before it or in it, "inest ei tamen ipsa mutabilitas, unde tenebresceret et frigesceret, nisi amore grandi tibi cohaerens tamquam semper meridies luceret et ferveret . . . O domus luminosa et speciosa . . . tibi suspiret peregrinatio mea" (*conf.* 12, 15, 21). And then Augustine cites Luke to indicate that he has left this house of God and has gone astray like a lost sheep (Lk 15:5).

In speaking of the heaven of heaven, Augustine is speaking about a spiritual creature, the mind of the heavenly city. Some citizens of this city never fell, never exercised their mutability, but ever remain in God's eternity without any distention into time. Others—we humans—fell down into bodies and times, became extended corporeally and distended temporally as the result of sin. But before sin, before the fall of the soul, either there was no time, or at least there was no time in which there was change and death. What Augustine seems to imply is the first alternative: we were all created in the heaven of heaven, created in that spiritual being before all times. But we fell away, and now we are returning, and our heart is restless until it once again rests in him.

CONCLUSION

We have seen that Augustine speaks of the Word having come as man to free man from time or to make men eternal. He understands this liberation of man from time not merely as giving man life without end, but as making man timeless through a participation in God's eternity. We have seen that time—as Augustine views it—is ambivalent. On the one hand, time is a creature, and as such it is something good.[32] On the other hand, there is also ample evidence that Augustine

---

32. In *lib. arb.* 3, 15, 42, Augustine even uses the passing character of times as an apologetic argument. "Quapropter omnia temporalia, quae in hoc rerum ordine ita lo-

regarded time as something ever perishing and ever causing to perish even the things and persons we love most.[33] We have seen that he links time with sin and mortality. Hence, the Augustinian view of time is certainly ambivalent.

In looking at some texts on the fall of the soul and time, we saw that like Plotinus, Augustine sees time as coming about through the fall of the soul into multiplicity. So too in looking at Augustine's discussion of the heaven of heaven, we saw that had man's soul not sinned and fallen away, he would have remained in unchanging contemplation of God—not immutable, but sharing in God's eternity. But man's soul fell—fell into body and into times, into manyness and distention, away from the *patria* for which he now longs and toward which he rises up to return.

Before drawing this paper to a close, I would like to draw one somewhat tentative conclusion and also to propose an even more guarded hypothesis. My tentative conclusion is that the ambivalent character of time from which, according to Augustine, the Word has come to set us free is due to Augustine's having thought out the concepts of time and eternity within the conceptual framework of *Ennead* 3, 7, where the origin of time is tied to the soul's entering the world of becoming through sin. His suggestion that time began with the soul's fall after its timeless existence in the heaven of heaven and his view of the soul's destiny as participating in eternity become more readily understandable once one sees that Augustine has thought this out within the Plotinian framework.

My even more guarded hypothesis is not merely that Augustine found in Plotinus the concept of eternity, but that it was through Augustine that the concept of eternity in the technical sense came into the thought of the Western Church. The classical definition of eternity

---

cata sunt, ut nisi deficiant, non possint praeteritis futura succedere, ut tota temporum in suo genere pulchritudo peragatur, absurdissime dicimus non debere deficere. Quantum enim acceperunt, tantum agunt, et tantum reddunt ei cui debent quod sunt in quantumcumque sunt." So too, if the first syllable did not pass, he argues, the whole word could not be heard, and no one would want to hear only the first syllable.

33. "[Q]uae temporalia et antequam sint non sunt, et cum sunt fugiunt, et cum fugerint non erunt. Itaque cum futura sunt, nondum sunt; cum autem praeterita sunt, jam non sunt. Quomodo igitur tenebuntur ut maneant, quibus hoc est incipere ut sint, quod est pergere ut non sint?" (*lib. arb.* 3, 7, 21); "tempora surripiunt quod amamus" (*vera rel.* 35, 65).

that prevailed among the great scholastics of the Middle Ages, that is, "interminabilis vitae tota simul et perfecta possessio," was formulated by Boethius (ca. 480–534/5)—almost a century after Augustine. However, the elements of the definition are all present in Augustine as well as in Plotinus before him. Prior to Augustine's time the Fathers generally mention eternity as one of the attributes of God, though it seems to entail in most cases no more than his having neither beginning nor end.[34] The idea of eternity involving not merely unending life, but life that is *tota simul,* does not clearly appear in the Fathers prior to the time of Augustine—at least in the West.[35] Though a great deal more research would be necessary to provide solid confirmation, I suggest that Augustine is the source of the concept of eternity in the thought of the Western Church, just as he is the source of the concept of spirituality in the West.[36] And as he owes the concept of spirituality to the Neoplatonic philosophy that he came into contact with in Milan, so I would suggest that he owes the concept of eternity to Plotinus as well.[37] That is, just as through the Neoplatonism he learned in the Milanese Church Augustine learned to conceive of God as spiritual, so from the same source he learned to think of God as not distended in time as well.

34. Marie Joseph Rouët de Journel's *Enchiridion Patristicum* (Freiburg: Herder, 1951) lists eleven entries on God's eternity prior to the time of Augustine. In most of them, however, God is said merely to be without beginning or end, without a source, unborn, and unmade. Some of these texts seem to indicate that eternity is radically other than time; however, none has explicitly the *tota simul* element.

35. On the other hand, in *METOUSIA TOU THEOU: Man's Participation in God's Perfections according to Saint Gregory of Nyssa* (Rome: Herder, 1966), 137–139, David Balás, S.O.Cist., seems to indicate Gregory's clear dependence upon Plotinus's conception of time and eternity. Furthermore, Gregory speaks of man's sharing in God's eternity so that memory and hope are excluded.

36. For the claim that Augustine and through him the whole Western Church came to conceive of God as immaterial or spiritual, see Verbeke, *L'évolution de la doctrine,* and Masai, "Les conversions de saint Augustin," 1–40.

37. The concepts of the spiritual and of the eternal have, after all, a conceptual affinity. For, as "spiritual" entails the absence of extension in length, breadth, and depth, "eternal" entails the absence of extension into past and future. As a spiritual substance is whole wherever it is, so an eternal substance is whole whenever it is. Since these concepts are in some sense correlative, it would seem that one would not be likely to conceive the eternal without conceiving the spiritual. Moreover, since Augustine came to conceive of the spiritual through his contact with the Neoplatonic philosophies current in the church of Milan, it would seem likely that he derived the concept of eternity from the same source and that, as the concept of spirituality came into the West through Augustine, so the concept of eternity came into the West through him as well.

After all, among the things that in the *conf.* Augustine admits that he found in the books of the Neoplatonists is that God is eternal: "quod enim ante omnia tempora et supra omnia tempora inconmutabiliter manet unigentus filius tuus coaeternus tibi et quia de plentitudine eius accipiunt animae, ut beatae sint, et quia particpatione manentis in se sapientiae renovantur, ut sapientes sint, est ibi" (*conf.* 7, 9, 14).[38] Though Augustine does not say that he learned from the Platonists that God is eternal and though it might seem that he is simply reporting that the *libri platonicorum* square with the teaching of the Church, there is reason to believe, as I have tried to argue, that he learned to think of God as eternal from his contact with Neoplatonism. For he does clearly state that the Platonists knew God and even that they were able to see him, albeit from afar. In fact, there is a startling parallel that he seems to draw between John the Evangelist and the Platonic philosophers in terms of their vision of God.[39] Admittedly, he emphasizes the pride of the philosophers who would not accept the Incarnation of the Word, who became for us the way of return to the Fatherland, but he does emphasize that they saw *idipsum* and *id quod est*—two of his favorite expressions for the God who truly is, because he is immutable, because his substance is eternity. Even though it would have been better not to see and yet to embrace the cross of Christ, nonetheless, they saw, he clearly says, the Word, *idipsum*.[40] And if they saw the goal whither we should go, the Fatherland, and the Selfsame, then they saw that eternity to which we can come because the Word came as man to free us from time.

The Platonists, however, refused to accept the need for Christ as

---

38. In his note, "Ce qu'Augustin dit avoir lu de Plotin," in BA 13, 686–687, A. Solignac lists the following texts from the *Enneads* as possible sources in Plotinus corresponding to this section in John: *Ennead* 5, 1, 4; 5, 1, 10; and 1, 6, 6, 1.

39. Augustine says that "quidem philosophi huius mundi" came to know God through creation. They saw whither they must go; "viderunt hoc quod dicit Iohannes, quia per Verbum Dei facta sunt omnia." And what is even more striking, he says, "Illud potuerunt videre quod est, sed viderunt de longe" (*Jo. Ev. tr.* 2, 4).

40. Of Augustine's interpretation of *in Idipsum*, which he found in his version of Ps 4:9, Gilson says, "Pour avoir lu dans cet *id ipsum*, décalque du *to auto* des Septante, l'immuable identité à soi-même de l'être vraiment être, il faut qu'Augustin ait trouvé dans la lecture de la Bible une irresistible provocation à se souvenir de Platon" (see "Notes sur l'être," 207). For a survey of the interpretation of *in Idipsum*, see Swetnam, "A Note on *In Idipsum* in St. Augustine."

the way to return. Though once in a blending of Plotinian thought and the parable of the prodigal, Augustine had said, "Non enim pedibus et spatiis locorum itur abs te aut reditur ad te aut vero filius ille tuus minor equos aut currus vel naves quaesivit aut evolat penna visibili aut moto poplite iter egit" (*conf.* 1, 18, 28),[41] by the time of the *Jo. Ev. tr.*, he maintains that we cannot cross the sea of this world to return to the Fatherland without a *lignum*—wood: the wood of a ship, the wood of the cross of Christ.[42]

If Augustine—and through Augustine the whole Western Church—learned to think of God as eternal in the technical sense of *tota simul* from Neoplatonism, as he—and the whole Western Church—learned from Neoplatonism to conceive of a spiritual substance, then it is not surprising that there are in Augustine's thought traces of the Plotinian conceptual scheme—traces that do not always fit comfortably with the Christian faith, for example, that there was no time before the fall, that times came to be as the result of the soul's fall, and that men were all once sharers in eternity, from which they have fallen into bodies and times. The theme of the Word having become man in order to free man from time, in other words, may well have remained a minor theme—not merely in Augustine, but in the theological tradition—precisely because it carries with it elements of Neoplatonic thought that the tradition chose not to develop as central to the articulation of the mission of the Word.

---

41. In *Ennead* 1, 6, 8, Plotinus says, "The Fatherland for us is there whence we have come. There is the Father. What is our course? What is to be the manner of our flight? Here there is no journeying for the feet; feet bring us only from land to land. Nor is it for coach or ship to bear us off. We must close our eyes and invoke a new manner of seeing" (*The Essential Plotinus,* trans. Elmer O'Brien [New York: Mentor Books, 1964], 42).

42. "Sic est enim tamquam videat quisque de longe patriam, et mare interiaceat; videt quo eat, sed non habet qua eat. . . . Ut ergo esset et qua iremus, venit inde ad quem ire volebamus. Et quid fecit? Instituit lignum quo mare transeamus. Nemo enim potest transire mare huius saeculi, nisi cruce Christi portatus" (*Jo. Ev. tr.* 2, 2). So too in the following column, he upbraids the philosophers for their pride: "noluerunt tenere humilitatem Christ, in qua navi securi pervenirent ad id quod longe videre potuerunt, et sorduit eis crux Christi. Mare transeundum est, et lignum contemnis."

14

THE HEAVEN OF HEAVEN AND THE UNITY OF AUGUSTINE'S *CONFESSIONES*

The question of the unity of the conf. *of Saint Augustine has been warmly debated by scholars, and although most now agree that the work is a unified work of great artistry, there remains considerable disagreement about how the unity of the work is to be conceived. Following themes developed by Robert O'Connell, I focused in this study upon the heaven of heaven in book 12 of the* conf. *and argued that Augustine's conception of the heaven of heaven offers further evidence for the influence of Plotinian philosophy on Augustine's thinking in the* conf. *I argued that it is the Plotinian understanding of the Christian faith that is best taken to unify the thirteen books of Augustine's masterpiece.*

At the 14th International Congress of Philosophy held in Vienna in 1968, John Cooper began his presentation by citing the German scholar Max Zepf, who had said of the *conf.*, "The entire work is divided into two parts which seem to have nothing whatsoever to do with each other. The biography of the first ten books is suddenly resolved into a dry exposition of the first chapter of Genesis. Who has not been compelled to shake his head and ask what purpose Augustine could have had in mind when he thus brought together such various materials."[1] Zepf's

1. Max Zepf, *Augustin's Confessiones,* Heidelberger Abhandlungen zur Phi-

rather critical remarks on the lack of unity in the *conf.* are not without some foundation. Augustine himself, after all, wrote in his *retr.*, "Books one to ten were written about me; the three others about the holy scriptures from where it says, 'In the beginning God made heaven and earth' (Gn 1:1) up to the repose of the seventh day."[2] How can a work that is divided into ten books of autobiography and three books of scriptural exegesis—and rather strange autobiography and even stranger exegesis at that—have the unity requisite for a great work of art—something almost every reader of the work takes the *conf.* to be?

The problem of the unity of the *conf.* is one which many scholars have addressed and to which they have given many quite different answers.[3] Some have, like Zepf, found nothing that unifies the work. John O'Meara claimed that the *conf.*, like many of Augustine's works, is "a badly composed book" and suggested that scholars who think otherwise "deny the evidence of their senses and forget that Augustine had no expectation of producing what has come to be regarded as a masterpiece."[4] Others have suggested a variety of unifying factors or themes. John Mourant, for example, finds in the later books "a continuation of a theme which dominates all the books of the *conf.*, namely, the praise of God."[5] He also finds in both parts the themes of confession and of searching for God, first in Augustine's own life and then in the Scriptures. Jean-Marie Le Blond finds memory as a unifying theme, claiming that the *conf.* are "une oeuvre de mémoire, de mémoire augustinienne: celle-ci comporte évidement l'évocation du passé, mais elle implique aussi le souvenir de soi dans le présent, et la tension vers l'avenir."[6] Thus

---

losophie und ihrer Geschichte 9 (Tubingen: J. C. B. Mohr, 1926), 3. For the English translation, see John C. Cooper, "Why Did Augustine Write Books XI–XIII of the Confessions?" *AS* 2 (1971): 37–46, here 37.

2. *Retr.* 2, 6,(23). The translations of Augustine's Latin are my own, except for the translation of the *Confessions* where I have used that by John K. Ryan, with frequent adaptations.

3. See Kenneth B. Steinhauser, "The Literary Unity of the *Confessions*," in *Augustine: From Rhetor to Theologian*, ed. Joanne McWilliam (Waterloo: Wilfred Laurier University Press, 1992), 15–30, for an excellent survey of previous accounts of the unity of the *Confessiones* as well as for solid arguments that Augustine did not leave the work in an unfinished state or one with which he was not satisfied.

4. John O'Meara, *The Young Augustine* (London: Longmans, Green, 1954), 13.

5. John A. Mourant, *Saint Augustine on Memory*, The Saint Augustine Lecture 1979 (Villanova: Villanova University Press, 1980), 64.

6. Le Blond, *Les conversions de saint Augustin*, 6.

the first nine books are memory of Augustine's past, the tenth memory of his present state, and the last three memory as stretched out to the future. Still others have paid scant attention to the final books. For example, Pierre Courcelle's important study of the *conf.* virtually ignores the final books. He says, "A partir du livre X, le sens même du mot confession va gauchir, ce qui permit à l'auteur d'ajouter des développements sans rapport avec le début: il va confesser sa science et son ignorance de la Loi divine."[7] In his monumental three-volume study of the *conf.*, James O'Donnell makes a sounder assessment when he says, "What is presented to us in the *Confessions* is the transformation of the traditional philosopher's ascent of the mind to the *summum bonum* into a uniquely Christian ascent that combines the two paths that Augustine had followed in his own life. The exegesis of a chapter of scripture that fills the last three books itself displays the union of the intellectual and exegetic, the Platonic and the Christian, approaches to God, setting a pattern that becomes the centre of Augustine's life's work, to be fulfilled only eschatologically—a goal anticipated but not reached on the last page of this text."[8]

What I want to do in this article is to take another look at what Augustine says about "the heaven of heaven," mainly in book 12 of the *conf.*, and to see how his discussion of this odd topic throws some light on the question of the unity of the work as a whole. In doing so, I by and large follow the interpretation of Robert O'Connell, whose books on Augustine I have for nearly a quarter century found most helpful in coming to understand the thought of the bishop of Hippo on many topics. In fact, I like to compare my enthusiasm on the discovery of O'Connell's book on the *conf.* to that of the British poet, John Keats, on first looking into Chapman's Homer.[9]

---

7. Courcelle, *Recherches sur les Confessions de saint Augustin*, 18.
8. James O'Donnell, *Augustine: Confessions* (Oxford: Oxford University Press, 1992), 1:xl.
9. John Keats, "On First Looking into Chapman's Homer," lines 8–14.
        Then felt I like some watcher of the skies
        When a new planet swims into his ken;
        Or like stout Cortez when with eagle eyes
        He star'd at the Pacific—and all his men
        Look'd at each other with a wild surmise—
        Silent, upon a peak in Darien.

SOME PRESUPPOSITIONS

I presuppose that the *conf.* is a great work of literary art—and I do not think Augustine was unaware of this when he was writing the work, as O'Meara believes. I presuppose that, as such, the work is not merely the addition of three books of an exegesis of the creation narrative in Genesis 1 to the ten books of autobiography. I presuppose that the unity of this work has to involve more than the recurrence of various themes in its different parts in the way various themes are taken up again in various parts of a symphony, for example, themes such as confession of sins, praise, and faith. Henri-Irénée Marrou once said, "Augustin compose mal,"[10] a remark that he found necessary to take back in his *Retractatio,* where he humbly described his earlier statement as: "jugement d'un jeune barbare ignorant et présomptueux."[11] In his *Retractatio* Marrou made the perceptive claim that Augustine composes in a musical manner.[12] There are, of course, in the *conf.* themes that first are played softly in the background and then reappear as a principal theme, but the recurrence of such themes is not enough, I think, to make the work a unified whole. Finally, I presuppose that I will not in this article resolve the question of the unity of the *conf.* At most, I want to propose what I think is a better solution or a good step on the way to a better solution, a solution that, as I have already indicated, I cannot claim as my own. O'Connell himself, in fact, suggests that his solution has been anticipated in different ways by John O'Meara and Georg Knauer:[13] by O'Meara, who saw Augustine as presenting a theory of human existence that was verified in Augustine's own life, and by Knauer, who saw that theory as *peregrinatio animae* or, as O'Connell puts it in the subtitle of his book, the odyssey of soul.

THE TWELFTH BOOK OF THE *CONFESSIONES*

At the beginning of book 11 Augustine announces that he is beginning to confess to God whatever he finds in God's books, all the won-

---

10. Marrou, *Saint Augustin et la fin de la culture antique,* 61.
11. Ibid., 665.
12. Ibid., 667.
13. O'Connell, *St. Augustine's Confessions,* 11.

derful things of God's law, "from that beginning in which you made heaven and earth up to the everlasting kingdom together with you in your holy city" (*conf.* 11, 2, 3). That is, he announces that he will confess to God what he finds in the whole biblical account of the history of salvation from creation to our eternal rest in heaven. Despite the sweeping cope of this plan, which would seem to embrace the whole of salvation history, the bishop of Hippo never quite gets beyond the first verse or two of Genesis 1, at least in books 11 and 12. He, of course, never intended anything like a commentary on the whole of the Bible, but rather a commentary on the Hexaemeron. The six days of creation provided him, as it had provided others of the Fathers, with an opportunity to distance himself from the Manichees as well as to present his understanding of the created world, along with the place of human beings in it and their destiny.

Book 11 begins with "In the beginning God made" and goes on to distinguish God's timeless eternity from the temporal duration of creatures, while book 12 takes up "heaven and earth" and presents a rather strange exegesis of these words in terms of the heaven of heaven and formless matter. In book 11 Augustine confronts the question posed by the Manichees, "What was God doing before he made heaven and earth?" (*conf.* 11, 10, 12).[14] He refuses to dismiss the question with the mocking reply that God "was preparing hell for those who pry into such deep subjects" (*conf.* 11, 12, 14), for it is a serious question that requires a serious answer every bit as much as did the other Manichaean question, "Where does evil come from?" (*conf.* 3, 7, 12), which Augustine could not satisfactorily answer before he came into contact with "certain books of the Platonists" (*conf.* 7, 9, 13).[15] A satisfactory answer to the question about what God was doing before creation requires the distinction between eternity and time, which Augustine draws in very Plotinian language and which he could not have drawn without contact with the thought of Plotinus.

In *Paradoxes of Time in St. Augustine,* I dealt chiefly with book 11 of the *conf.* and argued that Augustine's account of eternity as an im-

---

14. See Peters, "What Was God Doing before He Created the Heaven and the Earth?"
15. See my "The Aim of Augustine's Proof That God Truly Is," *International Philosophical Quarterly* 26 (1986): 253–268.

mutable present, all at once without past or future, is, like his account of time as a distention of the mind, something that he could have derived only from "certain books of the Platonists," which he read during the months prior to his baptism and which he continued to read and to meditate upon during the years immediately following his return to Africa.[16] That is, book 11, with its profound reflections on eternity and time, represents an attempt, and a successful one, to understand the biblical account of creation in terms of some features of Neoplatonic philosophy. Such a claim needs to be clearly and carefully understood. I do not mean that Neoplatonism replaces the biblical account or is blended with it to constitute a *tertium quid*. Nor do I mean that Neoplatonism as we find it in Plotinus is generally compatible with the Christian faith. Rather, certain features of Neoplatonic thought are used to come to some understanding of the biblical account so that the result is not a replacement of Christianity by Neoplatonism or a mélange of philosophical and biblical thought, but an understanding of what is presented in the biblical narrative—an *intellectus fidei* in the sense in which later thinkers, following Augustine, would describe theology.

In *Paradoxes of Time* I stressed that Augustine was the first Christian thinker—with the possible exception of Gregory of Nyssa[17]—to exploit the idea of divine eternity as whole all at once—*tota simul*.[18] Nor is this surprising, for if Augustine was the first in the Western Church to come to a clear conception of God as incorporeal or spiritual, as whole everywhere—*totus ubique*—it follows that there could hardly be another thinker prior to him who conceived of divine eternity as *tota simul*. And if Augustine derived the concept of eternity as "all at once": *omnia simul* from Plotinus, then, it is most plausible, I argued, that he derived from Plotinus the definition of time as "a distention or extension of the soul": *distentio animi*.

---

16. The question of how much of Plotinus—or possibly Porphyry—Augustine read before his baptism is warmly debated among scholars. Even if he read only a very few of the *Enneads* prior to his baptism, his initial enthusiasm for the books of the Platonists surely led him to read and ponder as much of Plotinus and Porphyry as he could lay his hands upon.

17. On this point see Balás, *METAOUSIA TOU THEOU*, as well as Richard Sorabji, *Time, Creation and the Continuum: Theories in Antiquity and the Early Middle Ages* (Ithaca: Cornell University Press, 1983).

18. *S.* 117, 10: "Totum ergo ibi simul."

In this article I want to turn to book 12 and the puzzling discussion of the heaven of heaven. Almost fifty years ago, Jean Pépin published his long and thorough study of the heaven of heaven,[19] in which he examined the expression as it emerged in Augustine's works, reached its most extensive development in the *conf.* and in *Gn. litt.*, and then soon faded almost completely out of his thought. In many respects Pépin's study is unsurpassable, and in his recent comments on book 12 he simply refers to the results of his previous article with regard to the heaven of heaven and turns to other topics.[20] Though in many respects Pépin's work on the meaning of *coelum coeli* cannot be surpassed, on the question of the relation of the heaven of heaven to the unity of the *conf.* I think something further can be said, perhaps nothing entirely new, but something at least, I hope, worth reflecting upon.

From Genesis 1:1 Augustine knows that God made heaven and earth, the heaven that he sees above and the earth below upon which he walks. But he asks, "Where is the heaven of heaven, O Lord, of which we hear in the words of the Psalm: 'The heaven of heaven is the Lord's, but the earth he has given to the children of men'?" (*conf.* 12, 2, 2). The heaven of heaven, Augustine infers, must be a heaven that we do not see and in relation to which the heaven and earth we do see are but earth. Augustine's exegesis, it should be noted, is here, however strange it may seem to us, not figurative or allegorical, but rather extremely literal, though "literal" meant something quite different for him than it does for us. For exegetes of the twentieth century the literal sense of a text means the sense that the human author intended; for Augustine to understand a text in the literal sense meant to take the words precisely as they sound without appeal to ordinary figures of speech—even without punctuation.[21] Hence, in a strictly literal sense, if Scripture speaks of a heaven and a heaven of heaven, there must be two heavens, one the heaven of the other.

Before continuing with the topic of the heaven of heaven, Augus-

---

19. See Jean Pépin, "Recherches sur le sens et les origines de l'expression *Caelum Caeli* dans le livre XII des *Confessions* de S. Augustin," *Bulletin du Cange* 23 (1953): 185–274.

20. See Luigi Franco Pizzolato and Giovanni Scanavino, eds., *"Le Confessioni" di Agostino d'Ippona: Libri X–XIII*. Commento di: Aimé Solignac, Eugenio Corsini, Jean Pépin, Alberto di Giovanni. Lectio Augustini (Palermo: Edizioni Augustinus, 1987), 67–95.

21. See *Gn. adv. Man.* 2, 2, 3.

tine turns to "the earth invisible and without order" of Genesis 1:2, which leads him into a meditation on formless matter. For from Wisdom 11:18 he knows that God made the world from unformed or unseen matter.²² But before God formed this unformed matter and introduced distinctions into it, "there was no thing, no color, no shape, no body, no spirit" (*conf.* 12, 3, 3). Yet it was not absolutely nothing; it was a certain formlessness without any distinctive character. Augustine's struggle to conceive unformed matter recalls his struggle to conceive an incorporeal substance, a struggle that he describes earlier in books 5 and 7 of the *conf.* and that is by far better known.²³ In both cases one must transcend the imagination or picture-thinking; as the incorporeal being of God or of the soul cannot be imagined, so the near nonbeing of formless matter cannot be imagined. Augustine once, presumably in his Manichaean days, pictured matter "as having countless different forms . . . forms foul and horrid in confused array, but still forms" (*conf.* 12, 6, 6). To think of matter correctly, he had to learn to "divest it utterly of every remnant of form" (*conf.* 12, 6, 6). Moreover, as Augustine attained the ability to conceive of incorporeal being through his contact with the books of the Platonists, he also attained the ability to conceive of unformed matter from his meditation on the books of the Platonists.²⁴ O'Connell singles out Plotinus's treatises on "The Nature and Source of Evil" and on "Matter"—*Enneads* 2, 8 and 2, 4.²⁵ Augustine tells us that, when we try to conceive matter by denying intelligible or sensible form of it, we strive "to know it by not knowing it or not to know it by knowing it": *vel nosse ignorando vel ignorare nossendo*—a formula that recalls Augustine's words about our knowledge of God, "who is known better by not knowing": *qui scitur melius nesciendo*.²⁶ His formula also recalls Plotinus's description of how matter is known, even echoing Plotinus's words "that which wants to be a thought about it will not be a thought but a sort of thoughtlessness; or rather the mental representation of it will be spurious not genuine."²⁷

22. Already in *Gn. adv. Man.* 1, 5, 9, Augustine shows that he is aware of the two readings.
23. See François Masai, "Les conversions de saint Augustin," for an account of the role of Augustine in introducing to the Latin West the concept of incorporeal being.
24. See Armstrong, "Spiritual or Intelligible Matter in Plotinus and St. Augustine."
25. O'Connell, *Confessions of St. Augustine*, 146.
26. *Ord.* 2, 16, 42.
27. *Ennead* 2, 4, 10. The translation is Armstrong's, 2:127.

Matter, for Augustine, turns out to be the very mutability of mutable things, a principle within both bodily and spiritual creatures: "The mutability of mutable things is itself receptive of all the forms into which mutable things are changed. And what is this? Is it a mind? A body? A kind of mind or body? If one could say 'a nothing something' *(nihil aliquid)* and 'it is and is not' *(est not est,)* I would say that it is such" (*conf.* 12, 6, 6). In fact, as Hilary Armstrong and Robert O'Connell have argued, Augustine derived this doctrine of matter, a matter that is both corporeal and spiritual, from Plotinus.[28]

I stress the Plotinian background to what Augustine says about matter, as I have stressed the Plotinian background of what Augustine said about eternity and time and about his coming to conceive of God and the soul as incorporeal beings, because I want also to stress the Plotinian background to what Augustine says about the heaven of heaven.

THE HEAVEN OF HEAVEN

In Genesis 1:1 the author of Genesis made no mention of times or days, and we are told that on the second day God made the firmament, that is, heaven of this earth. Hence, the heaven made before all mention of days must, Augustine tells us, be "some kind of intellectual creature" (*conf.* 12, 9, 9). Though it is not coeternal with God, it partakes of God's eternity, holding in check its mutability by a sweet and happy contemplation of God. God has spoken with a strong voice into Augustine's inner ear—an expression that is repeated later[29] and that makes a strong claim for the truth of what follows—that not even that intellectual creature is coeternal with God, that creature whose delight is God alone, which draws its nourishment from God, which has never asserted its mutability, but clings with all its powers to God, who is ever present to it. That creature neither has a future that it awaits, nor transfers what it remembers into the past; it is unaltered by change and not distended into times. This happy creature that clings to God's blessedness is, Augustine tells us, the heaven of heaven, God's own house contemplating God's delight without by any failure going out to some-

---

28. See O'Connell, *Confessions of St. Augustine*, 146, and Armstrong, "Spiritual or Intelligible Matter," 277–283.

29. See later in this paragraph as well as in the next and *conf.* 12, 15, 18, where he repeats the expression twice.

thing else, a pure mind most harmoniously one by the stabilizing peace of holy spirits, citizens of God's city in the heavenly places above these heavens (*conf.* 12, 11, 12). Hilary Armstrong comments, "Who except a Christian steeped in the thought of Plotinus would pass so naturally, in a single sentence, from speaking of the *spiritalis creatura,* the company of angels, as *coelum* and *domus Dei* to speaking of it as *mens* (*Conf.* XII, 11 and 15); and where else except in Plotinus can we find the conception of a Mind transcending the material world which is both one and many, a community of minds or spirits formed by and united in a single contemplation?"[30]

Like formless matter, this intellectual creature is immune from time. It has been so formed that, without any interruption of its contemplation, without interval of change, subject to change, but never changed, it enjoys eternity and immutability (*conf.* 12, 12, 15). The heaven of heaven, then, is "the intellectual heaven where it belongs to intellect to know all at once, not in part, not in a dark manner, not through a glass, but as a whole, in plain sight, face to face, not this thing now and that thing then, but . . . it knows all at once, without any passage of time" (*conf.* 12, 13, 16).

There are a number of things to note about this heaven of heaven. One, Augustine refers to it in the singular as a blessed creature, a mind most harmoniously one, but also in the collective plural as the home of blessed spirits, citizens of God's city. Two, the heaven of heaven is a creature and, hence, mutable, but by participating in eternity it has never exercised its mutability. Its intellect knows everything at once without any distention into the past and future. It checks its mutability by contemplating God. The strangeness of this participation in eternity where everything is all at once is not diminished by Augustine's claim that the destiny of the blessed in heaven involves a participation in such eternity. Elsewhere, in describing the salvific work of Christ, Augustine used the marvelous expression "calling temporal beings, making them eternal": *vocans temporales, faciens aeternos*—which, as I have argued, means quite literally that he calls us temporal beings and makes us partakers of his own eternal being,[31] so that the life of the blessed in heaven

---

30. Armstrong, "Spiritual or Intelligible Matter," 280, where he refers to *Ennead* 3, 7.
31. See *en. Ps.* 110, 10, and my "'Vocans temporales, faciens aeternos': St. Augustine on Liberation from Time," *Traditio* 49 (1985): 29–47.

is not one thing after another, but all at once—a quite unimaginable sort of destiny, which I confess I do not find immediately attractive.

Augustine confronts objectors, not ones who reject the Book of Genesis, presumably the Manichees, but those who praise it and yet claim that the Spirit of God did not intend that all this should be understood from the words Moses wrote. These Christian objectors are not identified, and four or five different ways of viewing the text of Genesis are pointed out. James O'Donnell suggests that the dialogue with the objectors "is both internal and imaginary: the real conflict is between different interpretations that A[ugustine] himself might choose to present."[32] Aimé Solignac, on the other hand, finds it more plausible that the objectors are real opponents who set their views against Augustine's.[33] O'Connell has offered a suggestion that strikes me as very plausible, namely, that these objectors who accepted the Book of Genesis, but insisted that Augustine's interpretation of the text was simply not what the author of Genesis, namely, Moses, intended, were those whom O'Connell calls "conservative" Catholic Christians,[34] those who found the Neoplatonic interpretation of Genesis that Augustine had brought back from Milan and was introducing to the African Church not to be false, but simply to be too farfetched or too philosophical to be an interpretation of what Moses meant. If, after all, Augustine really was—as has been very convincingly argued—the first Catholic thinker in the West—apart from the small group of Milanese Christian Neoplatonists, including Ambrose and Theodorus—to articulate a concept of God and the soul as incorporeal beings[35] and to articulate the concept of divine eternity as timeless duration, then the sort of claims that Augustine was making about eternity and time, about there being no time before God created, about the temporal distendedness of creatures, about an intellectual creature that, though mutable, checked its mutability by an uninterrupted contemplation of God, and about formless matter that, like God, could be known only by transcending the imagination—all these sorts of claims could not fail to strike the ordinary African Catholic as foreign not only to their Old Latin Bible,

---

32. O'Donnell, *Augustine: Confessions*, 3:318.
33. See his note, "Caelum caeli" in BA 14, 592–606, here 607.
34. See O'Connell, *Confessions of St. Augustine*, 18–19.
35. See Masai, "Les conversions de saint Augustin," 18–19, especially n34.

but to the old-fashioned Catholicism with which they had grown up, and to the Stoic corporealism that was the common philosophical patrimony of the Western Church.

THE FATHERLAND FROM WHICH WE FELL

Just what is the heaven of heaven? Or who are these spirits who populate this house of God, this heavenly city? In the *conf.* Augustine never explicitly identifies these spiritual creatures with the angels, though Armstrong did so in the passage I quoted. In fact, the term "angel" appears in only nineteen sentences in the whole of the work, and in book 12 there is but a single mention of an angel—and that in a biblical allusion. In this exposition of the six days of creation, Augustine makes no explicit mention of the creation of the angels, an odd fact, since in the creation accounts in *Gn. litt.* and in *civ. Dei* Augustine devotes considerable time to the creation of the angels and to the fall of some of them.[36] In the light of such considerations, it seems reasonable to suppose that the account of the heaven of heaven in the *conf.* in some sense takes the place of the accounts of the creation of the angels of *Gn. litt.* and *civ. Dei*. Aimé Solignac concludes that "il vaut mieux reconnaître que la notion du caelum caeli, telle que l'expriment les *Confessions,* reste malaisée à définir." But he adds that Augustine is thinking "à la Jérusalem céleste actuellement peuplée d'anges et séjour espéré des hommes spirituels."[37] There are, however, also reasons to think that, according to Augustine's thought at the time of the *conf.*, the heaven of heaven is not merely the present home of the angels who did not fall and the future home of the souls of the blessed, but was once the home of each of us, a home from which we have fallen and from which we are on pilgrimage.

In the paragraph after he introduced the heaven of heaven as an intellectual creature that checked its mutability by contemplation of God, Augustine says, "I fell away to these things *(defluxi ad ista)*. And I became darkened over, but from here, even from here I have loved you. I went astray *(erravi),* and I remembered you *(recordatus sum tui)*. I heard your voice behind me, calling me to return *(ut redirem)*" (*conf.* 12, 10, 10). In the penultimate chapter of book 11, just after coming to the

---

36. See *Gn. litt.* 4, 21, 38–35, 56 and *civ. Dei* 11, 9–15.
37. Solignac, "Caelum caeli," in BA 14, 597.

The Heaven of Heaven   271

realization that his life is a distention, Augustine says, while contrasting his condition with God's eternity, "But I leapt apart into times *(At ego in tempora dissilui)*" (*conf.* XI, 29, 39). O'Connell comments, "The background image is the one Augustine embodied in his description of the soul's fall, both in *De Genesi contra Manichaeos* and in the *De musica*."[38] So too, in chapter eleven of book 12, after describing the heaven of heaven as God's house and the pure mind of the blessed spirits, he prays that the soul that has wandered far from home *(peregrinatio)* may understand that, if she now longs for and seeks her God, she may dwell in God's house all the days of her life (*conf.* 12, 11, 13).

Again, in book 12 of the *conf.*, Augustine adds, "From here, then, may the soul which can understand how far above all times you are eternal when your house, which has not journeyed away from home, although it is not coeternal with you, does not, nonetheless, suffer any change of times because it unceasingly and unfailing clings to you" (*conf.* 12, 11, 13). Here the soul that has wandered far from home *(cuius peregrinatio longinqua facta est)* is contrasted with the house of God that has not gone off on a journey *(quae non peregrinata est)*, but remained unfailingly in contemplation of God. Surely, Augustine is saying that, unlike those blessed spirits who never flowed down, who never wandered away from the fatherland, the soul has flowed down and gone on a journey away from God's house, which it remembers and to which it is making its way back. Again, in arguing with those who find his interpretation of Genesis fanciful, he asks whether they deny "that there is a certain sublime creature which cleaves with so chaste a love to the true and truly eternal God that, though not coeternal with him, it still does not detach itself from him and does not flow down into any variation and change of times *(in nullam tamen temporum varietatem et vicissitudinem ab illo se resolvat et defluat)*" (*conf.* 12, 15, 19). Accordingly, he can go on to say to God's house, "O luminous and beautiful house . . . my wandering away from home sighs after you *(O domus luminosa et speciosa . . . tibi suspiret peregrinatio mea)*, and I say to him who made you that he should possess me too in you because he made me too. I have gone astray like a lost sheep, but on the shoulders of my shepherd, your builder, I hope to be carried back to you" (*conf.* 12, 15, 21). Note that

---

38. O'Connell, *Confessions of St. Augustine*, 143.

the image of the lost sheep that has wandered off *(erravi)* and the term *reportari* in its literal sense imply that Augustine's soul was once there.

Again, in prayer Augustine says to God, "Speak in my heart with truth, for you alone speak in that way.... I will enter my chamber and sing love songs to you, groaning with unspeakable groanings in my wandering *(peregrinatione)* and remembering *(recordans)* Jerusalem with my heart lifted up toward it, Jerusalem my fatherland, Jerusalem my mother and you who over her are ruler, enlightener, father, guardian, spouse, pure and strong delight, solid joy, all good things ineffable, all possessed at once *(simul omnia)*, because you are the one and the true good" (*conf.* 12, 16, 23).

We saw that Augustine identifies the heaven of heaven with the heavenly Jerusalem; here he sings love songs to it, groans on his journey away from it, and remembers it, his fatherland and his mother. All these images imply that he once was there, for one cannot love what one does not know, one cannot remember what one has not somehow experienced, and one cannot call his fatherland a land one has never known.

The theme of the soul's fall is taken up again in book 13, where Augustine speaks of the love of God poured out in our hearts as lifting us upward, while the weight of desire pulls us down. "The angel has flowed down *(defluxit)*; the soul of man has flowed down *(defluxit)*, and they have revealed the abyss of the whole spiritual creation in the dark depths, unless you had said, 'Let there be light,' and unless light was made and every obedient intelligence of your heavenly city clung to you and rested in your Spirit who is unchangeably borne over everything changeable. Otherwise, even the heaven of heaven would have been the dark abyss in itself" (*conf.* 13, 8, 9).

Hence, the heaven of heaven is not merely the present abode of the blessed angels and the future destiny of human souls of the blessed, but also the fatherland from which some angels fell and from which human souls fell, from which we souls are presently on pilgrimage, and to which we are returning.

SOME CONCLUDING REMARKS

First, in his study of the heaven of heaven, Jean Pépin devotes considerable attention to the sources of Augustine's doctrine; he finds the clearest analogies with the Augustinian *coelum coeli* in Philo and Origen.[39] Despite the similarities between them, he has to admit that it does not seem that Augustine could have known the texts of either Philo or Origen, unless one supposes a Latin translation of Origen of which little evidence remains that it existed and none that Augustine knew it.[40] We do know, on the other hand, that Augustine read Plotinus and was even wildly enthusiastic about having found in his philosophy a way to conceive of God and the soul as spiritual and of the difference between divine eternity and the temporal distention into which the soul has fallen. Moreover, in *Ennead* 3, 7, "On Eternity and Time," in describing the soul's contemplation of the eternal, Plotinus, it seems to me, anticipates what Augustine says about the heaven of heaven: "What then, if one does not depart at all from one's contemplation of [the eternal] but stays in its company, wondering at its nature and able to do so by a natural power which never fails? Surely one would be (would one not?) oneself on the move towards eternity and never falling away from it at all, that one might be like it and eternal, contemplating eternity and the eternal by the eternal in oneself."[41] Elements of Plotinus's thought have to be pruned away or adapted, but the idea is there. So too, later in section 12, Plotinus says, "Now if in our thought we were to make this power [of time] turn back again, and put a stop to this life . . . if this part of the soul turned back to the intelligible world and to eternity, and rested quietly there, what would there still be but eternity?"[42]

Hence, given all else that Augustine learned from Plotinus, I suggest that he also derived from Plotinus the idea of the heaven of heaven as a spiritual creature, not itself eternal, but partaking in eternity by contemplation of the eternal, as that place which is no place, from which we have fallen and to which we are making our return. But the terminology he derived with the Scriptures—and this is precisely the case with the terms "spirit" and "spiritual," as Masai has argued.[43] The concept is Neoplatonic, the terminology bibilical.

Second, if the heaven of heaven is not merely the present abode of the angels and the future home of the souls of the blessed, but also

---

39. See Pépin, "Recherches," 259–269.

40. See ibid., 268.

41. *Ennead* 3, 7, 5; tr. Armstrong, 317. See Solignac, "Caelum caeli," in BA 14, 593, where he points to *Ennead* 5, 8, 3, lines 27–36, where Plotinus speaks of a sensible heaven and an intelligible heaven.

42. Ibid., 12; tr. Armstrong, 343.

43. Masai, "Conversions de saint Augustin," 16–22.

the fatherland or homeland from which we souls have gone forth on pilgrimage or from which we have wandered away and to which we are making our return, certain things follow for the unity of the *conf.* One, it seems to me clear that books 10 to 13 have a unity that is more profound than is involved in merely continuing the theme of "confession"—no longer of sins, but of the marvelous works of God. What unifies these books is the extensive use of Neoplatonic philosophy as a means of coming to some understanding of the Christian faith, specifically an understanding of the origin, present state, and destiny of human beings. Neoplatonism provides a means of articulating that faith in a way that avoids some of the worst problems of the corporealist and time-bound thinking of the Stoics and the Manichees. Two, one has to see books 1 through 9 as more than mere autobiography. These books are rather the story of every human being written from a Neoplatonic Christian perspective—a view that at least in part explains why people have for centuries recognized themselves in the events of Augustine's life. Augustine is presenting a Neoplatonic understanding of existence, origin, and destiny of human beings. Where my understanding of the heaven of heaven—and O'Connell's—differs from that of others, such as Pépin, is chiefly with regard to the origin of the soul—a topic much in dispute among Augustinian scholars. Those opposed to any doctrine of the fall of the soul into these bodies from the heaven of heaven appeal to Augustine's statement in the *retr.* 1, 1, 3, that he did not know then—*(nec tunc sciebam)*—at the time of the *c. Acad.*—and he still does not know—*(nec adhuc scio)*—at the time of the *retr.*—the answer to the question about the soul's coming to be in the body.[44] Others, such as O'Connell, point out that such a statement does not preclude that he once thought that he knew the answer, that is, that at the time of the *conf.* he could still have thought he knew that each human soul was once in that heaven of heaven from which it has wandered off and to which it is making its return.

To establish that claim with any definitiveness, one would have to do much, much more than what I have done in this article. What I have tried to do is to get you to see, or at least to be open to seeing, that certain theses of a Christian Neoplatonism about human existence unify the *conf.* in a more profound way than has been generally acknowledged.

---

44. See O'Connell, *Early Theory*, 150.

BIBLIOGRAPHY

Works of Saint Augustine Cited
Contra Academicos. PL 32, 905–958; CCL 29, 3–61.
Contra adversarium legis et prophetarum. PL 42, 603–666; CCL 49, 35–131.
De anima et eius origine. PL 44, 475–548; CSEL 60, 303–419.
De animae quantitate. PL 32, 1035–80; CSEL 89, 131–231.
De beata vita. PL 32, 959–976, CSEL 63, 89–116; CCL 29, 65–85.
De civitate Dei. PL 41, 13–804; CCL 47.1, 1–314; 47.2, 321–866.
Confessiones. PL 32, 659–868; CSEL 33, 1–388; CCL 27, 1–273.
De consensu Evangelistarum. PL 34, 1041–1230; CSEL 43, 1–418.
De continentia. PL 40, 349–372; CSEL 41, 139–183.
De diversis quaestionibus octoginta tribus. PL 40, 11–100; CCL 44A, 11–249.
De doctrina Christiana. PL 34, 15–122; CSEL 89, 3–169; CCL 32, 1–167.
De duabus animabus. PL 34, 15–122; CSEL 25.1, 51–80.
Enchiridion ad Laurentium. PL 40, 231–290; CCL 46, 49–114.
Ennarationes in Psalmos. PL 36, 67–1028; 37, 1033–1966; CCL 38, 1–616; 39, 623–1417; 40, 1425–2196.
Epistulae. PL 33, 61–1094; CSEL 34.1, 1–125; 34.2, 1–746; 57, 1–656; 88, 3–138.
In epistulam Joannis. PL 35, 1977–2062.
Contra epistulam Manichaei quam vocant fundamenti. PL 42, 173–206; CSEL 25.1, 193–248.
Contra Felicem Manichaeum. PL 42, 519–552; CSEL 25.2, 801–852.
De fide et symbolo. PL 40, 181–196; CSEL 41, 3–32.
Acta contra Fortunatum Manichaeum. PL 42, 111–130; CSEL 25/1, 251–797.
De Genesi ad litteram. PL 34, 245–486; CSEL 28.1, 3–435.
De Genesi ad litteram imperfectus liber. PL 34, 219–246; CSEL 28.1, 457–503.
De Genesis adversus Manichaeos. PL 34, 173–220; CSEL 91, 67–172.
De haeresibus. PL 32, 593–656; CCL 45, 283–351.
De immortalite animae. PL 32, 1021–1034; CSEL 89, 101–128.
In Johannis evangelium tractatus. PL 35, 132–1975; CCL 36, 1–688.
De libero arbitrio. PL 32, 1221–1310; CSEL 74, 3–154; CCL 29, 211–321.
De magistro. PL 32, 1193–1220; CSEL 77.1, 3–55; CCL 29, 157–203.

Contra Maximinum Arianum. PL 42, 709–742.
De mendacio. PL 40, 487–578; CSEL 41, 413–466.
Contra mendacium. PL 40, 517–548; CSEL 41, 469–528.
De moribus ecclesiae Catholicae et de moribus Manichaeorum. PL 32, 1309–1378; CSEL 90, 3–156.
De musica. PL 32, 1081–1194.
De natura boni. PL 42, 551–572; CSEL 25.2, 855–889.
De ordine. PL 32, 977–1020; CSEL 63, 121–180; CCL 29, 89–137.
De peccatorum meritis et remissione et de baptismo parvulorum. PL 44, 109–200; CSEL 60, 3–151.
De praedestinatione sanctorum. PL 44, 959–992.
Contra Priscilianistas. PL 42, 669–678; CCL 49, 165–178.
Retractationes. PL 32, 553–656; CSEL 36, 7–204; CCL 57, 5–143.
Contra Secundinum Manichaeum. PL 42, 577–602; CSEL 25.2, 905–975.
De sermone Domini in monte. PL 34, 1229–1308; CCL 35, 1–188.
Sermones. PL 38, 23–1484; 39, 1493–1638, 1650–1652, 1655–1659, 1663–1669, 1671–1684, 1695–1697, 1701–1736.
Ad Simplicianum. PL 40, 349–372; CCL 44, 1–91.
Soliloquia. PL 32, 869–904; CSEL 89, 3–98.
Speculum. PL 34, 887–1040; CSEL 12, 3–285.
De spiritu et littera. PL 44, 201–246; CSEL 60, 155–229.
De Trinitate. PL 42, 817–1098; CCL 50, 25–380; 50A, 381–535.
De utiliate credendi. PL 42, 65–92; CSEL 25.1, 3–48.
De utilitate jejunii. PL 40, 707–716.
De vera religione. PL 34, 121–172; CSEL 77.2, 3–81; CCL 32, 187–260.

Translations Used

Augustine, Saint. *The Basic Writings of St. Augustine.* 2 vols. Edited by Whitney J. Oates. New York: Random House, 1948.

———. *Against the Academics.* Translated and annotated by John J. O'Meara. Westminster, Md.: Newman Press, 1950.

———. *Oeuvres de Saint Augustin.* Vol. 8. Translated by J. Pegon, S.J. Paris: Desclée de Brouwer, 1951.

———. *St. Augustine: Letters 165–203.* Translated by Sr. Wilfrid Parsons. Ancient Christian Writers 12. New York: Cima Publishing, 1955.

———. *The Confessions of St. Augustine.* Translated by John K. Ryan. Garden City, NY: Image Books, 1960.

———. *The Greatness of the Soul and The Teacher.* Translated by Joseph M. Colleran. Westminster, Md.: Newman, 1964.

———. *On the Free Choice of the Will.* Translated by Anna S. Benjamin and L. H. Hackstaff. Indianapolis: Library of the Liberal Arts, 1964.

———. *De Immortalitate Animae of Augustine: Text, Translation and Commentary.* Translated by C. W. Wolfskeel. Amsterdam: B. R. Grüner, 1977.

SECONDARY SOURCES

Alfaric, Prosper. *L'évolution intellectuelle de saint Augustin.* Paris: E. Nourry, 1918.
Altaner, B. "Augustinus und Gregor von Nazianz, Gregor von Nyssa." In *Kleine Patristische Schriften,* edited by G. Glockmann, 277–285. Berlin: Akademie Verlag, 1967.
Anderson, James F. *St. Augustine and Being: A Metaphysical Essay.* The Hague: M. Nijhoff, 1965.
Aquinas, Thomas. *Summa theologiae.* 3 vols. Turin: Marietti, 1952.
Arias, Luis. "El priscilianismo en san Agustin." *Augustinus* 25 (1980): 71–82.
Armstrong, A. H. "Spiritual or intelligible Matter in Plotinus and St. Augustine." In *Augustinus magister,* 1:277–283. Paris: Études Augustiniennes, 1954.
———. *Expectations of Immortality in Late Antiquity.* Milwaukee: Marquette University Press, 1987.
Aristotle. *The Basic Works of Aristotle.* Edited by Richard McKeon. New York: Random House, 1941.
Aubin, Paul. "L'image dans l'oeuvre de Plotin." *Recherches de science religieuse* 41 (1953): 348–379.
Ayers, Robert. "A Viable Theodicy for Christian Apologetics." *The Modern Schoolman* 52 (1975): 391–403.
Balás, David L. *METAOUSIA TOU THEOU: Man's Participation in God's Perfections according to Gregory of Nyssa.* Rome: Herder, 1966.
———. "Eternity and Time in Gregory of Nyssa's *Contra Eunomium.*" In *Gregor von Nyssa und die Philosophie,* edited by Heinrich Dörrie, Margarete Altenburger, and Uta Schramm, 128–155. Leiden: E. J. Brill, 1976.
Beierwaltes, W. *Plotin über Ewigkeit und Zeit.* Frankfurt am Main: V. Klostermann, 1967.
Berrouard, Marie-François. "Animalis homo," BA 71 (Paris, 1969), 837–838.
———. "Le Christ et la libération du temps," BA 72 (Paris, 1977), 850–851.
Beutler, R. "Porphyrios." In *Real-Encyclopädie den classischen Altertumswissenschaft,* vol. 22, pt. 1, cc. 284–285 (Stuttgart: Metzler, 1953).
Blic, Jacques de. "Platonisme et christianisme dans la conception augustinienne du Dieu createur." *Recherches de science religieuse* 30 (1940): 172–190.
Boethius, A. M. Severinus. *De consolatione philosophiae.* PL 63, 510–870.
Bourke, Vernon J. *Augustine's View of Reality.* Villanova: Villanova University Press, 1964.
———. *Joy in Augustine's Ethics.* Villanova: Villanova University Press, 1979.
———. "St. Augustine and the Cosmic Soul." *Giornale de Metafisica* 9 (1954): 431–440. Revised version appears in *Wisdom from St. Augustine.* Houston: Center for Thomistic Studies, 1984.
———. *Wisdom from St. Augustine.* Houston: Center for Thomistic Studies, 1984.
Boyer, Charles. "La preuve de Dieu Augustinienne." *Archives de philosophie* 7 (1930): 103–141.
———. *L'idée de vérité dans la philosophie de saint Augustin.* 2nd ed. Paris: Beauchesne, 1940.

Bradley, Francis H. *Appearance and Reality.* Oxford: Clarendon Press, 1930.
Brown, Peter. *Augustine of Hippo: A Biography.* Berkeley and Los Angeles: University of California Press, 1969.
———. *Augustine of Hippo: A Biography.* New ed. with epilogue. Berkeley and Los Angeles: University of California Press, 2000.
Burnaby, John. *Amor Dei: A Study of the Religion of St. Augustine.* London: Hodder and Stoughton, 1938.
Burns, J. Patout. "St. Augustine: The Original Condition of Humanity." In *Studia Patristica* 22, edited by E. A. Livingstone, 219–222. Leuven: Peeters, 1989.
Callahan, John F. *Four Views of Time in Ancient Philosophy.* Cambridge, Mass.: Harvard University Press, 1948.
Capánaga, Victorino, O.R.S.A. "La deificación en la soteriología agustiniana." In *Augustinus Mmagister,* 2:745–754. Paris: Études augustinienne, 1954–55.
Capello, Joseph. *S. Aurelii Augustini Confessionum Libri XIII.* Turin: Marietti, 1948.
Cayré, Fulbert. *Dieu présent dans la vie de l'esprit.* Paris: Desclée, De Brouwer, 1951.
Chadwick, Henry. *Priscillian of Avila: The Occult and the Charismatic in the Early Church.* Oxford: Oxford University Press, 1976.
Chaix-Ruy, J. "La cité de Dieu et la structure du temps." In *Augustinus magister.* Paris: Études augustinienne, 1954–55.
Chevalier, Irénée. *S. Augustin et la pensée grecque: Les relations trinitaires.* Fribourg: Librairie de l'université, 1940.
Clarke, W. Norris. "A New Look at the Immutability of God." In *God Knowable and Unknowable,* edited by Robert J. Roth, 43–72. New York: Fordham University Press, 1973.
Cooper, John C. "Why Did Augustine Write Books XI–XIII of the Confessions?" *Augustinian Studies* 2 (1971): 37–46.
Courcelle, Pierre. *Les lettres grecques en Occident de Macrobe à Cassiodore.* Paris: de Boccard, 1948.
———. *Recherches sur les Confessions de saint Augustin.* 2nd ed. Paris: de Boccard, 1968.
Cousineau, Robert-Henri. "Creation and Freedom: An Augustinian Problem: 'Quia voluit'? and/or 'Quia bonus'?" *Recherches Augustiniennes* 2 (1963): 253–271.
Dalmau, I. M. "De Deo Uno et Trino." In *Sacrae Theologiae Summa.* 4 vols. Madrid: Biblioteca de autores cristianos, 1958.
De Bruyne, Dom. "Itala de saint Augustin." *Revue Bénédictine* 30 (1913): 294–314.
Delhaye, Philippe. *Une controverse sur l'âme universelle au IXe siécle.* Analecta Mediaevalia Namurcensia 1. Namur: Centre d'études médiévales, 1950.
Descartes, René. *Oeuvres de Descartes.* Edited by Charles Adam and Paul Tannery. Paris: J. Vrin, 1964.
———. *Oeuvres Philosophiques.* Edited by Ferdinand Alquié. 3 vols. Paris: Garnier, 1967.
Du Roy, Olivier. *L'intelligence de la foi en la trinité selon s. Augustin: Genèse de sa théologie trinitaire iusqu'en 391.* Paris: Études augustiniennes, 1966.

Durandeaux, Jacques. *L'éternité dans la vie quotidienne: Essai sur les sources et la structure du concept d'éternité.* Bruges: Desclée de Brouwer, 1964.
Durrant, Michael. *Theology and Intelligibility.* London and Boston: Routledge and Kegan Paul, 1973.
Ferrari, Leo C. *The Conversions of Saint Augustine.* Villanova: Villanova University Press, 1984.
Flasch, Kurt. *Was ist Zeit?: Augustinus von Hippo, das XI. Buch der Confessiones.* Frankfurt am Main: V. Klostermann, 1993.
Folliet, Georges. "Etiam Peccata (De doctr. christ. III, xxiii, 33)." *Revue des études augustiniennes* 5 (1959): 450.
———. "'Deificari in otio': Augustin, *Epistula* 10, 2." *Recherches augustiniennes* 2 (1962): 225–236.
Fortin, Ernest. *Christianisme et culture philosophique au cinquième siècle: La querelle de l'âme humaine en Occident.* Paris: Études augustiniennes, 1959.
Galilei, Galileo. "Lettre à Christine de Lorraine, Grand-Duchesse de Toscane (1615), traduction et présentation par François Russo." *Revue d'histoire des sciences et de leurs applications* 17 (1964): 332–366.
Geach, Peter. *God and the Soul.* London: Routledge and Kegan Paul, 1969.
———. *Logic Matters.* Berkeley and Los Angeles: University of California Press, 1972.
Gilson, Etienne. *Philosophie et incarnation selon saint Augustin.* Montréal: Institut d'études médiévales, Université de Montréal, 1947.
———. *History of Christian Philosophy in the Middle Ages.* New York: Random House, 1955.
———. *The Christian Philosophy of St. Augustine.* Translated by L. E. M. Lynch. London: Victor Gollancz, 1960.
———. "Notes sur l'être et le temps chez saint Augustine." *Recherches Aaugustiniennes* 2 (1962): 205–223.
———. "Quasi Definitio Substantiae." In *St. Thomas Aquinas 1274–1974: Commemorative Studies,* edited by Armand A. Maurer, 1:111–129. Toronto: Pontifical Institute of Mediaeval Studies, 1974.
Grandgeorge, L. *Saint Augustine et le Neó-Platonisme.* Paris, 1896; reprint Frankfurt am Main: Minerva, 1967.
Guitton, Jean. *Le temps et l'éternité chez Plotin et saint Augustin.* 3rd rev. ed. Paris: J. Vrin, 1959.
Hadot, Ilsetraut. "The Spiritual Guide." In *Classical Mediterranean Spirituality,* 436–59. Vol. 15 of *World Spirituality: An Encyclopedic History of the Religious Quest.* New York: Crossroad, 1986.
Hadot, Pierre. *Exercises spirituels et philosophie antique.* Paris: Études augustiniennes, 1981.
Hartshorne, Charles. *Aquinas to Whitehead: Seven Centuries of Metaphysics of Religion.* Milwaukee: Marquette University Press, 1976.
Henry, Paul. *Plotin et l'Occident.* Louvain: Spicilegium Sacrum Lovaniense, 1934.

———. *La vision d'Ostie: Sa place dans la vie et l'oeuvre de saint Augustin*. Paris: J. Vrin, 1938.
Holte, Ragnar. *Béatitude et Sagesse: Saint Augustin et le problème de la fin de l'homme dans la philosophie ancienne*. Paris: Études augustiniennes, 1962.
Huftier, Maurice. *Le tragique de la condition chrétienne chez saint Augustin*. Paris: Desclée, 1964.
Hultgren, Gunnar. *Le commandement d'amour chez Augustin: Interprétation philosophique et théologique d'après les écrits de la période 386–400*. Paris: J. Vrin, 1939.
Jordan, Robert. "Time and Contingency in St. Augustine." *Review of Metaphysics* 8 (1954–55): 394–414.
Jourjon, Maurice. "L'homme image de Dieu selon Irenée de Lyon." *Christus* 31:24 (1984): 501–508.
———. "The Image of God according to Irenaeus." *Theology Digest* 32 (1985): 253–255.
La Croix, Richard R. "Augustine on the Simplicity of God." *New Scholasticism* 51 (1977): 453–469.
———. "Wainwright, Augustine and God's Simplicity." *New Scholasticism* 53 (1979): 124–127.
———. "Aquinas on God's Omnipresence and Timelessness." *Philosophy and Phenomenological Research* 42 (1982): 391–399.
Lawless, George. *Augustine of Hippo and His Monastic Rule*. Oxford: Clarendon Press, 1987.
Le Blond, Jean-Marie. *Les conversions de saint Augustin*. Paris: Aubier, 1950.
Lonergan, Bernard J. F. *Insight: A Study of Human Understanding*. London: Longmans, 1958.
Lossky, Vladimir. "Les elements de 'Théologie négative' dans la pensée de saint Augustin." In *Augustinus magister*, 1:575–581. Paris: Études augustiniennes, 1954.
Madec, Goulven. "Connaissance de Dieu et action de grâce. Essai sur les citations de l'*Ep. aux Romains* 1, 18–25 dans l'oeuvre de saint Augustin." *Recherches augustiniennes* 2 (1962): 273–309.
———. "L'*Hortensius* de Cicéron dans les livres XIII–XIV du *De Trinitate*." *Revue des études augustiniennes* 15 (1969): 167–171.
———. "A propos d'une traduction de *De ordine* II, v, 16." *Revue des études augustiniennes* 16 (1970): 179–185.
———. "La christianisation de l'hellenisme. Thème de l'histoire de la philosophie patristique." In *Humanisme et foi chrétienne: Mélanges scientifiques du centenaire de l'institut catholique de Paris*, 399–406. Paris: Beauchesne, 1976.
———. "Verus Philosophus Est Amator Dei: S. Ambroise, s. Augustin et la philosophie." *Revue des sciences philosophiques et théologiques* 61 (1977): 549–566.
Mandouze, André. *Saint Augustin: L'aventure de la raison et de la grâce*. Paris: Études augustiniennes, 1938.
Marcel, Gabriel. *Presence et immortalité*. Paris: Flammarion, 1959.

Markus, Robert A. "Augustine." In *The Cambridge History of Later Greek and Early Medieval Philosophy*, edited by A. H. Armstrong, 341–419. Cambridge: Cambridge University Press, 1967.

———. "Augustine, St." In *The Encyclopedia of Philosophy*, edited by Paul Edwards, 1:198–207. New York: Macmillan, 1967.

Marrou, Henri-Irénée. *L'ambivalence du temps de l'histoire chez saint Augustin*. Montreal: Institut d'études médiévales, Université de Montréal, 1950.

———. *St. Augustine and His Influence through the Ages*. New York: Harper and Brothers, 1957.

———. *Saint Augustin et la fin de la culture antique*. 4th ed. Paris: de Boccard, 1958.

Masai, François. "Les conversions de saint Augustin et les débuts du spiritualisme en Occident." *Le Moyen Âge* 67 (1961): 1–40.

McCool, Gerald A. "The Ambrosian Origen of St. Augustine's Theology of the Image of God in Man." *Theological Studies* 20 (1959): 62–81.

Meer, Frederick van der. *Augustine the Bishop: Church and Society at the Dawn of the Middle Ages*. New York: Harper, 1965.

Mourant, John A. *Augustine on Immortality*. Villanova: Augustinian Institute, 1969.

———. *Saint Augustine on Memory*. The Saint Augustine Lecture 1979. Villanova: Villanova University Press, 1980.

Mundle, C. W. K. "Time, Consciousness of." In *The Encyclopedia of Philosophy*, edited by Paul Edwards, 8:135–139. New York: Macmillan, 1967.

Murray, John C., S.J. *The Problem of God, Yesterday and Today*. New Haven: Yale University Press, 1964.

Nash, Ronald H. *The Light of the Mind: St. Augustine's Theory of Knowledge*. Lexington: University of Kentucky Press, 1969.

Nourrisson, Jean F. *La Philosophie de s. Augustin*. Paris: Didier et Cie, 1865.

Nygren, Anders. *Agape and Eros*. Philadelphia: Westminster, 1953.

O'Connell, Robert J. "Augustin et le stoicisme." *Recherches augustiniennes* 1 (1958): 67–89.

———. *St. Augustine's Early Theory of Man, A.D. 386–391*. Cambridge, Mass.: Belknap Press, 1968.

———. *St. Augustine's Confessions: The Odyssey of Soul*. Cambridge, Mass.: Belknap Press, 1969.

———. "Augustine's Rejection of the Fall of the Soul." *Augustinian Studies* 4 (1973): 1–32.

———. *Imagination and Metaphysics in St. Augustine*. Milwaukee: Marquette University Press, 1986.

———. "On Augustine's 'First Conversion' Factus Erectior (*De beata vita* 4)." *Augustinian Studies* 17 (1986): 15–29.

———. *The Origin of the Soul in St. Augustine's Later Works*. New York: Fordham University Press, 1987.

O'Daly, Gerard. *Augustine's Philosophy of Mind*. Berkeley and Los Angeles: University of California Press, 1987.

O'Donnell, James. *Augustine: Confessions*. 3 vols. Oxford: Oxford University Press, 1992.
O'Donovan, Oliver. *The Problem of Self-Love in St. Augustine*. New Haven: Yale University Press, 1980.
O'Meara, John J. *The Young Augustine*. London: Longmans, Green, 1954.
———. *Charter of Christendom: The Significance of the City of God*. New York: Macmillan, 1961.
Ommen, Thomas. "The Pre-Understanding of the Theologian." In *Theology and Discovery: Essays in honor of Karl Rahner,* edited by William Kelly, 231–261. Milwaukee: Marquette University Press, 1980.
Owens, Joseph. *The Doctrine of Being in Aristotelian Metaphysics*. Toronto: Pontifical Institute of Mediaeval Studies, 1951.
Pegis, Anton C. "The Second Conversion of St Augustine." In *Gesellschaft, Kultur, Literatur: Rezeption und Originalität im Wachsen einer europäisschen Literatur und Geistigkeit,* 79–93. Stuttgart: Anton Hiersemann, 1975.
Pelland, Gilles. *Cinq études d'Augustin sur le début de la Genèse*. Tournai: Desclée, 1972.
Pépin, Jean. "Recherches sur le sens et les origines de l'expression *Caelum Caeli* dans le livre XII des *Confessions* de S. Augustin." *Bulletin du Cange* 23 (1953): 185–274.
———. "A propos de l'histoire de l'exégèse allégorique: l'absurdité, signe de allégorie." *Studia Patristica* in *Texte un Untersuchungen* 63 (1955): 395–415.
Perl, Carl. *Die frühen Werke des heiligen Augustinus*. Paderborn, 1954.
Peter, Carl J. *Participated Eternity in the Vision of God: A Study of the Opinion of Thomas Aquinas and His Commentators on the Duration of the Acts of Glory*. Rome: Gregorian University Press, 1964.
Peters, E. "What Was God Doing before He Created the Heaven and the Earth?" *Augustiniana* 34 (1984): 53–74.
Philastrius. *Diversarum hereseon liber*. PL 12, 1111–1302.
Pizzolato, Luigi Franco, and Giovanni Scanavino, eds. *"Le Confessioni" di Agostino d'Ippona: Libri X–XIII*. Commento di: Aimé Solignac, Eugenio Corsini, Jean Pépin, Alberto di Giovanni. Lectio Augustini. Palermo: Edizioni Augustinus, 1987.
Plantinga, Alvin. *Does God Have a Nature?* Milwaukee: Marquette University Press, 1980.
Plato. *The Republic*. Translated by Paul Shorey. 2 vols. Cambridge, Mass.: Harvard University Press, 1946.
Plotinus. *Enneades* VI, Ire Partie. Paris: Belles lettres, 1963.
———. *The Essential Plotinus*. Translated by Elmer O'Brien. New York: Mentor Books, 1964.
———. *Enneads*. 6 vols. Translated by A. H. Armstrong. Cambridge, Mass.: Harvard University Press, 1966–87.
Pontifex, Mark. *St. Augustine: The Problem of Free Choice*. Westminster, Md.: Newman Press, 1955.

Portalié, Eugene. *A Guide to the Thought of Saint Augustine*. Translated by Ralph J. Bastian. Chicago: Regnery, 1960.

Rahner, Karl. "Philosophy and Theology." In *Theological Investigations*. Vol. 6. Baltimore: Helicon, 1969.

Ratrame de Corbie. *Liber de anima ad Odonem Bellovacensem*. Edited by D. C. Lambot, O.S.B. Analecta Mediaevalia Namurcensia 2. Namur: Godenne; Lille: Liard, 1951.

Raveaux, Thomas. "Aduersarium legis et prophetarum (Contra —)." In *Augustinus-Lexikon*, edited by Cornelius Mayer, vol. I, 1/2, 107–122. Basel: Schwabe, 1986–.

———. *Augustinus: Contra Adversarium Legis et Prophetarum. Analyse des Inhalts and Untersuchung des geistesgeschichtlichen Hintergrunds*. Würzburg: Augustinus Verlag, 1987.

Rivière, Jean. *Le dogme de la rédemption chez saint Augustin*. Paris: J. Gabalda, 1933.

Robles, Laureano. "San Agustin y la cuestión priscilianista sobre el origen del alma." *Augustinus* 25 (1980): 51–69.

Rohmer, Jean. "L'intentionalité des sensations chez saint Augustin." In *Augustinus magister*, 1:491–498. Paris: Études augustiniennes, 1954.

Rombs, Ronnie. *Saint Augustine and the Fall of the Soul: Beyond O'Connell and his Critics*. Washington, D.C.: The Catholic University of America Press, 2006.

Rouët de Journel, Marie Joseph. *Enchiridion Patristicum*. Freiburg: Herder, 1951.

Ruch, Michel. *L'Hortensius de Cicéron: Histoire et reconstitution*. Paris: Belles Lettres, 1958.

Russell, Bertrand. *Human Knowledge: Its Scope and Limits*. New York: Simon and Schuster, 1948.

Schumacher, William A. *Spiritus and Spirituales: A Study in the Sermons of Saint Augustine*. Mundelein, Ill.: St. Mary of the Lake Seminary, 1957.

Sejourné, P. "Les conversions de saint Augustine d'après le De Libero Arbitrio I." *Revue des sciences religieuses* 89–90 (1951): 359–360.

Smart, J. J. C. "Time." In *The Encyclopedia of Philosophy*, edited by John Edwards, 8:126–134. New York: Macmillan, 1967.

Smith, Thomas A. "Augustine in Two Gallic Controversies: Use or Abuse?" In *Augustine: Presbyter Factus Sum*, 43–55. New York: Peter Lang, 1993.

Solignac, Aimé. "Essai de Chronologie" BA 13 (Paris, 1962), 204–205.

———. "La doctrine manichéenne du 'cuneus,'" BA 13 (Paris, 1962), 674.

———. "Spirituels et charnels," BA 14 (Paris, 1962), 629–634.

Somers, H. "Image de Dieu. Les sources de l'exegèse augustinienne." *Revue des études augustiniennes* 7 (1961): 105–125.

Sorabji, Richard. *Time, Creation and the Continuum: Theories in Antiquity and the Early Middle Ages*. Ithaca: Cornell University Press, 1983.

Steinhauser, Kenneth B. "The Literary Unity of the Confessions." In *Augustine: From Rhetor to Theologian*, edited by Joanne McWilliam, 15–30. Waterloo: Wilfred Laurier University Press, 1992.

Stoop, J. A. A. A. *Die deificatio hominis in die Sermones en Epistulae van Augustinus*. Leiden: Luctur et Emergo, 1952.

Swetnam, James. "A Note on *In Idipsum* in St. Augustine." *The Modern Schoolman* 30 (1952–53): 328–331.
Swinburne, Richard. *The Coherence of Theism*. Oxford: Clarendon Press, 1977.
Tertullian, Quintus Septimus. *Adversus Hermogenem*. PL 2, 196–238.
———. *Adversus Praxean*. PL 2, 152–196.
———. *De carne Christi*. PL 2, 751–792.
———. *De praescriptione haereticorum*. PL 2, 9–74.
TeSelle, Eugene. *Augustine the Theologian*. New York: Herder and Herder, 1970.
Teske, Roland J. "Omniscience, Omnipotence, and Divine Transcendence." *New Scholasticism* 53 (1979): 277–294.
———. "Properties of God and the Predicaments in *De Trinitate* V." *The Modern Schoolman* 59 (1981): 1–19.
———. "The World-Soul and Time in St. Augustine." *AS* 14 (1983): 75–92.
———. "Spirituals and Spiritual Interpretation in St. Augustine." *AS* 15 (1984): 65–81.
———. "'*Vocans temporales, faciens aeternos*': St. Augustine on Liberation from Time." *Traditio* 41 (1985): 29–47.
———. "The Aim of Augustine's Proof That God Truly Is." *International Philosophical Quarterly* 26 (1986): 253–268.
———. "Love of Neighbor in St. Augustine." In *Atti III* of *Congresso internazionale su s. Agostino nel xvi centenario della conversione*. Rome: Augustinianum, 1987.
———. "*Homo spiritualis* in St. Augustine's *De Genesi contra Manichaeos*." *Studia Patristica* 22, edited by Elizabeth A. Livingstone, 351–355. Leuven: Peeters, 1989. A Spanish translation has appeared in *Augustinus* (Madrid) 36 (1991): 305–310.
———. "Rahner on the Relation of Nature and Grace." *Philosophy and Theology*, disk supplement 4, 4 (1989): 109–122.
———. "The Image and Likeness of God in St. Augustine's *De Genesi ad litteram liber imperfectus*." *Augustinianum* 30 (1990): 441–451.
———. "*Homo spiritualis* in St. Augustine's Confessions." In *Augustine: From Rhetor to Theologian*, edited by Joanne McWilliams, 67–76. Waterloo, Ontario: Wilfrid Laurier University Press, 1992.
———. "Origen and St. Augustine's First Commentaries on Genesis." In *Origenianum Quintum*, 179–185. Leuven: Peeters, 1992.
———. "Heresy and Imagination in St. Augustine." *Studia Patristica* 27, edited by Elizabeth A. Livingstone, 400–404. Leuven: Peeters, 1993.
———. "The Link between Faith and Time in St. Augustine." In *Augustine: Presbyter Factus Sum*, edited by J. Lienhard, E. Muller, and R. Teske, 195–206. New York: Peter Lang, 1993.
———. "St. Augustine and the Vision of God." In *Augustine: Mystic and Mystagogue*, edited by Frederick Van Fleteren and Joseph Schnaubelt, 287–308. New York: Peter Lang, 1994.

———. "The Criteria for Figurative Interpretation in St. Augustine." In *De doctrina christiana: A Classic of Western Culture*, edited by D. W. H. Arnold and P. Bright, 109–122. Notre Dame: University of Notre Dame Press, 1995.

———. "Ultimate Reality according to Augustine of Hippo." *Ultimate Reality and Meaning* 18 (1995): 20–33.

———. *Paradoxes of Time in Saint Augustine*. Milwaukee: Marquette University Press, 1996.

———. "Augustine and Jansenius on the State of Pure Nature." In *Augustinus in der Neuzeit*, edited by Kurt Flasch and Dominique de Courcelles, 161–174. Turnholt: Brepols, 1999.

———. "The Definition of Sacrifice in the *De ciuitate Dei*." In *Nova Doctrina Vetusque: Essays on Early Christianity in Honor of Fredric W. Schlatter, S.J.*, edited by Douglas Kries and Catherine Brown Tkacz, 153–167. New York: Peter Lang, 1999.

———. "Saint Augustine on Sacrifice in *Contra aduersarium legis et prophetarum*." In *Studia Patristica* 33, edited by E. A. Livingstone, 255–259. Leuven: Peeters, 1997. A Spanish translation has appeared in *Augustinus* (Madrid) 44 (1999): 277–281.

———. "St. Augustine, the Manichees, and the Bible." In *Augustine and the Bible*, edited by P. Bright, 208–221. Notre Dame, Ind.: Notre Dame University Press, 1999.

———. "The Heaven of Heaven and the Unity of St. Augustine's *Confessions*." *American Catholic Philosophical Quarterly* 74 (2000): 29–45.

———. "A Tribute to Robert J. O'Connell, S.J., 1925–1999." *Augustinian Studies* 31 (2000): 41–49.

———. "Augustine's Philosophy of Memory." In *Cambridge Companion to Augustine*, edited by Norman Kretzmann and Eleonore Stump, 148–158. Oxford: Oxford University Press, 2001.

———. "Augustine's Theory of Soul." In *Cambridge Companion to Augustine*, edited by Norman Kretzmann and Eleonore Stump, 116–123. Oxford: Oxford University Press, 2001.

———. "St. Augustine on the Good Samaritan." In *Augustine the Exegete*, edited by Frederick Van Fleteren and Joseph Schaubelt, 347–367. New York: Peter Lang, 2001.

———. "Augustine, St." In *The New Catholic Encyclopedia*, 1:850–868. Washington, D.C.: The Catholic University of America Press, 2003.

———. "Augustine and the Quaestiones et Responsiones Literature." In *Erotapokriseis: Early Christian Question-and-Answer Literature*, edited by Annelie Volgers and Claudio Zumagni, 127–144. Leuven: Peeters, 2004.

———. "Función de la segunda mitad de Confesiones 10." *Augustinus* (Madrid) 49 (2004): 377–388.

———. "Genesi ad litteram, de." In *Augustinus-Lexikon*, 3, Fasc. 1.2., 113–126. Basel: Schwabe, 2004.

———. "St. Augustine on the Humanity of Christ and Temptation." *Augustiniana* 54 (2004): 261–277.

———. "The Augustinianism of Prosper of Aquitaine Revisited." In *Studia Patristica* 43, edited by F. Young, M. Edwards, and P. Parvis, 491–503. Leuven: Peeters, 2006.

Testard, Maurice. *Saint Augustin et Ciceron*. Paris: Études augustiniennes, 1958.

Thimme, Wilhelm. *Augustins geistige Entwicklung in den ersten Jahren nach seiner 'Bekehrung,' 386–391*. Berlin: Trowitzsch und Sohn, 1908.

Van Bavel, T. J. "L'humanité du Christ comme lac parvulorum et comme via dans la spiritualité de saint Augustine." *Augustiniana* 7 (1957): 245–281.

Van Fleteren, Frederick. "Authority and Reason, Faith and Understanding in the Thought of St. Augustine." *Augustinian Studies* 4 (1973): 33–71.

———. "A Reply to O'Connell." *Augustinian Studies* 21 (1990): 127–137.

Verbeke, Gérard. *L'évolution de la doctrine du pneuma du stoïcisme à s. Augustin*. Paris: Desclée de Brouwer; Louvain: Institut supérieur de philosophie, 1945.

———. "Augustin et le stoicisme." *Recherches augustiniennes* 1 (1958): 67–89.

———. "L'immortalité de l'âme dans le 'De Anima' d'Avicenne: Une synthése de l'Aristotélisme et du Néoplatonisme." *Pensamiento* 25 (1969): 271–290.

Victorinus, Marius. *Adversus Arianos*. PL 8, 1039–1138.

Von Jess, Wilma G. "La simplicidad de Dios en el pensamiento agustiniano." *Augustinus* 19 (1974): 45–52.

Wainwright, William J. "Augustine on God's Simplicity: A Reply." *New Scholasticism* 53 (1979): 118–123.

Weil, E. "Remarques sur le 'matérialisme' des Stoiciens." In *Mélanges Alexandre Koyré*. Vol. 2, *L'aventure de l'esprit*, 556–572. Paris: Hermann, 1964.

Zepf, Max. *Augustin's Confessiones*. Heidelberger Abhandlungen zur Philosophie und ihrer Geschichte 9. Tubingen: J. C. B. Mohr, 1926.

Zimara, Coelestin, S.M.B. "Das Ineinanderspiel von Gottes Vorwissen und Wollen nach Augustinus." *Freiburger Zeitschrift für Philosophie and Theologie* 6 (1959): 271–299 and 371–334.

INDEX OF NAMES

Agaësse, P., 117n15, 159n13, 182n10
Alfaric, P., 137n20, 138n24
Altaner, B., 24n89
Alypius of Thagaste, 8
Ambrose of Milan, 3, 30, 36n20, 46, 49, 56–57, 62, 140, 141n34, 144n39, 201n9, 269
Anderson, J., 120n21, 125n29
Arians, 11n34, 23, 61n20
Arias, L., 200n8
Aristotle, 7, 24n87, 26, 93, 94n4, 112n1, 118, 120n21, 129, 139, 172n35, 202n15
Armstrong, A. H., 8–9, 192n61, 225–26n19, 228n28, 237n48, 253n30, 266n24, 266n27, 267, 267n28, 268, 268n23, 270, 273n41, 273n42
Ayers, R., 232n2

Balás, D., 24n89, 171n26, 256n35, 264n17
Bardy, G., 72n3, 146n43, 220n9, 221n10
Berrouard, M.-F., 54, 239n1
Boethius, A. M., 24n89, 151n51, 240n4, 256
Bourke, V., 76n3
Boyer, C., 27n2, 28n4, 156, 162n20
Bréhier, E., 42n32, 43n33, 112n1, 209n28
Brown, P., 14n48, 25, 63, 137n22, 139n31
Burnaby, J., 71n2
Burns, J. P., 181n1

Caelestinus (Celestine), 21–22, 76
Callahan, J., 149n47
Capánaga, V., 239n1
Capello, J., 33n15
Cassian, John, 23
Cayré, F., 16, 27n2
Chadwick, H., 173n38

Chaix-Ruy, J., 247n15
Christine of Lorraine, 21n75
Cicero, M. Tullius, 3, 5n3, 11, 24n85, 29n6, 73n5, 123, 137, 141
Clark, W. N., 132n1
Colleran, J., 198n4, 202n12, 205n17, 208n27, 218, 235n47
Consentius, 14, 19–20, 23,
Courcelle, P., 72n3
Cousineau, R. H., 156

David of Dinant, 29n6
De Lubac, H., 17
Descartes, R., 18, 64n29, 118n19, 209n29, 240n3, 278
Durandeaux, J., 240n4
Durrant, M., 94
Du Roy, O., 157n7, 159n12, 163

Epicureans, 170
Evodius, 38, 39n27, 41, 46, 75–76, 205–6, 213, 217

Fabricius, 167
Faustus of Riez, 23
Ferrari, Leo, 14n46, 14n47, 14n48
Filastrius of Brescia, 167
Fitzgerald, A., 1
Folliet, G., 9, 163n21
Fortin, E., 23n84
Fortunatus the Manichee, 35n19, 59, 139n31

Galileo Galilei, 20–21
Geach, P., 123n28, 136n17
Gilson, E., xiii, 13, 27n2, 27n3, 40n28, 41n30, 72n4, 85n32, 117n14, 121n23, 122,

287

288 Index of Names

Gilson, E. *(cont.)*
  125n29, 139n27, 151, 155–56, 158, 197n1, 198n3, 202n12, 207n25, 219n3, 226n21, 246, 252n27, 257n40
Gnostics, 170, 175
Grandgeorges, L., 125n31, 127n24
Gregory of Nyssa, 24, 171n26, 256n35, 264
Guitton, J., 239n1

Hadot, I., 8n17
Hadot, P., 8
Harnack, A. von, 167–68
Hartshorne, C., 132n4, 132n5
Hegel, G., 18
Hendrikx, E., 93–94
Henry, P., 133n1
Henry of Ghent, 26
Hilary, xiv
Hobbes, T., 29n6
Holte, R., 71n2
Huftier, M., 239n1, 246n11
Hultgren, G., 71n2

Irenaeus of Lyons, 142n36
Ithacus of Ossonuba, 173n38

Jerome of Bethlehem, 118, 197, 199–202
Job, 73n5
John the Evangelist, 51, 60, 176, 191, 257
Jordan, R., 130n35, 233n40, 235n45
Jourjon, M., 142n35
Julian of Eclanum, xi

Keats, J., 261
Kierkegaard, S., 18
Knauer.G., 262
Knöll, P., 11n34

LaCroix, R., 94–95, 97–99, 109–11, 114n6, 147n44
Lawless, G., 9n26
Le Blond, J.-M., 14n46, 137n19, 239n1, 246n12, 247n14, 248n16, n20, 252n27, 260
Leo the Great, xiv
Lienhard, J., 12n39
Lonergan, B., 46, 132n2
Lossky, V., 133n6

Maccarius Scotus, 184
Madec, G., 3, 4n1, 5n3, n5, 10n32, 11–12, 16n55

Manichees, 22, 23n80, 29–32, 34, 53n10, 56, 58, 63, 67, 71n3, 83, 86, 87n37, 89–90, 131, 132n5, 137, 138n23, 138n24, 138n26, 140–41, 143, 156, 160, 166, 169–73, 175–76, 189, 200, 232, 263, 269, 274
Mandouze, A., 8, 9n26
Marcel, G., 247n15
Marcion, 167–68, 170
Marrou, H.-I., 41n30, 72n3, 94n1, 162n21, 239n1, 243, 246n12, 247, 249n20, 249n22, 262
Masai, F., 14n46, 15–17, 22n78, 22n79, 23n80, 23–24n85, 28n4, 29–30, 31n11, 50n5, 51, 87n36, 137n19, 137n20, 138n23, 138n25, 141n34, 143n37, 149n46, 201, 291n9, 291n11, 215, 256n36, 266n23, 269n 35, 273
Maximinus the Arian, 23n81
Monica, 80n25, 109, 123, 138n24, 201
Mourant, J., 199n5, 260, 261n5
Muller, E., 12n39

Nebridius, 9, 234, 235–36n45
Neoplatonism, xi, 22n78, 25, 30, 32n12, 33, 34n17, 50, 55, 62–63, 65–66, 69–70, 72, 112n1, 125n29, 132, 137n20, 173n36, 256–58, 264, 274
Nicholas of Cusa, 133n6
Nourrisson, J., 198n1, 198n3
Nygren, A., 71n2

O'Connell, R., xi, 5n4, 21, 22n77, 23n82, 28n5, 31n10, 33, 35n18, 40n29, 41, 43n34, 44n35, 53n10, 54n11, 74n7, 75n12, 77n16, 86n35, 87n38, 105n24, 105n26, 122n26, 125n30, 132n4, 134n10, 138n24, 142n36, 150n47, 160n15, 177n53, 180–81, 192, 194n65, 199n6, 207n24, 217, 223n15, 224, 225n19, 229n29, 232n38, 234, 237, 249, 250n24, 252n27, 253n31, 259, 261–62, 266–67, 269, 271, 274
O'Donovan, O., 71n2
O'Meara, J., 32n12, 59n17, 129n37, 142n14, 147n37, 218n3, 224n14, 260, 262
Owens, J., 118n17

Parsons, W., 200n7
Paul the Apostle, 11, 14n48, 32n12, 51–53, 67, 70, 83–84, 87, 89, 90n40, 133n5
Paulinus of Nola, 53, 71
Pegis, A., 14n47
Pegon, J., 71n3

Index of Names

Pelagians, xii–xiv, 14n48
Pépin, J., 265
Perl, C., 27n1
Peter the Apostle, 20
Peters, E., 24n90, 169–70, 263n14
Plantinga, A., 29n6, 98, 99n15, 100n18
Plato, 5–7, 18, 27n3, 43n33, 129, 133n4, 159n12, 172n35, 218n3, 221, 257n40
Platonists, 3, 6n8, 7, 12, 30n9, 59, 68n36, 83n31, 131, 143–44, 149, 172, 257, 263–64, 266
Plotinus, xi, 5–7, 24, 30, 38, 40–41, 42n32, 43n33, n34, 44n36, 44n37, 45n38, 46, 51, 57, 75n12, 112–13n1, 122n25, 126n31, 129, 149–50n47, 151n51, 159n12, 160n14, 180, 192, 197, 198n4, 203n15, 206n23, 208–9, 214, 216, 217n1, 218, 219n4, 226n19, 227–29, 231n36, 232, 237–38, 239n1, 240n3, 240n4, 248–50, 253n28, 253n30, 255–56, 257n38, 258n41, 263–64, 267–68, 273
Pontifex, M., 27n1, 38n24
Porphyry, 7n15, 11n34, 112n1, 129, 218n3, 264n16
Priscillian, 173n38
Prosper of Aquitaine, xiv
Pseudo-Dionysius, 134n6
Pythagoras, 5

Rahner, K., 17, 17n56, 17n57, 113n3
Ratramus of Corbie, 184, 185n25
Raveaux, T., 167n12, 172n34, 173, 173n27
Rivière, J., 239n1
Robles, L., 200n8
Rohmer, J., 205
Rombs, R., xi, 217
Romanianus, 8, 71n3
Rouët de Journel, M. J., 256n34
Russell, B., 216, 227, 232–33
Russo, F., 21n5
Ruch, M., 5n3
Ryan, J. K., 27n1, 50n1, 56n14, 133n6, 123n16, 123n17, 124n18, 124n19, 234n44, 230n2, 250, 260n2

Sabellians, 11n34
Sallust, 172n35
Schumacher, W. A., 51n5, 53n8, 55, 62, 65
Secundinus the Manichee, 63

Sejourné, P., 28n5
Semi-Pelagians, xiv
Sheed, F., 56n14, 225n18
Simplicianus of Milan, 14, 14n48, 140
Simplicius, 112n1
Smart, J. J. C., 232n39
Smith, T., 23, 23n84
Socinians, 132n5
Socrates
Solignac, A., 33n14, 34n16, 53, 54n11, 62n21, 144n39, 159n13, 182n10, 219n4, 225n19, 227, 227n24, 228, 230n35, 234n43, 234n45, 235, 235n45, 236, 257n38, 265n20, 269–70, 270n3, 273n41
Solmsen, F., 209n30
Sorabji, R., 264n17
Steinhauser, K., 260n3
Stoicism, 22n78, 23n80, 34–35, 142n36
Stoics, 22, 131, 208, 274
Swetnam, J., 44n36, 122n27, 257n40
Swinburne, R., 131n2

Tertullian, Q. T., 19, 22, 23n83, 30n9, 33n15, 34, 57, 138, 141n34, 146n43, 202, 203n13
Testard, M., 23n85, 29n6
Theodorus, 269
Thimme, W., 206
Thomas Aquinas, 17, 26, 27n2, 47, 75n12, 117n14, 158n10, 239n1
Thonnard, F. J., 16, 27n1, 27n2, 38n24, 41n30, 42n33, 161n18, 205

Van Bavel, T. J., 54, 55n13, 65n32, 66n33
Van Fleteren, F., 11n34, 181
Verbeke, G., 22n78, 29, 30, 35n18, 50n4, 50n5, 51n5, 73n5, 138n25, 142n36, 143n37, 173n36, 201n9, 203n13, 215, 256n36
Vincentius Victor, 23, 128n36, 203
Von Jess, W., 147n44

Wainwright, W., 110n38
Weil, E., 22n78
Whitehead, A. N., 132n4, 132n5
Wolfskeel, C., 198n2, 198n3, 209

Zeno the Stoic, 23n8
Zepf, M., 259–60
Zimara, C., 161n18, 162n19

To Know God and the Soul: Essays on the Thought of Saint Augustine was designed and typeset in Garamond by Kachergis Book Design of Pittsboro, North Carolina. It was printed on 60-pound Natures Natural and bound by Thomson-Shore of Dexter, Michigan.

www.ingramcontent.com/pod-product-compliance
Lightning Source LLC
Chambersburg PA
CBHW051936290426
44110CB00015B/1996